The CalAware Guide to Open Meetings in California

The CalAware Guide to
Open Meetings in California

Terry Francke
General Counsel
Californians Aware

Californians Aware
Carmichael, California

Norman Rockwell Art Collection Trust, The Normal Rockwell Museum at Stockbridge, Massachusetts

Cover design by Kelly Muñiz de Francke

ISBN: 0-9769062-0-1

Printed in the United States of America

Californians Aware
2218 Homewood Way
Carmichael, CA 95608
Phone (916) 487-7000
Fax (916) 487-7999
info@calaware.org

Acknowledgments

This guide owes its existence to those whose help made it happen:

• with their review and advice on the text—Richard McKee and Dennis Winston;

• with their generous financial support for its publication—Cooper, White & Cooper, LLP, San Francisco; Burke, Williams & Sorensen, LLP, Los Angeles; and James McClatchy, Sacramento;

• and most of all those whose love, sacrifice and encouragement inspired and sustained its writing—my wife, Muffy, and my daughter and CalAware's executive director, Emily.

FOREWORD

By Richard McKee, President, Californians Aware

The envy of the modern world is the individual and collective freedom afforded the citizens of the United States of America. It flows from the protections provided by the Bill of Rights and the republican government embodied in the Constitution. Eleven score and nine years ago, when the war began, first to create, and later to preserve, protect and defend a government of, by, and for the people, hundreds of thousands gave their lives so their descendents could enjoy the liberties their victories ensured.

But the fight to preserve our representative form of government hasn't always been about military battles fought overseas, or even those joined from within. Rather, it is found in the electorate's active exercise of its right to the popular determination of local, state, and national policies, as opposed to accepting the edicts from those who would steal sovereignty from the people. To consistently exert one's rights to free speech and petition has proven one of the surest methods to avoid the loss of those rights to, instead, government in secret—of, by, and for a privileged few.

Fifty-two years ago, the California Legislature recognized a growing cancer in local government. It was a proliferation of secrecy, robbing the people of their knowledge of and involvement in the decision-making of their school boards, city councils, county supervisors, and the boards of special districts, all elected to represent the public's wishes. There was no need of a microscope to identify the pathology; just the naked eye was all that was required to recognize the stain left by secret, backroom deals.

The Legislature's remedy was a healthy dose of "sunshine." By enacting the Ralph M. Brown Act, the Legislature demanded openness in decision-making and guaranteed the people's right to involvement before those decisions were made. And since its creation in 1953, California's open meetings law has been amended in almost every legislative session to further reduce the employment of secrecy by local governments.

But what exactly are the people's rights when it comes to the operations of local legislative bodies? What notice is sufficient; what input is required; what information must be revealed? Just how can the people exercise the rights insured by the Brown Act?

The purpose of this book is to answer these questions. Similarly, the purpose of Californians Aware is to educate citizens on how to exercise their rights, so as to maintain an open and responsive government.

Californians Aware, a non-profit, 501(c)(3) corporation, was created in 2004 with a mission to educate everyone (i.e., the people, the media, and public officials) on public forum rights, so that public participation in governmental decision-making would be a welcome, positive, and effective experience.

Every year Californians Aware, existing only on contributions from individuals and groups supportive of the mission to enhance openness and public involvement in the determination of governmental policy, holds educational seminars on open government all over California.

This book, the first to be published by Californians Aware, is meant to provide interested members of the public, the media, local government officials, and the attorneys representing each of these groups, with a thorough understanding of the open meetings law. And this need could not be more obvious than to those observing or involved in local government over the past decade.

First, both local officials and the public are aware that the open meetings law exists. And second, neither group understands exactly what this law says.

In general, the public believes this law:

• is most restrictive, requiring virtually all agency business to be done in the open;

• gives every individual almost unlimited opportunities to address the governing body on any issue; and

• dictates that all records of the agency are immediately available to anyone for the asking.

On the other hand, elected and appointed officials tend to believe that:

• they are authorized to use closed sessions whenever presented with a sensitive, controversial, or potentially embarrassing issue, whether that issue is legal, financial, or disciplinary;

• the law allows public participation to be significantly restricted; and

• any document that is even remotely related to litigation or employee privacy is completely confidential.

Of course, the truth is that both perspectives are wrong, but neither is entirely wrong. If both sides are aware of this law, shouldn't both sides, on most occasions, be able to read the law and come to the same conclusion?

There's the real problem; *neither side reads the law.* Instead, both sides tune in to the "experts" of their choice to get a quick and easy-to-understand interpretation of their rights and obligations.

The public most often listens to newspapers and other media organizations that desire access to almost everything, despite some important privacy protections. On the other hand, elected tend to listen to public law attorneys who seem to have been hired in large measure to keep public officials from being embarrassed.

So wouldn't it be great if both sides could be treated to an unbiased introduction to the actual language of the open government law, and to the Legislature's intent when enacting each section? At least then, when the inevitable debate on interpretation comes, both sides would begin with the same set of facts.

The need for such an education on open meetings law is obvious even to the casual observer. Arguments over Brown Act issues are becoming more and more frequent, and are very emotional for both sides. And once lines are drawn in the sand, voices are raised, and charges exchanged, most rational discussion disappears and everyone's a loser.

For the public, the raised voices, finger-pointing, and name-calling only make elected officials less willing to listen to the arguments of those on the attack and more likely to retreat from doing business in the sunshine of the open meeting.

For the elected officials, secrecy breeds cynicism, and the appearance of corruption. The people are less likely trust officials when decisions seem to spring from nowhere, and the public has lost an opportunity to present its perspective because information was withheld.

The best answer is to avoid the confrontation in the first place.

The more open to public involvement a local government appears, the more trust and respect the public has for that government. And the more respect the people show for their government, the more willing that government is to invite and accept the people's participation.

Still, local agencies often decry the length and complexity of the Brown Act, saying they make unintentional violations inevitable. Yet they have no one to blame but themselves, since additions have only been made to plug the loopholes carved in the law by "creative" public agency executives attorneys, who interpret the law in a manner contrary to its intent, solely to support a desire for secrecy. They would rather focus on their justifying conclusion, "I believe the sensitivity of this issue demonstrates the need for a closed session;" than on the question, "Is it legally authorized and absolutely necessary that this issue be discussed in secret?"

So, throughout this text you will find not only the language of the Brown Act, but analysis and explanation of the cases and Attorney General's opinions that constitute the legal authority interpreting the law.

But the Legislature could not possibly anticipate every situation to be faced by every local legislative body. And the proliferation of new local agencies—regional government cooperatives, business improvement districts, joint powers insurance authorities, water suppliers, transportation authorities, land conservancies, air and water pollution boards, recycling authorities—along with some private entities that are being delegated public agency authority, means there will be new challenges to the people's ability to maintain control over its local governments.

Not only must the people and the media be more vigilant in monitoring these agencies created to do the people's business, but local agency officials must be more sensitive to their fundamental duty (especially after Proposition 59 of 2004) to keep the people informed about what its local governments are doing. The importance of this duty has been recognized by the courts on many occasions:

Information is necessary "'to ensure an informed citizenry, vital to the functioning of a democratic society, needed to check against corruption and to hold the governors accountable to the governed.'" *John Doe Agency v. John Doe Corp.* (1989) 493 U.S. 146, 152.

" 'A popular Government, without popular information, or the means of acquiring it, is but a Prologue to a Farce or a Tragedy; or, perhaps both. Knowledge will forever govern ignorance: And a people who mean to be their own Governors must arm themselves with the power which knowledge gives.' " *Environmental Protection Agency v. Mink* (1973) 410, U.S. 73, 110, 111, dissent of Justice Douglas, quoting James Madison.

Every failure of the people to demand the rights, as assured by the Brown Act, to information from and involvement in its local government, erodes the public's opportunity to maintain control over the government of its own creation. As the courts have cautioned:

""[O]fficials through devious ways are depriving us, the public, of our inalienable right to be present and to be heard at all deliberations of governmental bodies wherein decisions affecting the public are being made. ... [T]he public has the right to be present and to be heard during all phases of legislative enactment by any governmental agency. This right is a source of strength to our Country and must be protected at all costs."" *Sacramento Newspaper Guild v. Sacramento County Board of Supervisors* (1968) 263 Cal.App.2d 41, 49, 50; (footnotes and citation omitted.)

§ = section

CHAPTER SUMMARY

DETAILED TABLE OF CONTENTS

Closed Sessions

General Introduction

By Terry Francke

This guide presents the most thorough examination in print of the Ralph M. Brown Act—the open meeting law applicable to local government agencies—and the cases and Attorney General's opinions through which it is understood.

It also presents the texts of all other California open meeting laws, including the Bagley-Keene Act, which applies to meetings of state boards, commissions and other multi-member bodies in the executive branch.

Almost all the cases and Attorney General's opinions concerning open meeting laws deal with the Brown Act, now more than 50 years old, and accordingly, that statute gets by far the majority of this guide's attention. But because the Brown Act's provisions have so many counterparts in the Bagley-Keene Act, those parallel provisions are shown next to their corresponding Brown Act sections, to highlight how a court's understanding of the latter might apply to the former.

Predictable Questions

How do I find it? This guide, like most reference works, is not a book that most people would be inclined to sit down and read through. If, like most users, you come to it with a particular question or concern in mind, there are several pathways to an answer. Lawyers should have little trouble finding whatever help it may offer. For others, assuming that neither the table of contents nor the index provides a recognizable starting point, if you know a particular code section, or case name, or Attorney General's opinion number (perhaps because someone has cited it to you as a legal basis for doing or not doing something), the table of authorities beginning on page 289e leads you to the page or pages where those authorities are discussed. If what you want is just a current copy of the text of the laws, the Brown Act is reprinted on page 193 and the Bagley-Keene Act on page 220. Each section of the Government Code in these displays is linked to the section of this guide that discusses it.

What's the latest? This guide is published in September 2005 and is current as of then. For the rest of this year, new legal authorities including legislative amendments to the law, appellate cases and Attorney General's opinions will be posted on the updates page at the CalAware website, http://www.calaware.org, keyed to the chapter and page to which they pertain, and posted in most cases within days of when they are enacted or published. Any such late updates will be incorporated in the next printed edition.

Says who? In 15 years of interacting with local agency attorneys in panel discussions, instructional workshops and other occasions dealing with the Brown Act, it's my experience that the reading of the law reflected in this book agrees with that of government counsel something more than 99 percent of the time, especially where it's certain that we are applying the same statutes and case law to the same set of facts. Nonetheless, some may be tempted to dismiss this guide as biased and untrustworthy simply because it is the product of an organization committed to legally enforceable government transparency. To that disposition I have no compelling response, because it seems inherently prejudicial and resistant to persuasion. But if anyone can point to a statement in these pages that deviates from a reasonable reading of the law, I would be glad to hear of it, in order to amend either what is said or how it is said in later editions, or else to explain to the objector (and anyone else who cares) why no amendment seems necessary.

Where do you get that? Like any other statute, the Brown Act and other legislated rules in this guide have two levels of meaning. One is what you, I and others (lawyers or not) *think* a provision means. The other is what legal authorities say it means. It's the latter that counts, but among legal authorities there are degrees of weight and finality. From lowest to highest, then:

Attorney General's opinions, published and available to all, do not have the force of court decisions, but when they are cited, courts generally give them considerable respect. The opinions take the form of answers to particular questions, typically posed in a generalized, hypothetical form. There are a fair number of them referred to in this guide; see page 294 for a listing.

Superior Court decisions in the various county trial courts bind the plaintiff and defendant in a case (until and unless reversed on appeal) and no one else. They are not published and may not be cited to a court as case law. But they may informally provide a persuasive demonstration of how a court might rule in a future similar case.

Appellate court decisions that are published in the official legal reports not only bind the parties but provide one or more holdings or conclusions that are binding interpretations of the law for all those within their districts, until qualified, overturned or disapproved by a later decision of the same court or of the California Supreme Court. There are six districts of the California Court of Appeal, and half have smaller subregional divisions. Decisions of a given district of the Court of Appeal do not bind courts in other districts, which may reach different conclusions on the same or similar facts (these rare contradictory decisions may lead the California Supreme Court to take the later case up for review). Many appellate cases are not published because the deciding court, for a variety of reasons, does not see them as helpful precedent. Or sometimes, on request, the California Supreme Court orders an appellate case "de-published" after the fact if it does not consider it correct or useful precedent. In that instance, the decision continues to bind the parties but cannot be cited as case law. Most of the cases cited in this guide are from the appellate courts, and typically there is only one of these cases addressing a particular point in open meeting law. In that situation—where no other court has addressed the matter—the appellate case from any district is considered binding statewide until and unless another appellate court disagrees.

California Supreme Court decisions, all of which are published, are the final authorities on the meaning and effect of state statutes like the Brown Act and other open meeting laws in this guide. But the high court has dealt with only four open meeting law cases (two each on the Brown Act and the Bagley-Keene Act). Thus in practical terms, the case law on these statutes comes almost exclusively from the Court of Appeal (see above). Sometimes a federal law issue like the First Amendment will arise in a California public meeting. In such instances the matter may be dealt with in either a state or a federal court, and in the latter channel, the interpretive authorities may come from published decisions of the U.S. District Courts throughout the state, from the U.S. Court of Appeals for the Ninth Circuit, or from the U.S. Supreme Court.

Why should I care? This is a question that reporters often ask. They know why *they* care about the open meeting laws—keeping readers, listeners or viewers informed on what city hall or the school board is doing would be very difficult without them. But they sometimes want to remind the public why open government is important to ordinary citizens as well.

One way of looking at the answer is to consider how much of your quality of life is determined not in Washington, D.C. or Sacramento, where the broad policies are made, but in your home community, where they are put into effect—or maybe not. If public services like police, fire, public health and consumer protection, or schools, community colleges, parks, libraries, hospitals, electrical utilities, water supply, waste disposal, mosquito abatement and so forth are to be maintained, it's local agencies that do it. How well they do it is overseen in the first instance by local councils, boards and commissions. How much funding gets provided for personnel, equipment and other resources is also determined by these same bodies. In addition, just where you or others can locate homes, business structures or other uses of property—how growth controls and environmental protections are administered—these decisions are also locally determined.

Do you want them secretly determined, or with such suddenness that no one can see the decision point coming in time to make a difference?

If you're like most people, you probably have never had to exercise your right to go down to a government meeting, pay attention to what's being said and done, and make your voice heard. But if you should ever find your own rights, interests or activities so threatened by government officials (or those lobbying them) that you feel forced to find the officials poised to act, hear how they're being advised, address them in an open meeting (where your fellow citizens can see how you're treated), and know what effect your presence has had, you'll want laws like the Brown Act to be known, observed and respected. Meanwhile, while *you* may have no inclination to monitor government operations by observing officials acting in their collective meetings week to week, you probably want other watchdogs on a host of issues affecting your quality of life to be able to do so in your place.

Why should the average person care? Because government gives unique and, typically, controlling powers to other mostly average people. They do their best, but sometimes make mistakes, and once in a great while even do things that are highly questionable. This is true despite all the government transparency laws on the books. Can you imagine what things would be like without those laws?

1. Local Government Bodies: The Ralph M. Brown Act

The Ralph M. Brown Act (Government Code §54050 *et seq.*) is the California statute requiring open and publicized meetings of governing and advisory bodies in local government, at which members of the public not only may be present but also may address the body on matters relevant to its authority.

§ 1-1: Introduction

The Brown Act, in most respects the model for the separate law governing access to state agency boards and commissions also, has grown much lengthier and more complex than when enacted in the mid-20th century. But a glance at that early period shows that the initial purpose of the law was a reaction to many of the same concerns for secrecy that remain present in today's local government.

§ 1-1(a): Comparison with the Bagley-Keene Act

Whereas the Brown Act applies to local government councils, boards, commissions and the like, the Bagley-Keene Open Meeting Act (Government Code §11120 *et seq.*) applies to multi-member bodies in the executive branch of state government.

This guide focuses primarily on the Brown Act, which since its passage in 1953 has been interpreted in a relatively ample series of cases and Attorney General's opinions. In contrast, the Bagley-Keene Act has experienced relatively little case law or opinion interpretation. But the two statutes as a whole may be considered *in pari materia*, that is,

> although directed at different levels of government, they both seek to ensure that public agencies conduct their actions and deliberations openly. Most of the generic observations about legislative intent apply with equal force to both acts.

Funeral Security Plans Inc. v. State Board of Funeral Directors, 28 Cal. App. 4th 1470 (1994; depublished January 5, 1995). The California Supreme Court has dealt with the Brown Act and the Bagley-Keene Act only twice each; in one of the latter cases, while a dissenting opinion examined a number of Brown Act cases for comparison and contrast, the majority confined itself to the terse observation, "The two statutes are similar in some respects and dissimilar in others." *Regents of the University of California v. Superior Court* (Molloy) 20 Cal.4th 509, fn. 5 (1999). In the other case, the court engaged in an extensive comparison of the two statutes' treatment of the closed session on pending litigation, finding the purposes of the two provisions the same despite a small variation in language. *Southern California Edison Co. v. Peevey*, 31 Cal.4th 781 (2003).

When a particular provision of the Brown Act is paralleled by a corresponding provision in the Bagley-Keene Act, this guide shows the **Bagley-Keene Comparison**. This juxtaposition may lend insight in predicting a court's interpretation of a Bagley-Keene provision whose Brown Act counterpart has already been dealt with in case law or an Attorney General's opinion. The Bagley-Keene provisions *without* counterparts in the Brown Act, allowing closed sessions for particular bodies or purposes, are listed in § 2-1(a), page 217.

§ 1-1(b): The Original Statute

The following account of the origins of the Brown Act is taken from *The Right to Know: The Public's Access to Meetings and Records of Government Agencies*, Assembly Interim Committee on Government Organization, Vol. 12, No. 10 (1965), pp. 16-17, (footnotes omitted).

> The Assembly Interim Committee on Judiciary undertook a study in September 1952 initiated by its chairman, Assemblyman Ralph M. Brown, "to study and investigate 'loopholes' in the laws of this state, through which public boards, commissions, agencies and officials have suppressed information, the property of the public." The hearings held by the committee were primarily concerned with the practices of local governments in conducting closed meetings. "Your Secret Government," a series of articles by Michael Harris, was published in the *San Francisco Chronicle* at about this time focusing public attention on abuses at the local level. As a result of this and other testimony the committee concluded that:
>
>> There is a genuine and compelling need for legislative action of a nature designed to curb this misuse of democratic process by public bodies who would legislate in secret. Unless for proper security reasons, the public has the right to be present and to be heard during all phases of legislative enactment by any governmental agency. This right is a source of strength to our country and must be protected at all costs.
>
> Assembly Bill No. 339 introduced by Assemblyman Brown was supported by the California Newspaper Publishers Association and the League of California Cities. The bill was adopted by the Legislature and signed into law by Governor Earl Warren on

July 2, 1953.

As enacted, the Brown Act required that "all meetings of the legislative body of a local agency shall be open and public, and all persons shall be permitted to attend any meeting of the legislative body of a local agency…" (Section 54953, Government Code). Legislative body was defined as "the governing board, commission, directors or body of a local agency, or any board or commission thereof" (Section 54952), and local agency was defined as "a city, city and county, town, school district, municipal corporation, district, political subdivision, or any board, commission or agency thereof, or other local public agency" (Section 54951).

This was not a completely new statement of the law as it applied to most legislative bodies. It has been pointed out that the principle of open meetings had been recognized in the earliest law of the state. Richard Carpenter, General Counsel of the League of California has observed:

> The Brown Act was primarily a restatement of the law as it existed prior to 1953 and in fact from the formation of the first cities under the Constitution of 1849. Every charter we have examined requires council meetings to be public and the statutes under which general law cities operated also required meetings to be public…

A similar observation has been made with reference to counties. Stanford D. Herlick, County Counsel of San Bernardino County, has noted that county boards of supervisors have been governed by open meeting requirements "since shortly after the entrance of this state into the Union in 1850." To state, however, that the Brown Act was "but a reiteration of extant principles" is contrary to both the intent and the application of the law.

In Section 54950 it is declared to be the intent of the law that "actions be taken openly" and "deliberations be conducted openly." It is clear, both from the language of this section and from the report of the Assembly Interim Committee on Judiciary, that the Legislature intended a broader interpretation of the public meeting principle than had existed in the practices of local agencies and in prior case law.

In the committee's *Progress Report to the Legislature* certain practices used by legislative bodies to evade the requirements of a public meeting were cited, including the following:

> There is another "loophole" in the existing law through

> which government bodies have been secretly meeting and transacting business. They are meetings generally held before the official public meeting, under the guise of a variety of names, such as executive sessions, meetings of the committee of the whole, work sessions, and others.

The committee report cited specific instances of the use of these caucuses or prepublic meetings and observed: "At gatherings such as these, deliberations and determinations regarding matters affecting the public were made. The subsequent public meetings were mockery, a mere formality and a repetition of matters already decided at prepublic meetings."

The Judiciary Committee also expressed dissatisfaction with the interpretations of the courts in upholding the legality of meetings which are theoretically open to the public because the door to the room in which the meeting is held is unlocked.

In order to discourage the practice of conducting closed meetings, a provision was included in the Brown Act requiring notice to the public of any meeting not held at the regularly scheduled time and place (Gov. Code, Section 54956). An open meeting is open only in theory if the public has no knowledge of the time and place at which it is to be held. Existing law at the time of the passage of the Brown Act only required that the notice be sent to members of the legislative body in order to prevent secret action by a majority. The new notice provision clearly recognized the public's right of access to all meetings of the governing body of the local agency.

Another purpose of the new law was to provide uniform coverage for all local legislative bodies. Prior to its enactment many local legislative bodies were not covered by local meeting legislation. For example, elementary school boards were not required to hold public meetings, whereas they were mandatory for high school boards.

§ 1-1(c): The Legislature's Intent

The preamble to the Brown Act, Government Code Section 54950, states:

> In enacting this chapter, the Legislature finds and declares that the public commissions, boards and councils and the other public agencies in this State exist to aid in the conduct of the people's business. It is the intent of the law that their actions be taken

Bagley-Keene Comparison

Government Code §11120: It is the public policy of this state that public agencies exist to aid in the conduct of the people's business and the proceedings of public agencies be conducted openly so that the public may remain informed.

In enacting this article the Legislature

openly and that their deliberations be conducted openly.

The people of this State do not yield their sovereignty to the agencies which serve them. The people, in delegating authority, do not give their public servants the right to decide what is good for the people to know and what is not good for them to know. The people insist on remaining informed so that they may retain control over the instruments they have created.

finds and declares that it is the intent of the law that actions of state agencies be taken openly and that their deliberation be conducted openly.

The people of this state do not yield their sovereignty to the agencies which serve them. The people, in delegating authority, do not give their public servants the right to decide what is good for the people to know and what is not good for them to know. The people insist on remaining informed so that they may retain control over the instruments they have created.

§ 1-1(d): A Set of "Minimal Standards"

The Act does not preempt local governments' own public meeting policy-making. On the contrary, it expressly bestows on local officials the authority to be more accommodating to their constituents' desires for transparency than its own provisions require. Government Code §54953.7 states:

> Notwithstanding any other provision of law, legislative bodies of local agencies may impose requirements upon themselves which allow greater access to their meetings than prescribed by the minimal standards set forth in this chapter. In addition thereto, an elected legislative body of a local agency may impose such requirements on those appointed legislative bodies of the local agency of which all or a majority of the members are appointed by rounder the authority of the elected legislative body.

Accordingly, local jurisdictions have begun to adopt their own "sunshine" ordinances that provide more accommodating rules on access to public meetings and records (see Chapter 6).

§ 1-1(e) Conflict with Other State Laws

The Act has contained since its earliest days a declaration of its supersession of contrary statutes. Government Code §54958 states: "The provisions of his chapter shall apply to the legislative body of every local agency notwithstanding the conflicting provisions of any other state law."

Bagley-Keene Comparison
Government Code §11127: Each provision of this article shall apply to every state body unless the body is specifically excepted from that provision by law or is covered by any other conflicting provision of law.

A leading case has held with respect to Section 54958, however, that "(f)ailing to designate what if any laws are superseded, such a clause has no greater force than a repeal by implication; it subordinates or repeals existing law only to the extent that the two laws are irreconcilable." *Sacramento Newspaper Guild v. Sacramento County Board of Supervisors,*

263 Cal.App.2d 41 (1968). The court concluded, in that instance, that the Act did not repeal by implication the attorney-client privilege, and that accordingly local legislative bodies could meet in closed session to consult confidentially with their attorneys on pending litigation. In light of this conclusion, the Act was later amended more pointedly, not to identify "what if any laws were superseded," but rather to enumerate the only other statutes that would authorize a closed session not provided in the Act (see § 1-5(b)).

§ 1-2: Key Terms

The Act governs the conduct of a "legislative body" of a "local agency" in connection with its "meetings." "Action taken" in such meetings, if done in violation of certain provisions of the Act, may be subject to judicial nullification (§ 1-7(g)) or may, combined with other circumstances, subject members of the body to criminal prosecution (§ 1-7(a)).

§ 1-2(a): "Local Agency"

The Act defines "local agency" to mean "a county, city, whether general law or chartered, city and county, town, school district, municipal corporation, district, political subdivision, or any board, commission or agency thereof, or other local public agency." (Government Code §54951).

Bagley-Keene Comparison

Government Code §11121 defines the "state bodies" subject to the law to include:

(a) Every state board, or commission, or similar multimember body of the state that is created by statute or required by law to conduct official meetings and every commission created by executive order.
(b) A board, commission, committee, or similar multimember body that exercises any authority of a state body delegated to it by that state body.
(c) An advisory board, advisory commission, advisory committee, advisory subcommittee, or similar multimember advisory body of a state body, if created by formal action of the state body or of any member of the state body, and if the advisory body so created consists of three or more persons.
(d) A board, commission, committee, or similar multimember body on which a member of a body that is a state body pursuant to this section serves in his or her official capacity as a representative of that state body and that is supported, in whole or in part, by funds provided by the state body, whether the multimember body is organized and operated by the state body or by a private corporation.

Certain entities are expressly excluded, in Government Code §11121.1, from the definition of "state body":

Government Code §11121.1. As used in this article, "state body" does not include any of the following:
(a) State agencies provided for in Article VI of the California Constitution.
(b) Districts or other local agencies whose meetings are required to be open to the public pursuant to the Ralph M. Brown Act (Chapter 9 (commencing with Section 54950) of Part 1 of Division 2 of Title 5).

> (c) State agencies provided for in Article IV of the California Constitution whose meetings are required to be open to the public pursuant to the Grunsky-Burton Open Meeting Act (Article 2.2 (commencing with Section 9027) of Chapter 1.5 of Part 1 of Division 2 of Title 2).
> (d) State agencies when they are conducting proceedings pursuant to Section 3596.
> (e) State agencies provided for in Section 109260 of the Health and Safety Code, except as provided in Section 109390 of the Health and Safety Code.
> (f) State agencies provided for in Section 11770.5 of the Insurance Code.
> (g) The Credit Union Advisory Committee established pursuant to Section 14380 of the Financial Code.

Local vis-a-vis Regional or Statewide:

In *Torres v. Board of Commissioners*, 89 Cal.App.3d 545 (1979), in which it was an essential threshold issue to decide whether a local housing authority's board meetings were subject to the Brown Act or to the Bagley-Keene Open Meeting Act (governing "state bodies"—see Chapter 2 generally), the court held that

> a housing authority created by Health and Safety Code section 34200 et seq. is included within the statutory definition of a local agency under the Brown Act in that it is either an "other local public agency" or a "municipal corporation" or both, as those terms are used in Government Code section 54951.*****
>
> The term "municipal corporation" is broader than the term "city," particularly when the term "city" already appears in the applicable statute.*****
>
> In order to give meaning to the term "municipal corporation" in Government Code section 54951 we hold that such term is not restricted to its technical sense of a "city," general law or charter, but rather includes such entities as housing authorities.

Id. at 549 (citations omitted). The court also applied a pragmatic territorial test, noting that:

> a housing authority is local in scope and character, restricted geographically in its area of operation, and does not have statewide power or jurisdiction even though it is created by, and is an agent of, the state rather than of the city or county in which it functions. Respondents are correct in noting that no housing authority has

> statewide powers or jurisdiction and (that each) is in fact subject to some regulations by a state agency with statewide jurisdiction.

Id. at 550 (citations omitted).

Agency vis-a-vis Institution

Not every publicly significant institution on the community level is an "agency" within the meaning of the Act. The common element among the instances that define the term is one of governmental authority. Accordingly, the Attorney General has opined that a county central committee of a political party is not a local agency (59 Ops.Cal.Atty.Gen. 220 (1978)), and that neither is a county farm bureau, even with respect to a meeting at which its board is authorized to develop a list of candidates for appointment to the board of directors of a local water management agency (80 Ops.Cal.Atty.Gen. 270 (1997)). The opinion observed that the farm bureau

> is a nongovernmental, nonprofit corporation that was incorporated on January 1, 1933. It is one of 53 county farm bureaus comprising the California Farm Bureau Federation, which is, similarly, a nongovernmental, nonprofit corporation. As such, the Bureau does not fit within any of the categories of "local agencies" set forth in section 54951.

§ 1-2(b): "Legislative Body"

As defined in Government Code §54952, the term "legislative body" may refer to any of several entities having some connection with a local agency. Before turning to those definitions, however, it should be noted that the word "legislative" is a term of art. It is not confined to entities with rule-making or policy-setting authority, and in fact often applies to purely advisory groups. Nor does the Act apply only to the legislative actions of a body. If a body is covered at all, the Attorney General has opined that actions that are essentially executive or quasi-judicial fall under its requirements as well as purely legislative matters. 61 Ops.Cal. Atty. Gen. 220 (1978). But the body must be a "body"— a multimember collective. A court has held that the Act does not apply to a proceeding presided over by a single hearing officer. *Wilson v. San Francisco Municipal Railway*, 29 Cal.App.3d 870 (1973).

§ 1-2(b)(1): Governing Bodies and Bodies Established by Law

Government Code §54952 (a) provides: "The governing body of a local agency or any other local body created by state or federal statute" is a legislative body. Thus in a county, the board of supervisors is covered as the governing body, and the planning commission is covered as a body established by state law; in a city, the council and planning commission are covered likewise; in a school district, the board of trustees is the covered governing body; and in other governmental districts and agencies, the governing boards of directors or commissioners are covered. Courts have expressly held that the term "legislative body" applies to the board of the Orange County Employees Retirement System (*Freedom Newspapers, Inc. v. Orange County Employees Retirement System*, 6 Cal.4th 821 (1993)) and to the board of the Redevelopment Agency of the City of Stockton (*Stockton Newspapers, Inc. v. Redevelopment Agency*, 171 Cal.App.3d 95 (1985)).

§ 1-2(b)(2): Bodies Created by Legislative Bodies

Government Code §54952 (b) provides that "legislative body" also applies to:

> A commission, committee, board, or other body of a local agency, whether permanent or temporary, decision-making or advisory, created by charter, ordinance, resolution, or formal action of a legislative body. However, advisory committees, composed solely of the members of the legislative body that are less than a quorum of the legislative body are not legislative bodies, except that standing committees of a legislative body, irrespective of their composition, which have a continuing subject matter jurisdiction, or a meeting schedule fixed by charter, ordinance, resolution, or formal action of a legislative body are legislative bodies for purposes of this chapter.

This formulation raises two issues: the "formality" of the creating act by an existing body sufficient to bring the created body within the statute, and which internal and external, *ad hoc* and permanent committees are thereby subject to the Act.

Formal Creation by the Parent Body

As to the first issue, a court has held that when a city council designated two of its members to meet with two members of the planning commission to screen applicants for a vacancy on the commission, that initiative was a sufficiently "formal action" by the council to render the four-member screening committee a legislative body within the meaning of the Act. *Joiner v. City of Sebastopol*, 125 Cal.App.3d 799, 805 (1981). The court contrasted the facts at bar with another scenario, in which sub-quorum delegations from legislative bodies of two independent local agencies meet to exchange information or negotiate on matters of interest common to the agencies. The Attorney General had opined in an indexed letter that in such cases there was nothing more than a meeting between two sub-quorum pairs of officials, neither of which would have been subject to the Act's requirements in meeting separately, and which when meeting in combination did not trigger the Act either, since they did not constitute a new body "created" by action of either parent organization. In contrast, said the court:

> The representatives of the city council and the planning commission were not to "report back with information to their respective boards." Rather, they were as a "unitary body" to interview applicants and report, with recommendations, to the city council, which had sole legal responsibility for filling the vacancy. We conclude that the proposed meeting was to be of an "advisory committee" within the meaning of (the Brown Act).

Id. at 805. In a published opinion also cited in *Joiner*, the Attorney General opined that there may be situations in which delegations from independent local agencies may not only be meeting jointly to exchange information or negotiate but actually coalescing into a "unitary body," created by their respective parent organizations and given an identity and mission of its own, in which case the Act might apply. 64 Ops.Cal.Atty.Gen. 856 (1981).

Application to Community College Faculty and Student Bodies

The Attorney General has concluded that the phrase "created by charter, ordinance, resolution, or formal action of a legislative body" means that the Brown Act applies t two community college campus bodies: the faculty senate (66 Ops.Cal.Atty.Gen. 252 (1983)) and the student body association (75 Ops.Cal.Atty.Gen. 143 (1992)).

Creation/Appointment Distinction

A court has also held that where a school board's policy called for the creation of an advisory committee to hear parental complaints about the choice of curricular materials, and the superintendent was left the discretion to appoint the members, it was the board's policy—and thus the board—which "created" the committee, not the superintendent's power of appointment, and thus that committee was subject to the Act. *Frazer v. Dixon Unified School District*, 18 Cal.App.4th 781 (1993).

Structural/Functional Distinctions among Committees

The second issue concerns the creation of internal and external committees on the one hand, and *ad hoc* or standing committees on the other. The convoluted language of the second sentence beginning with "However" in subdivision (b) may lead to some confusion. The distinctions may more easily be seen in the following table, in which "internal" committees are subquorum elements (typically two members of a parent five-member body); "external" committees are those which may or may not include members of the parent body but also include members appointed from the staff, the community or both; "*ad hoc,*" meaning with a finite duration and subject matter to be investigated and reported back to the parent body, i.e. with no "continuing subject matter jurisdiction"; and "standing," meaning with a "continuing subject matter jurisdiction" and an indefinite or perennial existence.

	Internal Committee	**External Committee**
Ad Hoc	Not subject to the Act	Subject to the Act
Standing	Subject to the Act	Subject to the Act

Thus two members of a five-member body, for example, tasked to inquire into a situation and report back their findings and recommendations, and with no further assignment, are as an internal, *ad hoc* committee outside the Act's requirements. The three other varieties of committee are subject to the Act.

*Standing/*Ad Hoc *Distinction Applied*

Whether a subquorum committee of a legislative body is to be treated as a standing or an *ad hoc* committee is more than a simple matter of verbal designation. An Attorney General's opinion (79 Ops.Cal.Atty.Gen. 69 (1996)) concluded that the distinction depends on the scope of authority given to the committee, not formal declarations or disclaimers made in creating it.

> A public water district in Central California is governed by a seven member board of directors. The board has established a subcommittee of three members to advise the board on administrative matters as needed. The subcommittee has been in existence for several years and generally meets monthly, but it does not have a fixed meeting schedule and operates under the following rule:
>
> "The Administrative Committee shall consist of the three Directors appointed by the Chair and approved by the Board. This committee shall not exercise continuing subject matter jurisdiction. Its purpose shall be to advise the Board on administrative matters as appropriate. The Board of Directors shall not fix the meeting schedule of this committee. The committee may meet on the call of the chair or as decided by the members. Action taken

by the Administrative Committee shall be subject to final Board approval."
*****

The first question presented concerns whether a standing committee, composed of less than a quorum of the legislative body, has " continuing subject matter jurisdiction" for purposes of section 54952, subdivision (b), if it provides advice on budgets, audits, contracts, and personnel matters upon request of the legislative body. We conclude that the Act's requirements would be applicable to the subcommittee's meetings.

With respect to the application of the phrase "continuing subject matter jurisdiction" as used in section 54952, we are guided by well established principles of statutory construction.
*****

The courts have liberally construed the terms of the Act so as to effectuate its purposes. (See *Rowen v. Santa Clara Unified School Dist.* (1981) 121 Cal.App.3d 231, 235; *Sacramento Newspaper Guild v. Sacramento County Bd. of Suprs.* (1968) 263 Cal.App.2d 41, 48.)

We note that a "standing committee" is commonly defined as "a committee to consider subjects of a particular class arising during a stated period; specifically] a permanent committee of a legislative body ." (Webster's Third New Internat. Dict. (1971) p. 2224.) "Permanent" may be commonly defined as "to endure, remain." (*Id.* , at p. 1683.)

As for the phrase "continuing subject matter jurisdiction," we find that "continuing" means "needing no renewal" (Webster's, supra, at p. 493), "subject matter" means "matter presented for consideration" (*Id.* , at p. 2276), and "jurisdiction" means "power, right, or authority to hear . . . a cause" (*Id.* , at p. 1227).

Applying these common definitions in carrying out the Act's purposes, we believe that the subcommittee in question has the authority to hear and consider issues relating to budgets, audits, contracts, and personnel matters and that its authority needs no renewal. As such, it is a "legislative body" under the terms of section 54952, subdivision (b), and its meetings are subject to the Act's requirements of notice, a posted agenda, and public participation. Although under its local operating rule, the subcommittee "shall not exercise continuing subject matter jurisdiction," we do not find such rule provision to be determinative. The language of the local rule appears inconsistent at best and may not be used to thwart the purposes and requirements of the Act.

We thus follow function over form in carrying out the Legisla-

> ture's purposes. In particular, this subcommittee does not have a limited term, and it is not an ad hoc committee charged with accomplishing a specific task in a short period of time. Further, it is irrelevant for purposes of section 54952 that the subcommittee is advisory rather than decision making, that its meetings are called by the chair of the subcommittee rather than by formal action of the legislative body, or that some, but not all, of the matters under its jurisdiction are referred to it. The purpose of the subcommittee is to advise the legislative body when requested on those matters within its continuing subject matter jurisdiction.
>
> We conclude that the meetings of a standing committee composed of less than a quorum of a legislative body are subject to the notice, agenda, and public participation requirements of the Act, if the committee has the responsibility of providing advice on budgets, audits, contracts, and personnel matters upon request of the legislative body.

Exclusion of Sub-quorum Groups

This subdivision conveys the presumption (echoed elsewhere in the statute, although sometimes using the term "majority" and apparently using the terms interchangeably) that the Act applies only to the conduct of a quorum of a body. This principle is discussed thoroughly and adopted in *Henderson v. Board of Education*, 78 Cal.App.3d 875 (1978), which cites a consistent history of support for the concept in a line of Attorney General's opinions, and an early pronouncement in *Adler v. City Council*, 184 Cal.App.2d 763 (1960), in which the court stated:

> Ordinarily, a committee is composed of less than a quorum of the legislative body that has created it. In those cases the findings of such a committee have not been deliberated upon by a quorum of the legislative body and the necessity, as well as opportunity, for full public deliberation by the legislative body still remains. Thus the public's rights under the secret meeting law are protected. Therefore, meetings of committees of local agencies where such committees consist of less than a quorum of the members of the legislative body are not covered by the Act.

Id. at 771. Now, of course, the Act does cover standing committees.

§ 1-2(b)(3): Boards of Certain Private Corporations

Under Government Code §54952(c), "legislative body" also applies to bodies that govern private corporate entities, under varying circumstances, namely:

(1) A board, commission, committee, or other multimember body that governs a private corporation, limited liability company, or other entity that either:

(A) Is created by the elected legislative body in order to exercise authority that may lawfully be delegated by the elected governing body to a private corporation, limited liability company or other entity.

(B) Receives funds from a local agency and the membership of whose governing body includes a member of the legislative body of the local agency appointed to that governing body as a full voting member by the legislative body of the local agency.

Delegation to Business Corporation

The situation referred to in subparagraph (1)(A) was found to have obtained in *International Longshoremen's and Warehousemen's Union v. Los Angeles Export Terminal, Inc.*, 69 Cal.App.4th 1219 (1999). The underlying dispute had its origins when the Los Angeles Harbor Commissioners approved development of a large coal depot on Terminal Island, and thereafter proposed a complex joint "shareholders' agreement" with some 28 Japanese companies, six U.S. firms and the harbor department. Under the pact each party would share ownership in a new private, for-profit corporation, the Los Angeles Export Terminal (LAXT). That entity would build and operate a dry bulk handling facility for coal to be exported, on land leased from the harbor department.

The agreement and its ancillary 35-year harbor property lease were both approved by the Los Angeles City Council in 1993. Two years later when the complex was built, the board of LAXT entered into an operating agreement with Pacific Carbon Services Corporation (PCS). The ILWU attacked the agreement in court, alleging PCS was an anti-union employer whose hiring would mean substandard wages, conditions and benefits for LAXT workers. As part of its attack, ILWU contended that the LAXT board must meet openly as a legislative body subject to the Brown Act, had not done so at the time it formed the operating agreement with PCS, and thus left the agreement open to voiding by the court as a product of action taken in violation of the meeting law. The trial court agreed with ILWU and entered an order voiding all action taken by the LAXT board in the 90 days preceding the union's court challenge. It also awarded ILWU $60,000 in attorney's fees.

On appeal, the Second District ran the LAXT board's history, authority and structure through the Brown Act definitional formula for the kind of "legislative body" that would apply, and found what it concluded was a good fit, namely subparagraph (1)(A) of Government Code §54952(c). On the key issue of delegable authority, the court concluded, "Here, the City created LAXT to develop a coal facility on land leased from the Harbor Department, instead of developing the facility directly."

Delegation to Nonprofit Corporation

In *Epstein v. Hollywood Entertainment District II Business Improvement District*, 87 Cal.App.4th 862 (2001), the Second District stressed substance over form, applying the same analysis in noting how an assertedly private nonprofit group came into being. Los Angeles businessman Aaron Epstein, by virtue of his Hollywood Boulevard commercial address, was subject to an assessment by the Hollywood Entertainment District II Business Improvement District (HED2BID). That entity, established by the City of Los Angeles in 1998, was an extension of an earlier district that the city had set up in 1996. Epstein was galled to find that he was forced to subsidize a governmental entity run by a body whose business he could not monitor because its monthly meetings were closed to the public, not preceded by posted notice 72 hours in advance, and even sometimes held outside the business district entirely. The reason given was that neither the original improvement district nor the extension affecting Epstein, HED2BID, was operated by a publicly elected or appointed body. Instead, governance was in the hands of a nonprofit mutual benefit corporation, the Hollywood Entertainment District Property Owners Association (POA), which took the position that it was no different from any other trade or professional association—not subject to a sunshine law applicable to governmental agencies.

The POA board's organizing purpose, however, was to "develop and restore the public areas of the historic core of Hollywood, California, in order to make it a more attractive and popular destination for tourists, shoppers, business people and persons interested in culture and the arts." That the *raison d'etre* of this technically private group tracked the purposes of the public assessment districts—whose management plan's components addressed security, maintenance, marketing, streetscape and administration—was no accident. The papers documenting the city's establishment of the original HEDBID expressly referred to the future creation of a nonprofit association to be given governance authority. The management plan of HED2BID, the 1998 extension, explicitly stated that district programs "will be governed by the (POA), a non-profit corporation which was formed in 1996 to govern (HED1BID)." The management plan even incorporated the detailed bylaws of the POA.

Despite all this, the POA insisted it was outside the Brown Act for Epstein's purposes, since he was situated in HED2BID, which was created after the POA was established. It governed Epstein's district, the POA conceded, but nobody had "created" it to fill this function; it was just there to play the governing role when HED2BID came into being, and therefore Section 54952 (c) (1) (A) could not apply. This argument convinced the trial court, and Epstein was denied the declaration and injunction he had sought.

But on appeal the Second District reversed, finding Epstein entitled to the declaration that the Brown Act applied and an injunction ordering the POA to comply with it, based on the city's actions in establishing HED1BID and its adjacent extension along Hollywood Boulevard, HED2BId. The decisive language in these districts' organizing documents, which in the first instance anticipated creation of a nonprofit governing entity and in the second instance expressly referred to the POA by name and bylaws, was sufficient to show that the city had "created" the association to carry out delegated governing authority, the court reasoned. This was the case despite the fact that city officials themselves had not personally performed the POA's incorporation formalities, the court concluded. The city had, in the phrase applied in ILWU, supra, "played a role in bringing" the POA "into existence." In the court's words,

> The POA was not simply a pre-existing corporation that just "happened" to be available to administer the (assessment) funds for (HED2BID). Instead, the record indicates that the POA was formed and structured in such a way as to take over administrative functions that normally would be handled by City.

Id. at 864.

> City specifically provided in the first ordinance that (HED1BID) *would* be governed by a non-profit association, and even set forth a partial summary of the management and operation of such proposed association. Within days of the first ordinance's adoption, the POA's articles of incorporation were prepared, and less than a month later, were filed with the Secretary of State. The POA's sole purpose was to "develop and restore the public areas of the historic core of Hollywood." And it was the POA that did, in fact, take over governance of (HED1BID). Obviously, when City adopted the first ordinance creating HED1BID that called for the creation of a non-profit association to govern the (HED1BID) programs, the City "played a role in bringing the POA into existence."

Id. at 870 (emphasis in the original).

> Under these circumstances, we would improperly elevate form over substance if we were to treat the POA as a "pre-existing" private entity with which City just "happened" to decide to do business when it turned governance of (HED2BID) over to the

> POA. To turn a blind eye to such a subterfuge would allow City (and potentially, other elected legislative bodies in the future) to circumvent the requirements of the Brown Act, a statutory scheme designed to protect the public's interest in government. This we will not do.

Id. at 872.

Attorney General's Examples

In an opinion published prior to *ILWU* and *Epstein*, the Attorney General concluded that a nonprofit corporation formed by a community redevelopment agency for certain purposes would be covered:

> We are informed that some community redevelopment agencies provide money in their funds to nonprofit corporations for the purpose of increasing, improving, and preserving affordable housing. For example, one agency has formed a nonprofit corporation to administer its housing activities, with agency employees performing the activities on behalf of the corporation and the agency retaining approval power over the corporation's budget.
>
> Subdivision (c) of Government Code section 54952 includes within the definition of "legislative body" the governing board of a private corporation created by the agency's legislative body to exercise authority delegated by the agency or which receives funds from the agency and an agency member sits as a voting director of the corporation. In the facts presented here, the nonprofit corporation formed by the redevelopment agency would be subject to the Ralph M. Brown Act. We conclude that the governing board of a nonprofit corporation formed by a community redevelopment agency to carry out functions delegated to it by the agency must conduct its meetings in public, as well as a nonprofit corporation not created by the agency but where the corporation receives funds from the agency and a member of the agency's legislative body sits as a voting director of the corporation.

81 Ops.Cal.Atty.Gen. 281 (1998).

In a more recent opinion relying on *ILWU* and *Epstein*, the Attorney General concluded that the Act applied to meetings of the governing board of a private, nonprofit corporation that had been

> formed for the purpose of providing programming for a cable television channel set aside for educational use by a cable opera-

tor pursuant to its franchise agreement with a city and subsequently designated by the city to provide the programming services.
*****
In the present circumstances, the city council of the City (an elected legislative body of a local agency) played a role in bringing the Corporation into existence by (1) granting a franchise to Cablevision, (2) requiring Cablevision to set aside an educational channel, (3) designating the Corporation as the entity to operate the channel, and (4) indirectly providing the Corporation with an initial capitalization of $57,000. The term "created by" in section 54952, subdivision (c)(1)(A), means that the "City ' played a role in bringing' the [private corporation] ' into existence.' [Citation.]" (Epstein v. Hollywood Entertainment Dist. II Bus. Improvement Dist., supra, 87 Cal.App.4th at p. 870, citing International Longshoremen's & Warehousemen' s Union v. Los Angeles Export Terminal, Inc., supra, 69 Cal.App.4th at p. 295.)

The authority to operate the educational access channel was lawfully delegated to the Corporation by the city council of the City. … Here, the City has reserved the right to review and approve any guidelines the Corporation has concerning the use of Channel 21 and has reserved the right to terminate its authority previously delegated to the Corporation.

Both of the conditions of section 54952, subdivision (c)(1)(A), have therefore been met, resulting in the Corporation' s board coming within the meaning of a "legislative body" for purposes of the Brown Act's requirements.

85 Ops.Cal.Atty.Gen. 55 (2002).

Governmental Funding and Participation

The scenario described in subparagraph (1)(B), where the private organization "receives funds from a local agency and the membership of (its) governing body includes a member of the legislative body of the local agency appointed to that governing body as a full voting member by the legislative body of the local agency," has not been interpreted by a court. While it is sometimes assumed that the receipt of public funding by a nonprofit corporation should in and of itself subject its meetings or records to some special "sunshine" obligations, such is not the effect of the Brown Act or any other California statute. Subparagraph (1)(B), which requires more, would presumably apply when, for example:

- a city provides funding to a local chamber of commerce, a*nd*
- the city council appoints one of its members to sit on the chamber

board, *and*

- the council member sits on the board as a voting member.

Since this precise formula is so simple to avoid, it is likely that few funding relationships between local agencies and subsidized corporations—nonprofit or commercial—will leave all the elements in place for long unless those involved have an extraordinary commitment to public access and information.

The Attorney General, in the same opinion noted immediately above, found the formula to be fulfilled by a nonprofit corporation

> formed for the purpose of providing programming for a cable television channel set aside for educational use by a cable operator pursuant to its franchise agreement with a city and subsequently designated by the city to provide the programming services.***** The School District provides $200 annually towards the Corporation' s franchise fees. ***** Not only does the School District appoint three of the Corporation's five directors, it must approve the appointments of the other two directors as well. One of the District's trustees is a Corporation director with full voting rights. Hence, the Corporation' s board constitutes a "legislative body" as defined in section 54952, subdivision (c)(1)(B).

The Downey Phenomenon

Paragraph (2) of Government Code §54952(c) reflects legislation addressing a situation arising in the city of Downey. It states:

> Notwithstanding subparagraph (B) of paragraph (1), no board, commission, committee, or other multimember body that governs a private corporation, limited liability company, or other entity that receives funds from a local agency and, as of February 9, 1996, has a member of the legislative body of the local agency as a full voting member of the governing body of that private corporation, limited liability company, or other entity shall be relieved from the public meeting requirements of this chapter by virtue of a change in status of the full voting member to a nonvoting member.

This provision was added as part of a 1996 amendment to the Act that also specified that in order for the Brown Act to apply under the governmental funding definition, the subsidizing legislative body's delegate on the corporation's board must be a "full voting member" thereof. The purpose of the amendment as a whole was to relieve the Downey Community Hospital, a nonprofit corporation, from the open meeting consequences of its relationship to the city of Downey, which pursuant to a lease arrangement had the right to have its council members sit on the hospital board. These members had no voting power as directors, but prior to the 1996 amendment their mere presence on the board, coupled with the city's contribution of the dollar-a-year lease, was thought to make the hospital board subject to the Act. Adding the "full voting member" qualification solved that concern, and the language of paragraph (2) was intended to prevent entities that met the "full voting member" qualification as of early 1996 from removing the voting power of the agency member thereafter simply to escape coverage of the Act.

§ 1-2(b)(4): Boards of Certain Hospital Lessees

Under Government Code §54952(d), "legislative body" also applies to the board of a private corporation that leases and operates the medical facilities of a local hospital district as authorized in the Health and Safety Code, but only if the lease commenced after a certain date. The provision states that the Act governs:

> The lessee of any hospital the whole or part of which is first leased pursuant to subdivision (p) of Section 32121 of the Health and Safety Code after January 1, 1994, where the lessee exercises any material authority of a legislative body of a local agency delegated to it by that legislative body whether the lessee is organized and operated by the local agency or by a delegated authority.

This provision represents a compromise between two forces. The first were those who wished the Brown Act to apply to the boards of corporations which, pursuant to such special lease agreements, were operating hospitals established and still owned by local hospital districts. The second were those who argued that it was inappropriate, and not required by law, to subject these corporate boards to open meeting requirements, which were still applicable to the boards of the hospital districts themselves. Two districts of the Court of Appeal had split on this question, but only one of the opinions was left published. In *Yoffie v. Marin Hospital District*, 193 Cal.App.3d 743 (1987), the First District held that the lease agreement between a hospital district and a private corporation was not a "delegation of authority" of the kind which made the board of the latter a "legislative body" for purposes of the Act. In a case not long thereafter involving Desert Hospital in Palm Springs, the Fourth District held to the contrary in an opinion that was, however, ordered not to be published. The codified compromise grandfathers hospital lease agreements prior to 1994, in effect, outside the Brown Act consistent with the result in *Yoffie*, but with respect to leases commencing after January 1 of that year, provides that the Act shall apply, if the lease involves a delegation of "material" authority by the district to the lessee corporation.

§ 1-2(c): "Member" of a Legislative Body

While the Act does not define the term "member" of a legislative body, the contexts in which the term is used leave little doubt that it refers to those elected or appointed to the body. The Act does, however, extend the obligations imposed on members— and the exposure to enforcement actions—to individuals elected to serve as members who have not yet taken the oath of office. Government Code §54952.1 states:

> Any person elected to serve as a member of a legislative body who has not yet assumed the duties of office shall conform his or her conduct to the requirements of this chapter and shall be treated for purposes of enforcement of this chapter as if he or she has already assumed office.

Bagley-Keene Comparison
Government Code §11121.95: Any person appointed or elected to serve as a member of a state body who has not yet assumed the duties of office shall conform his or her conduct to the requirements of this article and shall be treated for purposes of this article as if he or she has already assumed office.

This provision deters a newly elected majority of a local body, for example, from meeting secretly to discuss and potentially decide matters of policy or other public business in the interim between their election and their being sworn in. It also would preclude a new member-elect of a five-member body, for example, from meeting with two incumbents who will remain on the body because their seats were not up for election.

§ 1-2(d): "Meeting"

Government Code §54952.2 defines "meeting" broadly, prohibits arrangements under which virtual meetings might otherwise be conducted, and enumerates certain circumstances under which the consequences of the broad definition will not arise. The first two provisions state:

> (a) As used in this chapter, "meeting" includes any congregation of a majority of the members of a legislative body at the same time and place to hear, discuss, or deliberate upon any item that is within the subject matter jurisdiction of the legislative body or the local agency to which it pertains.
> (b) Except as authorized pursuant to Section 54953, any use of direct communication, personal intermediaries, or technological devices that is employed by a majority of the members of the legislative body to develop a collective concurrence as to action to be taken on an item by the members of the legislative body is prohibited.

Bagley-Keene Comparison
Government Code §11122.5:
(a) As used in this article, "meeting" includes any congregation of a majority of the members of a state body at the same time and place to hear, discuss, or deliberate upon any item that is within the subject matter jurisdiction of the state body to which it pertains.
(b) Except as authorized pursuant to Section 11123, any use of direct communication, personal intermediaries, or technological devices that is employed by a majority of the members of the state body to develop a collective concurrence as to action to be taken on an item by the members of the state body is prohibited.

No Action Required

While a body's taking action at a meeting in violation of the Act can have some aggravating consequences (see § 1-7(a), (g)), it is not necessary that action be taken in order that a gathering be governed by the Act as a "meeting." Subdivision (a) makes it clear that the term applies although the sole activity of the body's members may be to discuss, deliberate or even hear a presentation on an item of business within their official jurisdiction.

No Formalities Required

The breadth of subdivision (a) makes it clear that what the "congregation" of the body's majority is called by those participating is not determinative; if the elements are fulfilled, the Act applies irrespective of how officials characterize the occasion. An early expression of this principle, as well as the notion above that a meeting is subject to the Act even in the absence of any action taken, occurs in the leading case of *Sacramento Newspaper Guild v. Sacramento County Board of Supervisors*, 263 Cal.App.2d 41 (1968), in which the court stated that in regulating meetings to ensure public access,

> a statute may push beyond debatable limits in order to block evasive techniques. An informal conference or caucus permits crystallization of secret decisions to a point just short of ceremonial acceptance. There is rarely any purpose to a nonpublic premeeting conference except to conduct some part of the decisional process behind closed doors. Only by embracing the collective inquiry and discussion stages, as well as the ultimate step of official action, can an open meeting regulation frustrate these evasive devices.
>
> *****
>
> As operative criteria, formality and informality are alien to the law's design, exposing it to the very evasions it was designed to prevent. Construed in the light of the Brown Act's objectives, the term "meeting" extends to informal sessions or conferences of the board members designed for the discussion of public business.

Id. at 50.

Consistent with this view, the Third District Court of Appeal concluded in a later case that a gathering of a quorum of a school board at a joint "Curriculum Council/Board Work Session," not open to the public, at which the trustees among others viewed a videotape concerning religious-based challenges to textbook materials, and at which discussion was held to bring the participants up to date on the review process for local parents' complaints, was a "meeting" within the meaning of the Act. The reason: it consisted of "collective acquisition and exchange of facts preliminary to the ultimate decision" on a pending dispute within the board's purview. *Frazer v. Dixon Unified School District*, 18 Cal.App.4th 781 (1993).

§ 1-2(d)(1): Serial Meetings

Subdivision (b) of Government Code §54952.2 codifies a principle previously recognized in two Attorney General's opinions and two cases. The Act may be violated by a deliberately orchestrated consensus process in which a majority of the body achieves a meeting of minds concerning action to be taken on (or not taken) an item without ever having been present to deal with it "at the same time and place" as specified in subdivision (a). In 63 Ops.Cal.Atty.Gen. 820 (1980), the Attorney General opined that it was a violation of the Act

> for members of a community redevelopment agency or their staff to hold a series of closed meetings with the city council or the city planning commission to convey information regarding the agency's business on or about the same date despite the fact that a quorum of any governmental body is not present at any given meeting.

Two years later an opinion reached the same conclusion on a somewhat different scenario:

> It would be a violation of the Ralph M. Brown Act for members of a city council to hold a series of closed discussions with citizens having matters of business pending before them to gather or convey information regarding those matters where the discussions are held on successive dates and are so planned to insure that a quorum of the council will not be present at any one meeting. 65 Ops.Cal.Atty.Gen. 63 (1982).

In *Stockton Newspapers, Inc. v. Stockton Redevelopment Agency*, 171 Cal.App.3d 95 (1985), the court directed the trial court to deny the defendants' motion for judgment on the pleadings, where a newspaper had sued for declaratory and injunctive relief, concluding that

> the alleged participation by defendants, a majority of the legislative body of the redevelopment agency, in a series of one-to-one nonpublic and unnoticed telephone conversations with the agency's attorney for the commonly agreed purpose of collectively deciding to approve the transfer of ownership in redevel-

> opment project property constitutes a "meeting" at which "action" was taken in violation of the Brown Act.

Id. at 105.

Citing *Stockton Newspapers* and the 1982 Attorney General's opinion, the California Supreme Court later observed in passing: "Of course the intent of the Brown Act cannot be avoided by subterfuge; a concerted plan to engage in collective deliberation on public business through a series of letters or telephone calls passing from one member of the governing body to the next would violate the open meeting requirement." *Roberts v. City of Palmdale*, 5 Cal.4th 363 (1993). The court distinguished that phenomenon from one in which a quorum simply receives information or advice from a city attorney via a memorandum, noting that the definitions of "meeting" or "session" were such as to " obviously imply collective action."

> We conclude that (the Brown Act authorization for closed sessions to allow attorney consultations on pending litigation) was intended to apply to collective action of local governing boards and not to the passive receipt by individuals of their mail.

Id. at 376.

Because of the variety of situations involving serial communications that may at some point implicate a quorum of the body, the Attorney General has devoted several paragraphs in that office's booklet, *The Brown Act: Open Meetings for Local Legislative Bodies* (1994), to a thoughtful discussion of the issues which bears quotation at length here.

> Once serial communications are found to exist, it must be determined whether the communications were used to develop a concurrence as to action to be taken. If the serial communications were not used to develop a concurrence as to action to be taken, the serial communications do not constitute a meeting and the Act is not applicable. In construing these terms, one should be mindful of the ultimate purposes of the Act— to provide the public with an opportunity to monitor and participate in the decision-making processes of boards and commissions. Accordingly, we think it is likely that a court would determine that matters which have been placed on an agenda are to be deliberated and acted upon by the legislative body in a public meeting. As such, substantive conversations amongst members concerning an agenda

item prior to a public meeting probably would be viewed as contributing to the development of a concurrence as to the ultimate action to be taken.

Conversations which advance or clarify a member's understanding of an issue, or facilitate an agreement or compromise amongst members, or advance the ultimate resolution of an issue, are all examples of communications which contribute to the development of a concurrence as to action to be taken by the legislative body. Accordingly, with respect to items that have been placed on an agenda or that are likely to be placed upon an agenda, members of legislative bodies should avoid serial communications of a substantive nature concerning such items.

This office does not think that the prohibition against serial meetings would prevent an executive officer from planning upcoming meetings by discussing times, dates, and placement of matters on the agenda. It also appears that an executive officer may receive spontaneous input from any of the board members with respect to these or other matters.

The problems arise when systematic communications begin to occur which involve members of the board acquiring substantive information for an upcoming meeting or engaging in debate, discussion, lobbying or any other aspect of the deliberative process either amongst themselves or with staff. For example, executive officers may wish to brief their members on policy decisions and background events concerning proposed agenda items. This office believes that a court would determine that such communications violate the Act, because such discussions are part of the deliberative process. If these communications are permitted to occur in private, a large part of the process by which members reach their decisions will have occurred outside the public eye. In this way, the public is able only to witness a shorthand version of the deliberative process, and its ability to monitor and contribute to the decision-making process will have been curtailed.

The express language of the statute concerning serial meetings largely codifies case law developed by the courts and the opinions issued by this office in the past. In *Frazer v. Dixon Unified School District, supra*, 18 Cal.App.4th 781, 796-798, the court concluded that the Act covers both deliberations and the taking of action. If a collective commitment were a necessary component of every meeting, the body could conduct most or all of its deliberation behind closed doors so long as the body did not actually reach agreement prior to consideration in public session. Accordingly, the court concluded that the collective acquisition of information constituted a meeting. The court cited briefing sessions as examples of deliberative meetings which are covered by the Act, and contrasted these sessions with activities that fall outside the purview of the Act, such as the passive receipt of an individual's mail or the solitary review of a memorandum by an individual board member.

Discussions by E-mail

Electronic mail has become such a universally adopted medium for personal, business and governmental use that it comes naturally as a means of communication among members of a legislative body as well. The Attorney General has addressed this reality in the context of the Brown Act in 84 Ops.Cal.Atty.Gen. 30 (2001). Given the novelty of the issue and the somewhat complicated qualification of the question posed, the analysis and conclusion of that opinion are here reprinted in their entirety, with italicized emphasis added to highlight question and answer.

> The Ralph M. Brown Act (Gov. Code, §§ 54950-54962; "Brown Act") generally requires the legislative body of a local public agency to hold its meetings open to the public. Agendas of the meetings must be posted, and members of the public must be given an opportunity to address the legislative body on any agenda item of interest to the public.
>
> The purposes of the Brown Act are thus to allow the public to attend, observe, monitor, and participate in the decision-making process at the local level of government. Not only are the Actions taken by the legislative body to be monitored by the public but also the deliberations leading to the Actions taken. (See *Roberts v. City of Palmdale* (1993) 5 Cal.4th 363, 373, 375; *Frazer v. Dixon Unified School Dist.* (1993) 18 Cal.App.4th 781, 795-797; *Stockton Newspaper, Inc. v. Redevelopment Agency* (1985) 171 Cal.App.3d 95, 100; *Sacramento Newspaper Guild v. Sacramento County Bd. of Suprs.* (1968) 263 Cal.App.2d 41, 45.) "The term 'deliberation' has been broadly construed to connote 'not only collective discussion, but the collective acquisition and exchange of facts preliminary to the ultimate decision.' [Citation.]" (*Rowen v. Santa Clara Unified School Dist.* (1981) 121 Cal.App.3d 231, 234; see *Roberts v. City of Palmdale, supra*, 5 Cal.4th at p. 376.)
>
> *The question presented for resolution concerns e-mail messages between members of the board of a local public agency. May a majority of the members e-mail each other to develop a collective concurrence as to action to be taken by the board without violating the Brown Act if the e- mails are sent to the secretary*

and chairperson of the agency, the e-mails are posted on the agency's Internet website, and a printed version of each e-mail is reported at the next public meeting of the agency? We conclude that such conditions would not be sufficient to prevent a violation of the Brown Act.

The statute governing our discussion is section 54952.2, subdivision (b), which provides:

"Except as authorized pursuant to Section 54953, any use of direct communication, personal intermediaries, or technological devices that is employed by a majority of the members of the legislative body to develop a collective concurrence as to action to be taken on an item by the members of the legislative body is prohibited."

Section 54953 concerns the use of teleconferencing procedures and has no application to the situation presented herein.

In analyzing the language of section 54952.2, we may apply well recognized principles of statutory construction. We are to "ascertain the intent of the Legislature so as to effectuate the purpose of the law." *(DuBois v. Workers' Comp. Appeals Bd.* (1993) 5 Cal.4th 382, 387.) "The words of the statute are the starting point." (*Wilcox v. Birtwhistle* (1999) 21 Cal.4th 973, 977.) "Words used in a statute . . . should be given the meaning they bear in ordinary use. [Citations.] If the language is clear and unambiguous there is no need for construction, nor is it necessary to resort to indicia of the intent of the Legislature . . . ." *(Lungren v. Deukmejian* (1988) 45 Cal.3d 727, 735.)

Applying these rules of construction to the terms of subdivision (b) of section 54952.2, we find that the sending of e-mails would be the "use of . . . technological devices." The statutory prohibition applies to such use "by a majority of the members of the legislative body." Anything less than a majority is not covered by the statute. (See *Roberts v. City of Palmdale*, *supra*, 5 Cal.4th at pp. 375- 377; *Frazer v. Dixon Unified School Dist.*, *supra*, 18 Cal.App.4th at p. 797.) Here, we are given that a majority of the board members are sending e-mails to each other.

As for the requirement that the e-mails be employed "to develop a collective concurrence as to action to be taken on an item," we note that such activity would include any exchange of facts (see *Roberts v. City of Palmdale*, *supra*, 5 Cal.4th at pp. 375-376; *Frazer v. Dixon Unified School Dist., supra*, 18 Cal.App.4th at p. 796) or, as we have previously explained in our pamphlet on the Brown Act, substantive discussions "which advance or clarify a member's understanding of an issue, or facilitate an agreement or compromise amongst members, or advance the ultimate resolution of an issue" (Cal. Dept. of Justice, *The Brown Act, Open Meetings For Local Legislative Bodies* (1994), p. 12) regarding an agenda item.

We find no distinction between e-mails and other forms of communication such as leaving telephone messages or sending letters or memorandums. If e-mails are employed to develop a collective concurrence by a majority of board members on an agenda item, they are subject to the prohibition of section 54952.2, subdivision (b). Application of the statute in such circumstances furthers the "broad policy of the Act to ensure that local governing bodies deliberate in public." (*Roberts v. City of Palmdale, supra*, 5 Cal.4th at p. 373; see *Frazer v. Dixon Unified School Dist., supra*, 18 Cal.App.4th at pp. 794-795; *Stockton Newspapers, Inc. v. Redevelopment Agency, supra*, 171 Cal.App.3d at p. 100; *Sacramento Newspaper Guild v. Sacramento County Board of Suprs., supra*, 263 Cal.App.3d at p. 45).

We recognize that the three conditions of (1) concurrently sending copies of the e-mails to the secretary and chairperson of the agency, (2) concurrently posting the e-mails on the agency's Internet website, and (3) reporting the contents of the e-mails at the agency's next public meeting would allow the deliberations to be conducted "in public" to some extent. Nevertheless, the deliberations would not be conducted as contemplated by the Brown Act. Members of the public who do not have Internet access would be unable to monitor the deliberations as they occur. All debate concerning an agenda item could well be over before members of the public could be given an opportunity to participate in the decision-making process. (See *Frazer v. Dixon Unified School Dist., supra*, 18 Cal.App.4th at p. 794; Cal. Dept. of Justice, *The Brown Act, Open Meetings For Local Legislative Bodies, supra*, p. 12.) Subdivision (b) of section 54952.2 is straightforward and unambiguous. The proposed conditions satisfy neither the specific language nor all the critical purposes of the statute.

We thus conclude that a majority of the board members of a local public agency may not e-mail each other to develop a collective concurrence as to action to be taken by the board without violating the Brown Act even if the e-mails are also sent to the secretary and chairperson of the agency, the e-mails are posted on the agency's Internet website, and a printed version of each e-mail is reported at the next public meeting of the board.

§ 1-2(d)(2): Gatherings That Are Not "Meetings" *Per Se*

Given the inclusive definition of "meeting" in subdivision (a) of Government Code §54952.2, subdivision (c) below exempts several situations. The first, in paragraph (1), simply clarifies that whatever may be the consequence of serial communications taken as a whole, members are otherwise free individually to communicate with whomever they please. The other paragraphs apply to occasions on which a quorum or majority of a body may be present but the mere fact of that congregation, without more, does not invoke the Act's formalities. Paragraph (2) might apply to a conference of the League of California Cities; paragraph (3) might apply to a candidates' forum sponsored by the League of Women Voters; paragraph (4) might apply to the attendance of a city council at an open and noticed meeting of the city parks commission, or of the county board of supervisors; paragraph (5) might apply to a school board's presence at a groundbreaking ceremony or an employee's retirement party; and paragraph (6) might apply to the presence of county supervisors other than those on the board's legislation committee, at a meeting of that sub-quorum standing committee. The Attorney General has concluded in 81 Ops.Cal.Atty.Gen. 156 (1998), however, that with respect to paragraph (6), "Members of the legislative body of a local public agency may not ask questions or make statements ... (or) sit in special chairs on the dais while attending a meeting of a standing committee of the legislative body 'as observers.'"

Bagley-Keene Comparison
Government Code §11122.5:
(c) The prohibitions of this article do not apply to any of the following:
(1) Individual contacts or conversations between a member of a state body and any other person.
(2) The attendance of a majority of the members of a state body at a conference or similar gathering open to the public that involves a discussion of issues of general interest to the public or to public agencies of the type represented by the state body, provided that a majority of the members do not discuss among themselves, other than as part of the scheduled program, business of a specified nature that is within the subject matter jurisdiction of the state body. This paragraph is not intended to allow members of the public free admission to a conference or similar gathering at which the organizers have required other participants or registrants to pay fees or charges as a condition of attendance.
(3) The attendance of a majority of the

(c) Nothing in this section shall impose the requirements of this chapter upon any of the following:
(1) Individual contacts or conversations between a member of a legislative body and any other person.
(2) The attendance of a majority of the members of a legislative body at a conference or similar gathering open to the public that involves a discussion of issues of general interest to the public or to public agencies of the type represented by the legislative body, provided that a majority of the members do not discuss among themselves, other than as part of the scheduled program, business of a specified nature that is within the subject matter jurisdiction of the local agency. Nothing in this paragraph is intended to allow members of the public free admission to a conference or similar gathering at which the organizers have required other participants or registrants to

pay fees or charges as a condition of attendance.

(3) The attendance of a majority of the members of a legislative body at an open and publicized meeting organized to address a topic of local community concern by a person or organization other than the local agency, provided that a majority of the members do not discuss among themselves, other than as part of the scheduled program, business of a specific nature that is within the subject matter jurisdiction of the legislative body of the local agency.

(4) The attendance of a majority of the members of a legislative body at an open and noticed meeting of another body of the local agency, or at an open and noticed meeting of a legislative body of another local agency, provided that a majority of the members do not discuss among themselves, other than as part of the scheduled meeting, business of a specific nature that is within the subject matter jurisdiction of the legislative body of the local agency.

(5) The attendance of a majority of the members of a legislative body at a purely social or ceremonial occasion, provided that a majority of the members do not discuss among themselves business of a specific nature that is within the subject matter jurisdiction of the legislative body of the local agency.

(6) The attendance of a majority of the members of a legislative body at an open and noticed meeting of a standing committee of that body, provided that the members of the legislative body who are not members of the standing committee attend only as observers.

members of a state body at an open and publicized meeting organized to address a topic of state concern by a person or organization other than the state body, provided that a majority of the members do not discuss among themselves, other than as part of the scheduled program, business of a specific nature that is within the subject matter jurisdiction of the state body.

(4) The attendance of a majority of the members of a state body at an open and noticed meeting of another state body or of a legislative body of a local agency as defined by Section 54951, provided that a majority of the members do not discuss among themselves, other than as part of the scheduled meeting, business of a specific nature that is within the subject matter jurisdiction of the other state body.

(5) The attendance of a majority of the members of a state body at a purely social or ceremonial occasion, provided that a majority of the members do not discuss among themselves business of a specific nature that is within the subject matter jurisdiction of the state body.

(6) The attendance of a majority of the members of a state body at an open and noticed meeting of a standing committee of that body, provided that the members of the state body who are not members of the standing committee attend only as observers.

§ 1-2(e): "Action Taken"

The Act in Government Code §54952.6 defines "action taken" to mean "a collective decision made by a majority of the members of a legislative body, a collective commitment or promise by a majority of the members of a legislative body to make a positive or a negative decision, or an actual vote by a majority of the members of a legislative body when sitting as a body or entity, upon a motion, proposal, resolution, order or ordinance." The rationale for this expansive definition was explained by the

Bagley-Keene Comparison
Government Code §11122:
As used in this article "action taken" means a collective decision made by the members of a state body, a collective commitment or promise by the members of the state body to make a positive or negative decision or an actual vote by the members of a state body when sitting as a body or entity upon a motion, proposal, resolution, order or similar action.

court in *Stockton Newspapers, Inc. v. Redevelopment Agency*, 171 Cal.App.3d 95 (1985):

> Following a narrow judicial construction of the word "meeting" (*Adler v. City Council* (1960) 184 Cal.App.2d 763 [7 Cal.Rptr. 805]), the Legislature amended the Brown Act to make clear that legislative action within the Act was not necessarily limited to action taken at a formal meeting
> *****
> Reviewing the effect of the 1961 amendments, the Attorney General observed there is "little, if any, strength left" to the decision in *Adler v. City Council*, supra. (42 Ops.Cal.Atty.Gen. 61, 67 (1963).) Since the law as amended "prohibits secret gatherings at which a majority of the members of the legislative body agree or agree to agree," it is highly unlikely that "a California court would persist in maintaining that a majority of the members of a local legislative body, without complying with the statute ... could nevertheless meet together in a so-called 'informal,' 'study,' 'discussion,' [']informational, 'fact finding' or 'pre-council' gathering for the avowed purpose of discussing items of general importance irrespective of whether the individual members of the legislative body intend or do not intend to take 'action' at such a gathering."

Id. at 101.

Proof of "action taken" is an essential element for the civil remedy of judicial nullification (see § 1-7(g)) or for a criminal prosecution (see § 1-7(a)). Any "action taken" at an emergency meeting of a body must be communicated to interested members of the local media as soon as possible (see § 1-3(g)). Absent advance written notice to an employee of the agency concerning whom specific complaints and charges are discussed in a closed session, any "action taken" in the session is deemed null and void (see § 1-5(b)(4)). "Action taken" in closed session, if not contingent for its finality on the approval of another party or of a court, or to administrative appeal process, must generally be reported in open session at the same meeting (see § 1-5(a)(3)).

§ 1-3: Requirements for Meetings

If the Act applies to a meeting, certain requirements and prerequisites condition when, where and how the proceeding is to be conducted, and how the costs of such provisions are to be accounted for in making any claims to the state for reimbursement.

§ 1-3(a): Local Siting

The Act sets constraints in subdivisions (b), (c) and (d) of Government Code §54954 on where a body may hold its meetings. The general rule is that they must be held within the local agency's territory, but there are several exceptions for local bodies in general (b) and for school boards (c) and certain joint powers authorities (d) in particular. The purpose of these restrictions, adopted in 1994 legislation, was to end the practice of some local bodies which held "retreats" at locations distant from their home communities, thereby making it difficult, costly or even impossible for constituents to attend. By definition, any meeting held other than at the place adopted by the body for its regular meetings would constitute a special meeting, and for such occasions there are particular notice and other requirements (see § 1-3(f)).

(b) Regular and special meetings of the legislative body shall be held within the boundaries of the territory over which the local agency exercises jurisdiction, except to do any of the following:

(1) Comply with state or federal law or court order, or attend a judicial or administrative proceeding to which the local agency is a party.

(2) Inspect real or personal property which cannot be conveniently brought within the boundaries of the territory over which the local agency exercises jurisdiction provided that the topic of the meeting is limited to items directly related to the real or personal property.

(3) Participate in meetings or discussions of multiagency significance that are outside the boundaries of a local agency's jurisdiction. However, any meeting or discussion held pursuant to this subdivision shall take place within the jurisdiction of one of the participating local agencies and be noticed by all participating agencies as provided for in this chapter.

(4) Meet in the closest meeting facility if the local agency has no meeting facility within the boundaries of the territory over which the local agency exercises jurisdiction, or at the principal office of the local agency if that office is located outside the territory over which the agency exercises jurisdiction.

(5) Meet outside their immediate jurisdiction with elected or appointed officials of the United States or the State of California when a local meeting would be impractical, solely to discuss a legislative or regulatory issue affecting the local agency and over which the federal or state officials have jurisdiction.

(6) Meet outside their immediate jurisdiction if the meeting takes place in or nearby a facility owned by the agency, provided that the topic of the meeting is limited to items directly related to the facility.

(7) Visit the office of the local agency's legal counsel for a closed session on pending litigation held pursuant to Section 54956.9, when to do so would reduce legal fees or costs.

(c) Meetings of the governing board of a school district shall be held within the district except under the circumstances enumerated in subdivision (b), or to do any of the following:

(1) Attend a conference on nonadversarial collective bargaining techniques.

(2) Interview members of the public residing in another district with reference to the trustees' potential employment of the superintendent of that district.

(3) Interview a potential employee from another district.

(d) Meetings of a joint powers authority shall occur within the territory of at least one of its member agencies, or as provided in subdivision (b). However, a joint powers authority which has members throughout the state may meet at any facility in the state which complies with the requirements of Section 54961.

(e) If, by reason of fire, flood, earthquake, or other emergency, it shall be unsafe to meet in the place designated, the meetings shall be held for the duration of the emergency at the place designated by the presiding officer of the legislative body or his or her designee in a notice to the local media that have requested notice pursuant to Section 54956, by the most rapid means of communication available at the time.

With respect to the issue raised in subdivision (b), paragraph (1), a court has concluded that nothing in the Act prevents a legislative body from attending a court-ordered settlement conference. *Sigala v. Anaheim City School Dist.*, 15 Cal.App.4th 661 (1993).

§ 1-3(b): Nondiscriminatory Facilities

The Act states, in Government Code §54961, subdivision (a):

No legislative body of a local agency shall conduct any meeting in any facility that prohibits the admittance of any person, or persons, on the basis of race, religious creed, color, national origin, ancestry, or sex, or which is inaccessible to disabled persons, or where members of the public may not be present without making a payment or purchase. This section shall apply to every local agency as defined in Section 54951.

Bagley-Keene Comparison

Government Code §11131: No state agency shall conduct any meeting, conference, or other function in any facility that prohibits the admittance of any person, or persons, on the basis of race, religious creed, color, national origin, ancestry, or sex, or that is inaccessible to disabled persons, or where members of the public may not be present without making a payment or purchase. As used in this section, "state agency" means and includes every state body, office, officer, department, division, bureau, board, council, commission, or other state agency.

11123.1. All meetings of a state body that are open and public shall meet the protections and prohibitions contained in Section 202 of the Americans with Disabilities Act of 1990 (42 U.S.C. Sec. 12132), and the federal rules and regulations adopted in implementation thereof.

The "inaccessible to disabled persons" language might preclude holding a meeting in a private home or any other structure not architecturally compliant with the Americans with Disabilities Act. This point is expressly reinforced by §54953.2, which states:

All meetings of a legislative body of a local agency that are open and public shall meet the protections and prohibitions contained in Section 202 of the Americans with Disabilities Act of 1990 (42 U.S.C. Sec. 12132), and the federal rules and regulations adopted in implementation thereof.

(See reference to the ADA under *Accommodations for the Disabled* in §1-3 (e)).

The "payment or purchase" language would prevent a body from holding a meeting in a restaurant or other dining area, for example, if citizens attending would have to order something to be allowed to remain. As for an admission charge by the body itself, Government Code §54956.6 states: "No fees may be charged by the legislative body of a local agency for carrying out any provision of this chapter, except as specifically authorized by this chapter."

§ 1-3(c): Teleconferences

Pursuant to subdivision (b) of Government Code §54953, a body may hold a meeting in which one or more of the members are linked to the discussion by telephone or video conferencing technology, but with some significant limitations. A quorum of the body, whether convened in one place or distributed over separate, conference-linked sites, must remain within the territory of the agency. The agenda for the meeting must list all teleconference locations, and, in effect, each of these locations must comport with the Act's requirements for a meeting. At each location there must be an agenda posted, and the public must be admitted, and must have the opportunity to address the body via the conference link. All votes must be by roll call. Otherwise, anything that can be done in a conventional meeting may be done at a teleconferenced meeting. The provision states:

(b)(1) Notwithstanding any other provision of law, the legislative body of a local agency may use teleconferencing for the benefit of the public and the legislative body of a local agency in connection with any meeting or proceeding authorized by law. The teleconferenced meeting or proceeding shall comply with all requirements of this chapter and all otherwise applicable provisions of law relating to a specific type of meeting or proceeding.

(2) Teleconferencing, as authorized by this section, may be used for all purposes in connection with any meeting within the subject matter jurisdiction of the legislative body. All votes taken during a teleconferenced meeting shall be by rollcall.

Bagley-Keene Comparison

Government Code §11123:

(b) (1) This article does not prohibit a state body from holding an open or closed meeting by teleconference for the benefit of the public and state body. The meeting or proceeding held by teleconference shall otherwise comply with all applicable requirements or laws relating to a specific type of meeting or proceeding, including the following:

(A) The teleconferencing meeting shall comply with all requirements of this article applicable to other meetings.

(B) The portion of the teleconferenced meeting that is required to be open to the public shall be audible to the public at the location specified in the notice of the meeting.

(C) If the state body elects to conduct a

meeting or proceeding by teleconference, it shall post agendas at all teleconference locations and conduct teleconference meetings in a manner that protects the rights of any party or member of the public appearing before the state body. Each teleconference location shall be identified in the notice and agenda of the meeting or proceeding, and each teleconference location shall be accessible to the public. The agenda shall provide an opportunity for members of the public to address the state body directly pursuant to Section 11125.7 at each teleconference location.

(D) All votes taken during a teleconferenced meeting shall be by rollcall.

(E) The portion of the teleconferenced meeting that is closed to the public may not include the consideration of any agenda item being heard pursuant to Section 11125.5.

(F) At least one member of the state body shall be physically present at the location specified in the notice of the meeting.

(2) For the purposes of this subdivision, "teleconference" means a meeting of a state body, the members of which are at different locations, connected by electronic means, through either audio or both audio and video. This section does not prohibit a state body from providing members of the public with additional locations in which the public may observe or address the state body by electronic means, through either audio or both audio and video.

(3) If the legislative body of a local agency elects to use teleconferencing, it shall post agendas at all teleconference locations and conduct teleconference meetings in a manner that protects the statutory and constitutional rights of the parties or the public appearing before the legislative body of a local agency. Each teleconference location shall be identified in the notice and agenda of the meeting or proceeding, and each teleconference location shall be accessible to the public. During the teleconference, at least a quorum of the members of the legislative body shall participate from locations within the boundaries of the territory over which the local agency exercises jurisdiction. The agenda shall provide an opportunity for members of the public to address the legislative body directly pursuant to Section 54954.3 at each teleconference location.

(4) For the purposes of this section, "teleconference" means a meeting of a legislative body, the members of which are in different locations, connected by electronic means, through either audio or video, or both. Nothing in this section shall prohibit a local agency from providing the public with additional teleconference locations.

§ 1-3(d): "Open and Public" Meeting

The central mandate of the Act is found in subdivision (a) of Government Code §54953: "All meetings of the legislative body of a local agency shall be open and public, and all persons shall be permitted to attend any meeting of the legislative body of a local agency, except as otherwise provided in this chapter." The exceptions are discussed below in § 1-5.

Bagley-Keene Comparison
Government Code §11123:
(a) All meetings of a state body shall be open and public and all persons shall be permitted to attend any meeting of a state body except as otherwise provided in this article.

Secret Balloting

As a corollary, subdivision (c) states: "(c) No legislative body shall take action by secret ballot, whether preliminary or final."

Grand Jury Testimony

Without defining whether such an occasion constitutes a "meeting," Government Code §54953.1 states, "The provisions of this chapter shall not be construed to prohibit the members of the legislative body of a local agency from giving testimony in private before a grand jury, either as individuals or as a body."

Reaction to Disruption

If a meeting is disrupted, the body may as a last resort limit public attendance pursuant to Government Code §54957.9:

> In the event that any meeting is willfully interrupted by a group or groups of persons so as to render the orderly conduct of such meeting unfeasible and order cannot be restored by the removal of individuals who are willfully interrupting the meeting, the members of the legislative body conducting the meeting may order the meeting room cleared and continue in session. Only matters appearing on the agenda may be considered in such a session. Representatives of the press or other news media, except those participating in the disturbance, shall be allowed to attend any session held pursuant to this section. Nothing in this section shall prohibit the legislative body from establishing a procedure for readmitting an individual or individuals not responsible for willfully disturbing the orderly conduct of the meeting.

Bagley-Keene Comparison

Government Code §11126.5:

In the event that any meeting is willfully interrupted by a group or groups of persons so as to render the orderly conduct of such meeting unfeasible and order cannot be restored by the removal of individuals who are willfully interrupting the meeting the state body conducting the meeting may order the meeting room cleared and continue in session. Nothing in this section shall prohibit the state body from establishing a procedure for readmitting an individual or individuals not responsible for willfully disturbing the orderly conduct of the meeting. Notwithstanding any other provision of law, only matters appearing on the agenda may be considered in such a session. Representatives of the press or other news media, except those participating in the disturbance, shall be allowed to attend any session held pursuant to this section.

Arrest of Disruptive Persons

In what appears to be the only case addressing criminal disruption of a meeting governed by the Brown Act in the First Amendment context, a court concluded that the free speech rights of a protesting citizen at a school board meeting were not violated when he was arrested and removed for dumping several 13-gallon bags of trash on a tarp he spread on the meeting room floor. The defendant, David McMahon, was a resident complaining of the repeated littering of his property by students from a nearby high school. After getting no satisfactory help from Albany Unified School District officials despite previous complaints, he brought garbage bags full of student-scattered trash to a school board meeting and dumped it in front of the trustees during a regular meeting. When he persisted in doing so, the superintendent summoned police and had them remove McMahon under citizen's arrest, after which they cited him for violating Penal Code §403, disturbing a lawful assembly. They then released him, and no charges were filed. McMahon sued the district and various individuals on several grounds, including false arrest, and lost in a jury trial. On appeal, seeking a directed verdict in his favor, he argued that under the leading case of *In re Kay*, 1 Cal.3d 930 (1970), his conduct was protected speech. But the court in *McMahon v. Albany Unified School District*, 104 Cal.App.4th 1275 (2002) noted that the bounds of protected speech—verbal or symbolic—at an official business meeting of a government body are often more confined that those at a speech or political rally, and dependent to a key degree on what is the normally expected conduct at such meetings:

> McMahon claims that no custom or usage, of which he knew or should have known, prevented him from dumping gallons of garbage onto the schoolroom floor. Sufficient evidence supports the jury's finding to the contrary.
>
> The record indicates that McMahon freely discussed a range of subjects at the school board meetings, including trash in school neighborhoods. Previously he had illustrated his point by holding up a bag of discarded items he had collected. None of this conduct was unacceptable within the context of meetings held in Cornell Elementary School's multipurpose room. The jury concluded, however, that dumping trash on the tarp and floor was another matter. The room served as the school's cafeteria and student assembly room, and was used after school for childcare. When McMahon started emptying the bag, Principal Boyan expressly cautioned him: "Kids are in this room tomorrow . . . ." The jury reasonably concluded that dumping trash is not an accepted element of meetings regularly held in a room where children eat and congregate, and thus violated the customs and usages of those meetings. Although McMahon told the audience that the bags contained drug paraphernalia and bottles of alcohol, he now describes the contents as innocuous. His assertion is irrelevant. McMahon dumped garbage. It was well within the jury's province to conclude that McMahon's conduct exceeded the bounds of constitutionally protected speech ...

Id. at 1286. The court expressly upheld as correct the following set of instructions, given to the jury that convicted McMahon, which were tailored to the standards of *In re Kay*:

> For a violation of Penal Code section 403, *disturbing a lawful assembly*, the following elements must exist:

> 1. Mr. McMahon must have substantially impaired the conduct of the meeting;
> 2. by intentionally committing acts;
> 3. in violation of implicit customs or usages for the governance of the meeting of which he knew or, as a reasonable person should have known.
>
> If you find by a preponderance of the evidence that such facts are true, you must find that there was proper cause to arrest Mr. McMahon.
>
> If you find that such facts are not true, you must find that there was not proper cause to arrest Mr. McMahon. That is, if you find that Mr. McMahon was arrested because of his expression (speech)—which can include activities—and not because of his conduct alone, then he would not have been properly arrested.
>
> If you find that the standard of conduct for the Board of Education meeting lies in doubt, in determining whether Mr. McMahon violated implicit customs or usages for the governance of the meeting, a warning and request that Mr. McMahon curtail his conduct should precede an arrest. You may consider whether or not a warning or request was directed to Mr. McMahon to cease his activities, and if none, whether there was an opportunity for such a request to be directed to him. If you find that no warning was given and there was an opportunity to give such a request than [*sic*] the arrest is unlawful.
>
> In the crime of *disturbing a lawful assembly* there must exist a union or joint operation of act or conduct and general criminal intent. General criminal intent does not require an intent to violate the law. When a person intentionally does that which the law declares to be a crime he is acting with general criminal intent, even though he may not know that his act or conduct is unlawful.

Id. at 1285 (emphasis in the original). One of McMahon's other causes of action in an earlier related lawsuit had sought a declaratory judgment that the trustees had violated the Brown Act

> in adjourning the Board meeting when plaintiff was . . . criticizing their policies relating to trash and public safety, and going into closed session and arranging for the arrest of plaintiff, effecting the arrest of plaintiff, and then resuming the Board Meeting after plaintiff's criticism could not longer be heard.

The court noted that in its earlier unpublished opinion in that case it had decided that "(t)he chance that the relevant conduct would recur can properly be regarded as remote, thus the grant of relief was unnecessary in the context of litigation the court was simultaneously ending."

Id. at 1294.

§ 1-3(e): Notice of Regular Meetings

The notice requirements for regular meetings—those on a pre-adopted schedule fixed by action of the body—prescribe the location and timing for posting the agenda and also limit the body's ability to discuss or act on matters not on the agenda. A body must adopt a regular meeting schedule, with exceptions for committees. Subdivision (a) of Government Code §54954 states:

Bagley-Keene Comparison
Government Code §11125:
(a) The state body shall provide notice of its meeting to any person who requests that notice in writing. Notice shall be given and also made available on the Internet at least 10 days in advance of the meeting, and shall include the name, address, and telephone number of any person who can provide further information prior to the meeting, but need not include a list of witnesses expected to appear at the meeting. The written notice shall additionally include the address of the Internet site where notices required by this article are made available.

(b) The notice of a meeting of a body that is a state body shall include a specific agenda for the meeting, containing a brief description of the items of business to be transacted or discussed in either open or closed session. A brief general description of an item generally need not exceed 20 words. A description of an item to
be transacted or discussed in closed session shall include a citation of the specific statutory authority under which a closed session is being held. No item shall be added to the agenda subsequent to the provision of this notice, unless otherwise permitted by this article.

(c) Notice of a meeting of a state body that complies with this section shall also constitute notice of a meeting of an advisory body of that state body, provided that the business to be discussed by the advisory body is covered by the notice of the meeting of the state body, provided that the specific time and place of the advisory body's meeting is announced during the open and public state body's meeting, and provided that the advi-

Each legislative body of a local agency, except for advisory committees or standing committees, shall provide, by ordinance, resolution, bylaws, or by whatever other rule is required for the conduct of business by that body, the time and place for holding regular meetings. Meetings of advisory committees or standing committees, for which an agenda is posted at least 72 hours in advance of the meeting pursuant to subdivision (a) of Section 54954.2, shall be considered for purposes of this chapter as regular meetings of the legislative body.

The notice requirements are set forth in Government Code §54954.2:

(a) At least 72 hours before a regular meeting, the legislative body of the local agency, or its designee, shall post an agenda containing a brief general description of each item of business to be transacted or discussed at the meeting, including items to be discussed in closed session. A brief general description of an item generally need not exceed 20 words. The agenda shall specify the time and location of the regular meeting and shall be posted in a location that is freely accessible to members of the public. If requested, the agenda shall be made available inappropriate alternative formats to persons with a disability, as required by Section 202 of the Americans with Disabilities Act of 1990 (42 U.S.C. Sec. 12132), and the federal rules and regulations adopted in implementation thereof. The agenda shall include information regarding how, to whom, and when a request for disability-related modification or accommodation, including auxiliary aids or services may be made by a person with a disability who requires a modification or accommodation in order to participate in the public meeting.

No action or discussion shall be undertaken on any item not appearing on the posted agenda, except that members of a legislative body or its staff may briefly respond to statements made or questions posed by persons exercising their public testimony rights under Section 54954.3. In addition, on their own initiative or in response to questions posed by the public, a member of a legislative body or its staff may ask a question for clarification, make a brief announcement, or make a brief report on his or her own activities. Furthermore, a member of a legislative body, or the body itself, subject to rules or procedures of the legislative body, may provide a reference to staff or other resources for factual information, request staff to report back to the body at a subsequent meeting concerning any matter, or take action to direct staff to place a matter of business on a future agenda.

(b) Notwithstanding subdivision (a), the legislative body may take action on items of business not appearing on the posted agenda under any of the conditions stated below. Prior to discussing any item pursuant to this subdivision, the legislative body shall publicly identify the item.

(1) Upon a determination by a majority vote of the legislative body that an emergency situation exists, as defined in Section 54956.5.

(2) Upon a determination by a two-thirds vote of the members of the legislative body present at the meeting, or, if less than two-thirds of the members are present, a unanimous vote of those members present, that there is a need to take immediate

sory body's meeting is conducted within a reasonable time of, and nearby, the meeting of the state body.

(d) A person may request, and shall be provided, notice pursuant to subdivision (a) for all meetings of a state body or for a specific meeting or meetings. In addition, at the state body's discretion, a person may request, and may be provided, notice of only those meetings of a state body at which a particular subject or subjects specified in the request will be discussed.

(e) A request for notice of more than one meeting of a state body shall be subject to the provisions of Section 14911.

(f) The notice shall be made available in appropriate alternative formats, as required by Section 202 of the Americans with Disabilities Act of 1990 (42 U.S.C. Sec. 12132), and the federal rules and regulations adopted in implementation thereof, upon request by any person with a disability. The notice shall include information regarding how, to whom, and by when a request for any disability-related modification or accommodation, including auxiliary aids or services may be made by a person with a disability who requires these aids or services in order to participate in the public meeting.

11125.3. (a) Notwithstanding Section 11125, a state body may take action on items of business not appearing on the posted agenda under any of the conditions stated below:

(1) Upon a determination by a majority vote of the state body that an emergency situation exists, as defined in Section 11125.5.

(2) Upon a determination by a two-thirds vote of the state body, or, if less than two-thirds of the members are present, a unanimous vote of those members present, that there exists a need to take immediate action and that the need for action came to the attention of the state body subsequent to the agenda being posted as specified in Section 11125.

(b) Notice of the additional item to be considered shall be provided to each member of the state body and to all parties that have requested notice of its meetings as soon as is practicable after a determination of the need to consider the item is made, but shall be delivered in a manner that allows it to be received by the members and by newspapers of general circulation and radio or television stations at least 48 hours before the time of the meeting specified in the notice.

Notice shall be made available to newspapers of general circulation and radio or television stations by providing that notice to all national press wire services. Notice shall also be made available on the Internet as soon as is practicable after the decision to consider additional items at a meeting has been made.

11125.9. Regional water quality control boards shall comply with the notification guidelines in Section 11125 and, in addition, shall do both of the following:

(a) Notify, in writing, all clerks of the city councils and county boards of supervisors within the regional board's jurisdiction of any and all board hearings at least 10 days prior to the hearing. Notification shall include an agenda for the meeting with contents as described in subdivision (b) of Section 11125 as well as the name, address, and telephone number of any person who can provide further information prior to the meeting, but need not include a list of witnesses expected to appear at the meeting. Each clerk, upon receipt of the notification of a board hearing, shall distribute the notice to all members of the respective city council or board of supervisors within the regional board's jurisdiction.

(b) Notify, in writing, all newspapers with a circulation rate of at least 10,000 within the regional board's jurisdiction of any and all board hearings, at least 10 days prior to the hearing. Notification shall include an agenda for the meeting with contents as described in subdivision (b) of Section 11125 as well as the name, address, and telephone number of any person who can provide further information prior to the meeting, but need not include a list of witnesses expected to appear ...

action and that the need for action came to the attention of the local agency subsequent to the agenda being posted as specified in subdivision (a).

(3) The item was posted pursuant to subdivision (a) for a prior meeting of the legislative body occurring not more than five calendar days prior to the date action is taken on the item, and at the prior meeting the item was continued to the meeting at which action is being taken.

Accommodations for the Disabled

The provision of the Americans with Disabilities Act (ADA) referenced by the Brown Act in subdivision (a) above states:

> Subject to the provisions of this subchapter, no qualified individual with a disability shall, by reason of such disability, be excluded from participation in or be denied the benefits of the services, programs, or activities of a public entity, or be subjected to discrimination by any such entity.

The "appropriate alternative format" phrase does not appear in the ADA, but interpretive regulations issued by the U.S. Department of Justice provide the following rules for government agencies in their communications with the disabled in general.

Title 28 Code of Federal Regulations
Chapter 1, Part 35, Subpart E, Communications

35.160 General.

(a) A public entity shall take appropriate steps to ensure that communications with applicants, participants, and members of the public with disabilities are as effective as communications with others.

(b)(1) A public entity shall furnish appropriate auxiliary aids and services where necessary to afford an individual with a disability an equal opportunity to participate in, and enjoy the benefits of, a service, program, or activity conducted by a public entity.

(2) In determining what type of auxiliary aid and service is necessary, a public entity shall give primary consideration to the requests of the individual with disabilities.

35.161 Telecommunication devices for the deaf (TDD's).

Where a public entity communicates by telephone with applicants and beneficiaries, TDD's or equally effective telecommunication systems shall be used to communicate with individuals with impaired hearing or speech.

35.162 Telephone emergency services.

Telephone emergency services, including 911 services, shall provide direct access to individuals who use TDD's and computer modems.

35.163 Information and signage.

(a) A public entity shall ensure that interested persons, including persons with impaired vision or hearing, can obtain information as to the existence and location of accessible services, activities, and facilities.

(b) A public entity shall provide signage at all inaccessible entrances to each of its facilities, directing users to an accessible entrance or to a location at which they can obtain information about accessible facilities. The international symbol for accessibility shall be used at each accessible entrance of a facility.

35.164 Duties.

This subpart does not require a public entity to take any action that it can demonstrate would result in a fundamental alteration in the nature of a service, program, or activity or in undue financial and administrative burdens. In those circumstances where personnel of the public entity believe that the proposed action would fundamentally alter the service, program, or activity or would result in undue financial and administrative burdens, a public entity has the burden of proving that compliance with this subpart would result in such alteration or burdens. The decision that compliance would result in such alteration or burdens must be made by the head of the public entity or his or her designee after considering all resources available for use in the funding and operation of the service, program, or activity and must be accompanied by a written statement of the reasons for reaching that conclusion. If an action required to comply with this subpart would result in such an alteration or such burdens, a public entity shall take any other action that would not result in such an alteration or such burdens but would nevertheless ensure that, to the maximum extent possible, individuals with disabilities receive the benefits or services provided by the public entity.

Closed Session Meeting Topics

The agenda must disclose not only items to be dealt with in open session, but closed session items as well. The content of such agenda descriptions that will create a safe harbor against any challenge on the basis of allegedly inadequate information are set forth in statutory examples discussed in connection with the various types of closed session described below (see § 1.5).

Committee Meeting Notices

In subdivision (a) of Government Code §54954, advisory and standing committees are excused from adopting regular meeting schedules, but if they do post their agendas 72 hours in advance, their meetings are deemed regular meetings. If they do not adopt a regular meeting schedule, their meetings are presumably subject to the special meeting notice requirements (see § 1-3(f)).

Free Accessibility

The Act does not require the posting of more than one copy of the agenda, but that copy, at least, must be posted where it is "freely accessible to" the public. The Attorney General has concluded that weekend hours may be counted as part of the 72-hour period for the posting of an agenda prior to the regular meeting of the legislative body of a local agency, but that posting the agenda in a public building that is locked outside business hours would not satisfy the statutory requirement. 78 Ops.Cal.Atty.Gen. 327 (1995).

§ 1-3(e)(1): Adequacy of Agenda Descriptions

A regular meeting agenda is required to provide a "brief general description of each item of business to be transacted or discussed" at the meeting. The "brief general description" can be just that—brief and general, usually satisfied within 20 words—but it should be a description, not a code phrase unintelligible to the public, or an empty category label appearing without further elaboration on every agenda. As stated in the 1994 edition of the Attorney General's *The Brown Act: Open Meetings for Local Legislative Bodies*: "The purpose of the brief general description is to inform interested members of the public about the subject matter under consideration so that they can determine whether to monitor or participate in the meeting of the body." This does not mean that the agenda description need educate the reader about all aspects of an item—such would often be impossible in any "brief" or "general" way, and the law clearly assumes that citizens who have a particular interest in a given subject matter will take steps to find out more about the proposal in advance, or to attend the meeting, or both. But it does mean, among other things, that when it is possible to use a few words to *alert* the public to an obviously consequential or controversial proposal, a failure to do just that may violate the law if its effect is to leave those most likely to care unaware and with lowered guard.

The leading example of this defect was identified in *Carlson v. Para-*

dise Unified School District, 18 Cal.App.3d 196 (1971) as violating not the Brown Act but a comparable public notice provision, Education Code §966, which if anything was considerably less imposing than the current Brown Act language. It simply called for the posting of "a list of items that will constitute the agenda." The offending school board listed "Continuation school site change"—just those four words—as one item, but its literally hidden agenda, executed at that meeting and maintained despite parents' immediate entreaties, was not only to transfer the continuation program to an elementary school campus, but to relocate the elementary school program—and students—elsewhere. The court, affirming a trial court order that enjoined this shift on the basis that the board acted without jurisdiction in violating a mandatory notice statute, remarked that the "school site change" listing

> . . . was entirely inadequate notice to a citizenry which may have been concerned over a school closure. On this point alone, the agenda item, while not deceitful, was entirely misleading and inadequate to show the whole scope of the board's intended plans. It would have taken relatively little effort to add to the agenda that this "school site change" also included the discontinuance of elementary education at Canyon View and the transfer of those students to Ponderosa School.

Id. at 200.

No Prediction of Action Required

If a proposal is sufficiently described, the agenda need not state in advance the precise decision the body would make. "The agenda item made it clear," stated the court in *Phillips v. Seely,* 43 Cal.App.3d 104, 119 (1974), "that the board was to hear and consider an offer to supply public defender services to the county . . . where the subject matter to be considered is sufficiently defined to apprise the public of the matter to be considered and notice has been given in the manner required by law, the governing body is not required to give further special notice of what action it might take."

The Fair Warning Standard

General titling or captioning is insufficient if it fails to communicate the essence of a specific and unusual proposal. A court held that a school board agenda item worded "Resolution Regarding Certificated Employees" was unacceptably vague in that it "could have referred to any number of routine resolutions concerning certificated employees and cannot be said to have given fair warning" of what was actually on the table

—"that a reduction in staff or termination of employees would be considered." *Campbell Elementary Teachers Association v. Abbott,* 76 Cal.App.3d 796, 805 (1978).

Novel Change in Proposal to be Highlighted

Truly different options introduced into a repeatedly noticed proposal must be highlighted. Where several alternatives for a proposed school desegregation plan had been defined through previous meetings and hearings, the California Supreme Court held, a routinely repeated agenda item that referred exclusively to those established options was misleading for a meeting at which a new option was presented with significantly different consequences, such as school closures never before contemplated. Moreover, the fact that the new option and the staff's intention to air it at the meeting had received considerable media publicity did not legally mitigate the misleading character of the agenda, which nonetheless referred only to the first three options. *Santa Barbara School District v. Superior Court,* 13 Cal.3d 315 (1975).

Other Laws May Require More Detail

Agenda descriptions must comply with any special statutory requirements for specificity. For example, a provision of the Health and Safety Code required, prior to a board of supervisors' closure of certain county health care facilities, a hearing preceded by a notice 30 days in advance containing "a detailed list of the proposed reductions or changes, by facility and service (including) … the amount and type of each proposed change, the expected saving, and the number of persons affected." Accordingly, the initial timely notice giving citizens only a few of these specifics was legally insufficient, and the corrective notice, published only a week before the hearing, while sufficiently detailed, was untimely. *Smith v. Board of Supervisors*, 216 Cal.App.3d 862 (1989).

No Need to Identify Sexual Misconduct Victims

Government Code §54961, subdivision (b) states: "No notice, agenda, announcement, or report required under this chapter need identify any victim or alleged victim of tortious sexual conduct or child abuse unless the identity of the person has been publicly disclosed."

§ 1-3(e)(2): Action Prohibited on Nonagendized Items

Even the clearest agenda language is of limited use to the public if, at the meeting, the body is free to take action on business not listed at all. The latter portion of Government Code §54954.2 attempts to preclude unwarranted surprise action, or even extensive discussion by the members of a nonagendized item, while allowing flexibility to address unforeseen and urgent matters. On the one hand, members of the body may provide brief informational reports on their own personal activities, make announcements, and interact with public speakers and staff for informational or procedural purposes, including the addition of an item to a future agenda. On the other hand, they may not indulge in policy discussions or take substantive action of any kind on a nonagendized item without making certain findings by a specified vote.

The first situation permitting consideration of, and action on, nonagendized items is one of "emergency." Within the narrow meaning discussed in § 1-3(g) below, an emergency would justify a meeting on one hour's notice to the media. Here the body must find by a majority vote that there exists a condition of disruption to public facilities that "severely impairs" public health, safety or both.

The more ordinary second situation—but if properly observed, still quite rare—is when the body is able to find, by a supermajority or unanimous vote, that immediate action is required by an exigency unknown to the agency at the time the agenda was posted. The table below shows the votes required to make such a finding by members of a body comprising five, six or seven members in total, depending on how many are present.

	All Present	6 Present	5 Present	4 Present	3 Present
5 Member Body	4 votes	N.A.	4 votes	4 votes	3 votes
6 Member Body	4 votes	4 votes	4 votes	4 votes	no quorum
7 Member Body	5 votes	4 votes	4 votes	4 votes	no quorum

Only one case has addressed how pressing such urgency must be, but it illustrates that when presented with the issue, a court may conclude that a body's finding of the need for immediate action was contrary to fact and inadequate as a matter of law. The court in *Cohan v. City of Thousand Oaks,* 30 Cal.App.4th 547, 556 (1994) concluded that a bona fide "urgent action" situation was not created by a crowd at a city council demanding the overturn of an unpopular planning commission ruling not included on the agenda, especially where the council knew in advance that the ruling was controversial and that time was running out to appeal.

§ 1-3(f): Notice of Special Meeting

If a body needs to address a matter that it deems pressing enough not to wait for the next scheduled regular meeting, or an issue that deserves extensive consideration without the press of other business, or if it needs otherwise to convene at some time or place other than its adopted meeting time or site, it may depart from its regular meeting schedule and convene at some other time or place pursuant to Government Code Section §54956:

A special meeting may be called at any time by the presiding officer of the legislative body of a local agency, or by a majority of the members of the legislative body, by delivering written notice to each member of the legislative body and to each local newspaper of general circulation and radio or television station requesting notice in writing. The notice shall be delivered personally or by any other means and shall be received at least 24 hours before the time of the meeting as specified in the notice. The call and notice shall specify the time and place of the special meeting and the business to be transacted or discussed. No other business shall be considered at these meetings by the legislative body. The written notice may be dispensed with as to any member who at or prior to the time the meeting convenes files with the clerk or secretary of the legislative body a written waiver of notice. The waiver may be given by telegram. The written notice may also be dispensed with as to any member who is actually present at the meeting at the time it convenes.

The call and notice shall be posted at least 24 hours prior to the special meeting in a location that is freely accessible to members of the public.

Bagley-Keene Comparison
Government Code §11125.4:

(a) A special meeting may be called at any time by the presiding officer of the state body or by a majority of the members of the state body. A special meeting may only be called for one of the following purposes where compliance with the 10-day notice provisions of Section 11125 would impose a substantial hardship on the state body or where immediate action is required to protect the public interest:

(1) To consider "pending litigation" as that term is defined in subdivision (e) of Section 11126.

(2) To consider proposed legislation.

(3) To consider issuance of a legal opinion.

(4) To consider disciplinary action involving a state officer or employee.

(5) To consider the purchase, sale, exchange, or lease of real property.

(6) To consider license examinations and applications.

(7) To consider an action on a loan or grant provided pursuant to Division 31 (commencing with Section 50000) of the Health and Safety Code.

(8) To consider its response to a confidential final draft audit report as permitted by Section 11126.2.

(b) When a special meeting is called pursuant to one of the purposes specified in subdivision (a), the state body shall provide notice of the special meeting to each member of the state body and to all parties that have requested notice of its meetings as soon as is practicable after the decision to call a special meeting has been made, but shall deliver the notice in a manner that allows it to be received by the members and by newspapers of general circulation and radio or television stations at least 48 hours before the time of the special meeting specified in the notice. Notice shall be made available to newspapers of general circulation and radio or television stations by providing that notice to all national press wire services. Notice shall also be made available on the Internet within the time periods required by this section. The notice shall specify the time and place of the special meeting and the business to be transacted. The written notice shall additionally specify the address of the Internet Web site where notices required by this article are made available. No other business shall be considered at a special meeting by the state body. The written notice may be dispensed with as to any member who at or prior to the time the meeting convenes files with the clerk or secretary of the state body a written waiver of notice. The waiver may be given by telegram, facsimile transmission, or similar means. The written notice may also be dispensed with as to any member who is actually present at the meeting at the time it convenes. Notice shall be required pursuant to this section regardless of whether any action is taken at the special meeting.

(c) At the commencement of any special meeting, the state body must make a finding in open session that the delay necessitated by providing notice 10 days prior to a meeting as required by Section 11125 would cause a substantial hardship on the body or that immediate action is required to protect the public interest.

The finding shall set forth the specific facts that constitute the hardship to the body or the impending harm to the public interest. The finding shall be adopted by a two-thirds vote of the body, or, if less than two-thirds of the members are present, a unanimous vote of those members present. The finding shall be made available on the Internet. Failure to adopt the finding terminates the meeting.

Brief General Description

A court has held that the statutory requirement that the agenda for a regular meeting contain a “brief general description” of each item (see § 1-3(e) above) applies to notices of special meetings as well:

> We do not understand section 54956 to allow a City to omit the "brief general description" required by section 54954.2. Section 54956 requires the notice to "specify . . . the business to be transacted or discussed." Section 54954.2 requires the agenda to give

> "a brief general description of each item of business to be transacted or discussed." The word "specify" means "to name or state explicitly or in detail." (Webster's Collegiate Dict. (10th ed. 1993 p. 1129.) We cannot conceive of how a City could "specify" an item of business without providing a "brief general description" of that item of business. In our view, section 54956's requirement that the notice "specify" is intended to refer back to section 54954.2's requirement that an agenda provide a "description."

Moreno v. City of King, 127 Cal.App.4th 17, 26 (2005).

Notice to Local Media

The Attorney General has concluded that a newspaper or broadcast station need not receive the written notice unless it has submitted a written request for such alerts (62 Ops.Cal.Atty.Gen 658 (1979)), but that if such a request has been submitted, the fact that the discussion will take place entirely in closed session does not excuse the notice. 43 Ops.Cal. Atty. Gen. 79 (1964).

§ 1-3(g): Notice of Emergency Meeting; "Dire" Emergencies

The briefest period of advance notice is for an "emergency" meeting, with rules prescribed in §54956.5:

> (a) For purposes of this section, "emergency situation" means both of the following:
>
> (1) An emergency, which shall be defined as a work stoppage, crippling activity, or other activity that severely impairs public health, safety, or both, as determined by a majority of the members of the legislative body.
>
> (2) A dire emergency, which shall be defined as a crippling disaster, mass destruction, terrorist act, or threatened terrorist activity that poses peril so immediate and significant that requiring legislative body to provide one-hour notice before holding an emergency meeting under this section may endanger the public health, safety, or both, as determined by a majority of the members of the legislative body.
>
> (b) (1) Subject to paragraph (2), in the case of an emergency situation involving matters upon which prompt action is necessary due to the disruption or threatened disruption of public facilities, a legislative body may hold

Bagley-Keene Comparison

Government Code §11125.5:

(a) In the case of an emergency situation involving matters upon which prompt action is necessary due to the disruption or threatened disruption of public facilities, a state body may hold an emergency meeting without complying with the 10-day notice requirement of Section 11125 or the 48-hour notice requirement of Section 11125.4.

(b) For purposes of this section, "emergency situation" means any of the following, as determined by a majority of the members of the state body during a meeting prior to the emergency meeting, or at the beginning of the emergency meeting:

(1) Work stoppage or other activity that severely impairs public health or safety, or both.

(2) Crippling disaster that severely impairs public health or safety, or both.

(c) However, newspapers of general circulation and radio or television stations that have requested notice of meetings pursuant to Section 11125 shall be notified by the presiding officer of the state body, or a designee thereof, one hour prior to the emeran emergency meeting without complying with either the 24-hour notice requirement or the 24-hour posting requirement of Section 54956 or both of the notice and posting requirements

(2) Each local newspaper of general circulation and radio or television station that has requested notice of special meetings pursuant to Section 54956 shall be notified by the presiding officer of the legislative body, or designee thereof, one hour prior to the emergency meeting, or, in the case of a dire emergency, at or near the time that the presiding officer or designee notifies the members of the legislative body of the emergency meeting. This notice shall be given by telephone and all telephone numbers provided in the most recent request of a newspaper or station for notification of special meetings shall be exhausted. In the event that telephone services are not functioning, the notice requirements of this section shall be deemed waived, and the legislative body, or designee of the legislative body, shall notify those newspapers, radio stations, or television stations of the fact of the holding of the emergency meeting, the purpose of the meeting, and any action taken at the meeting as soon after the meeting as possible.

(c) During a meeting held pursuant to this section, the legislative body may meet in closed session pursuant to Section 54957 if agreed to by a two-thirds vote of the members of the legislative body present, or, if less than two-thirds of the members are present, by a unanimous vote of the members present.

(d) All special meeting requirements, as prescribed in Section 54956 shall be applicable to a meeting called pursuant to this section, with the exception of the 24-hour notice requirement.

(e) The minutes of a meeting called pursuant to this section, a list of persons whom the presiding officer of the legislative body, or designee of the legislative body, notified or attempted to notify, a copy of the rollcall vote, and any actions taken at the meeting shall be posted for a minimum of 10 days in a public place as soon after the meeting as possible.

gency meeting by telephone. Notice shall also be made available on the Internet as soon as is practicable after the decision to call the emergency meeting has been made. If telephone services are not functioning, the notice requirements of this section shall be deemed waived, and the presiding officer of the state body, or a designee thereof, shall notify those newspapers, radio stations, or television stations of the fact of the holding of the emergency meeting, the purpose of the meeting, and any action taken at the meeting as soon after the meeting as possible.

(d) The minutes of a meeting called pursuant to this section, a list of persons who the presiding officer of the state body, or a designee thereof, notified or attempted to notify, a copy of the rollcall vote, and any action taken at the meeting shall be posted for a minimum of 10 days in a public place, and also made available on the Internet for a minimum of 10 days, as soon after the meeting as possible.

11125.6. (a) An emergency meeting may be called at any time by the president of the Fish and Game Commission or by a majority of the members of the commission to consider an appeal of a closure of or restriction in a fishery adopted pursuant to Section 7710 of the Fish
and Game Code. In the case of an emergency situation involving matters upon which prompt action is necessary due to the disruption or threatened disruption of an established fishery, the commission may hold an emergency meeting without complying with the 10-day notice requirement of Section 11125 or the 48-hour notice requirement of Section 11125.4 if the delay necessitated by providing the 10-day notice of a public meeting required by Section 11125 or the 48-hour notice required by Section 11125.4 would significantly adversely impact the economic benefits of a fishery to the participants in the fishery and to the people of the state or significantly adversely impact the sustainability of a fishery managed by the state.

(b) At the commencement of an emergency meeting called pursuant to this section, the commission shall make a finding in open session that the delay necessitated by providing notice 10 days prior to a meeting as required by Section 11125 or 48 hours prior to a meeting as required by Section 11125.4 would significantly adversely impact the economic benefits of a fishery to the participants in the fishery and to the people of the state or significantly adversely impact the sustainability of a fishery managed by the state. The finding shall set forth the specific facts that constitute the impact to the economic benefits of the fishery or the sustainability of the fishery. The finding shall be adopted by a vote of at least four members of the commission, or, if less than four of the members are present, a unanimous vote of those members present. Failure to adopt the finding shall terminate the meeting.

(c) Newspapers of general circulation and radio or television stations that have requested notice of meetings pursuant to Section 11125 shall be notified by the presiding officer of the commission, or a designee thereof, one hour prior to the emergency meeting by telephone.

(d) The minutes of an emergency meeting called pursuant to this section, a list of persons who the president of the commission, or a designee thereof, notified or attempted to notify, a copy of the rollcall vote, and any action taken at the meeting shall be posted for a minimum of 10 days in a public place as soon after the meeting as possible.

Timing of Media Notice

The main practical difference between an "emergency" and a "dire emergency" within the meaning of this section—since both involve a present and serious threat of some kind to public health or safety—is whether the meeting must be held only after an hour's telephone notice to the media on record as desiring notice, or whether it may be started as soon as possible, with the media alerted as soon as members of the body have been notified. If the situation is caused by a work stoppage, for example, one-hour notice would probably be required because that situation is one specified for an emergency but not a dire emergency procedure. But if some other human causation (negligent, criminal or terrorist) or "act of God" is one that "poses peril so immediate and significant that requiring the legislative body to provide one-hour notice before holding an emergency meeting under this section may endanger the public health, safety, or both," then the hour's advance media notice may be dispensed with. But this judgment is not a matter of the personal discretion of the staff or even the body's presiding officer; it can be decided only by a majority of the body.

Although an emergency meeting my include a closed session authorized by Government Code §54957—if agreed by a supermajority vote of the members—it is likely that what the Legislature intended here was not a personnel discussion of some kind but rather the other function recognized by that section as needing confidentiality, namely to confer "with the Attorney General, district attorney, agency counsel, sheriff, or chief of police, or their respective deputies, or a security consultant or a security operations manager, on matters posing a threat to the security of public buildings, a threat to the security of essential public services, including water, drinking water, wastewater treatment, natural gas service, and electric service, or a threat to the public's right of access to public services or public facilities."

§ 1-3(i): Notice of Adjournment, Continuance

The final general notice provisions deal with procedures for alerting the public that a meeting has been adjourned, or a hearing continued, to a later time. Ironically, those present at the time of adjournment or continuance probably do not need notice other than that announced by the chair, while those absent at that point would have little reason to inquire or check for a posted notice.

Adjournments

Government Code §54955 states:

> The legislative body of a local agency may adjourn any regular, adjourned regular, special or adjourned special meeting to a time and place specified in the order of adjournment. Less than a quorum may so adjourn from time to time. If all members are absent from any regular or adjourned regular meeting the clerk or secretary of the legislative body may declare the meeting adjourned to a stated time and place and he shall cause a written notice of the adjournment to be given in the same manner as provided in Section 54956 for special meetings, unless such notice is waived as provided for special meetings. A copy of the order or notice of adjournment shall be conspicuously posted on or near the door of the place where the regular, adjourned regular, special or adjourned special meeting was held within 24 hours after the time of the adjournment. When a regular or adjourned regular meeting is adjourned as provided in this section, the resulting adjourned regular meeting is a regular meeting for all purposes. When an order of adjournment of any meeting fails to state the hour at which the adjourned meeting is to be held, it shall be held at the hour specified for regular meetings by ordinance, resolution, bylaw, or other rule.

Bagley-Keene Comparison

Government Code §11128.5:

The state body may adjourn any regular, adjourned regular, special, or adjourned special meeting to a time and place specified in the order of adjournment. Less than a quorum may so adjourn from time to time. If all members are absent from any regular or adjourned regular meeting, the clerk or secretary of the state body may declare the meeting adjourned to a stated time and place and he or she shall cause a written notice of the adjournment to be given in the same manner as provided in Section 11125.4 for special meetings, unless that notice is waived as provided for special meetings. A copy of the order or notice of adjournment shall be conspicuously posted on or near the door of the place where the regular, adjourned regular, special, or adjourned special meeting was held within 24 hours after the time of the adjournment. When a regular or adjourned regular meeting is adjourned as provided in this section, the resulting adjourned regular meeting is a regular meeting for all purposes. When an order of adjournment of any meeting fails to state the hour at which the adjourned meeting is to be held, it shall be held at the hour specified for regular meetings by law or regulation.

Continuances

Government Code §54955.1 states:

> Any hearing being held, or noticed or ordered to be held, by a legislative body of a local agency at any meeting may by order or notice of continuance be continued or recontinued to any subsequent meeting of the legislative body in the same manner and to the same extent set forth in Section 54955 for the adjournment of meetings; provided, that if the hearing is continued to a time less than 24 hours after the time specified in the order or notice of hearing, a copy of the order or notice of continuance of hearing shall be posted immediately following the meeting at which the order or declaration of continuance was adopted or made.

Bagley-Keene Comparison
Government Code §11129:
Any hearing being held, or noticed or ordered to be held by a state body at any meeting may by order or notice of continuance be continued or recontinued to any subsequent meeting of the state body in the same manner and to the same extent set forth in Section 11128.5 for the adjournment of meetings. A copy of the order or notice of continuance shall be conspicuously posted on or near the door of the place where the hearing was held within 24 hours after the time of the continuance; provided, that if the hearing is continued to a time less than 24 hours after the time specified in the order or notice of hearing, a copy of the order or notice of continuance of hearing shall be posted immediately following the meeting at which the order or declaration of continuance was adopted or made.

§ 1-3(j): Notice of Tax or Assessment Hearing

The most comprehensive notice mandate in the Act, requiring both general notification to the community and direct written alerts to affected individuals, is required when an agency is contemplating imposing new revenue burdens on the public. The procedures, which call for both a "meeting" and a separate "hearing" on a proposed new or increased general tax or assessment, are described in Government Code §54954.6:

> (a)(1) Before adopting any new or increased general tax or any new or increased assessment, the legislative body of a local agency shall conduct at least one public meeting at which local officials shall allow public testimony regarding the proposed new or increased general tax or new or increased assessment in addition to the noticed public hearing at which the legislative body proposes to enact or increase the general tax or assessment.
>
> For purposes of this section, the term "new or increased assessment" does not include any of the following:
>
> (A) A fee that does not exceed the reasonable cost of providing the services, facilities, or regulatory activity for which the fee is charged.
>
> (B) A service charge, rate, or charge, unless a special district's principal act requires the service charge, rate, or charge to conform to the requirements of this section.
>
> (C) An ongoing annual assessment if it is imposed at the same or lower amount as any previous year.
>
> (D) An assessment that does not exceed an assessment formula or range of assessments previously specified in the notice given to the public pursuant to subparagraph (G) of paragraph (2) of subdivision (c) and that was previously adopted by the agency or approved by the voters in the area where the assess-

ment is imposed.

(E) Standby or immediate availability charges.

(2) The legislative body shall provide at least 45 days' public notice of the public hearing at which the legislative body proposes to enact or increase the general tax or assessment. The legislative body shall provide notice for the public meeting at the same time and in the same document as the notice for the public hearing, but the meeting shall occur prior to the hearing.

Tax Notice

The notice regarding a tax involves both a newspaper advertisement and a personal mailing to any taxpayer who has gone on record requesting it.

(b)(1) The joint notice of both the public meeting and the public hearing required by subdivision (a) with respect to a proposal for a new or increased general tax shall be accomplished by placing a display advertisement of at least one-eighth page in a newspaper of general circulation for three weeks pursuant to Section 6063 and by a first-class mailing to those interested parties who have filed a written request with the local agency for mailed notice of public meetings or hearings on new or increased general taxes. The public meeting pursuant to subdivision (a) shall take place no earlier than 10 days after the first publication of the joint notice pursuant to this subdivision. The public hearing shall take place no earlier than seven days after the public meeting pursuant to this subdivision. Notwithstanding paragraph (2) of subdivision (a), the joint notice need not include notice of the public meeting after the meeting has taken place. The public hearing pursuant to subdivision (a) shall take place no earlier than 45 days after the first publication of the joint notice pursuant to this subdivision. Any written request for mailed notices shall be effective for one year from the date on which it is filed unless a renewal request is filed.

Renewal requests for mailed notices shall be filed on or before April 1 of each year. The legislative body may establish a reasonable annual charge for sending notices based on the estimated cost of providing the service.

(2) The notice required by paragraph (1) of this subdivision shall include, but not be limited to, the following:

(A) The amount or rate of the tax. If the tax is proposed to be increased from any previous year, the joint notice shall separately state both the existing tax rate and the proposed tax rate increase.

(B) The Activity to be taxed.

(C) The estimated amount of revenue to be raised by the tax annually.

(D) The method and frequency for collecting the tax.

(E) The dates, times, and locations of the public meeting and hearing described in subdivision (a).

(F) The phone number and address of an individual, office, or organization that interested persons may contact to receive additional information about the tax.

Assessment Notice

The notice regarding an assessment involves a personal mailing to all affected property owners on the assessment roll.

(c)(1) The joint notice of both the public meeting and the public hearing required by subdivision (a) with respect to a proposal for a new or increased assessment on real property shall be accomplished through a mailing, postage prepaid, in the United States mail and shall be deemed given when so deposited. The public meeting pursuant to subdivision (a) shall take place no earlier than 10 days after the joint mailing pursuant to this subdivision. The public hearing shall take place no earlier than seven days after the public meeting pursuant to this subdivision. The envelope or the cover of the mailing shall include the name of the local agency and the return address of the sender. This mailed notice shall be in at least 10-point type and shall be given to all property owners proposed to be subject to the new or increased assessment by a mailing by name to those persons whose names and addresses appear on the last equalized county assessment roll or the State Board of Equalization assessment roll, as the case may be.

(2) The joint notice required by paragraph (1) of this subdivision shall include, but not be limited to, the following:

(A) The estimated amount of the assessment per parcel. If the assessment is proposed to be increased from any previous year, the joint notice shall separately state both the amount of the existing assessment and the proposed assessment increase.

(B) A general description of the purpose or improvements that the assessment will fund.

(C) The address to which property owners may mail a protest against the assessment.

(D) The phone number and address of an individual, office, or organization that interested persons may contact to receive additional information about the assessment.

(E) A statement that a majority protest will cause the assessment to be abandoned if the assessment act used to levy the assessment so provides. Notice shall also state the percentage of protests required to trigger an election, if applicable.

(F) The dates, times, and locations of the public meeting and hearing described in subdivision (a).

(G) A proposed assessment formula or range as described in subparagraph (D) of paragraph (1) of subdivision (a) if applicable and that is noticed pursuant to this section.

(3) Notwithstanding paragraph (1), in the case of an assessment that is proposed exclusively for operation and maintenance expenses imposed throughout the entire local agency, or exclusively for operation and maintenance assessments proposed to be levied on 50,000 parcels or more, notice may be provided pursuant to this subdivision or pursuant to paragraph (1) of subdivision (b) and shall include the estimated amount of the assessment of various types, amounts, or uses of property and the information required by subparagraphs (B) to (G), inclusive, of paragraph (2) of subdivision (c).

(4) Notwithstanding paragraph (1), in the case of an assessment proposed to be levied pursuant to Part 2 (commencing with Section 22500) of Division 2 of the Streets and Highways Code by a regional park district, regional park and open-space district, or regional open-space district formed pursuant to Article 3 (commencing with Section 5500) of Chapter 3 of Division 5 of, or pursuant to Division 26 (commencing with Section 35100) of, the Public Resources Code, notice may be provided pursuant to paragraph (1) of subdivision (b).

(d) The notice requirements imposed by this section shall be construed as additional to, and not to supersede, existing provisions of law, and shall be applied concurrently with the existing provisions so as to not delay or prolong the governmental decisionmaking process.

(e) This section shall not apply to any new or increased general tax or any new or increased assessment that requires an election of either of the following:

(1) The property owners subject to the assessment.

(2) The voters within the local agency imposing the tax or assessment.

(f) Nothing in this section shall prohibit a local agency from holding a consolidated meeting or hearing at which the legislative body discusses multiple tax or assessment proposals.

(g) The local agency may recover the reasonable costs of public meetings, public hearings, and notice required by this section from the proceeds of the tax or assessment. The costs recovered for these purposes, whether recovered pursuant to this subdivision or any other provision of law, shall not exceed the reasonable costs of the public meetings, public hearings, and notice.

(h) Any new or increased assessment that is subject to the notice and hearing provisions of Article XIIIC or XIIID of the California Constitution is not subject to the notice and hearing requirements of this section.

§ 1-3(k): Mandated Cost Claim Limitation

To preclude local agencies from filing inflated claims for reimbursement for "state mandated costs" involved in agenda preparation and other work done to conform with the Act, and to avoid the suspension of the mandate to prepare agendas when claims exceed the state's budgeted appropriations, Government Code §54954.4. cautions that such claims should be calculated and reviewed conservatively:

(a) The Legislature hereby finds and declares that Section 12 of Chapter 641 of the Statutes of 1986, authorizing reimbursement to local agencies and school districts for costs mandated by the state pursuant to that act, shall be interpreted strictly. The intent of the Legislature is to provide reimbursement for only those costs which are clearly and unequivocally incurred as the direct and necessary result of compliance with Chapter 641 of the Statutes of 1986.

(b) In this regard, the Legislature directs all state employees and officials involved in reviewing or authorizing claims for reimbursement, or otherwise participating in the reimbursement process, to rigorously review each claim and authorize only those claims, or parts thereof, which represent costs which are clearly and unequivocally incurred as the direct and necessary result of compliance with Chapter 641 of the Statutes of 1986 and for which complete documentation exists. For purposes of Section 54954.2, costs eligible for reimbursement shall only include the Actual cost to post a single agenda for any one meeting.

(c) The Legislature hereby finds and declares that complete, faithful, and uninterrupted compliance with the Ralph M. Brown Act (Chapter 9 (commencing with Section 54950) of Part 1 of Division 2 of Title 5 of the Government Code) is a matter of overriding public importance. Unless specifically stated, no future Budget Act, or related budget enactments, shall, in any manner, be interpreted to suspend, eliminate, or otherwise modify the legal obligation and duty of local agencies to fully comply with Chapter 641 of the Statutes of 1986 in a complete, faithful, and uninterrupted manner.

Claimed Costs Must Be for "Mandated" Service

The California Supreme Court has held that costs associated with the meetings of school site parental advisory committees, required for several bilingual and other supplementary education programs subsidized by special state funding, are not "mandated" for purposes of reimbursement because the programs themselves are not mandated, however highly desirable they may be to school districts.

In essence, claimants assert that their participation in the education-related programs here at issue is so beneficial that, as a practical matter, they feel they must participate in the programs, accept program funds, and—by virtue of Government Code section 54952 and Education Code section 35147—incur expenses

> necessary to comply with the procedural conditions imposed on program participants. Although it is completely understandable that a participant in a funded program may be disappointed when additional requirements (with their attendant costs) are imposed as a condition of continued participation in the program, just as such a participant would be disappointed if the total amount of the annual funds provided for the program were reduced by legislative or gubernatorial action, the circumstance that the Legislature has determined that the requirements of an ongoing elective program should be modified does not render a local entity's decision whether to continue its participation in the modified program any less voluntary. We reject the suggestion, implicit in claimants' argument, that the state cannot legally provide school districts with funds for voluntary programs, and then effectively reduce that funding grant by requiring school districts to incur expenses in order to meet conditions of program participation.

Department of Finance v. Commission on State Mandates, 30 Cal.4th 727, 753 (2003). This case raises the issue of whether costs for agenda preparation and other activities required by the Brown Act can be legitimately claimed for reimbursement if they are incurred in connection with meetings of legislative bodies that are not themselves mandated by the Act or some other law, e.g. advisory committees voluntarily created by governing bodies as a matter of discretion.

Certain Mandates No Longer Reimbursable?

AB 138 of 2005, a trailer bill signed by the Governor in connection with the 2005-2006 State Budget, approved as this guide was going to press, repealed and re-enacted two Brown Act provisions requiring:

- preparation and posting of regular meeting agendas with "brief general descriptions" of the business to be addresses (see § 1-3(e)(1)), and
- subsequent and public disclosure of actions taken in closed session (see § 1-5(a)(3)).

The bill declared that "Sections 54954.2 and 54957.1 of the Government Code are necessary to implement and reasonably within the scope of paragraph (1) of subdivision (b) of Section 3 of Article I of the California Constitution." It directed the Commission on State Mandates to revisit the test claims under which these Brown Act mandates were originally approved for reimbursement to local agencies, to reconsider whether these were still reimbursable mandates in light of Proposition 59 of 2004. The underlying notion was that, since the state is required to reimburse the cost of only those mandates created by acts of the Legislature or executive order, these mandates were no longer reimbursable.

§ 1-4: Rights of the Public

In addition to the procedural formalities imposed on legislative bodies, the Act gives citizens several rights in support of their ability to enjoy informed and meaningful participation in meetings subject to the statute.

§ 1-4(a): Access to Meeting-Related Documents

Because the agenda listing concerning a given item need only be a "brief general description," it is often vital that the public be able to learn details of what is being proposed for action or what is covered in a certain report. For that, journalists and other citizens rely on the agenda packet—the total compilation of backup memoranda and other materials that are delivered to the body prior to a meeting to educate them on the pending business. There is no question that these documents are accessible (by and large) under the California Public Records Act; but the Brown Act reinforces that point and stresses the immediacy with which access must be provided upon distribution to the body. Government Code §54957.5 states:

(a) Notwithstanding Section 6255 or any other provisions of law, agendas of public meetings and any other writings, when distributed to all, or a majority of all, of the members of a legislative body of a local agency by any person in connection with a matter subject to discussion or consideration at a public meeting of the body, are disclosable public records under the California Public Records Act (Chapter 3.5 (commencing with Section 6250) of Division 7 of Title 1), and shall be made available upon request without delay. However, this section shall not include any writing exempt from public disclosure under Section 6253.5, 6254, or 6254.7.

(b) Writings that are public records under subdivision (a) and that are distributed during a public meeting shall be made available for public inspection at the meeting if prepared by the local agency or a member of its legislative body, or after the meeting if prepared by some other person.

(c) Nothing in this chapter shall be construed to prevent the legislative body of a local agency from charging a fee or deposit for a copy of a public record pursuant to Section 6257.

Bagley-Keene Comparison

Government Code §11125.1:

(a) Notwithstanding Section 6255 or any other provisions of law, agendas of public meetings and other writings, when distributed to all, or a majority of all, of the members of a state body by any person in connection with a matter subject to discussion or consideration at a public meeting of the body, are disclosable public records under the California Public Records Act (Chapter 3.5 (commencing with Section 6250) of Division 7 of Title 1), and shall be made available upon request without delay. However, this section shall not include any writing exempt from public disclosure under Section 6253.5, 6254, or 6254.7 of this code, or Section 489.1 or 583 of the Public Utilities Code.

(b) Writings that are public records under subdivision (a) and that are distributed to members of the state body prior to or during a meeting, pertaining to any item to be considered during the meeting, shall be made available for public inspection at the meeting if prepared by the state body or a member of the state body, or after the meeting if prepared by some other person. These writings shall be made available in appropriate alternative formats, as required by Section 202 of the Americans with Disabilities Act of 1990 (42 U.S.C. Sec. 12132), and the federal rules and regulations adopted in implementation thereof, upon request by a person with a disability.

(c) In the case of the Franchise Tax Board, prior to that state body taking final action on any item, writings pertaining to that item that are public records under subdivision (a) that are distributed to members of the state body by board staff or individual members prior to or during a meeting shall be:

(1) Made available for public inspection at that meeting.

(2) Distributed to all persons who request notice in writing pursuant to subdivision (a) of Section 11125.

(3) Made available on the Internet.

(d) Prior to the State Board of Equalization taking final action on any item that does not involve a named tax or fee payer, writings pertaining to that item that are public records under subdivision (a) that are prepared and distributed by board staff or individual members to members of the state body prior to or during a meeting shall be:

(1) Made available for public inspection at that meeting.

(2) Distributed to all persons who request or have requested copies of these writings.

(3) Made available on the Internet.

(e) Nothing in this section shall be construed to prevent a state body from charging a fee or deposit for a copy of a public record pursuant to Section 6253, except that no surcharge shall be imposed on persons with disabilities in violation of Section 202 of the Americans with Disabilities Act of 1990 (42 U.S.C. Sec. 12132), and the federal rules and regulations adopted in implementation thereof. The writings described in subdivision (b) are subject to the requirements of the California Public Records Act (Chapter 3.5 (commencing with Section 6250) of Division 7 of Title 1), and shall not be construed to limit or delay the public's right to inspect any record required to be disclosed by that act, or to limit the public's right to inspect any record covered by that act. This section shall not be construed to be applicable to any writings solely because they are properly discussed in a closed session of a state body. Nothing in this article shall be construed to require a state body to place any paid advertisement or any other paid notice in any publication.

(f) "Writing" for purposes of this section means "writing" as defined under Section 6252.

(d) This section shall not be construed to limit or delay the public's right to inspect or obtain a copy of any record required to be disclosed under the requirements of the California Public Records Act (Chapter 3.5 (commencing with Section 6250) of Division 7 of Title 1). Nothing in this chapter shall be construed to require a legislative body of a local agency to place any paid advertisement or any other paid notice in any publication.

Scope of Available Documents

The access rights effective "without delay" in this section pertain to documents made available to the body by "any person"—not just the staff—and attach not only if the documents are distributed in connection with a particular impending meeting, but even "in connection with *a matter subject to discussion or consideration* at a public meeting"—that is, in connection with any matter that is not so confidential that it may be discussed in a closed session. The access right "without delay" is thus triggered whenever anyone distributes documents that are not legally confidential to a majority of a body. It is not confined to agenda packets prepared as such by the staff and handed out shortly before the meeting.

Delay Not Authorized

Local agencies sometimes cite these provisions when withholding requested documents until they have been distributed to the body, but the language in subdivision (d) indicates strongly to the contrary. Even before the Brown Act expressly conferred a right of access to agenda packets, the Attorney General's office advised a member of the Assembly (Index Letter 77-67): "Assuming a 'routine' agenda packet contains no legally privileged or confidential information, it is available under the general provisions of the California Public Records Act, in the district's office, as soon as assembled and even prior to distribution to the body."

Confidential Distribution

A "confidential" packet may be withheld, the index letter added, "if, in fact, the documents therein are exempt from disclosure under the California Public Records Act"—for example, a copy of a memorandum reprimanding an employee for unsatisfactory performance, which would probably be exempt from Public Records Act disclosure as a matter of personal privacy. On the other hand, the practice of school superintendents and others—of sending separate and secret "eyes only" packets to inform their boards of matters that are not confidential as a matter of law cannot be justified under either the Brown Act or the Public Records Act, at least once a request for disclosure has been made under the latter.

Subscription to Agenda Packets

Government Code §54954.1 requires that citizens be allowed to subscribe, in effect, to "agenda packets"—the term is undefined—for an annually renewable fee. It states:

> Any person may request that a copy of the agenda, or a copy of all the documents constituting the agenda packet, of any meeting of a legislative body be mailed to that person. If requested, the agenda and documents in the agenda packet shall be made available in appropriate alternative formats to persons with a

disability, as required by Section 202 of the Americans with Disabilities Act of 1990 (42 U.S.C. Sec. 12132), and the federal rules and regulations adopted in implementation thereof. Upon receipt of the written request, the legislative body or its designee shall cause the requested materials to be mailed at the time the agenda is posted pursuant to Section 54954.2 and 54956 or upon distribution to all, or a majority of all, of the members of a legislative body, whichever occurs first. Any request for mailed copies of agendas or agenda packets shall be valid for the calendar year in which it is filed and must be renewed following January 1 of each year. The legislative body may establish a fee for mailing the agenda or agenda packet, which fee shall not exceed the cost of providing the service. Failure of the requesting person to receive the agenda or agenda packet pursuant to this section shall not constitute grounds for invalidation of the Actions of the legislative body taken at the meeting for which the agenda or agenda packet was not received.

Accommodations for the Disabled

See discussion of the second sentence's requirement in § 1-3(e) above.

§ 1-4(b): Free and Anonymous Attendance

Those attending a meeting may not be charged a fee for admission or any other exercise of rights under the Act, nor may they be required to identify themselves as a condition to admission. Government Code §54956.6 states: "No fees may be charged by the legislative body of a local agency for carrying out any provision of this chapter, except as specifically authorized by this chapter." Government Code §54953.3 states:

A member of the public shall not be required, as a condition to attendance at a meeting of a legislative body of a local agency, to register his or her name, to provide other information, to complete a questionnaire, or otherwise to fulfill any condition precedent to his or her attendance.
If an attendance list, register, questionnaire, or other similar document is posted at or near the entrance to the room where the meeting is to be held, or is circulated to the persons present during the meeting, it shall state clearly that the signing, registering, or completion of the document is voluntary, and that all persons may attend the meeting regardless of whether a person signs, registers, or completes the document.

Bagley-Keene Comparison
Government Code §11126.7:
No fees may be charged by a state body for providing a notice required by Section 11125 or for carrying out any provision of this article, except as specifically authorized pursuant to this article.

Bagley-Keene Comparison
Government Code §11124:
No person shall be required, as a condition to attendance at a meeting of a state body, to register his or her name, to provide other information, to complete a questionnaire, or otherwise to fulfill any condition precedent to his or her attendance.
If an attendance list, register, questionnaire, or other similar document is posted at or near the entrance to the room where the meeting is to be held, or is circulated to persons present during the meeting, it shall state clearly that the signing, registering, or completion of the document is voluntary, and that all persons may attend the meeting regardless of whether a person signs, registers, or completes the document.

The anonymity right attaches to attendance at a meeting. As for those who wish to address the body, however (see below) it is a widespread if not universal practice to require them to identify themselves for the record.

Weapons Barred

Penal Code §171b makes it a crime punishable by up to a year in jail time to bring into a meeting governed by the Brown Act or the Bagley-Keene Open Meeting Act a firearm, or any of a wide variety of clubbing or edged weapons, or tear gas or taser gun devices, but exempts peace officers and duly authorized building security guards.

§ 1-4(c): Addressing the Legislative Body

Of all the Act's entitlements to those attending meetings, it is the right to address the body that raises the most questions and conflicts. Government Code §54954.3 provides:

> (a) Every agenda for regular meetings shall provide an opportunity for members of the public to directly address the legislative body on any item of interest to the public, before or during the legislative body's consideration of the item, that is within the subject matter jurisdiction of the legislative body, provided that no action shall be taken on any item not appearing on the agenda unless the Action is otherwise authorized by subdivision (b) of Section 54954.2. However, the agenda need not provide an opportunity for members of the public to address the legislative body on any item that has already been considered by a committee, composed exclusively of members of the legislative body, at a public meeting wherein all interested members of the public were afforded the opportunity to address the committee on the item, before or during the committee's consideration of the item, unless the item has been substantially changed since the committee heard the item, as determined by the legislative body. Every notice for a special meeting shall provide an opportunity for members of the public to directly address the legislative body concerning any item that has been described in the notice for the meeting before or during consideration of that item.

Bagley-Keene Comparison

Government Code §11125.7:

(a) Except as otherwise provided in this section, the state body shall provide an opportunity for members of the public to directly address the state body on each agenda item before or during the state body's discussion or consideration of the item. This section is not applicable if the agenda item has already been considered by a committee composed exclusively of members of the state body at a public meeting where interested members of the public were afforded the opportunity to address the committee on the item, before or during the committee's consideration of the item, unless the item has been substantially changed since the committee heard the item, as determined by the state body. Every notice for a special meeting at which action is proposed to be taken on an item shall provide an opportunity for members of the public to directly address the state body concerning that item prior to action on the item. In addition, the notice requirement of Section 11125 shall not preclude the acceptance of testimony at meetings, other than emergency meetings, from members of the public, provided, however, that no action is taken by the state body at the same meeting on matters brought before the body by members of the public.

(b) The state body may adopt reasonable regulations to ensure that the intent of subdivision (a) is carried out, including, but not limited to, regulations limiting the total amount of time allocated for public comment on particular issues and for each individual speaker.

(c) The state body shall not prohibit public criticism of the policies, programs, or services of the state body, or of the Acts or omissions of the state body. Nothing in this subdivision shall confer any privilege or protection for expression beyond that otherwise provided by law.

(d) This section is not applicable to closed sessions held pursuant to Section 11126.

(e) This section is not applicable to decisions regarding proceedings held pursuant to Chapter 5 (commencing with Section 11500), relating to administrative adjudication, or to the conduct of those proceedings.

(f) This section is not applicable to hearings conducted by the State Board of Control pursuant to Sections 13963 and 13963.1.

(g) This section is not applicable to agenda items that involve decisions of the Public Utilities Commission regarding adjudicatory hearings held pursuant to Chapter 9 (commencing with Section 1701) of Part 1 of Division 1 of the Public Utilities Code. For all other agenda items, the commission shall provide members of the public, other than those who have already participated in the proceedings underlying the agenda item, an opportunity to directly address the commission before or during the commission's consideration of the item.

(b) The legislative body of a local agency may adopt reasonable regulations to ensure that the intent of subdivision (a) is carried out, including, but not limited to, regulations limiting the total amount of time allocated for public testimony on particular issues and for each individual speaker.

(c) The legislative body of a local agency shall not prohibit public criticism of the policies, procedures, programs, or services of the agency, or of the Acts or omissions of the legislative body. Nothing in this subdivision shall confer any privilege or protection for expression beyond that otherwise provided by law.

Scope of Comment at Regular versus Special Meetings

At a regular meeting the public must be allowed to address not only agenda items but any item they choose within the body's jurisdiction. But at special meetings public comment may be confined to the specific topic or topics contained in the meeting notice.

Matters Open to Comment at an Earlier Hearing

The body's authority to preclude comment on a matter considered at an earlier hearing applies only if that hearing was conducted by a committee of the body and "all interested members of the public" were given the opportunity to comment. Thus if the committee cut off comment while there were were still speakers waiting to be heard, they cannot be denied a chance to address the full body when the item is taken up there.

Application to Multiple-Session Meetings

Occasionally a meeting will be adjourned or a hearing continued, with attention to the agenda to resume at a later time. A court has concluded that the public's entitlement to address the body on matters *not* on the agenda need be accommodated at no more than one of these meeting segments. In a case brought by a speaker complaining of being denied such multiple speaking opportunities before a municipal library commission, the court analyzed similar provisions in both the Brown Act and the city's own sunshine ordinance thus:

> When the Brown Act and the Sunshine Ordinance are read in their entirety, we conclude that the lawmaking bodies clearly contemplated circumstances in which continuances and multiple sessions of meetings to consider a published agenda would be required, and thus they mandated that a single general public comment period be provided per agenda, in addition to public comment on each agenda item as it is taken up by the body.
>
> *****
>
> The Library Commission fully adhered to the language of these enactments and the Legislature's intent embedded in the statutes by hearing public comment on every agenda item taken up at the May 16th meeting. When the commission then lost its quorum … the meeting on the May 16th agenda was continued for a period not to exceed the prescribed five-day limit with notice of the continued hearing time and date posted on the door of the meeting place within 24 hours. Further, the commission provided public comment on every remaining agenda item at the session held on May 21st, including providing for general public comment. Thus, the Library Commission did all that was required under both the plain meaning of pertinent provisions of the Brown Act and the Sunshine Ordinance, and in accordance with the Legislature's purpose in facilitating and providing for public participation in legislative decisionmaking.

Chafee v. San Francisco Library Commission, 115 Cal.App.4th 461, 469 (2004).

Reasonable Time Limits

The body's principal control over public comment is in its use of time limits. The Act does not prescribe those limits but states simply that they are to be "reasonable . . . to ensure that the intent" of accommodating public comment "is carried out." The Attorney General has concluded that five minutes per speaker may be "reasonable" under the circumstances (75 Ops.Cal.Atty.Gen. 89 (1992)), but many if not most agencies appear to keep the per speaker limit to three minutes per agenda item.

Viewpoint Neutrality and "Equal Time"

More important than the amount of time permitted is that the time limits be administered neutrally and evenhandedly. Clearly giving more time to citizens on one side of a controversial topic than those on the other, for example, is not "reasonable," as the court noted in *Leventhal v. Vista Unified School Dist.*, 973 F.Supp. 951 (1997).

> In *Rosenberger v. Rector & Visitors of Univ. of Va.*, the Supreme Court explained: When the government targets not subject matter but particular views taken by speakers on a subject, the violation of the First Amendment is all the more blatant. Viewpoint discrimination is thus an egregious form of content discrimination. The government must abstain from regulating speech when the specific motivating ideology is the rationale for the restriction.

Id. at 960 (citations omitted).

In *Kindt v. Santa Monica Rent Control Board*, 67 F.3d 266 (1995) the court was presented with a claim that the plaintiff's free speech rights had been violated when, due to his failure to submit speaker cards in advance to address specific topics raised by other speakers under the same agenda heading, he was relegated to the general "oral communications" speaker period later in the meeting. He argued that the later opportunity left him with a smaller audience and that the three-minute time limit deprived him of the chance to make a more extended response to points made by other speakers addressing a specific agenda item. The court stated that "Kindt was not entitled to an 'equal time' response period to rebut the views of the Item 4 speakers *at the moment they concluded their remarks*" (emphasis added) On the other hand, the court noted in footnote 6, "Had the evidence shown that those promoting certain viewpoints ... could speak under Item 4 and those promoting opposing viewpoints could not, this would be a different, and more difficult, case."

Restricted Scope of Comments Permitted

The authority to limit citizen speech to matters within the body's "subject matter jurisdiction"—matters on which the body has authority to act—does not conflict with the First Amendment or the free speech guarantee of the California Constitution, the Attorney General has concluded, in 78 Ops.Cal.Atty.Gen. 218 (1995). The opinion's rationale notes the public forum analysis in *White v. City of Norwalk* (see page 72). The opinion was "prompted by the refusal of a legislative body to permit public comment regarding the personal life of one of its members—a matter outside the subject matter jurisdiction of the legislative body."

Maintaining Order vs. Impermissibly Restraining Speech

With increasing specificity over a series of cases, federal courts confronted with reconciling the meeting management rights reserved to local bodies under §54954.3 with speakers' claims to protected expression have attempted to classify the statutory public comment period as some kind of forum for speech—a classification with significance as to how much official control may be exerted over what is said, and how, and when. This forum analysis as a First Amendment methodology is described in *Leventhal, supra*, as follows:

> Although the doctrine's roots can be traced back to dicta in the Supreme Court's decision in *Hague v. CIO*, 307 U.S. 496, 515, 59 S.Ct. 954, 963-64, 83 L.Ed. 1423 (1939), the modern categorical approach began with *Perry Education Ass'n v. Perry Local Educators' Ass'n*, 460 U.S. 37, 103 S.Ct. 948, 74 L.Ed.2d 794 (1983). In *Perry*, the Court identified three distinct types of fora: first, "traditional" public fora--"places which by long tradition or government fiat have been devoted to assembly and debate;" second, "limited" public fora-- "public property which the State has opened for use by the public as a place for expressive activity;" and third, "nonpublic" fora--property not dedicated in any significant way to free or open communication. *Id.* at 45-46, 103 S.Ct. at 954-56.
>
> Under this categorical system, the state's ability to regulate speech depends on the nature of the forum. The government's power to restrict expression in traditional public fora, the *Perry* Court explained, is extremely limited: "reasonable time, place and manner regulations are permissible, and a content-based prohibition must be narrowly drawn to effectuate a compelling state interest." *Id.* at 46, 103 S.Ct. at 955-56. The Court imposed similar restraints on speech in limited public fora: "Although a State is not required to indefinitely retain the open character of the facility, as long as it does so it is bound by the same standards as apply in a traditional public forum." *Id.* In nonpublic fora, the government may restrict expression only if the regulation is reasonable and viewpoint-neutral.

973 F.Supp. at 956, 957.

Even prior to the debut of its forum classifications in *Perry*, the Supreme Court had concluded that where a state "sunshine" law required school board meetings to be open to the public, and where the board conceded that any citizen could address the board on the topic of teacher pay negotiations, a forum had been created such that the First Amendment gave teachers and their representatives the right to be heard on the same issues, despite the fact that negotiations on those issues were pending outside the public meeting process. "Where the State has opened a forum for direct citizen involvement, it is difficult to find justification for excluding teachers who make up the overwhelming proportion of school employees and who are most vitally concerned with the proceedings," the court stated in *City of Madison Joint School District v. Wisconsin Employment Relations Commission*, 429 U.S. 167 (1976). Thus arguably in any local governmental meeting open by law to the public and where citizens are permitted to address the body, a "limited" or "designated" public forum has been created. Several courts have concluded as much with respect to public comment rights under the Brown Act.

The Ninth Circuit, in a case involving several incidents occurring in Norwalk City Council meetings prior to 1986, when the Act was amended to mandate for the first time that the public be allowed to address the body, was faced with a speech forum created not by state law but by local ordinance. Citing *Madison*, the court observed:

> City Council meetings like Norwalk's, where the public is afforded the opportunity to address the Council, are the focus of highly important individual and governmental interests. Citizens have an enormous first amendment interest in directing speech about public issues to those who govern their city. It is doubtless partly for this reason that such meetings, once opened, have been regarded as public forums, albeit limited ones.

White v. City of Norwalk, 900 F.2d 1421, 1425 (1990)

On the other hand, the court emphasized that the council had an agenda to be dealt with and that "(p)ublic forum or not, the usual first amendment antipathy to content-oriented control of speech cannot be imported into the Council chambers intact." The plaintiff had been ruled out of order on several occasions while addressing the council, escorted to his seat and even twice ejected from the meeting room, and the council's justification was that he had been behaving disruptively, in violation of the public speaker ordinance, by being overly lengthy, repetitious or off-topic. In his action for an injunction and damages for violation of his speech rights, the court held that the council was warranted in its curtailment of his remarks, which in the meeting environment could be disruptive even if not a breach of the peace:

> A speaker may disrupt a Council meeting by speaking too long,

> by being unduly repetitious, or by extended discussion of irrelevancies. The meeting is disrupted because the Council is prevented from accomplishing its business in a reasonably efficient manner. Indeed, such conduct may interfere with the rights of other speakers.

Id. at 1426.

At the same time, the court accepted the saving construction offered by the city that its speaker ordinance, which prohibited "personal, impertinent, slanderous or profane remarks," could be the basis for warning, ejection or prosecution only when and if such remarks were made while engaging in disorderly conduct which itself disrupted the meeting. The plaintiff had argued that the content-prohibitive clause read alone was fatally vague and overbroad.

Five years later the Ninth Circuit dealt with a case brought by a Santa Monica landlord who had been repeatedly ejected from meetings of the municipal rent control board, usually for interrupting or distracting speakers with comments or applause from the audience. He brought a civil rights action based on these incidents and also arguing unlawful viewpoint discrimination among speakers, in that the board would not recognize his right to make statements immediately rebutting those of other speakers on particular topics, but forced him to wait until the general period for comments on matters not on the agenda, toward the end of the meeting. In *Kindt v. Santa Monica Rent Control Board*, 67 F.3d 266 (1995), the parties apparently made no mention of the Brown Act. Ironically, one of Kindt's main sources of criticism of the board was its practice of permitting both members of the board and citizen speakers to address any number of matters having nothing to do with rent control: foreign aid to El Salvador, abortion clinic defense, labor-management controversies, nuclear testing protests, and demonstrations opposing the Gulf War. The Brown Act permits bodies to limit public comments to matters within their subject matter jurisdiction (Government Code §54954.3), but does not mandate such a limit. The court noted that the board sometimes passed resolutions before allowing comment from the public (which would violate the Brown Act) but concluded that such practice did not violate the First Amendment because it was done without regard for the viewpoints involved. Moreover, the court observed:

> It seems to us that the highly structured nature of city council and city board meetings makes them fit more neatly into the nonpublic forum niche. But as we intimated in *City of Norwalk*, the important thing is not whether we call the meetings highly regulated

> limited public fora or nonpublic fora. The fact remains that limitations on speech at those meetings must be reasonable and content neutral, but that is all they need be.

Id. at 270. Two U.S. District Court cases have since explicitly held the Brown Act's public comment requirements as having created a limited public forum for First Amendment analysis. In *Baca v. Moreno Valley Unified School Dist.*, 936 F.Supp. 719 (1996), the court cited the Act's open meeting and public speaker provisions and stated:

> Thus, by opening school board meetings to public comment "on any item of interest to the public, before or during the legislative body's consideration of the item, that is within the subject matter jurisdiction of the legislative body," Govt. Code, § 54954.3(a), the California Legislature has designated school board meetings as limited public fora, i.e., fora open to the public in general, but limited to comments related to the school board's "subject matter." Therefore, the open sessions of District's Board meetings are limited public fora, and any regulation of speech in such fora must be reviewed in light of the nature of the fora.

Id. at 728. In footnote 11 to this statement, the court observed that

> to the extent that defendants rely on *Kindt v. Santa Monica Rent Control Bd.*, 67 F.3d 266, 270 (9th Cir. 1995) to argue that a California school board meeting is a "non-public forum," such reliance is misplaced, because the Brown Act specifically creates a public forum, albeit one limited to comments related to school boards' "subject matter."

The court reasoned that given the existence of even a limited public forum, the school board's rule prohibiting "charges or complaints against any employee of the district" by citizen speakers in open session was an unconstitutional prior restraint on speech and subject to injunction, since

> the applicable standard of review for testing the constitutionality of regulations of speech in a designated, limited public forum is the same standard which applies to regulation of speech in a traditional public forum ...This means that even in a limited public forum, before the state can enforce "[any] content-based exclusion it must show that its regulation is necessary to serve a compelling state interest and that it is narrowly drawn to achieve that end," and that although "[r]easonable time, place and manner regula-

> tions are permissible," they must be "content- neutral, ... narrowly tailored to serve a significant government interest, and leave open ample channels of communication.

Id. at 730. The court concluded that the board's policy did impose content-based restrictions which were not narrowly drawn to effectuate a compelling state interest. The only interest asserted by the board to be "compelling" was that of protecting its employees' privacy and reputations. This interest, given the absolutely privileged character of the occasion under state law—speech at an open governmental meeting—could not be vindicated by defamation or privacy actions. The reputation/privacy protection interest is, in this context, outweighed by the public's interest in vigorous public speech, as evidenced in the Legislature's enactment of the meeting privilege itself and its creation of the speech forum at meetings, as well as the state constitution's ban on censorship of even defamatory speech, the court noted. It granted a permanent injunction against enforcement of the policy barring criticism of employees.

In *Leventhal v. Vista Unified School District*, 973 F.Supp. 951 (1997), the court held that a school board's bylaw providing that "[c]omplaints against an individual employee will not be heard at open Board meetings unless the individual employee consents," when used to prevent citizens from criticizing the superintendent, failed "even under the more deferential standard of review applied to speech restrictions in nonpublic fora," where speech regulations "will survive a constitutional challenge only if they are 'reasonable in light of the purpose served by the forum and are viewpoint neutral.'" *Id.* at 960. The challenged bylaw, said the court,

> effectuates a classic form of viewpoint discrimination. As the *Baca* court noted, the regulation "allows expression of two points of view (laudatory and neutral) while prohibiting a different point of view (negatively critical) on a particular subject matter (District employees' conduct or performance)." ... This system engenders discussion artificially geared toward praising (and maintaining) the status quo, thereby foreclosing meaningful public dialogue and, ultimately, dynamic political change.

Ibid. The court noted that the board's application of the bylaw had a particularly one-sided effect in that Superintendent Gyves and Board member Vervynck

> criticized several non-employee speakers ... Yet members of the community at large cannot respond to these charges, even to discuss the same subject matter or issue, if Board President Hubbard

> determines that their comments relate to a "personnel issue." In other words, the Bylaw permits the expression of one viewpoint ("complaints" or "charges" against members of the public) but not another ("complaints" or "charges" against District employees). Accordingly, even if the Board meetings were nonpublic fora, the Bylaw operates in direct violation of the First Amendment.

Ibid.

§ 1-4(d): Photography, Recording, Broadcast

In *Nevens v. City of Chino*, 233 Cal.App.2d 775 (1965), the court held that the defendant could not bar a newspaper reporter from using a battery-operated, unobtrusive tape recorder to preserve the proceedings of its council meetings. Relying neither on the First Amendment nor on the Brown Act, but rather finding the prohibition analogous to use of pencil and paper to record public proceedings, the court observed:

> It is true that a city council has an absolute right to adopt and enforce such rules and regulations as are necessary to protect its public meetings. (Gov. Code, § 36813.) For example, the council has unquestioned power to prohibit any disturbance at its meetings. Furthermore, the city could properly prevent the use of municipal electricity, or any similar product, in a recording machine operated by a reporter. And the rights of others in the audience should not be infringed; that is to say, a rule could be made that a reporter cannot occupy any more space than any other citizen. But the plaintiff says that his machine is silent and unobtrusive and that it does not interfere in any way with the meetings of the council; it is not claimed that he uses electricity of the city, or that he interferes with the auditory rights of other citizens. The court can take judicial notice that there have been developed during recent years more than one variety of noiseless tape recorder. The Action of the city council is too arbitrary and capricious, too restrictive and unreasonable ... It bars what clearly should be permitted in making an accurate record of what takes place at such meetings.
>
> Accuracy in reporting the transactions of a public governing body should never be penalized, particularly in a democracy, where truth is often said to be supreme. Governmental measures based upon police power should always be well defined and reasonably exercised. And here reason is down-graded. If a shorthand record of such a meeting is more accurate than long hand notes, then the use of shorthand is to be approved...; and if the

making of a tape record is a still better method of memorializing the Acts of a public body it should be encouraged.

As no one is harmed, the use of a silent tape recorder operated exclusively by the person interested in making such a record must be permitted. The general rule approved in *Wrather-Alvarez Broadcasting, Inc. v. Hewicker*, 147 Cal.App.2d 509, 514, is applicable: "We conclude that petitioner or his assistant is authorized at any public hearing in the court where he is rightfully in attendance to take such notes as he may desire concerning the proceedings in any form selected by him so long as it does not interfere with the orderly conduct of the proceedings."

Id. at 778, 779 (citations omitted). This rationale has been codified and expanded in two Brown Act sections of the Government Code, pertaining to recording media in general and also to live broadcast:

§54953.5.

(a) Any person attending an open and public meeting of a legislative body of a local agency shall have the right to record the proceedings with an audio or video tape recorder or a still or motion picture camera in the absence of a reasonable finding by the legislative body of the local agency that the recording cannot continue without noise, illumination, or obstruction of view that constitutes, or would constitute, a persistent disruption of the proceedings.

§54953.6.

No legislative body of a local agency shall prohibit or otherwise restrict the broadcast of its open and public meetings in the absence of a reasonable finding that the broadcast cannot be accomplished without noise, illumination, or obstruction of view that would constitute a persistent disruption of the proceedings.

Bagley-Keene Comparison

Government Code §11124.1 states:

(a) Any person attending an open and public meeting of the state body shall have the right to record the proceedings with an audio or video tape recorder or a still or motion picture camera in the absence of a reasonable finding by the state body that the recording cannot continue without noise, illumination, or obstruction of view that constitutes, or would constitute, a persistent disruption of the proceedings.

****

(c) No state body shall prohibit or otherwise restrict the broadcast of its open and public meetings in the absence of a reasonable finding that the broadcast cannot be accomplished without noise, illumination, or obstruction of view that would constitute a persistent disruption of the proceedings.

§ 1-4(e): Access to Official Tapes

In addition to the right to record open meetings, those interested in the content of recordings made by the agency itself are given the right to inspect and copy them in subdivision (b) of Government Code §54953.5:

Any tape or film record of an open and public meeting made for whatever purpose by or at the direction of the local agency shall be subject to inspection pursuant to the California Public Records Act (Chapter 3.5 (commencing with Section 6250) of Division 7 of Title 1), but, notwithstanding Section 34090, may be

Bagley-Keene Comparison
Government Code §11124.1 states:

(b) Any tape or film record of an open and public meeting made for whatever purpose by or at the direction of the state body shall be subject to inspection pursuant to the California Public Records Act (Chapter 3.5 (commencing with Section 6250) of Division 7 of Title 1), but may be erased or destroyed 30 days after the taping or recording. Any inspection of an audio or video tape recording shall be provided without charge on an audio or video tape player made available by the state body.

erased or destroyed 30 days after the taping or recording. Any inspection of a video or tape recording shall be provided without charge on a video or tape player made available by the local agency.

§ 1-4(f): Access to Minutes

The Act does not require the preservation of minutes, or mention them in any respect other than in connection with discussions and actions in closed session, as noted in § 1-5(a)(1) below. But there is little question that minutes of the open and public portions of a meeting subject to the Act are documents accessible under the California Public Records Act, at least at the time when they are submitted for approval to the body (see § 1-4(a) above).

§ 1-5: Exceptions from the Open Meeting Requirement

The Act in Government Code §54953 (a) states: "All meetings of the legislative body of a local agency shall be open and public, and all persons shall be permitted to attend any meeting of the legislative body of a local agency, except as otherwise provided in this chapter." There are 19 situations expressly authorized or referenced in the Act in which a closed session excluding the public is permissible.

Exclusion of Nonessential Persons

The Attorney General has consistently taken the position in published opinions that closed sessions must exclude all persons whose participation is not essential to the business at hand. Most recently, this principle was applied to the question of an alternate member of a Local Agency Formation Commission's presence in a closed session where the regular member is already present:

> In the pamphlet, *The Brown Act, Open Meetings For Local Legislative Bodies* (Cal. Dept. of Justice, 1994), we examined whether various interested persons could attend a closed meeting under the Ralph M. Brown Act:
>
>> In 46 Ops.Cal.Atty.Gen. 34 (1965), this office also concluded that meetings could not be semi-closed. Thus, certain interested members of the public may not be admitted to a closed session while the remainder of the public is excluded. Nor would it be proper for an investigative committee of a grand jury performing its duties of investigating the county's business to be admitted to a closed session. (I.L. 70-184.) As a general rule, closed sessions may involve only the membership of the body in question plus any additional support staff which may be required (e.g., attorney required to provide legal advice; supervisor may be required in connection with disciplinary proceeding; labor negotiator required for consultation). Persons without an official role in the meeting should not be present.
>
> Unless sitting in place of an absent or disqualified regular member, an alternate member may not attend a closed session without converting the session into an unauthorized "semi-closed meeting." A may not enact parliamentary rules that contravene statutory law, in this case, the Ralph M. Brown Act. (See *Dyna-Med, Inc. v. Fair Employment & Housing Com.*, supra, 43 Cal.3d at 1389; *Morris v. Williams* (1967) 67 Cal.2d 733, 748; *Mason,*

> *supra*, at pp. 30-31). Returning to the analogy of a jury, we believe exclusion from a closed session would be similar to alternate jurors being excluded from jury deliberations required by law to be conducted in closed session. (See Pen. Code, §§ 1089, 1137-1138; Code Civ. Proc., §§ 233-234.)]… therefore, we conclude that an alternate member of a LAFCO may not attend a closed session when not serving in place of a regular member.

82 Ops.Cal.Atty.Gen. 29 (1999).

Inclusion of Selected Non-officials via Committee

Despite the the principle stated above, the Attorney General has opined that the Brown Act is not violated under an arrangement that allows non-officials into closed sessions—so long as the closed sessions are held by committees of which the non-officials have been made members, and thus at least temporarily "official." In 80 Ops.Cal.Atty.Gen. 308 (1997) the conclusion was:

> Where the board of trustees of a school district has formed a committee, known as the district liaison council, consisting of eight representatives from the community, seven employees of the district, and one student, to interview candidates for the office of district superintendent and to make a recommendation to the board, the sessions of the committee held to perform such delegated duties are not required to be open to members of the public.

The reasoning was that the committee formed in this manner would be subject to the Brown Act, but that as such it would be entitled to hold a closed session to interview employment applicants, discuss their merits, and adopt recommendations. Thus the confidential personnel decision-making process from which non-officials would ordinarily be excluded because they could not sit in on the board's closed sessions is made available to non-officials simply by designating them as members of a board-created committee and allowing them their own closed sessions.

§ 1-5(a): Closed Session Rules in General

The Act sets forth procedural requirements applying to most if not all closed sessions. The minutes kept of such sessions are not public records, but the public is entitled to some minimal advance notice of the topics to be dealt with, and if action is taken it must likewise be disclosed, and any documents approved become public records thereafter.

§ 1-5(a)(1): Closed Session Minutes and Confidentiality

The Act authorizes the body to preserve minutes (by summary, transcript or electronic recording) of its closed sessions, and if it does so, provides that the minutes are not public records. They are available only to members of the body itself or to a court in a proceeding challenging the legality of discussions or actions undertaken in the closed session. Government Code §54957.2 states:

> (a) The legislative body of a local agency may, by ordinance or resolution, designate a clerk or other officer or employee of the local agency who shall then attend each closed session of the legislative body and keep and enter in a minute book a record of topics discussed and decisions made at the meeting. The minute book made pursuant to this section is not a public record subject to inspection pursuant to the California Public Records Act (Chapter 3.5 (commencing with Section 6250) of Division 7 of Title 1), and shall be kept confidential. The minute book shall be available only to members of the legislative body or, if a violation of this chapter is alleged to have occurred at a closed session, to a court of general jurisdiction wherein the local agency lies. Such minute book may, but need not, consist of a recording of the closed session.
>
> (b) An elected legislative body of a local agency may require that each legislative body all or a majority of whose members are appointed by or under the authority of the elected legislative body keep a minute book as prescribed under subdivision (a).

Bagley-Keene Comparison

Government Code §11126.1 states:

> The state body shall designate a clerk or other officer or employee of the state body, who shall then attend each closed session of the state body and keep and enter in a minute book a record of topics discussed and decisions made at the meeting. The minute book made pursuant to this section is not a public record subject to inspection pursuant to the California Public Records Act (Chapter 3.5 (commencing with Section 6250) of Division 7 of Title 1), and shall be kept confidential. The minute book shall be available to members of the state body or, if a violation of this chapter is alleged to have occurred at a closed session, to a court of general jurisdiction. Such minute book may, but need not, consist of a recording of the closed session.

Confidentiality of Matters Learned in Closed Session

The Act also expressly prohibits "leaks" to the public of information gained by members of the body, agency employees or others present in a lawfully closed session, if the information is "specifically related" to the lawful purpose of the closed session. The body may waive this confidentiality and authorize disclosure. Members of the body or others present making unauthorized disclosures may be referred to the grand jury (although such violations are not a crime); employees doing likewise may be disciplined, if previously informed of the confidentiality requirement; and finally, anyone present may be subject to an injunction if necessary to stop the leaks. Government Code §54963 states:

> (a) A person may not disclose confidential information that has been acquired by being present in a closed session authorized by Section 54956.7, 54956.8, 54956.86, 54956.87, 54956.9, 54957, 54957.6, 54957.8, or 54957.10 to a person not entitled to receive it, unless the legislative body authorizes disclosure of that

confidential information.

(b) For purposes of this section, "confidential information" means a communication made in a closed session that is specifically related to the basis for the legislative body of a local agency to meet lawfully in closed session under this chapter.

(c) Violation of this section may be addressed by the use of such remedies as are currently available by law, including, but not limited to:

(1) Injunctive relief to prevent the disclosure of confidential information prohibited by this section.

(2) Disciplinary action against an employee who has willfully disclosed confidential information in violation of this section.

(3) Referral of a member of a legislative body who has willfully disclosed confidential information in violation of this section to the grand jury.

(d) Disciplinary action pursuant to paragraph (2) of subdivision (c) shall require that the employee in question has either received training as to the requirements of this section or otherwise has been given notice of the requirements of this section.

Protections for Whistleblowers

Such sanctions are not available, however (see subdivisions (e) and (f) below), against those who:

• confidentially report suspected violations of the lawful scope of closed session discussions to a grand jury or a district attorney; or

• publicly voice an opinion about the propriety or lawfulness of an action taken in closed session; or

• reveal information learned in a closed session that is not confidential because it is not "specifically related" to the lawful basis for the closed session; or

• are protected by either of two more general whistleblower statutes. Of those, Labor Code §1102.5 prohibits employers, private or public, from either preventing workers from reporting violations of law (based on "reasonable cause" for belief) to a government or law enforcement agency, or punishing them for having done so. Government Code §53296 applies to public employees of local agencies in particular, protecting them from "reprisal" by the employing agency for having made a sworn written complaint to their superiors containing evidence of "gross mismanagement or a significant waste of funds, an abuse of authority, or a substantial and specific danger to public health or safety."

(e) A local agency may not take any action authorized by subdivision (c) against a person, nor shall it be deemed a violation of this section, for doing any of the following:

(1) Making a confidential inquiry or complaint to a district attorney or grand jury concerning a perceived violation of law, including disclosing facts to a district attorney or grand jury that are necessary to establish the illegality of an action taken by a legislative body of a local agency or the potential illegality of an action that has been the subject of deliberation at a closed session if that action were to be taken by a legislative body of a local agency.

(2) Expressing an opinion concerning the propriety or legality of actions taken by a legislative body of a local agency in closed session, including disclosure of the nature and extent of the illegal or potentially illegal action.

(3) Disclosing information acquired by being present in a closed session under

this chapter that is not confidential information.

(f) Nothing in this section shall be construed to prohibit disclosures under the whistleblower statutes contained in Section 1102.5 of the Labor Code or Article 4.5 (commencing with Section 53296) of Chapter 2 of this code.

Joint Powers Agency Disclosure

In certain circumstances the content of a closed session of the governing body of a joint powers agency may be disclosed by one of its members to his or her "home" legislative body, for example to a city council of a city that is a partner to the joint powers agreement that formed the agency and that has a council member sitting on the agency's board and was present in the closed session (see §1-5 (b) (8)).

No Criminal Penalty

The Attorney General has opined that a city may not adopt an ordinance making it a misdemeanor for those present during a duly conducted closed session of a city council to publicly disclose the substance of any discussion properly held during the session unless so authorized by the council. 76 Ops.Cal.Atty.Gen. 289 (1993). That opinion in part relies on the conclusion that such conduct by members of the body or employees may be already subject to misdemeanor prosecution for any "willful omission to perform any duty enjoined by law upon any public officer, or person holding any public trust or employment, where no special provision is made for the punishment of such delinquency" pursuant Government Code §1222. But that prospect has been greatly reduced if not eliminated by the fact that the legislation adding Section 54963 above to the Brown Act, AB 1945 of 2002 (Simitian), in its original version would have made unauthorized disclosures from closed session a misdemeanor. That penalty was removed by the author in the bill's first hearing in the Assembly Local Government Committee, at which point the current sanctions were substituted instead.

Access to Minutes or Recordings by Members of the Body

In *Hamilton v. Town of Los Gatos*, 213 Cal.App.3d 1050 (1989), the court held that despite the right of access to closed session tapes granted in this section to members of the legislative body, certain considerations under the law governing conflicts of interest precluded a member from exercising that prerogative in an unusual circumstance. A town council member who owned business property within a downtown parking assessment district created by the city abstained from discussing or voting on issues connected with the district after receiving a city attorney's opinion, backed by an advisory letter from the Fair Political Practices Commission, that to involve himself in those matters would constitute a conflict of interest under Government Code Section 87100. He also absented himself from a closed session with the city attorney to address litigation by members of the community challenging formation of the district as unconstitutional, although he was not among the plaintiffs. But he then asked the city clerk to obtain a copy of the tape recording of that closed session, and was refused. The trial court denied his petition for a writ of mandate on several grounds, including that allowing him to review the discussion even in retrospect would be inconsistent with his conflicted status under the Political Reform Act. The appellate court agreed, stating:

> Despite Hamilton's insistence that nothing improper could come of his silent observation of the closed session, or his later acquisition of the tape, we are concerned with how this might look to the public. To permit a financially interested council member to be privy, unnecessarily, to confidential information which might affect his business interests gives the appearance of impropriety. In our society, information is power. The council member might use the confidential information to his advantage personally, or he might disclose the information improperly to others interested in the decision. Furthermore, the disqualified member's mere presence, or knowledge thereafter, might also subtly influence the decisions of other council members who must maintain an ongoing relationship with him.
>
> We acknowledge Hamilton's point that dissent is a necessary part of our political system, and that the public has a right to be kept informed concerning public matters. In this instance, however, we believe that the policy of promoting unbiased governmental decisions outweighs the public's right to know or to have all of its representatives be fully informed or actively participate in all governmental decisions. The Legislature has already determined that public officials can in certain circumstances be excluded from governmental decisions, and that the public can be denied access to certain council discussions. Hamilton's presence was not necessary to the council discussion, and we feel the best path is to deny him access to the tape.
>
> In this particular case, our conclusion is based in large part on the fact that the reason for the closed session was to have the town council confer with legal counsel about the parking issues.***** In the case where a council member is disqualified from participation in a decision because of a financial conflict of interest, it does not appear to be in the best interest of the town to have that council member present at discussions between the council and its attorney concerning that decision. The attorney, as well as the other

> council members, might not feel as free to disclose everything necessary when a "biased" public official were present. The council members and attorney might feel similarly inhibited where they are aware that a "biased" council member can later obtain a tape recording of the attorney-council discussion. The town might thus be denied effective assistance of counsel.
>
> In these circumstances, we believe the policy and rule against participation by a council member with a conflict should be construed to prohibit the council member from obtaining a tape recording of a closed session between the council and its attorney, where the council met to discuss litigation related to the disqualified council member's area of conflict. We therefore conclude that Hamilton was properly denied access to the tape under section 87100.

Id. at 1058, 1059. This exception to the member's general right of access, the court recognized, was a narrow one. It disagreed with the trial court's conclusion that the plaintiff could have been kept out of the closed session or away from the tape recording thereof on grounds of the attorney-client privilege alone:

> If we had concluded that section 87100 did not bar Council Member Hamilton from obtaining the tape despite his disqualification from active participation in the closed session, the attorney-client privilege would offer the town no further protection from disclosure. Hamilton would have had the right to be a silent spectator at the closed session, or to obtain the tape, simply by virtue of his membership on the council. The attorney-client privilege would not have come into play, as Hamilton would have stood, not in the shoes of the general public, but in the shoes of a full council member/"client."

Ibid., fn. 7.

Access by the Public When the Session Was Unlawfully Closed

The confidentiality of closed session minutes assumes that the recorded discussion was lawful to occur in the closed session to begin with. Where such was not the case, in a closed session of a county's claims settlement committee not held as an attorney-client consultation on pending litigation, a court held that the minutes were accessible to a newspaper as public records, protected neither by the Brown Act nor the attorney-client privilege.

The County's claims settlement committee discussed the Clemens' settlement in a session closed to the public. The Brown Act does not, however, authorize the holding of closed sessions by legislative bodies for the purpose of discussing settlement claims. Thus, the committee's secret meeting was in clear violation of the Brown Act. County's argument that the closed session minutes are exempt under section (54957.2) is also unfounded as that section does not apply to closed sessions held in violation of the Act.

County further argues the minutes of the claim's settlement committee meeting should be protected from disclosure by attorney-client privileges because county counsel was present as both legal counsel and committee member. While the Brown Act has been interpreted to allow closed sessions for the purpose of confidential attorney-client consultation ... the mere presence of county counsel at a meeting will not turn deliberations regarding the settlement of a tort claim into "confidential" attorney-client communications. As stated in the *Sacramento Newspaper Guild* case, "Neither the attorney's presence nor the happenstance of some kind of lawsuit may serve as the pretext for secret consultations whose revelation will not injure the public interest."

Register Division of Freedom Newspapers, Inc. v. County of Orange, 158 Cal.App.3d 893, 907(1984).

§ 1-5(a)(2): Notice of Closed Session Topics

The Act permits closed sessions in certain defined circumstances, not to keep the public in the dark about the issues being dealt with by a legislative body, but to avoid the ill effects of one kind or another which might result from having to expose the full discussion itself to indiscriminate public attention. Accordingly, bodies must provide some information about the general nature of the closed session discussion in advance, by a statement in open session, by a listing on the posted agenda, or—typically—by both. After the closed session, if action was taken of the kind that must immediately be disclosed, that disclosure must be made in open session. The Act makes it clear, therefore, that a body's meeting cannot begin in closed session. The closed session in every instance must be preceded by an announcement which informs the public, even if only by reference to the posted agenda, of the nature of the discussion to take place in closed session. Government Code §54957.7 states:

(a) Prior to holding any closed session, the legislative body of the local agency shall disclose, in an open meeting, the item or items to be discussed in the closed session. The

Bagley-Keene Comparison
Government Code §11126:
(a) Prior to holding any closed session, the state body shall disclose, in an open meeting, the general nature of the item or

items to be discussed in the closed session. The disclosure may take the form of a reference to the item or items as they are listed by number or letter on the agenda. If the session is closed pursuant to paragraph (2) of subdivision (d) of Section 11126, the state body shall state the title of, or otherwise specifically identify, the proceeding or disciplinary action contemplated. However, should the body determine that to do so would jeopardize the body's ability to effectuate service of process upon one or more unserved parties if the proceeding or disciplinary action is commenced or that to do so would fail to protect the private economic and business reputation of the person or entity if the proceeding or disciplinary action is not commenced, then the state body shall notice that there will be a closed session and describe in general terms the purpose of that session. If the session is closed pursuant to subparagraph (A) of paragraph (2) of subdivision (e) of Section 11126, the state body shall state the title of, or otherwise specifically identify, the litigation to be discussed unless the body states that to do so would jeopardize the body's ability to effectuate service of process upon one or more unserved parties, or that to do so would jeopardize its ability to conclude existing settlement negotiations to its advantage.

(b) In the closed session, the state body may consider only those matters covered in its disclosure.

(c) The disclosure shall be made as part of the notice provided for the meeting pursuant to Section 11125 or pursuant to subdivision (a) of Section 92032 of the Education Code and of any order or notice required by Section 11129.

(d) If, after the agenda has been published in compliance with this article, any pending litigation (under subdivision (e) of Section 11126) matters arise, the postponement of which will prevent the state body from complying with any statutory, court-ordered, or other legally imposed deadline, the state body may proceed to discuss those matters in closed session and shall publicly announce in the meeting the title of, or otherwise specifically identify, the litigation to be discussed, unless the body states that to do so would jeopardize the body's ability to effectuate service of process upon one or more unserved parties, or that to do so would jeopardize its ability to conclude existing settlement negotiations to its advantage. Such an announcement shall be deemed to

disclosure may take the form of a reference to the item or items as they are listed by number or letter on the agenda. In the closed session, the legislative body may consider only those matters covered in its statement. Nothing in this section shall require or authorize a disclosure of information prohibited by state or federal law.

(b) After any closed session, the legislative body shall reconvene into open session prior to adjournment and shall make any disclosures required by Section 54957.1 of action taken in the closed session.

(c) The announcements required to be made in open session pursuant to this section may be made at the location announced in the agenda for the closed session, as long as the public is allowed to be present at that location for the purpose of hearing the announcements.

comply fully with the requirements of this section.

(e) Nothing in this section shall require or authorize a disclosure of names or other information that would constitute an invasion of privacy or otherwise unnecessarily divulge the particular facts concerning the closed session or the disclosure of which is prohibited by state or federal law.

(f) After any closed session, the state body shall reconvene into open session prior to adjournment and shall make any reports, provide any documentation, and make any other disclosures required by Section 11125.2 of action taken in the closed session.

(g) The announcements required to be made in open session pursuant to this section may be made at the location announced in the agenda for the closed session, as long as the public is allowed to be present at that location for the purpose of hearing the announcement.

The California Supreme Court has interpreted the last sentence of subdivision (a) of Section 11126 above—a provision of the Bagley-Keene Act—to authorize the California Public Utilities Commission to decline to disclose on its closed session (pending litigation) agenda the fact that it proposed to discuss its litigation with a regulated electric utility, Southern California Edison. The P.U.C. was also not required to announce, after the closed session, that it had taken action in the closed session to approve a settlement with Edison allowing the company to extend the charging of a temporary higher consumer fee rate that had been due to lapse. The court stated:

> Under the quoted provision, a body may decline to identify the litigation under discussion closed session if the body states that to identify it would jeopardize the conclusion of an advantageous settlement. Were the body required, after its closed-session deliberations *but before actually concluding* the settlement, to announce publicly the proposed settlement and the name of the litigation, the protective purpose of Government Code section 11126.3, subdivision (a) would be defeated. The Legislature clearly intended ... that a state body be able to keep private the identity of litigation it is considering settling until it has "conclude[d]" the settlement (assuming the body believes privacy is strategically necessary to the ... negotiations). Construing the closely related provisions of Government Code section 11126, subdivision (e)(1) to require a public identification of the proposed settlement *before* it has been con-

cluded, would defeat that purpose and could not have been the legislative intent.

In this case PUC strictly followed the procedure mandated in Government Code section 11126.3, subdivision (a), noting in the closed-session agenda item, "Case name unspecified. (Disclosure of case name would jeopardize existing settlement negotiations.) (Gov. Code Sec. 11126(e)(2)(A).)" To require PUC, under Government Code section 11126, subdivision (e)(1), to reconvene in open session and publicly announce it was considering settling SCE's federal litigation would subject PUC to the potential loss of the very negotiating equality that Government Code section 11126.3, subdivision (a) was designed to preserve. Reading Government Code section 11126, subdivision (e)(1) in statutory context, therefore, we conclude it authorized PUC not only to discuss, but also to conclude the settlement in closed session.

Southern California Edison Co. v. Peevey, 31 Cal.4th 781, 801 (2003) (emphasis in the original).

§ 1-5(a)(3): Disclosure of Closed Session Action

In all but a few instances, the Act requires that a body disclose the nature of any action taken in closed session and the vote breakdown. In some cases, where the body's own action disposes of the matter, the disclosure must be immediate —by a specific announcement. In other situations, where there is some other party to negotiations or litigation whose approval is needed for closure, or some other event which will officially signal the commencement of an approved action (such as the filing of litigation), the disclosure can be deferred until that point, and even then need not be pointedly announced but simply revealed upon inquiry. Government Code §54957.1 states:

> (a) The legislative body of any local agency shall publicly report any action taken in closed session and the vote or abstention of every member present thereon ... *****
>
> (d) Nothing in this section shall be construed to require that the legislative body approve actions not otherwise subject to legislative body approval.
>
> (e) No action for injury to a reputational, liberty, or other personal interest may be commenced by or on behalf of any employee or former employee with respect to whom a disclosure is made by a legislative body in an effort to comply with this section.

§ 1-5(a)(4): Access to Documents after Closed Session

As soon as a closed session action is disclosed, any written material approved as part of the closed session action (contracts, leases, memoranda of understanding, litigation settlements, et cetera) is likewise disclosable on request. Subdivisions (b) and (c) of §54957.1 state:

> (b) Reports that are required to be made pursuant to this section may be made orally or in writing. The legislative body shall provide to any person who has submitted a written request to the legislative body within 24 hours of the posting of the agenda, or to any person who has made a standing request for all documentation as part of a request for notice of meetings pursuant to Section 54954.1 or 54956, if the requester is present at the time the closed session ends, copies of any contracts, settlement agreements, or other documents that were finally approved or adopted in the closed session. If the Action taken results in one or more substantive amendments to the related documents requiring retyping, the documents need not be released until the retyping is completed during normal business hours, provided that the presiding officer of the legislative body or his or her designee orally summarizes the substance of the amendments for the benefit of the document requester or any other person present and requesting the information.
>
> (c) The documentation referred to in paragraph (b) shall be available to any person on the next business day following the meeting in which the Action referred to is taken or, in the case of substantial amendments, when any necessary retyping is complete.

§ 1-5(b): Authorized Closed Sessions

A legislative body may not hold a closed session simply because there appears to be a good reason for doing so. Government Code §54962 states:

> Except as expressly authorized by this chapter, or by Sections 1461, 1462, 32106, and 32155 of the Health and Safety Code or Sections 37606 and 37624.3 of the Government Code as they apply to hospitals, or by any provision of the Education Code pertaining to school districts and community college districts, no closed session may be held by any legislative body of any local agency.

Bagley-Keene Comparison

Government Code §11132: Except as expressly authorized by this article, no closed session may be held by any state body.

Despite this language, the Attorney General concluded in 79 Ops.Cal.Atty.Gen. 124 (1996) that the Brown Act restriction on closed sessions does not apply to the hearings of a county board of supervisors when acting as the county board of equalization or to the hearings of an assessment appeals board. This view, based on legislative history of other statutes, led the opinion writer to decide that "it is evident that the Legislature has never considered the Brown Act, with its 'exclusivity' provisions, to be applicable to county boards of equalization or assessment appeals boards." Otherwise, however, the Attorney General has concluded in 88 Ops.Cal.Atty.Gen. 16 (2005):

> The Legislature's addition of section 54962 has effectively eliminated the possibility of finding an implied authorization for a closed session. Confidential communication privileges defined in other statutes, such as in the Public Records Act (§§ 6250-6276.48) and

the Evidence Code, no longer provide a basis for excluding the public during a legislative body's meetings.

Agenda Listings and Action Disclosures

For the sake of convenience, the following review of each type of closed session authorized under the Act includes references to the corresponding "safe harbor" agenda listing, if any set forth in the statute (*Suggested Agenda Listing*) as well as what if any information about action taken in that closed session must be communicated to the public (*Subsequent Action Disclosure*).

§ 1-5(b)(1): Conference with Counsel on Pending Litigation

In the most frequently cited case interpreting the Act, *Sacramento Newspaper Guild v. Sacramento County Bd. of Supervisors*, 263 Cal.App.2d 41 (1968), among the issues the court was asked to decide was whether the statute, which at that time had not yet been amended expressly to authorize a closed session to confer with counsel, was subject to an implied exception to permit public bodies to exercise the attorney-client privilege at least as to matters whose public discussion would hamper to agency's ability to protect and pursue its legal interests. The court observed:

> Public agencies are constantly embroiled in contract and eminent domain litigation and, with the expansion of public tort liability, in personal injury and property damage suits. Large-scale public services and projects expose public entities to potential tort liabilities dwarfing those of most private clients. Money actions by and against the public are as contentious as those involving private litigants. The most casual and naive observer can sense the financial stakes wrapped up in the conventionalities of a condemnation trial. Government should have no advantage in legal strife; neither should it be a second-class citizen. We reiterate what we stated in the supersedeas aspect of this suit… : "Public agencies face the same hard realities as other civil litigants. An attorney who cannot confer with his client outside his opponent's presence may be under insurmountable handicaps. A panoply of constitutional, statutory, administrative and fiscal arrangements covering state and local government expresses a policy that litigating public agencies strive with their legal adversaries on fairly even terms. We need not pause for citations to demonstrate the obvious. There is a public entitlement to the effective aid of legal counsel in civil litigation. Effective aid is impossible if opportunity for confidential legal advice is banned."

Id. at 56 (citation omitted). The court noted that closed sessions were desirable not only for the defense or prosecution of litigation, but for attorney and client to confer on the resolution of such disputes by other means.

> Settlement and avoidance of litigation are particularly sensitive activities, whose conduct would be grossly confounded, often made impossible, by undiscriminating insistence on open lawyer-client conferences. In settlement advice, the attorney's professional task is to provide his client a frank appraisal of strength and weakness, gains and risks, hopes and fears. If the public's "right to know" compelled admission of an audience, the ringside seats would be occupied by the government's adversary, delighted to capitalize on every revelation of weakness…

Ibid (footnote, citation omitted). After deciding that the evidence was "thin" that the Legislature had deliberately intended that public bodies have no means of confidential consultation with their attorneys, the court concluded that at least a limited-scope closed session was both necessary and consistent with the Act. Referring to the statutory privilege and the Brown Act, the court stated:

> The two enactments are capable of concurrent operation if the lawyer-client privilege is not overblown beyond its true dimensions. As a barrier to testimonial disclosure, the privilege tends to suppress relevant facts, hence is strictly construed. *****
>
> As a barrier against public access to public affairs, it has precisely the same suppressing effect, hence here too must be strictly construed. As noted earlier, the assurance of private legal consultation is restricted to communications "in confidence." Private clients, relatively free of regulation, may set relatively wide limits on confidentiality; public board members, sworn to uphold the law, may not arbitrarily or unnecessarily inflate confidentiality for the purpose of deflating the spread of the public meeting law. Neither the attorney's presence nor the happenstance of some kind of lawsuit may serve as the pretext for secret consultations whose revelation will not injure the public interest.

Id. at 58 (citation omitted).

When the Legislature added to the Act Government Code §54956.9, codifying the exception permitting such closed sessions, it emphasized that for purposes of the Act, "all expressions of the lawyer-client privilege other than those provided in this section are hereby abrogated. This section is the exclusive expression of the lawyer-client privilege for purposes of conducting closed-session meetings pursuant to this chapter." Pursuant to the section, a body may use a closed session to consult with its attorney on a specific threat of litigation against it, on the advisability of taking legal action itself, or on the progress of court action or settlement negotiations in an ongoing case. Government Code §54956.9 states:

Nothing in this chapter shall be construed to prevent a legislative body of a local agency, based on advice of its legal counsel, from holding a closed session to confer with, or receive advice from, its legal counsel regarding pending litigation when discussion in open session concerning those matters would prejudice the position of the local agency in the litigation.

For purposes of this chapter, all expressions of the lawyer-client privilege other than those provided in this section are hereby abrogated. This section is the exclusive expression of the lawyer-client privilege for purposes of conducting closed-session meetings pursuant to this chapter. For purposes of this section, "litigation" includes any adjudicatory proceeding, including eminent domain, before a court, administrative body exercising its adjudicatory authority, hearing officer, or arbitrator.

For purposes of this section, litigation shall be considered pending when any of the following circumstances exist:

(a) Litigation, to which the local agency is a party, has been initiated formally.

(b) (1) A point has been reached where, in the opinion of the legislative body of the local agency on the advice of its legal counsel, based on existing facts and circumstances, there is a significant exposure to litigation against the local agency.

(2) Based on existing facts and circumstances, the legislative body of the local agency is meeting only to decide whether a closed session is authorized pursuant to paragraph (1) of this subdivision.

For purposes of paragraphs (1) and (2), "existing facts and circum-

Bagley-Keene Comparison

Government Code §11126

(e) (1) Nothing in this article shall be construed to prevent a state body, based on the advice of its legal counsel, from holding a closed session to confer with, or receive advice from, its legal counsel regarding pending litigation when discussion in open session concerning those matters would prejudice the position of the state body in the litigation.

(2) For purposes of this article, all expressions of the lawyer-client privilege other than those provided in this subdivision are hereby abrogated. This subdivision is the exclusive expression of the lawyer-client privilege for purposes of conducting closed session meetings pursuant to this article. For purposes of this subdivision, litigation shall be considered pending when any of the following circumstances exist:

(A) An adjudicatory proceeding before a court, an administrative body exercising its adjudicatory authority, a hearing officer, or an arbitrator, to which the state body is a party, has been initiated formally.

(B) (i) A point has been reached where, in the opinion of the state body on the advice of its legal counsel, based on existing facts and circumstances, there is a significant exposure to litigation against the state body.

(ii) Based on existing facts and circumstances, the state body is meeting only to decide whether a closed session is authorized pursuant to clause (i).

(C) (i) Based on existing facts and circumstances, the state body has decided to initiate or is deciding whether to initiate litigation.

(ii) The legal counsel of the state body shall prepare and submit to it a memorandum stating the specific reasons and legal authority for the closed session. If the closed session is pursuant to paragraph (1), the memorandum shall include the title of the litigation. If the closed session is pursuant to subparagraph (A) or (B), the memorandum shall include the existing facts and circumstances on which it is based. The legal counsel shall submit the memorandum to the state body prior to the closed session, if feasible, and in any case no later than one week after the closed session. The memorandum shall be exempt from disclosure pursuant to Section 6254.25.

(iii) For purposes of this subdivision, "litigation" includes any adjudicatory proceeding, including eminent domain, before a court, administrative body exercising its adjudicatory authority, hearing officer, or arbitrator.

(iv) Disclosure of a memorandum required under this subdivision shall not be deemed as a waiver of the lawyer-client privilege, as provided for under Article 3 (commencing with Section 950) of Chapter 4 of Division 8 of the Evidence Code.

§11131.5. No notice, agenda, announcement, or report required under this article need identify any victim or alleged victim of crime, tortious sexual conduct, or child abuse unless the identity of the person has been publicly disclosed.

stances" shall consist only of one of the following:

(A) Facts and circumstances that might result in litigation against the agency but which the agency believes are not yet known to a potential plaintiff or plaintiffs, which facts and circumstances need not be disclosed.

(B) Facts and circumstances, including, but not limited to, an accident, disaster, incident, or transactional occurrence that might result in litigation against the agency and that are known to a potential plaintiff or plaintiffs, which facts or circumstances shall be publicly stated on the agenda or announced.

(C) The receipt of a claim pursuant to the Tort Claims Act or some other writ- ten communication from a potential plaintiff threatening litigation, which claim or communication shall be available for public inspection pursuant to Section 54957.5.

(D) A statement made by a person in an open and public meeting threatening litigation on a specific matter within the responsibility of the legislative body.

(E) A statement threatening litigation made by a person outside an open and public meeting on a specific matter within the responsibility of the legislative body so long as the official or employee of the local agency receiving knowledge of the threat makes a contemporaneous or other record of the statement prior to the meeting, which record shall be available for public inspection pursuant to Section 54957.5. The records so created need not identify the alleged victim of unlawful or tortious sexual conduct or anyone making the threat on their behalf, or identify a public employee who is the alleged perpetrator of any unlawful or tortious conduct upon which a threat of litigation is based, unless the identity of the person has been publicly disclosed.

(F) Nothing in this section shall require disclosure of written communications that are privileged and not subject to disclosure pursuant to the California Public Records Act (Chapter 3.5 (commencing at Section 6250) of Division 7, Title 1).

(c) Based on existing facts and circumstances, the legislative body of the local agency has decided to initiate or is deciding whether to initiate litigation.

Prior to holding a closed session pursuant to this section, the legislative body of the local agency shall state on the agenda or publicly announce the subdivision of this section that authorizes the closed session. If the session is closed pursuant to subdivision (a), the body shall state the title of or otherwise specifically identify the litigation to be discussed, unless the body states that to do so would jeopardize the agency's ability to effectuate service of process upon one or more unserved parties, or that to do so would jeopardize its ability to conclude existing settlement negotiations to its advantage.

A local agency shall be considered to be a "party" or to have a "significant exposure to litigation" if an officer or employee of the local agency is a party or has significant exposure to litigation concerning prior or prospective activities or alleged activities during the course and scope of that office or employment, including litigation in which it is an issue whether an activity is outside the course and scope of the office or employment.

Privileged Memoranda for Non-litigation Matters

When a legislative body chooses to confer personally with its attorney, the only subject matter permitted for a closed session is "pending litigation." As for privileged communications on matters not involving litigation, a legislative body may receive completely confidential information or advice from its attorney in the form of a written memorandum. *Roberts v. City of Palmdale,* 5 Cal.4th 363 (1993).

Attorney Consultation Required

The closed session is for a communication between attorney and client: "to confer with, or receive advice from, its legal counsel." The body may not discuss litigation in closed session under this heading unless its legal counsel is a party to the discussion, at least by conference call.

Exception Available to Non-governing Bodies

The Attorney General has opined that while in general a body may not use a closed session to discuss cases to which it is not and would not be a party, the governing body of the agency may not be the only legislative body entitled to a closed session. For example, a county's airport advisory committee—not just the board of supervisors—might hold a closed session with its attorney to discuss litigation involving the county airport. 67 Ops.Cal.Atty.Gen. 111 (1984). On the other hand, if the specialized body opts to discuss the litigation openly, that fact does not preclude the governing body from discussing that matter in closed session. 69 Ops. Cal.Atty.Gen. 232 (1986).

Exception Not Available for Hypothetical or Contingent Threats

The Attorney General has opined that the attorney's advice to a body as to the lawfulness or legal implications of a proposed action not yet taken is not appropriate for a closed session, because the public is entitled to know what this advice is in order to evaluate the performance of the body. 36 Ops.Cal.Atty.Gen. 175 (1960). The mere possibility that a body's action might be challenged in court does not suffice as a defined threat that would justify discussing the proposed action in closed session, since that rationale would justify a "litigation" session on any matter. 71 Ops.Cal.Atty.Gen. 96 (1988).

Application of the Exception to Settlement Discussions

The Attorney General has opined that a body may not use a closed session on pending litigation to meet directly with the adverse party or its representative to negotiate a settlement; the negotiation must be handled by its attorney in a separate setting. 62 Ops.Cal.Atty.Gen. 150 (1979). A body may, however, use a closed litigation session not only to confer with counsel about a settlement but to deliberate and approve the settlement or a settlement offer (75 Ops. Cal. Atty. Gen. 14 (1992); *Southern California Edison Co. v. Peevey*, 31 Cal.4th 781, 801 (2003)).

Suggested Agenda Listings

The Act sets forth a safe harbor provision suggesting content for disclosure language on the meeting agenda which, if employed to alert the public as to the subject matter of the closed session, will insulate the agency against liability for providing a substantively inadequate description of the closed session's purpose. Government Code §54954.5 states:

> For purposes of describing closed session items pursuant to Section 54954.2, the agenda may describe closed sessions as provided below. No legislative body or elected official shall be in violation of Section 54954.2 or 54956 if the closed session items were described in substantial compliance with this section. Substantial compliance is satisfied by including the information provided below, irrespective of its format.*****
>
> (c) With respect to every item of business to be discussed in closed session pursuant to Section 54956.9:
>
> CONFERENCE WITH LEGAL COUNSEL--EXISTING LITIGATION
>
> (Subdivision (a) of Section 54956.9)
>
> Name of case: (Specify by reference to claimant's name, names of parties, case or claim numbers)
>
> or
>
> Case name unspecified: (Specify whether disclosure would jeopardize service of process or existing settlement negotiations)
>
> CONFERENCE WITH LEGAL COUNSEL--ANTICIPATED LITIGATION
>
> Significant exposure to litigation pursuant to subdivision (b) of Section 54956.9: (Specify number of potential cases)
>
> (In addition to the information noticed above, the agency may be required to provide additional information on the agenda or in an oral statement prior to the closed session pursuant to subparagraphs (B) to (E), inclusive, of paragraph (3) of subdivision (b) of Section 54956.9.)
>
> Initiation of litigation pursuant to subdivision (c) of Section 54956.9: (Specify number of potential cases)

Disclosure of Threats prior to Session

When a closed session is scheduled under "significant exposure to litigation," unless the facts and circumstances creating the threat are not yet known to the likely plaintiffs, they must be accessible to the public. In *California Alliance for Utility etc. Education v. City of San Diego*, 56 Cal.App.4th 1024 (1997) the court noted

> the important balance which the Brown Act attempts to draw between the requirement that public business be conducted in public and the practical need public agencies have for confidentiality when attempting to make rational decisions about the legal strength of arguments asserted by an actual or probable adversary… The Brown Act attempts to draw that balance by, among

> other devices, requiring disclosure to the public of facts and circumstances which show that a public discussion of a particular matter is prejudicial to the agency's interests.

Id. at 1030. The result is a significant addition to the general agenda listing requirements. As noted on page 22 of the Attorney General's guide, *The Brown Act: Open Meetings for Local Legislative Bodies,* under §54956.9(b)(3) there are requirements for supplementary oral or written announcements, in effect, in four such situations:

• If there has been no kind of communication yet from the likely plaintiffs but the agency is aware of something that is likely to prompt a litigation threat—some accident, disaster, incident or transaction such as a contract dispute—"the facts must be publicly stated on the agenda or announced" prior to the closed session.

• If a claim or some other written threat of litigation has been received, the document is a public record and "reference to the claim or communication must be publicly stated on the agenda or announced" prior to the closed session.

• When the closed session is triggered by a litigation threat made in an open and public meeting, "reference to the statement must be publicly stated on the agenda or announced" prior to the closed session.

• When an oral threat of litigation is made outside a meeting, it may not be made the basis of a closed session unless the official who became aware of it makes a memo explaining what was saId. The memo is a public record and "reference to the claim or communication must be publicly stated on the agenda or announced" prior to the closed session.

Subsequent Action Disclosures

The required disclosures of any action taken are set forth in Government Code §54957.1:

> (a) The legislative body of any local agency shall publicly report any action taken in closed session and the vote or abstention of every member present thereon, as follows:
>
> *****
>
> (2) Approval given to the body's legal counsel to defend, or seek or refrain from seeking appellate review or relief, or to enter as an amicus curiae in any form of litigation as the result of a consultation under Section 54956.9 shall be reported in open session at the public meeting during which the closed session is held. The report shall identify, if known, the adverse party or parties and the substance of the litigation. In the case of approval given to initiate or intervene in an action, the announcement need not identify the Action, the defendants, or other particulars, but shall specify that the direction to initiate or intervene in an action has been given and that the Action, the defendants, and the other particulars shall, once formally commenced, be disclosed to any person upon inquiry, unless to do so would jeopardize the agency's ability to effectuate service of process on one or more unserved parties, or that to do so would jeopardize its ability to conclude

existing settlement negotiations to its advantage.

(3) Approval given to the body's legal counsel of a settlement of pending litigation as defined in Section 54956.9, at any stage prior to or during a judicial or quasi-judicial proceeding shall be reported after the settlement is final, as specified below:

(A) If the body accepts a settlement offer signed by the opposing party, the body shall report its acceptance and identify the substance of the agreement in open session at the public meeting during which the closed session is held.

(B) If final approval rests with some other party to the litigation or with the court, then as soon as the settlement becomes final, and upon inquiry by any person, the local agency shall disclose the fact of that approval, and identify the substance of the agreement.

§ 1-5(b)(2): Conference with Agent on Employee Negotiations

A body may go into closed session to confer with its own bargaining agent on the progress of negotiations with an employee bargaining unit or even with individual executive, management or other "unrepresented" employees, concerning wages or other compensation, or (in the case of an organized employee unit) issues which must under state law be submitted to collective bargaining. A court has said that this section, "by permitting the governing body to meet in secret with its negotiating team during collective bargaining, underscores the Legislature's intent to assign the governing body the central role of directing the meet and confer process so as to achieve binding labor-management agreements." *Voters for Responsible Retirement v. Board of Supervisors*, 8 Cal.4th 765, fn. 5 (1994). Government Code §54957.6 states:

Bagley-Keene Comparison

Government Code §11126:

(c). Nothing in this article shall be construed to do any of the following:

•••••

(17) Prevent a state body, or boards, commissions, administrative officers, or other representatives that may properly be designated by law or by a state body, from holding closed sessions with its representatives in discharging its responsibilities under Chapter 10 (commencing with Section 3500), Chapter 10.3 (commencing with Section 3512), Chapter 10.5 (commencing with Section 3525), or Chapter 10.7 (commencing of Section 3540) of Division 4 of Title 1 as the sessions relate to salaries, salary schedules, or compensation paid in the form of fringe benefits. For the purposes enumerated in the preceding sentence, a state body may also meet with a state conciliator who has intervened in the proceedings.

(a) Notwithstanding any other provision of law, a legislative body of a local agency may hold closed sessions with the local agency's designated representatives regarding the salaries, salary schedules, or compensation paid in the form of fringe benefits of its represented and unrepresented employees, and, for represented employees, any other matter within the statutorily-provided scope of representation. Closed sessions of a legislative body of a local agency, as permitted in this section, shall be for the purpose of reviewing its position and instructing the local agency's designated representatives. Closed sessions, as permitted in this section, may take place prior to and during consultations and discussions with representatives of employee organizations and unrepresented employees.

Closed sessions with the local agency's designated representative regarding the salaries, salary schedules, or compensation paid in the form of fringe benefits may include discussion of an agency's available funds and funding priorities, but only insofar as these discussions relate to providing instructions to the local agency's designated representative.

Closed sessions held pursuant to this section shall not include final action on the proposed compensation of one or more unrepresented employees.

For the purposes enumerated in this section, a legislative body of a local agency may also meet with a state conciliator who has intervened in the proceedings.

(b) For the purposes of this section, the term "employee" shall include an officer or an independent contractor who functions as an officer or an employee, but shall not include any elected official, member of a legislative body, or other independent contractors.

Represented and Unrepresented Employees

There are two somewhat different situations covered by this section.

• One is the body's conference with its bargaining agent when he or she is negotiating with an organized employee unit—a union or association. In this situation the body not only may review its position and provide instructions to the negotiator, but may actually vote in closed session to approve a final package including compensation elements. The vote and the contents of the package, as noted below, need not be disclosed until the employee unit has ratified its acceptance.

• The other situation is one in which the bargaining is being conducted with one or more "unrepresented" (nonunion) individual employees—typically chief executives or key department heads. This provision was added to the section after a court concluded that the salaries of individual employees could not be deliberated and set in a closed session on performance evaluation (*San Diego Union v. City Council of San Diego*, 146 Cal.App.3d 947 (1983)). In such cases the agency's "representative" may actually be a member of the body itself. But it is important to note three limitations.

First, this closed session is authorized only when the body is actually bargaining with the unrepresented employee(s). If instead it is unilaterally discussing a non-negotiated pay increase for one or more individual employees, for example, no closed session is permitted. In such a case, the court's discussion in *San Diego Union,* concluding that discussions of employee salaries are to be segregated from performance evaluation and conducted openly, would apply:

> Salaries and other terms of compensation constitute municipal budgetary matters of substantial public interest warranting open discussion and eventual electoral public ratification. Public visibility breeds public awareness which in turn fosters public activism politically and subtly encouraging the governmental entity to permit public participation in the discussion process. It is difficult

> to imagine a more critical time for public scrutiny of its governmental decision-making process than when the latter is determining how it shall spend public funds. With ever-increasing demands on public funds which have dwindled so drastically since the passage of Proposition 13, secrecy cannot be condoned in budgetary determinations, including the establishment of salaries. Granted, evaluating a specific employee's performance is a matter within the ambit of the "personnel exception" in light of the 1982 amendment to section 54957; however, upon the determination a particular public employee is deserving of a salary increase, various other factors must be considered such as available funds, other city funding priorities, relative compensation of similar positions within the city and in other jurisdictions, before determining the salary increase. Each of these considerations is of acute public interest.
>
> Further, there is no basis for the apparent underlying assumption of the City Council's argument that it cannot evaluate the performance of the cited public employees without also establishing their salaries in executive session. Consistent with both the "personnel exception" as to the evaluation of performance of a particular employee and the general mandate of the Brown Act, we envision the two-step process of an executive session evaluating the performance of the public employee and a properly noticed, open session for setting that particular employee's salary as a facile matter, not negatively affecting the review process. Common sense compels the conclusion that oblique references to discussions of salaries for specific individuals within executive sessions evaluating the performance of that public employee would not violate the Brown Act so long as the specific discussions as to the amount of salary increase are reserved for a properly noticed, public meeting.

Id. at 955, 956.

Second, since the purpose of the closed session is to allow the body to discuss its position without revealing it to the other side, the body may not negotiate directly with an affected employee in closed session.

Finally, any final action on compensation for an unrepresented employee must be in open session.

Suggested Agenda Listings

The Act sets forth a safe harbor provision suggesting content for disclosure language on the meeting agenda which, if employed to alert the public as to the subject matter of the closed session, will insulate the agency against liability for providing a substantively inadequate description of the closed session's purpose. Government Code §54954.5 states:

> For purposes of describing closed session items pursuant to Section 54954.2, the agenda may describe closed sessions as provided below. No legislative body or elected official shall be in violation of Section 54954.2 if the closed session items were described in substantial compliance with this section. Substantial compliance is satisfied by including the information provided below, irrespective of its format.
>
> *****
>
> (f) With respect to every item of business to be discussed in closed session pursuant to Section 54957.6:
>
> CONFERENCE WITH LABOR NEGOTIATORS
>
> Agency designated representatives: (Specify names of designated representatives attending the closed session) (If circumstances necessitate the absence of a specified designated representative, an agent or designee may participate in place of the absent representative so long as the name of the agent or designee is announced at an open session held prior to the closed session.)
>
> Employee organization: (Specify name of organization representing employee or employees in question)
>
> Or
>
> Unrepresented employee: (Specify position title of unrepresented employee who is the subject of the negotiations)

Subsequent Action Disclosures

The required disclosures of any action taken are set forth in Government Code §54957.1:

> (a) The legislative body of any local agency shall publicly report any action taken in closed session and the vote or abstention of every member present thereon, as follows:
>
> *****
>
> (6) Approval of an agreement concluding labor negotiations pursuant to Section 54957.6 shall be reported after the agreement is final and has been accepted or ratified by the other party. The report shall identify the item approved and the other party or parties to the negotiation.

Special Rules for School Districts

School districts are subject to a different union bargaining law than that governing other local agencies. The Rodda Act provides school boards with more flexibility in how they meet and confer—even allowing them to negotiate directly, outside the Brown Act, with their employee organizations—but provides its own special controls to assure that the public is kept informed of the issues under discussion and allowed to express its views in timely fashion. Education Code §3549.1 states:

> All the proceedings set forth in subdivisions (a) to (d), inclusive, shall be exempt from the provisions of ... the Ralph M. Brown Act ... unless the parties mutually agree otherwise:
>
> (a) Any meeting and negotiating discussion between a public school employer and a recognized or certified employee organization.

(b) Any meeting of a mediator with either party or both parties to the meeting and negotiating process.

(c) Any hearing, meeting, or investigation conducted by a factfinder or arbitrator.

(d) Any executive session of the public school employer or between the public school employer and its designated representative for the purpose of discussing its position regarding any matter within the scope of representation and instructing its designated representatives.

But there are safeguards in the Rodda Act supporting public awareness and participation. As the California Supreme Court has noted, that statute

> recognizes the importance of public participation in decisions affecting the educational process even as to matters clearly within the scope of representation. Initial contract proposals made by both sides must be presented at a public meeting and thereafter become matters of public record. The public must be allowed a reasonable time to become informed of the proposals and to express its views at a public meeting prior to commencement of employer-employee negotiation. Any new subject introduced into the collective bargaining process must be made public within 24 hours and the public must be informed of any votes cast upon the subject by the employer…
>
> *****
>
> Thus, although the public is excluded from actual negotiating sessions … its opportunity to be fully informed and to express its views is preserved.

San Mateo City School District v. Public Employment Relations Board, 33 Cal.3d 850, 864 (1983) (citations omitted). The provisions the court referred to are in Education Code §§3547 and 3547.5:

Education Code §3547

(a) All initial proposals of exclusive representatives and of public school employers, which relate to matters within the scope of representation, shall be presented at a public meeting of the public school employer and thereafter shall be public records.

(b) Meeting and negotiating shall not take place on any proposal until a reasonable time has elapsed after the submission of the proposal to enable the public to become informed and the public has the opportunity to express itself regarding the proposal at a meeting of the school employer.

(c) After the public has had the opportunity to express itself, the public school employer shall, at a meeting which is open to the public, adopt its initial proposal.

(d) New subjects of meeting and negotiating arising after the presentation of initial proposals shall be made public within 24 hours. If a vote is taken on such subject by the public school employer, the vote thereon by each member voting shall also be made public within 24 hours.

(e) The board may adopt regulations for the purpose of implementing this section, which are consistent with the intent of the section; namely that the public be informed of the issues that are being negotiated upon and have full opportunity to express their views on the issues to the public school employer, and to know of the positions of their elected representatives.

Education Code §3547.5. Before a public school employer enters into a written agreement with an exclusive representative covering matters within the scope of representation, the major provisions of the agreement, including, but not limited to, the costs that would be incurred by the public school employer under the agreement for the current and subsequent fiscal years, shall be disclosed at a public meeting of the public school employer in a format established for this purpose by the Superintendent of Public Instruction.

§ 1-5(b)(3): Conference with Agent on Property Negotiations

A body may go into closed session to confer with its agent about the price or terms of payment being negotiated with some other party for a real estate transaction—a sale, rental or lease, for example, of some interest in land, buildings or other structures. Government Code §54956.8 states:

Notwithstanding any other provision of this chapter, a legislative body of a local agency may hold a closed session with its negotiator prior to the purchase, sale, exchange, or lease of real property by or for the local agency to grant authority to its negotiator regarding the price and terms of payment for the purchase, sale, exchange, or lease.

However, prior to the closed session, the legislative body of the local agency shall hold an open and public session in which it identifies the real property or real properties which the negotiations may concern and the person or persons with whom its negotiator may negotiate.

For the purpose of this section, the negotiator may be a member of the legislative body of the local agency.

For purposes of this section, "lease" includes renewal or renegotiation of a lease.

Nothing in this section shall preclude a local agency from holding a closed session for discussions regarding eminent domain proceedings pursuant to Section 54956.9.

Bagley-Keene Comparison
Government Code §11126:
c). Nothing in this article shall be construed to do any of the following:
•••••
(7) (A) Prevent a state body from holding closed sessions with its negotiator prior to the purchase, sale, exchange, or lease of real property by or for the state body to give instructions to its negotiator regarding the price and terms of payment for the purchase, sale, exchange, or lease.
(B) However, prior to the closed session, the state body shall hold an open and public session in which it identifies the real property or real properties that the negotiations may concern and the person or persons with whom its negotiator may negotiate.
(C) For purposes of this paragraph, the negotiator may be a member of the state body.
(D) For purposes of this paragraph, "lease" includes renewal or renegotiation of a lease.
(E) Nothing in this paragraph shall preclude a state body from holding a closed session for discussions regarding eminent domain proceedings pursuant to subdivision (e).

Negotiations Must Be Under Way

This closed session is not intended to be used to discuss the pluses or minuses of a merely potential property transaction, or the selection of properties to be sought or put on the market, or likely buyers, sellers or other interested parties, or any other topic antecedent to a specific negotiation, about a particular parcel or building, with a particular party. Section 54956.8 assumes that authority has already been given in open session to enter into negotiation with all these particulars already determined —because the session must be preceded by a statement identifying the property and the other party to the negotiations. The only topics authorized for discussion in the closed session are the price and the terms of payment to be sought or offered.

Property Identification Must Be Specific

The phrase "identifies the real property or real properties which the negotiations may concern" is not satisfied by a listing of all possible properties that might be subject of negotiations. The Attorney General concluded, in 73 Ops. Cal. Atty. Gen. 1 (1990) that the apparent purpose of the prior identification requirement

> was to provide the members of the public an opportunity to comment or to take pertinent action in favor of or opposition to a particular acquisition . . . In order for any such comment or action to be relevant and appropriately directed, however, the property to be considered at a particular closed session of the board, as well as "the person or persons with whom its negotiator may negotiate," must be specifically identified.

Proper Scope of Discussion

In *Shapiro v. City Council of San Diego*, 96 Cal.App.4th 904 (2002) the Court of Appeal agreed with the trial court that the San Diego Council had violated the Brown Act in including discussion of a variety of "related" issues in a series of closed sessions held to consult with its agent in real property negotiations concerning a large redevelopment project to create a new baseball park. The trial judge had cited and criticized several deviations in the topics of discussion reflected in the minutes of various closed sessions, summarizing in its declaratory judgment:

> The defendant City Council's discussion of the following topics in closed sessions on the dates specified, is outside the scope of and so violates its duty under section 54956.8 to limit topics to instructions to its negotiators regarding the price and terms of payment for the purchase, sale, exchange or lease of specific real property by or for the City of San Diego:
>
> Closed session: Improper topics
>
> Dec. 1, 1998 - briefing on land acquisition matters, design

work of architect engineers, and infrastructure and parking developments

Dec. 8, 1998 - general MOU discussion

Jan. 11, 1999 - authority to hire ballpark manager

Jan. 19, 1999 - need to hire a project director for the ballpark project

Feb. 16, 1999 - capping interim expenses and environmental impact report (EIR), issues of alternative sites, traffic and parking

Mar. 30, 31, 1999 - financing of the ballpark project

Jun. 29, 1999 - naming rights in the ballpark, pending litigation

Aug. 3, 1999 - EIR

Sept. 14, 1999 - homeless and effects of redevelopment on homeless

Sept. 28, 1999 - obtaining consultants.

Id. at 909. Coupled with its declaratory judgment, the court issued an injunction prohibiting such practices in the future. The city appealed, arguing both that the injunction was an unauthorized remedy and that the court had misinterpreted the disclosure requirements and scope of discussion for real property closed sessions. On the lawfulness of its agenda descriptions, the city argued that since the Brown Act's "safe harbor" formula requires only disclosure of whether the discussions will concern price, or terms of payment, or both, anything other than those issues need not be disclosed. The Fourth District disagreed.

> The City Council says that since the safe harbor language of section 54954.5, subdivision (b) does not require the City to identify topics that go beyond a purchase or sale transaction into related areas, then it need not provide any such notice, even if such things will inevitably come up in discussion as part of the overall consideration of whether to purchase certain properties, as part of the overall redevelopment transaction. The City Council contends it is unreasonable to require notice to be given of such topics as transient occupancy taxes or environmental impact report mitigation requirements, even though such factors are often important considerations in the decision of whether to carry out such a purchase transaction of real property, and are reasonably related to the subject purchase decisions.
>
> We believe the City Council's view that no detailed disclosures should be required before closed sessions may be held to discuss a complex overall real estate based transaction is inconsistent with the express statutory requirements of section 54956.8 (real property which is the subject of the negotiations and the person with whom

> the negotiator will negotiate must both be identified) and section 54954.2, subdivision (a) (the legislative body must post an agenda containing a brief general description of each item of business to be transacted or discussed at the meeting, including items to be discussed in closed session).

Id. at 920. On the other hand, the court concluded that the city's notion of what could be included in a real property closed session was erroneously inflated to begin with.

> The City Council argues for a "rule of reason" to allow background discussions, questions and answers during closed session, if they are reasonably related to the purpose of giving direction to a legislative body's negotiator, even though a different project or proposed agreement would still remain outside the scope of the negotiations under way. The City contends that matters of importance for the agreement being negotiated must be allowed, even if that topic is not specifically set forth in the agenda for the closed session. For example, financing should be an exception to the disclosure requirement, according to the City.

Id. at 922. The city's "rule of reason" argument took its cue from the dissent of California Supreme Court Justice Janice Rogers Brown in *Regents of the University of California v. Superior Court (Molloy)*, 20 Cal.4th 509, 537 (1999), an opinion that expressed strong skepticism about the Legislature's efforts in the open meeting laws to constrain the collegiality and "deliberative process" of government bodies by rules insisting on public proceedings and disclosures. But the Court of Appeal observed:

> Even assuming such a balancing process is appropriate in this instance, when we compare, as did the trial court, the published agendas with the confidential minutes for the closed sessions, we can only conclude that such a balance should be struck in favor of public disclosure in this instance, in compliance with both the letter and the spirit of the Brown Act. As found by the trial court, the agenda items noticed related only to City negotiations with designated representatives from the Padres and the Port District regarding real property interests in the East Village area, or Qualcomm Stadium, or the Centre City East area. Under the plain language of section 54956.8, the City Council gave notice of its intent to hold a closed session with its negotiator, prior to the purchase or other transaction of real property, to the extent that the local agency wished to grant authority to its nego-

> tiator regarding the price and terms of payment for the purchase/transaction. Under section 54954.2, subdivision (a), members of the legislative body or its staff may ask questions for clarifications or report on related activities, etc. However, there is nothing in the statutory scheme that grants an unlimited scope of authority to the City Council, in conducting such business, to determine what discussions it may deem to be related background information that is essential to the particular transaction in real property, for purposes of giving instructions to a negotiator about that transaction.
>
> In this case, the actual discussions in closed session extended to topics such as briefing on land acquisition matters, design work of architects, engineers, and infrastructure and parking developments. Also, such topics as capping interim expenses, environmental impact report (EIR) considerations, issues of alternative sites, traffic, naming rights, expert consultants and staff were discussed. Such policy considerations as the impact of the ballpark project on the homeless were discussed at closed session. All these topics confirm the City' s position that this redevelopment project, as memorialized in the MOU and related agreements, is indeed a complex real estate based transaction. That characterization, however, does not negate the requirements of the Brown Act when agenda items are noticed concerning real estate interests, such as purchase and sale of real property on which the anticipated development will be located.

Id. at 923. In affirming the judgment issuing the injunction, the court concluded:

> The City Council cannot claim substantial compliance under the safe harbor provisions of section 54954.5, subdivision (b), when its anticipated project discussions exceed the scope of the safe harbor notice provisions, and do not involve a specific and identifiable piece of property under discussion, but rather range far afield of a specific buying and selling decision that the negotiator is instructed to work toward.
>
> If we were to accept the City' s interpretation of the Brown Act in this respect, we would be turning the Brown Act on its head, by narrowly construing the open meeting requirements and broadly construing the statutory exceptions to it. That would be incorrect. We do not denigrate the important consideration of confidentiality in negotiations. However, we believe that in this case, the City Council is attempting to use the Brown Act as a shield against public disclosure of its consideration of important public policy issues, of the type that are inevitably raised whenever such a large public redevelopment real

estate based transaction is contemplated. The important policy considerations of the Brown Act, however, must be enforced, even where particular transactions do not fit neatly within its statutory categories. In this case, the trial court reached an appropriate balance in applying the Brown Act to this particular set of circumstances.

Id. at 924.

Suggested Agenda Listing

The Act sets forth a safe harbor provision suggesting content for disclosure language on the meeting agenda which, if employed to alert the public as to the subject matter of the closed session, will insulate the agency against liability for providing a substantively inadequate description of the closed session's purpose. Government Code §54954.5 states:

> For purposes of describing closed session items pursuant to Section 54954.2, the agenda may describe closed sessions as provided below. No legislative body or elected official shall be in violation of Section 54954.2 if the closed session items were described in substantial compliance with this section. Substantial compliance is satisfied by including the information provided below, irrespective of its format.
>
> *****
>
> (b) With respect to every item of business to be discussed in closed session pursuant to Section 54956.8:
>
> CONFERENCE WITH REAL PROPERTY NEGOTIATORS
>
> Property: (Specify street address, or if no street address, the parcel number or other unique reference, of the real property under negotiation)
>
> Agency negotiator: (Specify names of negotiators attending the closed session) (If circumstances necessitate the absence of a specified negotiator, an agent or designee may participate in place of the absent negotiator so long as the name of the agent or designee is announced at an open session held prior to the closed session.)
>
> Negotiating parties: (Specify name of party (not agent))
>
> Under negotiation: (Specify whether instruction to negotiator will concern price, terms of payment, or both)

Subsequent Action Disclosures

The required disclosures of any action taken are set forth in Government Code §54957.1:

> (a) The legislative body of any local agency shall publicly report any action taken in closed session and the vote or abstention of every member present thereon, as follows:
>
> *****
>
> (1) Approval of an agreement concluding real estate negotiations pursuant to Section 54956.8 shall be reported after the agreement is final, as specified below:
>
> (A) If its own approval renders the agreement final, the body shall report that approval and the substance of the agreement in open session at the public meeting during which the closed session is held.
>
> (B) If final approval rests with the other party to the negotiations, the local agency shall disclose the fact of that approval and the substance of the agree-

ment upon inquiry by any person, as soon as the other party or its agent has informed the local agency of its approval.

§ 1-5(b)(4): Employee Hiring, Evaluation, Discipline, Dismissal

Perhaps the most frequently invoked variety of closed session is often referred to as dealing with "personnel." The only risk in using that term (it is not used in any of the open meeting laws) is that it may embody or encourage the mistaken notion that any issue dealing with staff or staffing—or indeed any embarrassing situation somehow involving a particular employee—is eligible for closed session. As the language of the sections below suggest, however, the permissible topics are far narrower. Government Code §54957 states:

(b) (1) Subject to paragraph (2), nothing contained in this chapter shall be construed to prevent the legislative body of a local agency from holding closed sessions during a regular or special meeting to consider the appointment, employment, evaluation of performance, discipline, or dismissal of a public employee or to hear complaints or charges brought against the employee by another person or employee unless the employee requests a public session.

(2) As a condition to holding a closed session on specific complaints or charges brought against an employee by another person or employee, the employee shall be given written notice of his or her right to have the complaints or charges heard in an open session rather than a closed session, which notice shall be delivered to the employee personally or by mail at least 24 hours before the time for holding the session. If notice is not given, any disciplinary or other action taken by the legislative body against the employee based on the specific complaints or charges in the closed session shall be null and void.

(3) The legislative body also may exclude from the public or closed meeting, during the examination of a witness, any or all other witnesses in the matter being investigated by the legislative body.

(4) For the purposes of this subdivision, the term "employee" shall include an officer or an independent contractor who functions as an officer or an employee but shall not include

Bagley-Keene Comparison

Government Code §11126.

(a) (1) Nothing in this article shall be construed to prevent a state body from holding closed sessions during a regular or special meeting to consider the appointment, employment, evaluation of performance, or dismissal of a public employee or to hear complaints or charges brought against that employee by another person or employee unless the employee requests a public hearing.

(2) As a condition to holding a closed session on the complaints or charges to consider disciplinary action or to consider dismissal, the employee shall be given written notice of his or her right to have a public hearing, rather than a closed session, and that notice shall be delivered to the employee personally or by mail at least 24 hours before the time for holding a regular or special meeting. If notice is not given, any disciplinary or other action taken against any employee at the closed session shall be null and void.

(3) The state body also may exclude from any public or closed session, during the examination of a witness, any or all other witnesses in the matter being investigated by the state body.

(4) Following the public hearing or closed session, the body may deliberate on the decision to be reached in a closed session.

(b) For the purposes of this section, "employee" does not include any person who is elected to, or appointed to a public office by, any state body. However, officers of the California State University who receive compensation for their services, other than per diem and ordinary and necessary expenses, shall, when engaged in that capacity, be considered employees. Furthermore, for purposes of this section, the term employee includes a person exempt from civil service pursuant to subdivision (e) of Section 4 of Article VII of the California Constitution.

11128. Each closed session of a state body shall be held only during a regular or special meeting of the body.

any elected official, member of a legislative body or other independent contractors. Nothing in this subdivision shall limit local officials' ability to hold closed session meetings pursuant to Sections 1461, 32106, and 32155 of the Health and Safety Code or Sections 37606 and 37624.3 of the Government Code. Closed sessions held pursuant to this subdivision shall not include discussion or action on proposed compensation except for a reduction of compensation that results from the imposition of discipline.

No Place for Impersonal Personnel Decisions

The fact that a personnel policy discussion may affect staff morale does not qualify it for closed session. The Attorney General has opined that a general consideration of the need for one or more new positions does not warrant a closed session, although the evaluation of an existing employee's performance—which may lead to such a discussion—is one of the recognized exceptions. 63 Ops. Cal. Atty. Gen. 153 (1980). These topics, although they may be closely linked, should be segregated, with the policy question discussed openly, if only to avoid a misleading agenda listing. A court has held that a school board's discussion and decision on staff cutbacks or layoffs as a general result of declining pupil attendance, and the need to eliminate certain positions, although it may certainly affect identifiable employees, is not a merit-specific matter. Such deliberations, driven by economic or other impersonal forces, must be conducted openly. *Santa Clara Federation of Teachers v. Governing Board,* 116 Cal.App.3d 831 (1981).

Exception Applicable to Former Employees

Sometimes a body may be required to revisit a previous dismissal. Although at that point the person in question is no longer an employee, a court has found a closed session justifiable in such circumstances. *Cozzolino v. City of Fontana,* 136 Cal.App.2d 608 (1955).

Employee and Independent Contractor Distinguished

A court held, prior to an amendment of the Act expressly excluding independent contractors from the definition of "employee" for purposes of closed sessions, that the common law distinctions between the terms were to be read into the designation "employee." The result was that a school board could not lawfully discuss contracting with a consortium of real estate specialists in closed session under §54957. *Rowen v. Santa Clara Unified School District.*, 121 Cal.App.3d 231 (1981).

Employee and Public Official Distinguished

A court held, prior to the amendment to the statute expressly excluding elected officials and members of legislative bodies from the definition of "employee" for purposes of closed sessions, that the board of directors of a public museum was authorized under §54957 to hold a closed session to elect its chairman and vice chairman. The current language renders obsolete the authority of *Edgar v. Oakland Museum Advisory Commission*, 36 Cal.App.3d 73 (1973).

Exception Includes Consideration of Nominations

A court has held that the scope of discussion and action permissible in closed session pursuant to §54957 includes the selection of three nominees for a municipal position subject to appointment by the mayor, and that because nomination is not an action to "appoint" or "employ," the body making the nominations need not identify them publicly prior to the mayor's appointment. *Gillespie v. San Francisco Public Library Commission*, 67 Cal.App.4th 1165 (1998).

Exception Includes Consideration of Disability Retirement

The Attorney General has concluded, in 88 Ops.Cal.Atty.Gen. 16 (2005), that a county retirement board may use a closed session under this provision to review an application for a disability retirement, including the employee's medical records, since in doing so,

> it is determining whether the applicant's "employment" should continue or should be terminated due to the claimed disability. (§ 54957, subd. (b)(1).) The board's determination thus constitutes an "[a]ction taken to . . . affect the employment status" of the applicant.

Exception Excludes Employees Not Reporting to the Body

If it is the chief executive officer of the agency rather than the governing body who hires, evaluates and terminates the employees, the body has no authority to meet in closed session concerning the staff, the Attorney General opined in 85 Ops.Cal.Atty.Gen. 77 (2002). Since a county superintendent of schools employs the staff of a county department of education, the opinion noted,

> We find no substantial reason for a board, which is neither the employer of, nor disciplinary authority for, certificated or classified employees of the superintendent, to meet in closed session for the purpose of considering the superintendent's appointment, employment, performance evaluation, discipline, or dismissal of such employees."

The opinion said county school boards could not meet in closed session to discuss the employees' compensation either.

Exception is Available to Citizen Advisory Committees

The Attorney General has opined that a citizens' advisory committee comprising community representatives, district employees and a student, appointed by a school board to screen candidates for employment as superintendent, may conduct closed sessions under §54957 to interview the applicants, deliberate and formulate recommendations to the board. 80 Ops.Cal.Atty.Gen. 308 (1997).

Performance Evaluation May Include Preliminaries

A court has concluded that the body's authority to hold a closed session to evaluate an employee's performance includes authority to design an evaluation process behind closed doors as well, reasoning that doing so may well reflect on the employee's past performance. In *Duval v. Board of Trustees*, 93 Cal.App.4th 902 (2001) the plaintiffs argued that a school board had violated the Act in using a closed session, listed as concerning performance evaluation, to discuss a form it would use to evaluate the superintendent. The Sixth District found otherwise:

> (W)e conclude "evaluation" may properly include consideration of the criteria for such evaluation, consideration of the process for conducting the evaluation, and other preliminary matters, to the extent those matters constitute an exercise of defendant's discretion in evaluating a particular employee. In some circumstances, a public employer might be bound by a collective bargaining agreement to evaluate certain employees pursuant to fixed criteria or by use of a particular form. In that instance, a determination to employ the required criteria does not reflect a "personnel decision" by the employer. By contrast, in circumstances such as the present case, the selection of criteria, the establishment of a fact-gathering mechanism, and a designation of particular areas of emphasis in the evaluation each might reflect the board's initial perception of the superintendent's performance since the last evaluation. That is, the evaluation commonly would be tailored to issues arising from the superintendent's actual discharge of her duties through time. As such, these preliminary considerations are an integral part of the Actual evaluation of the superintendent and are properly a part of defendant's "consider[ation] [of] the ... evaluation of performance" of the superintendent.

Id. at 909. This interpretation should probably be confined to its facts, or at least to the situation in which an incumbent employee's performance record is to be evaluated. Its logic would not seem to extend to situations in which the employing body is setting up performance goals for a new employee, a process that would not involve references to previous shortcomings.

Performance Evaluation May Be Event-Specific

The court in *Duval* above also concluded that closed sessions for performance evaluation need not be confined to an annual review:

> We disagree that "evaluation of performance" is as narrow as plaintiffs suggest. In the context of section 54957, the phrase "to consider the ... evaluation of performance" clearly is meant to extend to all employer consideration of an employee's discharge of his or her job duties after "appointment" or "employment" of the employee, up to (but excluding) "discipline" or "dismissal" of the employee. Nothing in the language of section 54957, adopted to permit "the majority of personnel matters to be discussed freely and candidly in closed session," indicates that "evaluation of performance" is limited to the annual or periodic comprehensive, formal, and structured review of job performance commonly envisioned in a typical personnel manual or employment contract. We conclude the phrase "evaluation of performance" encompasses a review of an employee's job performance even if that review involves particular instances of job performance rather than a comprehensive review of such performance. Accordingly, we conclude plaintiffs' allegations ... do not show a Brown Act violation.

Id. at 909. The court's phrase, "up to (but excluding) 'discipline' or 'dismissal'" highlights an important distinction, because consideration of discipline or dismissal would implicate those "specific complaints and charges" the discussion of which in closed session must be preceded in most cases by a 24-hour advance notice to the affected employee (see below).

Notice Confined to Complaints and Charges "Hearing"

While §54957 gives employees, in effect, the right to 24-hour minimum advance written notice of any closed session in which "specific complaints or charges" against them are to be discussed so that they may elect to have the discussion in open session, the Attorney General has opined (78 Ops.Cal.Atty.Gen. 218, (1995)), and courts have ruled, that this right does not apply to the decision by a school board not to retain a probationary employee, at least where "complaints or charges" as such are not under discussion. Negative comments included in the written evaluation of a community college librarian did not constitute "complaints or charges" for purposes of invoking the notice requirement concerning the closed session at which the district board decided not to grant her permanent status, the court held in *Furtado v. Sierra Community College,* 68 Cal.App.4th 876 (1998). Similarly, the court in *Fischer v. Los Angeles Unified School District* 70 Cal.App.4th 87 (1999) concluded that by the time a recommendation against retaining several probationary teachers reached the school board, any "specific complaints or charges" had already been dealt with at the level of administrative appeal, and were not part of the board's deliberation:

> The definition of "specific complaints or charges brought against an employee by another person or employee" does not correspond to the "notice of unsatisfactory act" or other notice of specific charges which Hudson, Sternfeld, Jackson, and Fischer received. The probationary teachers had an opportunity to respond to those charges in conferences and meetings with district administrative personnel. Summaries of those conferences were provided for the probationary teachers' review. In some instances, a probationary teacher was given the opportunity to bring a representative of his choice to the meeting to discuss specific charges and the possible recommendation of dismissal. This was the stage at which specific complaints and charges were brought against an employee. As a matter of law, the Board did not hear specific complaints and charges when it made its determination to nonreelect the probationary teachers.

Id. at 100.

In another variation of this restrictive approach, the court in *Bollinger v. San Diego Civil Service Commission*, 71 Cal.App.4th 568 (1999) concluded that since the statute refers to the employee's right to have complaints or charges "heard" in open session, if the body is not conducting an evidentiary hearing but simply deliberating whether to ratify the recommendations of a prior administrative hearing, the right to notice does not apply. One justice noted that the case did not decide whether, if the employee had requested an open and public hearing at the time (he did not, although orally informed that the hearing officer's recommendations would be considered in closed session), the board would have violated the Act in refusing to grant him the hearing.

"Hearing" Triggered by Factfinding

But in *Morrison v. Housing Authority Board*, 107 Cal.App.4th 860 (2003), the court held that a "hearing," for purposes of the employee notice right, occurred when a board on its own initiative decided to conduct an accusatory inquiry into the facts of an employee's alleged misconduct instead of making a decision based on a hearing officer's factfinding.

> Under their contract with Morrison's union the commissioners could have elected to hear Morrison's appeal themselves rather than referring it to a hearing officer for an advisory report. Had they chosen initially to hear the appeal themselves, it is beyond dispute Morrison would have had the right to demand an open proceeding under section 54957, subdivision (b)(2) because the commissioners were acting under subdivision (b)(1) to "hear complaints or charges brought against [an] employee by another person or employee[.]" We see no reason why the result should be any different when the commissioners, having initially opted to employ an independent hearing officer, decide to reject the hearing officer's findings as to the facts and the credibility of the witnesses and make their own factual findings and credibility determinations. This is particularly true where, as here, the hearing officer had found the main charge against Morrison to be without merit—so to impose the discipline they did the commissioners had to evaluate the charges and find valid a charge the hearing officer rejected. Here the commissioners not only inserted themselves into the shoes of the hearing officer they walked in the exact opposite direction.
>
> The result we reach is in accord with the Legislative intent the "deliberations" of a public agency "be conducted openly." The term "deliberation" has been broadly construed to connote "'not only collective discussion, but the collective acquisition and exchange of facts preliminary to the ultimate decision.'" In making its own evaluation of the complaint against Morrison based on the record, the commissioners engaged in a "collective acquisition and exchange of facts" within the meaning of section 54950.
>
> Finally, requiring the commissioners' fact-finding to be conducted openly upon the demand of the employee is consistent with maintaining the three-way balance the Legislature sought to achieve between the public's interest in "remaining informed" and "retain[ing] control over the instruments [it] created," the agency's interest in being able to discuss personnel matters "freely and candidly in closed session," and the employee's interest in "an open session to defend against specific complaints or charges . . .

> and thus to clear his or her name." It has long been the law of this state that "the people have the right to know what is going on in their courts." The Brown Act applies this principle to proceedings by public agencies. The interests of the public and the accused employee in a public hearing are much the same as the interests of the public and an accused criminal in a public trial; that the public may see the employee receives a fair hearing and is not unjustly disciplined based on the evidence; and that the presence of interested spectators keep the triers of fact alive to a sense of their responsibility and to the importance of their function. In addition, as previously mentioned, the accused employee may wish to publicly clear her name. In the employee discipline context, the value competing against the public's "right to know what is going on" is not a right to take evidence in secret, but the need for free and candid discussion of the Action the agency should take in light of that evidence. As one commentator has noted, "it makes a good deal of sense for any governmental body to retain a zone of privacy within which its members can air internal disagreements."
>
> Having determined the Brown Act required the commissioners to conduct their fact-finding in open session at Morrison's request, we conclude the commissioners violated the Act when they failed to do so.

Id. at 874. The court remanded the matter to the commission, either to "adopt the hearing officer's findings of fact or … substitute their own evidentiary findings after a hearing held in conformity with the notice requirements of section 54957, subdivision (b)."

"Complaints and Charges" as Accusatory Presentation

The court in *Bell v. Vista Unified School District*, 82 Cal.App.4th 672 (2000) held that a high school head football coach had been denied his rights when his school board employer held a closed session, without giving him the 24-hour written notice, to consider disciplining him. The California Interscholastic Federation (CIF) had imposed a one-year suspension on Bell's school's athletic program as the result of his involvement in the transfer of a foreign student, ineligible under CIF rules, into the school in order to join the football team. He did receive a written notice on the day of the closed session informing him that the board would be considering the school's probation and asking him to stand by in case the trustees had any questions on the matter—a request that he declined on advice of his attorney—but he was not informed orally or in writing that the board would consider disciplining him. In the closed session the board permanently stripped him of his coaching assignment, with no loss in pay or tenure in his teaching position. The Court of Appeal affirmed the judgment of the trial court that the failure to notify Bell as specified in Section 54957 violated the Brown Act and rendered the discipline imposed on him null and voId. The court stated:

> Here, the CIF finding that Bell had violated CIF rule 510, rendering (the transferred student) ineligible and (Bell's school) on one-year athletic probation, upon presentation to the Board evolved into a "complaint or charge" brought by other employees ... and another person (a CIF official). Once (the other employees) presented the CIF's undue influence finding to the Board as a basis for disciplining Bell, that finding essentially became an accusation—an indictment brought against him with potential disciplinary consequences. As such, Bell was entitled to the opportunity to respond to it, so as to put it in proper factual context, to clear his name and to avoid imposition of discipline. Granted, Bell had testified at the CIF hearing; however, the focus of that hearing was John's eligibility, not whether Bell's conduct giving rise to the CIF rule 510 violation warranted individual discipline by (the school district). In any event, the Board apparently considered the matter without the benefit of a written transcript of the CIF hearing, relying primarily on the representations of (the complaining employees). Under such circumstances, Bell should have been afforded the opportunity to present his version of the facts regarding his role and the roles of other employees including those who directly and indirectly presented the CIF finding to the Board. Only within that context could the Board meaningfully evaluate the complaint or charge and, if necessary, later decide upon appropriate discipline.

Id. at 683.

No Correction Demand Required for Failure to Notify Employee

A court has held that a city council, in failing to notify its finance director that it would be addressing charges against him in closed session, left its decision to fire him null and void, despite his failure to demand a cure or correction (see page 170). Roberto Moreno, finance director for King City, was fired after the city council was presented with a memorandum by the city manager in closed session, detailing five alleged instances of misconduct. Moreno did not learn of this decision, or even that he had been accused of wrongdoing, until six days later, when the city manager presented him with a copy of the charges at 7:45 a.m., with termination effective at close of business the same day. When Moreno sued for wrongful termination he argued among other things that the manner of his firing involved several violations of the Brown Act. The trial court, and the Court of Appeal as well, agreed with his contentions that:

• the notice for the special meeting closed session at which the firing occurred, in stating only "Per Government Code Section 54957: Public Employee (employment contract)," was a violation of the requirement that special meeting notices must "specify…the business to be transacted or discussed." The law could have been satisfied, the Sixth District concluded, if the notice had used the standard Brown Act formulation: "Public Employee Dismissal."

• Moreno was entitled to a written notice, 24 hours in advance of the closed session, that the council would be discussing "specific complaints or charges" against him, and that absent that alert, the council's action in firing him was properly declared null and voId. The city manager testified that he had presented the council with the written allegations, but insisted that he had not "discussed" them in the closed session. But the Sixth District ruled that it was a fair inference that the council had discussed the charges before deciding to fire Moreno.

• the council's agenda notice at a later meeting, noting under the consent calendar that Moreno had presented a tort claim against the city, did not serve as a "cure or correction" sufficient to undo the original failure of notice. In any event, the Brown Act does not require an employee to demand cure or correction when he or she was never given notice of a closed session to discuss complaints or charges; it simply provides that such a failure renders any adverse action taken as a result to be null and voId.

Moreno v. City of King, 127 Cal.App.4th 17 (2005).

Compensation Not to be Addressed

Deliberation on the appropriate pay increase for an employee may not be folded into a closed session review of his or her performance, nor may pay-setting be part of a closed session deliberation on hiring. A closed evaluation session may be used to decide whether an employee merits *any* pay increase, but not how much (see *San Diego Union v. City Council of San Diego*, 146 Cal.App.3d 947 (1983), discussed in § 1-5(b)(2) above). But as noted in that discussion, if the body has a representative actually bargaining with the employee individually on compensation issues, a closed session may be used to consult with that agent on progress and provide negotiation instructions. In that scenario, final action on the pay increase must be in open session.

Closed Session on Deferred Compensation Withdrawals

The Act does, however, permit a closed session to accommodate private discussion of a particular kind of employee hardship. Government Code §54957.10 states:

> Notwithstanding any other provision of law, a legislative body of a local agency may hold closed sessions to discuss a local agency employee's application for early withdrawal of funds in deferred compensation plan when the application is based on financial hardship arising from an unforeseeable emergency due to illness, accident, casualty, or other extraordinary event, as specified in the deferred compensation plan.

Suggested Agenda Listings

The Act sets forth a safe harbor provision suggesting content for disclosure language on the meeting agenda which, if employed to alert the public as to the subject matter of the closed session, will insulate the agency against liability for providing a substantively inadequate description of the closed session's purpose. Government Code §54954.5 states:

> For purposes of describing closed session items pursuant to Section 54954.2, the agenda may describe closed sessions as provided below. No legislative body or elected official shall be in violation of Section 54954.2 if the closed session items were described in substantial compliance with this section. Substantial compliance is satisfied by including the information provided below, irrespective of its format.
>
> *****
>
> (e) With respect to every item of business to be discussed in closed session pursuant to Section 54957:
>
> *****
>
> PUBLIC EMPLOYEE APPOINTMENT
> Title: (Specify description of position to be filled)
> PUBLIC EMPLOYMENT
> Title: (Specify description of position to be filled)
> PUBLIC EMPLOYEE PERFORMANCE EVALUATION
> Title: (Specify position title of employee being reviewed)
> PUBLIC EMPLOYEE DISCIPLINE/DISMISSAL/RELEASE
> (No additional information is required in connection with a closed session to consider discipline, dismissal, or release of a public employee. Discipline includes potential reduction of compensation.)

Subsequent Action Disclosures

The required disclosures of any action taken are set forth in Government Code §54957.1:

> (a) The legislative body of any local agency shall publicly report any action taken in closed session and the vote or abstention of every member present thereon, as follows:
>
> *****
>
> (5) Action taken to appoint, employ, dismiss, accept the resignation

Bagley-Keene Comparison
Government Code §11125.2: Any state body shall report publicly at a subsequent public meeting any action taken, and any rollcall vote thereon, to appoint, employ, or dismiss a public employee arising out of any closed session of the state body.

> of, or otherwise affect the employment status of a public employee in closed session pursuant to Section 54957 shall be reported at the public meeting during which the closed session is held. Any report required by this paragraph shall identify the title of the position. The general requirement of this paragraph notwithstanding, the report of a dismissal or of the nonrenewal of an employment contract shall be deferred until the first public meeting following the exhaustion of administrative remedies, if any.

Disclosure of Employee Discipline under the Public Records Act

While the Brown Act does not mandate the disclosure of complaints of serious misconduct alleged to have been committed by public employees, or what if anything the public agency did about the complaints, the California Public Records Act (Government Code §6250 *et seq.*) does require release of records containing such information, on request, according to the only two appellate cases that have considered the issue. Complaints about the performance of public employees (other than peace officers) are public if they lead to disciplinary action (*AFSCME v. Regents*, 80 Cal. App. 3d 913 (1978)) or even, discipline or not, if they are "well-founded." *Bakersfield City School District v. Superior Court*, 118 Cal.App.4th 1041 (2004). Thus while legislative bodies are not required to take the initiative in publicizing complaints alleging employee misbehavior, or the outcome of any investigation into them, or any discipline imposed, the employee in question does not have a privacy right that requires denial of a public records request for the information.

Reportability of Decisions Not to Act

While the Act requires disclosures of action taken that change the employment status of the employee, the Attorney General has opined that decisions not to take these actions need not be reported, since a primary reason for the "personnel exception" to the Ralph M. Brown Act is to avoid undue publicity and embarrassment to the affected employee.

> It is patent that to require a public report on all "action taken" in executive session on "'personnel matters" could effectively destroy the "personnel exception." For example, a report would be required that it had been decided not to dismiss an employee even if the possible dismissal was not a matter of public knowledge. Such an announcement would run completely counter to the purpose of section 54957 with respect to personnel executive sessions.

63 Ops.Cal.Atty.Gen. 215 (1980)

§ 1-5(b)(5): Consultation on Threats to Public Security or Access

The Act permits a legislative body to meet in closed session with certain public officials, employees or consultant concerning threats to the security of, or to public access to, certain public facilities or resources. Government Code §54957 states:

> (a) Nothing contained in this chapter shall be construed to prevent the legislative body of a local agency from holding closed sessions with the Attorney General, district attorney, agency counsel, sheriff, or chief of police, or their respective deputies, or a security consultant or a security operations manager, on matters posing a threat to the security of public buildings, a threat to the security of essential public services, including water, drinking water, wastewater treatment, natural gas service, and electric service, or a threat to the public's right of access to public services or public facilities.

Bagley-Keene Comparison

Government Code §11126:

(c). Nothing in this article shall be construed to do any of the following:

•••••

(18) (A) Prevent a state body from holding closed sessions to consider matters posing a threat or potential threat of criminal or terrorist activity against the personnel, property, buildings, facilities, or equipment, including electronic data, owned, leased, or controlled by the state body, where disclosure of these considerations could compromise or impede the safety or security of the personnel, property, buildings, facilities, or equipment, including electronic data, owned, leased, or controlled by the state body.

(B) Notwithstanding any other provision of law, a state body, at any regular or special meeting, may meet in a closed session pursuant to subparagraph (A) upon a two-thirds vote of the members present at the meeting.

(C) After meeting in closed session pursuant to subparagraph (A), the state body shall reconvene in open session prior to adjournment and report that a closed session was held pursuant to subparagraph (A), the general nature of the matters considered, and whether any action was taken in closed session.

(D) After meeting in closed session pursuant to subparagraph (A), the state body shall submit to the Legislative Analyst written notification stating that it held this closed session, the general reason or reasons for the closed session, the general nature of the matters considered, and whether any action was taken in closed session. The Legislative Analyst shall retain for no less than four years any written notification received from a state body pursuant to this subparagraph.

This provision originally authorized closed sessions only with the specified law enforcement officials, and did not refer to threats to "essential public services" of any kind. It was directed at government building "sit-ins" and other acts of obstructive civil disobedience characteristic of the late 1960s, and once those demonstrations tapered off, became a vestigial oddity for the next three decades, rarely if ever invoked, much less interpreted by a court. The anxiety provoked by the events of September 11, 2001 led to the addition of the language directed at the security of "essential public services" and the expanded category of those with whom the consultation is authorized. It is likely this type of closed session that is referred to in the recently added authority for emergency meetings to deal with imminent threats of terrorism (see § 1-3(g) above).

Suggested Agenda Listing

The Act sets forth a safe harbor provision suggesting content for disclosure language on the meeting agenda which, if employed to alert the public as to the subject matter of the closed session, will insulate the agency against liability for providing a substantively inadequate description of the closed session's purpose. Government Code §54954.5 states:

> For purposes of describing closed session items pursuant to Section 54954.2, the agenda may describe closed sessions as provided below. No legislative body or elected official shall be in violation of Section 54954.2 if the closed session items were described in substantial compliance with this section. Substantial compliance is satisfied by including the information provided below, irrespective of its format.
>
> *****
>
> (e) With respect to every item of business to be discussed in closed session pursuant to Section 54957:
>
> THREAT TO PUBLIC SERVICES OR FACILITIES
>
> Consultation with: (Specify name of law enforcement agency and title of officer, or name of applicable agency representative and title)

Subsequent Action Disclosure

None is required, but since the purpose of the session is consultation, not action, any action taken to adopt an emergency ordinance or other policy, for example, would need to be done in open session in any event.

§ 1-5(b)(6): License Application Appeal

The resort to this kind of closed session is relatively rare, since it is relevant only to local agencies—mainly cities and counties—that issue licenses for which an individual's personal criminal history is an eligibility issue; even in those jurisdictions the involvement of a legislative body in a question of this kind will be infrequent. Government Code §54956.7 states:

> Whenever a legislative body of a local agency determines that it is necessary to discuss and determine whether an applicant for a license or license renewal, who has a criminal record, is sufficiently rehabilitated to obtain the license, the legislative body may hold a closed session with the applicant and the applicant's attorney, if any, for the purpose of holding the discussion and making the determination. If the legislative body determines, as a result of the closed session, that the

issuance or renewal of the license should be denied, the applicant shall be offered the opportunity to withdraw the application. If the applicant withdraws the application, no record shall be kept of the discussions or decisions made at the closed session and all matters relating to the closed session shall be confidential. If the applicant does not withdraw the application, the legislative body shall take action at the public meeting during which the closed session is held or at its next public meeting denying the application for the license but all matters relating to the closed session are confidential and shall not be disclosed without the consent of the applicant, except in an action by an applicant who has been denied a license challenging the denial of the license.

Suggested Agenda Listings

The Act sets forth a safe harbor provision suggesting content for disclosure language on the meeting agenda which, if employed to alert the public as to the subject matter of the closed session, will insulate the agency against liability for providing a substantively inadequate description of the closed session's purpose. Government Code §54954.5 states:

For purposes of describing closed session items pursuant to Section 54954.2, the agenda may describe closed sessions as provided below. No legislative body or elected official shall be in violation of Section 54954.2 if the closed session items were described in substantial compliance with this section. Substantial compliance is satisfied by including the information provided below, irrespective of its format.

*****

(a) With respect to a closed session held pursuant to Section 54956.7:
LICENSE/PERMIT DETERMINATION
Applicant(s): (Specify number of applicants)

Subsequent Action Disclosure

If the body grants or renews the license, there is no requirement to announce that fact, but it would be a matter of public record just as with any other applicant. There would be nothing, however, to link the licensee with the closed session on rehabilitation. If the body is inclined to deny the license or renewal, the applicant has the choice discreetly to withdraw the application, with nothing more to be sald. If he or she insists on public action, the body has that option as well.

§ 1-5(b)(7): Discussion of State Audit Report

The Bureau of State Audits conducts investigations and issues reports on a wide variety of California governmental programs and activities. Most audits are at the bureau's discretion, triggered by requests or complaints or its own concern, and most focus on statewide agencies and programs. Occasionally a local government program or activity will be audited. In late 2004, for example, of some 17 audits in progress, three concerned or affected particular local agencies.

Effective January 1, 2005, the legislative body of a local agency is permitted to hold a closed session to discuss and prepare responses to a state auditor's tentative final report of an audit of that agency. This provision was added to allow the legislative body to participate in formulating a response to the audit to incorporate into the final report, which until final is confidential under other law. Government Code §54956.75 states:

Bagley-Keene Comparison
Government Code §11126.2:
(a) Nothing in this article shall be construed to prohibit a state body that has received a confidential final draft audit report from the Bureau of State Audits from holding closed sessions to discuss its response to that report.
(b) After the public release of an audit report by the Bureau of State Audits, if a state body meets to discuss the audit report, it shall do so in an open session unless exempted from that requirement by some other provision of law.

(a) Nothing contained in this chapter shall be construed to prevent the legislative body of a local agency that has received a confidential final draft audit report from the Bureau of State Audits from holding closed sessions to discuss its response to that report.
(b) After the public release of an audit report by the Bureau of State Audits, if a legislative body of a local agency meets to discuss the audit report, it shall do so in an open session unless exempted from that requirement by some other provision of law.

Suggested Agenda Listing

The Act sets forth a safe harbor provision suggesting content for disclosure language on the meeting agenda which, if employed to alert the public as to the subject matter of the closed session, will insulate the agency against liability for providing a substantively inadequate description of the closed session's purpose. Government Code §54954.5 states:

> For purposes of describing closed session items pursuant to Section 54954.2, the agenda may describe closed sessions as provided below. No legislative body or elected official shall be in violation of Section 54954.2 if the closed session items were described in substantial compliance with this section. Substantial compliance is satisfied by including the information provided below, irrespective of its format.
>
> *****
>
> (k) With respect to every item of business to be discussed in closed session pursuant to Section 54956.75:
>
> AUDIT BY BUREAU OF STATE AUDITS

Subsequent Action Disclosure

Other than to discuss its response to the report, no action is authorized within this closed session. Any response actually approved would appear in the final public report.

§ 1-5(b)(8): Joint Powers Agency Impact Issues

Cities and other local agencies may enter into "joint powers" agreements with one another creating new "joint powers agencies" (JPAs) to accomplish common, typically regionally significant, objectives. The resulting JPA has its own board comprising members of the constituent agencies. For example, a JPA created by several cities will have a board comprising representatives of those cities, often (but not always) city council members. The JPA board and the city councils are all governed by the Brown Act. Any discussion held by the JPA board in open session is easily reported by the council members back to their respective cities. Until 2004, however, the Brown Act was viewed as an obstacle to the same reporting back of JPA board closed session discussions, because there was simply no authority for a city council, for example, to hold closed sessions to discuss the confidential discussions of any other entity, JPA or not. As a result of 2004 legislation, however, effective January 1, 2005, certain matters from lawfully closed JPA board sessions may be reported back to the constituent agency bodies in their own closed sessions, if those matters would have a certain decided impact on those constituent agencies. Cities are used as the example here, but the legislation opens this procedure to any local government agency that is party to a joint powers agreement. Government Code Section 54956.96 states:

> (a) Nothing in this chapter shall be construed to prevent the legislative body of a joint powers agency formed pursuant to Article 1 (commencing with Section 6500) of Chapter 5 of Division 7 of Title 1, from adopting a policy or a bylaw or including in its joint powers agreement provisions that authorize either or both of the following:
>
> (1) All information received by the legislative body of the local agency member in a closed session related to the information presented to the joint powers agency in closed session shall be confidential. However, a member of the legislative body of a member local agency may disclose information obtained in a closed session that has direct financial or liability implications for that local agency to the following individuals:
>
> (A) Legal counsel of that member local agency for purposes of obtaining advice on whether the matter has direct financial or liability implications for that member local agency.
>
> (B) Other members of the legislative body of the local agency present in a closed session of that member local agency.
>
> (2) Any designated alternate member of the legislative body of the joint powers agency who is also a member of the legislative body of a local agency member and who is attending a properly noticed meeting of the joint powers agency in lieu of a local agency member's regularly appointed member to attend closed sessions of the joint powers agency.
>
> (b) If the legislative body of a joint powers agency adopts a policy or a bylaw or includes provisions in its joint powers agreement pursuant to subdivision (a), then the legislative body of the local agency member, upon the advice of its legal counsel, may conduct a closed session in order to receive, discuss, and take action concerning information obtained in a closed session of the joint powers agency pursuant to paragraph (1) of subdivision (a).

The Problem Addressed

AB 2782, the legislation adding this closed session authority to the Brown Act, is the result of a problem exemplified by the following excerpt from the bill's Senate Floor Analysis:

SunLine Transit is a JPA formed by nine Coachella Valley cities and Riverside County to provide public transportation services. In 2003, a series of newspaper reports revealed administrative problems within the JPA, including allegations of false documents, illegal financial maneuvers, conflicts of interest, contract violations and audit irregularities. As a result, the JPA board placed the general manager and chief financial officer on administrative leave. The JPA board held a series of closed session meetings regarding the situation. Because the discussions occurred in closed session and thus were confidential under the Brown Act, the primary source of information to the public, including local officials not on the JPA board, was the news media.

Frustrated by their lack of access to information discussed in closed session of a JPA they created, some local officials in the Coachella Valley want the boards of member agencies of a JPA to have access to the JPA's closed session information.

JPA Board Authorization

The closed session provided in this section is authorized only by a formal policy or bylaw adopted by the JPA board, an action that must be taken only in an open session of that board.

Qualifying Reports

The only matters confidentially reportable to the legislative body of the participating local agency in this closed session are those that have "direct financial or liability implications for that agency." The provision clearly contemplates that the question of whether an issue meets that definition, and thus can be reported to the participating agency's body, is one that must be determined in consultation with agency's legal counsel, who is authorized to be given the information in order to make that determination. It is only upon the legal counsel's advice that such a closed session may be held.

Suggested Agenda Listings

The Act sets forth a safe harbor provision suggesting content for disclosure language on the meeting agenda which, if employed to alert the public as to the subject matter of the closed session, will insulate the agency against liability for providing a substantively inadequate description of the closed session's purpose. Government Code §54954.5 states:

> For purposes of describing closed session items pursuant to Section 54954.2, the agenda may describe closed sessions as provided below. No legislative body or elected official shall be in violation of Section 54954.2 if the closed session items were described in substantial compliance with this section. Substantial compliance is satisfied by including the information provided below, irrespective of its

format.

*****

(j) With respect to every item of business to be discussed in closed session pursuant to Section 54956.96:

CONFERENCE INVOLVING A JOINT POWERS AGENCY (Specify by name)

Discussion will concern: (Specify closed session description used by the joint powers agency.) Name of local agency representative on joint powers agency board: (Specify name)

(Additional information listing the names of agencies or titles of representatives attending the closed session as consultants or other representatives.)

Subsequent Action Disclosure

There is no specific safe harbor provision for disclosing action taken in such a closed session. Typically one would expect that the principal outcome would be guidance or instructions given to the local agency's representative on the JPA board, and that the guidance would be reflected in that representative's participation in the next relevant closed session of the JPA board on the matter. If the result is that the body needs to take some action of its own beyond such guidance, then depending on the nature of the Action other provisions of the Brown Act would determine whether the Action must be done publicly or in closed session, and if the latter, under what type of agenda listing and with what kind of subsequent action disclosure.

§ 1-5(b)(9): Student Discipline and Expulsion

Government Code §54962 authorizes local educational bodies to hold a closed session for any purpose for which one is permitted or required by the Education Code. Under that code a school board, county board of education or community college district board not must use a closed session to consider discipline, suspension or expulsion of a pupil or student unless the student or his or her parent requests an open hearing. Even if the hearing in general is public due to such a request, however, whatever discussion would reveal information from the records of another student must be taken into closed session. The Education Code requires that the body's final action be in open session, and that any suspension or expulsion must be kept available as a public record including, in the case of an expulsion, the cause, but this has been held to conflict with federal law.

Suspension or Other Disciplinary Action

A school board's discussion of proposed discipline short of expulsion, including suspension, must be conducted openly if the affected student so requests. But a closed session is required for any portion of the discussion that would disclose information from some other student's personnel file. In such circumstances there is no distinction between the "hearing" of the charges and response on the one hand and the board's deliberation on the other. The latter must be in open session. Education Code §35146 states:

> Notwithstanding the provisions of Section 35145 of this code and Section 54950 of the Government Code, the governing body of a school district shall, unless a request by the parent has been made pursuant to this section, hold closed sessions if the board is considering the suspension of, or disciplinary action or any other action except expulsion in connection with any pupil of the school district, if a public hearing upon such question would lead to the giving out of information concerning school pupils which would be in violation of Article 5 (commencing with Section 49073) of Chapter 6.5 of Part 27 of this code.
>
> Before calling such closed session of the governing board of the district to consider these matters, the governing board of the district shall, in writing, by registered or certified mail or by personal service, if the pupil is a minor, notify the pupil and his or her parent or guardian, or the pupil if the pupil is an adult, of the intent of the governing board of the district to call and hold such closed session. Unless the pupil, or his or her parent, or guardian shall, in writing, within 48 hours after receipt of such written notice of intention, request that the hearing of the governing board be held as a public meeting, then the hearing to consider such matters shall be conducted by the governing board in closed session. If such written request is served upon the clerk or secretary of the governing board, the meeting shall be public except that any discussion at such meeting that might be in conflict with the right to privacy of any pupil other than the pupil requesting the public meeting or on behalf of whom such meeting is requested, shall be in closed session. Whether the matter is considered at a closed session or at a public meeting, the final action of the governing board of the school district shall be taken at a public meeting and the result of such action shall be a public record of the school district.

Expulsion

A school board's expulsion session reverses the rules above. If, that is, the student requests an open session, there is no provision for closing a portion of it to protect other students, but the board may go into closed session to deliberate after the open "hearing." The same rules apply to a county school board's hearing on appeals of expulsion decisions. Education Code §48918 states:

> The governing board of each school district shall establish rules and regulations governing procedures for the expulsion of pupils. These procedures shall include, but are not necessarily limited to, all of the following:
>
> *****
>
> (c) Notwithstanding Section 54593 of the Government Code and Section 35145 of this code, the governing board shall conduct a hearing to consider the expulsion of a pupil in a session closed to the public, unless the pupil requests, in writing, at least five days prior to the date of the hearing, that the hearing be conducted at a public meeting. Regardless of whether the expulsion hearing is conducted in a closed or public session, the governing board may meet in closed session for the purpose of deliberating and determining whether the pupil should be expelled.
>
> If the governing board or the hearing officer or administrative panel appointed under subdivision (d) to conduct the hearing admits any other person to a closed deliberation session, the parent or guardian of the pupil, the pupil, and the counsel of the pupil also shall be allowed to attend the closed deliberations.
>
> (d) In lieu of conducting an expulsion hearing itself, the governing board may

contract with the county hearing officer, or with the Office of Administrative Hearings of the State of California pursuant to Chapter 14 (commencing with Section 27720) of Part 3 of Division 2 of Title 3 of the Government Code and Section 35207 of this code, for a hearing officer to conduct the hearing. The governing board also may appoint an impartial administrative panel of three or more certificated persons, none of whom are members of the board or employed on the staff of the school in which the pupil is enrolled. The hearing shall be conducted in accordance with all of the procedures established under this section.

*****

(i) Whether an expulsion hearing is conducted by the governing board or before a hearing officer or administrative panel, final action to expel a pupil shall be taken only by the governing board in a public session. Written notice of any decision to expel or to suspend the enforcement of an expulsion order during a period of probation shall be sent by the superintendent of schools or his or her designee to the pupil or the pupil's parent or guardian, and shall be accompanied by notice of the right to appeal the expulsion to the county board of education and of the obligation of the parent, guardian, or pupil under subdivision (b) of Section 48915.1, upon the pupil's enrollment in a new school district, to inform that district of the expulsion.

(j) The governing board shall maintain a record of each expulsion, including the cause therefore. Records of expulsions shall be a nonprivileged, disclosable public record . . .

Expulsion Appeals to County Board

With respect to expulsion appeals taken to the county school board, Education Code §48920 states:

Notwithstanding the provisions of Section 54950 of the Government Code and Section 35145 of this code, the county board of education shall hear an appeal of an expulsion order in closed session, unless the pupil requests, in writing, at least five days prior to the date of the hearing, that the hearing be conducted in a public meeting. Upon the timely submission of a request for a public meeting, the county board of education shall be required to honor the request. Whether the hearing is conducted in closed or public session, the county board may meet in closed session for the purpose of deliberations. If the county board admits any representative of the pupil or the school district, the board shall, at the same time, admit representatives from the opposing party.

Community College Students

Education Code §72122 allows community college district boards to to use a closed session to deliberate student suspension or other discipline under essentially the same conditions (other than parental involvement) as noted above for public school pupils. The rules are the same as for school board hearings on discipline short of expulsion: if an open hearing is held at the request of the affected student, it must be closed to the extend necessary to protect other students. There is no authority, however, for a closed post-hearing session to deliberate a decision.

Naming Expelled Students

The Attorney General has opined that, pursuant to Education Code Section 48918, a school board's expulsion action, taken in public session, must name the affected student. 80 Ops.Cal.Atty.Gen. 85 (1997). But the

Court of Appeal has concluded that the federal Family Education Rights and Privacy Act (FERPA) "preempts section 48918, in that section 48918 requires the public disclosure of student expulsion records while FERPA conditions the receipt of federal funds on protecting students and their parents from disclosure of this very type of record." *Rim of the World Unified School District v. Superior Court*, 104 Cal.App.4th 1393 (2002).

Suggested Agenda Listings

The Brown Act does not include suggested agenda listings for these types of closed sessions, but neither does it exempt them from providing some kind of agenda notice. A procedure that would probably comply would be simply to list "Pupil Suspension," "Pupil Expulsion" or something similar if the student has not requested an open hearing, and if he or she has done so, to name him or her as well.

§ 1-5(b)(10): Student Records Challenges

The Education Code provisions that make student records confidential also allow the pupil or his or her parents or guardian to challenge the accuracy or completeness of these records. Because the challenge itself involves a discussion of protected information, any portion of it that requires the challenger to appear before a school or community college district board is protected by the allowance for a closed session consistent with the pupil's privacy rights. With respect to school boards, Education Code §49070 states:

> Following an inspection and review of a pupil's records, the parent of a pupil or former pupil of a school district may challenge the content of any pupil record.
>
> (a) The parent of a pupil may file a written request with the superintendent of the district to correct or remove any information recorded in the written records concerning his or her child which the parent alleges to be any of the following:
>
> Inaccurate.
>
> An unsubstantiated personal conclusion or inference.
>
> A conclusion or inference outside of the observer's area of competence.
>
> Not based on the personal observation of a named person with the time and place of the observation noted.
>
> Misleading.
>
> In violation of the privacy or other rights of the pupil.
>
> (b) Within 30 days of receipt of a request pursuant to subdivision (a), the superintendent or the superintendent's designee shall meet with the parent and the certificated employee who recorded the information in question, if any, and if the employee is presently employed by the school district. The superintendent shall then sustain or deny the allegations . . .
>
> If the superintendent denies any or all of the allegations and refuses to order the correction or the removal of the information, the parent may, within 30 days of the refusal, appeal the decision in writing to the governing board of the school district.
>
> (c) Within 30 days of receipt of an appeal pursuant to subdivision (b), the governing board shall, in closed session with the parent and the certificated em-

ployee who recorded the information in question, if any, and if the employee is presently employed by the school district, determine whether or not to sustain or deny the allegations . . .

Essentially identical provisions for closed sessions of community college district boards are found in Education Code §78232.

Suggested Agenda Listing

The Brown Act does not include suggested agenda listings for these types of closed sessions, but neither does it exempt them from providing some kind of agenda notice. A procedure that would probably comply would be simply to list "Pupil Records Correction Appeal" or something similar.

Subsequent Action Disclosures

There is no requirement for an action disclosure, and in any event no meaningful disclosure could be effected consistent with the student privacy provisions of the Education Code.

§ 1-5(b)(11): Medical Privileges and Quality of Care

A hospital's consideration of whether to grant privileges to a physician to have his or her patients admitted there is to some degree comparable to the process for hiring employees, in that it involves issues of personal fitness and professional accomplishment. In such situations the Brown Act, as applied to public hospital boards, defers to other laws permitting closed sessions to hear physicians' appeals from decisions denying or canceling privileges, or to conduct hearings on the reports of medical audit or quality assurance committees that may reflect adversely on physicians with privileges. With respect to hospital district boards, the Health & Safety Code states:

§32150. The board of directors shall adopt reasonable rules and regulations, or bylaws, providing for appellate review of any action, decision, or recommendation of the medical staff affecting the professional privileges of any member of, or applicant for membership on, the medical staff ...

§32155. The board of directors may order that the hearing pursuant to this article . . . be held in private or executive session, provided, that an applicant or medical staff member whose staff privileges are the direct subject of a hearing may request a public hearing. Deliberations of the board of directors in connection with matters pertaining to this article may be held in executive session.

Concerning municipal hospitals, Government Code §37624.3 states:

The governing body of the hospital may order that the hearing pursuant to this article . . . be held in private or executive session, provided, that an applicant or medical staff member whose staff privileges are the direct subject of a hearing may request a public hearing. Deliberations of the governing body in connection with matters pertaining to this article may be held in executive session.

Suggested Agenda Listing

The Act sets forth a safe harbor provision suggesting content for disclosure language on the meeting agenda which, if employed to alert the public as to the subject matter of the closed session, will insulate the agency against liability for providing a substantively inadequate description of the closed session's purpose. Government Code §54954.5 states:

Bagley-Keene Comparison
Government Code §11126 (f):
In addition to subdivisions (a), (b), and (c), nothing in this article shall be construed to do any of the following: (1) Prevent a state body operating under a joint powers agreement for insurance pooling from holding a closed session to discuss a claim for the payment of tort liability or public liability losses incurred by the state body or any member agency under the joint powers agreement.

> For purposes of describing closed session items pursuant to Section 54954.2, the agenda may describe closed sessions as provided below. No legislative body or elected official shall be in violation of Section 54954.2 if the closed session items were described in substantial compliance with this section. Substantial compliance is satisfied by including the information provided below, irrespective of its format.
>
> *****
>
> (h) With respect to every item of business discussed in closed session pursuant to Section 54962 and Sections ... 32155 of the Health and Safety Code or ... 37624.3 of the Government Code:
>
> HEARINGS
>
> Subject matter: (Specify whether testimony/deliberation will concern staff privileges, report of medical audit committee, or report of quality assurance committee)

Subsequent Action Disclosures

No specific disclosure requirements are provided for in the Act.

§ 1-5(b)(12): Insurance Pools and Liability Claims

When local agencies have entered into a joint powers agreement to maintain a common liability insurance pool, this exemption is available to any of their legislative bodies individually, or to the body that governs the pool agency. Comparable in some respects to the exemption for discussion of pending litigation, this provision does not require consultation with an attorney—it authorizes closed session discussion and action by the body's members alone on claims affecting liability and workers' compensation insurance. Government Code §54956.95 states:

> (a) Nothing in this chapter shall be construed to prevent a joint powers agency formed pursuant to Article 1 (commencing with Section 6500) of Chapter 5 of Division 7 of Title 1, for purposes of insurance pooling, or a local agency member of the joint powers agency, from holding a closed session to discuss a claim for the payment of tort liability losses, public liability losses, or workers' compensation liability incurred by the joint powers agency or a local agency member of the joint powers agency.
>
> (b) Nothing in this chapter shall be construed to prevent the Local Agency Self-Insurance Authority formed pursuant to Chapter 5.5 (commencing with Section 6599.01) of Division 7 of Title 1, or a local agency member of the authority, from

holding a closed session to discuss a claim for the payment of tort liability losses, public liability losses, or workers' compensation liability incurred by the authority or a local agency member of the authority.

(c) Nothing in this section shall be construed to affect Section 54956.9 with respect to any other local agency.

Suggested Agenda Listing

The Act sets forth a safe harbor provision suggesting content for disclosure language on the meeting agenda which, if employed to alert the public as to the subject matter of the closed session, will insulate the agency against liability for providing a substantively inadequate description of the closed session's purpose. Government Code §54954.5 states:

For purposes of describing closed session items pursuant to Section 54954.2, the agenda may describe closed sessions as provided below. No legislative body or elected official shall be in violation of Section 54954.2 if the closed session items were described in substantial compliance with this section. Substantial compliance is satisfied by including the information provided below, irrespective of its format.

*****

(d) With respect to every item of business to be discussed in closed session pursuant to Section 54956.95:

LIABILITY CLAIMS

Claimant: (Specify name unless unspecified pursuant to Section 54961)

Agency claimed against: (Specify name)

Subsequent Action Disclosure

The required disclosures of any action taken are set forth in Government Code §54957.1:

(a) The legislative body of any local agency shall publicly report any action taken in closed session and the vote or abstention of every member present thereon, as follows:

*****

(4) Disposition reached as to claims discussed in closed session pursuant to Section 54956.95 shall be reported as soon as reached in a manner that identifies the name of the claimant, the name of the local agency claimed against, the substance of the claim, and any monetary amount approved for payment and agreed upon by the claimant.

§ 1-5(b)(13): Joint Drug Law Enforcement Operations

Where a "multijurisdictional drug law enforcement agency" has been formed it typically comprises the sheriff's department and one or more police departments in a county, and operations may be planned and executed in concert with state or federal agencies. This closed session is permitted only for the discussion of specific investigations or operations. Administrative and policy matters are reserved for open session, as with any other local agency body. Government Code §54957.8 states:

Nothing contained in this chapter shall be construed to prevent the legislative body of a multijurisdictional drug law enforcement agency, or an advisory body of a multijurisdictional drug law enforcement agency, from holding closed sessions to discuss the case records of any ongoing criminal investigation of the multijurisdictional drug law enforcement agency or of any party to the joint powers agreement, to hear testimony from persons involved in the investigation, and to discuss courses of action in particular cases.

"Multijurisdictional drug law enforcement agency," for purposes of this section, means a joint powers entity formed pursuant to Article 1 (commencing with Section 6500) of Chapter 5 of Division 7 of Title 1, which provides drug law enforcement services for the parties to the joint powers agreement.

The Legislature finds and declares that this section is within the public interest, in that its provisions are necessary to prevent the impairment of ongoing law enforcement investigations, to protect witnesses and informants, and to permit the discussion of effective courses of action in particular cases.

Suggested Agenda Listing

The Act sets forth a safe harbor provision suggesting content for disclosure language on the meeting agenda which, if employed to alert the public as to the subject matter of the closed session, will insulate the agency against liability for providing a substantively inadequate description of the closed session's purpose. Government Code §54954.5 states:

For purposes of describing closed session items pursuant to Section 54954.2, the agenda may describe closed sessions as provided below. No legislative body or elected official shall be in violation of Section 54954.2 if the closed session items were described in substantial compliance with this section. Substantial compliance is satisfied by including the information provided below, irrespective of its format.

*****

(g) With respect to closed sessions called pursuant to Section 54957.8:
CASE REVIEW/PLANNING

Subsequent Action Disclosure

There is no requirement specified in the Act to disclose action taken.

§ 1-5(b)(14): Hospital Trade Secrets and Quality of Care

Hospital districts, originally established to cope with a scarcity of private medical facilities, now say they find themselves competing with them, at least in the more affluent suburban areas. To meet that competition they must occasionally consider expanding or upgrading what they offer the public—a new program, service or facility, for example. Laying the groundwork for a specific project often requires market research, and this closed session is primarily intended to allow the hospital district board to review and discuss that market research—a "trade secret" that would be equally valuable to competing hospitals. The statute bars the taking of any action in this type of closed session. Also prohibited is discussion or deliberation of changes in ownership or management of the district's assets, including the hospital, or of the dissolution of the district itself. Another exception permits closed hearings in any public hospital on the reports of medical audit or quality assurance committees which may reflect adversely on physicians with privileges.

Health Care Facility Trade Secrets

Health & Safety Code §32106:

(a) Except as provided in this section, Section 32155, or the Ralph M. Brown Act (Chapter 9 (commencing with Section 54950) of Part 1 of Division 2 of Title 5 of the Government Code) all of the sessions of the board of directors, whether regular or special, shall be open to the public, and a majority of the members of the board shall constitute a quorum for the transaction of business.

(b) The board of directors may order that a meeting held solely for the purpose of discussion or deliberation, or both, of reports involving district trade secrets be held in closed session. Except as provided in this subdivision, the closed session shall meet all applicable requirements of Chapter 9 (commencing with Section 54950) of Division 2 of Title 5 of the Government Code, including Section 54957.7.

(c) "Health care facility trade secrets," as used in this section, means a "trade secret," as defined in subdivision (d) of Section 3426.1 of the Civil Code, and in addition meets all of the following:

1. Is necessary to initiate a new district service or program or add a district health care facility.

2. Would, if prematurely disclosed, create a substantial probability of depriving the district of a substantial economic benefit.

(d) The exception provided in subdivision (b) to the general open meeting requirements for a meeting of the board of directors, shall not apply to a meeting where there is action taken, as defined in Section 54952.6 of the Government Code.

(e) Nothing in this section shall be construed to permit the board of directors to order a closed meeting for the purposes of discussing or deliberating, or to permit the discussion or deliberation in any closed meeting of any proposals regarding:

1. The sale, conversion, contract for management, or leasing of any district health care facility or the assets thereof, to any for-profit or nonprofit entity, agency, association, organization, governmental body, person, partnership, corporation, or other district.

2. The conversion of any district health care facility to any other form of ownership by the district.

3. The dissolution of any district.

Quality of Care in County Hospitals

Health & Safety Code §1461: Notwithstanding any other provisions of law, the board of directors of any hospital subject to this chapter may order that any hearings on the reports of hospital medical audit or quality assurance committees be held in closed session. An applicant or medical staff member whose staff privileges are the direct subject of a hearing may request a public hearing. Deliberations of the board of directors in connection with matters pertaining to these hearings may be held in closed session.

Quality of Care in District Hospitals

Health & Safety Code §32155. The board of directors may order that the hearing pursuant to this article, and hearings on the reports of the hospital medical audit or quality assurance committees, be held in private or executive session, provided, that an applicant or medical staff member whose staff privileges are the direct subject of a hearing may request a public hearing. Deliberations of the board of directors in connection with matters pertaining to this article may be held in executive session.

Suggested Agenda Listings

The Act sets forth a safe harbor provision suggesting content for disclosure language on the meeting agenda which, if employed to alert the public as to the subject matter of the closed session, will insulate the agency against liability for providing a substantively inadequate description of the closed session's purpose. Government Code §54954.5 states:

> For purposes of describing closed session items pursuant to Section 54954.2, the agenda may describe closed sessions as provided below. No legislative body or elected official shall be in violation of Section 54954.2 if the closed session items were described in substantial compliance with this section. Substantial compliance is satisfied by including the information provided below, irrespective of its format.
>
> *****
>
> (h) With respect to every item of business discussed in closed session pursuant to Section 54962 and Sections 1461, 32106, and 32155 of the Health and Safety Code or Sections 37606 and 37624.3 of the Government Code:
>
> REPORT INVOLVING TRADE SECRET
>
> Discussion will concern: (Specify whether discussion will concern proposed new service, program, or facility)
>
> Estimated date of public disclosure: (Specify month and year)
>
> HEARINGS
>
> Subject matter: (Specify whether testimony/deliberation will concern staff privileges, report of medical audit committee, or report of quality assurance committee)

Subsequent Action Disclosure

There is no requirement to disclose action taken in the closed hearings.

§ 1-5(b)(15): Health Care Service Plan Trade Secrets

Like the boards of local public hospitals (see section above) the bodies governing "local initiative" health plans—established in nine counties to offer managed health care to Medi-Cal beneficiaries—to discuss a species of trade secrets in closed session, to preserve the plan's ability to compete with private providers. Government Code §54956.87 states:

> (a) Notwithstanding any other provision of this chapter, the records of a health plan that is licensed pursuant to the Knox-Keene Health Care Service Plan Act of 1975 (Chapter 2.2(commencing with Section 1340) of Division 2 of the Health and Safety Code) and that is governed by a county board of supervisors, whether paper records, records maintained in the management information system, or records in any other form, that relate to provider rate or payment determinations, allocation or distribution methodologies for provider payments, formulae or calculations for these payments, and contract negotiations with providers of health care for alternative rates are exempt from disclosure for a period of three years after the contract is fully executed. The transmission of the records, or the information contained therein in an alternative form, to the board of supervisors shall not constitute a waiver of exemption from disclosure, and the records and information once transmitted to the board of supervisors shall be subject to this same exemption.
>
> (b) Notwithstanding any other provision of law, the governing board of a health

plan that is licensed pursuant to the Knox-Keene Health Care Service Plan Act of 1975 (Chapter 2.2 (commencing with Section 1340) of Division 2 of the Health and Safety Code) and that is governed by a county board of supervisors may order that a meeting held solely for the purpose of discussion or taking action on health plan trade secrets, as defined in subdivision (c) of Section 32106 of the Health and Safety Code, shall be held in closed session. The requirements of making a public report of action taken in closed session, and the vote or abstention of every member present, may be limited to a brief general description without the information constituting the trade secret.

(c) The governing board may delete the portion or portions containing trade secrets from any documents that were finally approved in the closed session held pursuant to subdivision (b) that are provided to persons who have made the timely or standing request.

(d) Nothing in this section shall be construed as preventing the governing board from meeting in closed session as otherwise provided by law.

(e) The provisions of this section shall not prevent access to any records by the Joint Legislative Audit Committee in the exercise of its powers pursuant to Article 1 (commencing with Section 10500) of Chapter 4 of Part 2 of Division 2 of Title 2. The provisions of this section also shall not prevent access to any records by the Department of Corporations in the exercise of its powers pursuant to Article 1 (commencing with Section 1340) of Chapter 2.2 of Division 2 of the Health and Safety Code.

(f) For purposes of this section, "health plan trade secret" means a trade secret, as defined in subdivision (d) of Section 3426.1 o the Civil Code, that also meets both of the following criteria:

(1) The secrecy of the information is necessary for the health plan to initiate a new service, program, marketing strategy, business plan, or technology, or to add a benefit or product.

(2) Premature disclosure of the trade secret would create a substantial probability of depriving the health plan of substantial economic benefit or opportunity.

Suggested Agenda Listing

The Act provides no specific "safe harbor" agenda listing, but consistent with the one required for "hospital trade secrets," a sufficient wording would probably be "Discussion/action involving plan trade secret."

Subsequent Action Disclosure

See the final sentence of subdivision (b).

§ 1-5(b)(16): Acceptance of Gifts by Community College Trustees

A community college district board is permitted a closed session to discuss a gift which has been offered to the district by a donor seeking to preserve his or her anonymity. The confidentiality is apparently intended to encourage wealthy benefactors, who may prefer to keep a low profile. Education Code §72111: "The governing board of a community college

Bagley-Keene Comparison
Government Code §11126:

(c). Nothing in this article shall be construed to do any of the following:

....

(5) Prevent any closed session to consider the conferring of honorary degrees, or gifts, donations, and bequests that the donor or proposed donor has requested in writing to be kept confidential.

district may hold closed sessions … to consider gifts from a donor who wants to remain anonymous."

Suggested Agenda Listing

The Brown Act does not include a suggested agenda listing for this type of closed session, but neither does it exempt it. A procedure that would probably comply would be simply to list "Consideration of Gift" or something similar.

Subsequent Action Disclosures

Action taken to accept a gift would be required to be in open session.

§ 1-5(b)(17): Honorary Degrees by Community College Trustees

A community college district board may wish to confer an honorary degree on a person, but in order to do so it would ordinarily prefer to be able to discuss the candidate candidly and with due regard for his or her privacy and dignity. A closed session for this purpose is permitted by Education Code §72122, which states: "The governing board of a community college district may hold closed sessions to consider the conferring of honorary degrees ..."

Bagley-Keene Comparison See previous section.

Suggested Agenda Listing

The Brown Act does not include a suggested agenda listing for this type of closed session, but neither does it exempt it. A procedure that would probably comply would be simply to list "Consideration of Conferral of Honorary Degree" or something similar.

Subsequent Action Disclosure

The Brown Act does not specifically require a disclosure of the action taken in this kind of closed session, but if the decision is affirmative, a resolution to that affect would occur in open session.

§ 1-5(b)(18): Health Plan Complaints

Local public hospitals that contract with the state to provide Medi-Cal services to patients may get complaints about those services, expressed by patients directly to the governing board. The Act permits such bodies to allow the complainants to express themselves in closed session if they are concerned for their medical privacy. Government Code §54956.86 states:

> Notwithstanding any other provision of this chapter, a legislative body of a local agency which provides services pursuant to Section 14087.3 of the Welfare and

Institutions Code may hold a closed session to hear a charge or complaint from a member enrolled in its health plan if the member does not wish to have his or her name, medical status, or other information that is protected by federal law publicly disclosed. Prior to holding a closed session pursuant to this section, the legislative body shall inform the member, in writing, of his or her right to have the charge or complaint heard in an open session rather than a closed session.

Suggested Agenda Listing

The Act sets forth a safe harbor provision suggesting content for disclosure language on the meeting agenda which, if employed to alert the public as to the subject matter of the closed session, will insulate the agency against liability for providing a substantively inadequate description of the closed session's purpose. Government Code §54954.5 states:

> For purposes of describing closed session items pursuant to Section 54954.2, the agenda may describe closed sessions as provided below. No legislative body or elected official shall be in violation of Section 54954.2 if the closed session items were described in substantial compliance with this section. Substantial compliance is satisfied by including the information provided below, irrespective of its format.
>
> *****
>
> (i) With respect to every item of business to be discussed in closed session pursuant to Section 54956.86:
>
> CHARGE OR COMPLAINT INVOLVING INFORMATION PROTECTED BY FEDERAL LAW
>
> (No additional information is required in connection with a closed session to discuss a charge or complaint pursuant to Section 54956.86.)

Subsequent Action Disclosure

The Brown Act does not specifically require a disclosure of the action taken, if any, in this kind of closed session.

§ 1-5(b)(19): Pension Fund Investments

Effective January 1, 2005, Government Code 54956.81 states:

> Notwithstanding any other provision of this chapter, a legislative body of a local agency that invests pension funds may hold a closed session to consider the purchase or sale of particular, specific pension fund investments. All investment transaction decisions made during the closed session shall be made by rollcall vote entered into the minutes of the closed session as provided in subdivision (a) of Section 54957.2.

Bagley-Keene Comparison

Government Code §11126:

(c). Nothing in this article shall be construed to do any of the following:

•••••

(16) Prevent a state body that invests retirement, pension, or endowment funds from holding closed sessions when considering investment decisions. For purposes of consideration of shareholder voting on corporate stocks held by the state body, closed sessions for the purposes of voting may be held only with respect to election of corporate directors, election of independent auditors, and other financial issues that could have a material effect on the net income of the corporation. For the purpose of real property

investment decisions that may be considered in a closed session pursuant to this paragraph, a state body shall also be exempt from the provisions of paragraph (7) relating to the identification of real properties prior to the closed session.

The Problem Addressed

The Senate Floor Analysis for AB 2234 of 2004, which added this provision, stated:

> Some ... county retirement boards have discussed specific investments (of county employee retirement funds) in open session and found market movements in the days following the public discussion. In San Joaquin County, the retirement board discussed the intent to purchase a downtown Stockton building as both a headquarters and investment. Following the discussion, the price of the property was bid up and the retirement system was no longer able to remain in the bidding process. In Orange County, a public discussion was held regarding the potential sale of a portion of the retirement system's bond portfolio. The following day, sales occurred in the bond market that were potentially reflective of a large institutional investor poised to sell.

Not Limited to County Retirement Boards

Despite AB 2234's focus on county retirement boards in other provisions, Section 549956.81 is available to any "legislative body of a local agency that invests pension funds."

Secret Rollcall Vote

While investment purchase or sale decisions must be disclosed as such at a forthcoming public meeting, the actual vote on the decision is to be made by roll call, and unlike any other action vote in closed session, is recorded only in the closed session minutes, which are confidential.

Suggested Agenda Listing

The Brown Act does not include a suggested agenda listing for this type of closed session, but neither does it exempt it. A procedure that would probably comply would be simply to list "Retirement Fund Investment Transaction" or something similar.

Subsequent Action Disclosure

The required disclosures of any action taken are set forth in Government Code §54957.1:

> (a) The legislative body of any local agency shall publicly report any action taken in closed session and the vote or abstention of every member present thereon, as follows:
>
> *****
>
> (7) Pension fund investment transaction decisions made pursuant to Section 54956.81 shall be disclosed at the first open meeting of the legislative body held after the earlier of the close of the investment transaction or the transfer of pension fund assets for the investment transaction.

§ 1-6: Dealing with Violations without Going to Court

For various reasons, getting public officials to comply with the Brown Act is seldom if ever accomplished most quickly, reliably or lastingly through legal action. The preferred alternatives are in most cases education, publicity, complaints to the grand jury or district attorney, or seeking a clarifying opinion from the Attorney General.

§ 1-6(a): Educating the Legislative Body

Twenty-five years of close observation lead this author to conclude that most violations of the Brown Act trace to mistake rather than intentional misconduct—lack of information about the law or positive misinformation, sometimes attributable to faulty counseling by legal advisors. While many city councils, school boards and other local agencies provide their legislative bodies with periodic training in compliance with the Brown Act, the quality of that training is hard to assess from the outside. Given the variety of mistaken impressions of the law that seem to account for most detected violations, however, an apparent violation presents an opportunity for education as the best correction, if the body is open to it. Sometimes, if the training provider is the same attorney who shares the responsibility for the violation in having counseled the erring body that a certain course of action was defensible, it may be desirable to have a training session conducted by an outside attorney experienced in the Brown Act. This can be done without recrimination or discomfort for anyone, especially if the body's attorney is part of the process. Of course periodic training involving those known for Brown Act experience, as a preventive measure, would seem preferable to corrective training, since it would be presented without a background of recent controversy. In any event, before attempting to educate the body or any of the officials that it relies on, it may be helpful to check one's concerns, impressions or questions about the Brown Act with an attorney experienced with that law. This is a service offered to journalists, public officials or attorneys, and other citizens free of charge and on a confidential basis by Terry Francke, general counsel of Californians Aware, at (916) 487-7000 or terry@calaware.org.

§ 1-6(b): Mobilizing Change through Publicity

In any number of contexts, sometimes in order to show any movement at all, a legislative body needs to be aware that its constituency is informed of the need for change and of its resistance to providing it. If, in the open meetings context, a body having violated the Brown Act is not open to simple corrective education because it is mistakenly convinced of the correctness of the approach being questioned—or at least convinced that its approach will weather an individual's criticism—press publicity may be effective. Most newspapers take the Brown Act quite seriously, if for no other reason than that many (but not all) violations of the law prevent them from doing their job. Also, the press can readily convert a citizen's accusation of a Brown Act violation into a story that substitutes for the account that would have been written about the "open and public" discussion or action that did not take place. Journalists often point to the truism that the fact that all airplanes that took off today landed safely does not produce reportable news—another way of explaining why a disproportionate amount of what gets reported as news is bad news. Accordingly, a statement from an authoritative and credible source that even a small number of the planes that landed safely today may not do so tomorrow is not only reportable news, but a major story. News is often about things going wrong, or even being perceived likely to go wrong. That makes a complaint about a suspected Brown Act violation natural material for at least an initial story, especially if it comes from a source not previously identified as critical of everything the body does. The story may even prompt an editorial. And an elected official who too often provides the public at large with media-supported suggestions that he or she is disdainful of the Brown Act (and thus of public accountability) is simply arming a future electoral challenger or, in extreme cases, a recall organizer. An experienced city attorney not long ago advised public officials that the real "teeth" in the Brown Act were provided not by the statute itself but by the reality that publicized perceived violations can be politically damaging. In that perspective, political damage is not simply a threat to the prospects of a local official interested in a political career. It is also the loss of good will and confidence that any official needs in order to advance his or her constructive agenda.

With these considerations in mind, a person or group convinced that a serious Brown Act violation has occurred or is about to occur, and having exhausted efforts to persuade the officials responsible (or having concluded from experience that attempted persuasion would be futile), may well if time permits find the local press a forceful ally and a far preferable recourse than more formal options. But in approaching a reporter or editor, such a complainant needs to present essentially the same case for concern as would be required in those more formal, official channels: A clear and concise statement of the relevant facts (what has happened or is about to happen), an informed notion of what the Brown Act requires or prohibits (reference to one or more particular code sections will save time and minimize mistaken conclusions), and a statement of why the facts and the law show a true conflict. As noted in § 1-6(a) above, helping clarify such matters is a service offered to journalists, public officials or attorneys, and other citizens, free of charge and on a confidential basis, by Terry Francke, general counsel of Californians Aware, at (916) 487-7000 or terry@calaware.org.

§ 1-6(c): Complaint to Grand Jury

California grand juries regularly accept, and address in their annual final reports, complaints alleging Brown Act violations. These reports can have a corrective publicity effect comparable to that arising from ordinary press coverage, although typically with less of an edge because of their delayed, once-a-year release and the fact that pending that release, the grand jury can say nothing about the matter, or even confirm that an investigation is under way. Furthermore, the legislative body may simply deny that it violated the law, and a grand jury has no power to compel correction.

On the other hand, grand juries might react to what they conclude are serious and intentional violations by using their accusation authority to charge public officials with "willful or corrupt misconduct in office." An accusation, only rarely issued, is somewhat comparable to a criminal indictment in that it alleges misconduct by, and may lead to punishment of, particular individuals—including members of a local legislative body. The possible defendants include, under Government Code §3060, "any officer of a district, county, or city," accused of "misconduct in office occurring at any time within the six years immediately preceding the presentation of an accusation by the grand jury." (Section 3074). The punishment resulting from a grand jury accusation and a resulting conviction is removal from office; in this sense the accusation process can be thought of as comparable to an impeachment. An accusation proceeding is tried to a jury by the district attorney, "in all respects in the same manner as the trial of an indictment," (Government Code §3070), and a conviction, as with a criminal offense, may be appealed.

The district attorney may not dismiss an accusation for political or other extra-legal motives, but may make a motion to dismiss in the interest of justice if, for example, the accusation "is concurred in by less than the required number of grand jurors, is barred by the statute of limitations, is brought against a public official not subject to section 3060, or is not supported by sufficient, admissible evidence." *Bradley v. Lacy*, 53 Cal.App.4th 883 (1997) In the accusation dealt with in *Bradley*—one charging a county supervisor with both leaking information about a settlement to the press and violating the Brown Act in holding a series of unlawful private meetings with other (unaccused) supervisors—the superior court subsequently dismissed the case in the interest of justice. The court found several incurable defects, in that:

- the document was undated and unsigned;
- there was no indication that the required number of grand jurors had

voted to return the accusation;

- the witnesses were not named;
- there was no transcript of the grand jury investigation leading to the accusation; and
- none of the three counts of the document stated a valid ground for the accusation of official misconduct.

As to what constitutes "willful misconduct in office," most of the handful of reported cases supporting a conviction (none dealing with the Brown Act) have involved conduct that was flatly criminal or nearly so. That pattern argues against prosecuting officials for being simply careless or incompetent, concluded the Fourth District Court of Appeal in *Steiner v. Superior Court*, 50 Cal.App.4th 1771 (1996):

> To adopt the district attorney's proposed negligence standard would have ominous public policy implications. It would effectively make the district attorney a performance monitor of elected officials, and allow him to subject them to the expense and rigors of accusation and trial if he deemed their performance to fall below that of the "reasonable" public official. In plain terms, he could try to oust them for getting a C minus on their report cards. We cannot believe the Legislature intended to give the district attorney that power when it enacted section 3060. The procedure must be reserved for serious misconduct, such as that found in the cases we have reviewed, misconduct that involves criminal behavior or, at least, *a purposeful failure to carry out mandatory duties of office*.

Id. at 1782 (emphasis added).

§ 1-6(d): Complaint to District Attorney

The district attorney is authorized not only to prosecute criminal violations of the Brown Act (see Section 1-7(a)) but also to file suit for any of the civil remedies provided under the Act (see Sections 1-7(b)-(e)). But short of litigation, the district attorney's office can also investigate complaints and issue public findings concerning, and/or admonitions to, offending local agencies. There is no legal hazard in doing so. In *Ingram v. Flippo*, 74 Cal.App.4th 1280, (1999), the district attorney of Monterey County investigated a complaint that members of a school board had violated the Brown Act, and had subsequently issued a press release stating that several board members had committed minor violations. In a defamation lawsuit brought by one of the trustees said to be at fault, the court concluded that Government Code §821.6 provided immunity for these statements. That provision states:

A public employee is not liable for injury caused by his instituting or prosecuting any judicial or administrative proceeding within the scope of his employment, even if he acts maliciously and without probable cause.

The court concluded, "We believe that the statements made in the press release were part of the prosecution process as that term is understood in the context of section 821.6. The District Attorney's conduct thus constitutes an exercise of prosecutorial discretion even though he decided not to prosecute an action at the time." *Id.* at 1283.

Such investigations and announcements, even if, as is typical, they rule out prosecution, can be a very effective control over the more easily determined violations. Some district attorneys have committed special resources to Brown Act complaint investigations. The Public Integrity Division of the Los Angeles County District Attorney's Office reported in February 2004 that it had reviewed 122 such complaints since its establishment in 2001. Late in 2004, within the span of a few weeks, investigations resulted in District Attorney Steve Cooley's letters announcing the finding of violations by the Beverly Hills City Council and the county Board of Supervisors. Other district attorneys' offices with public integrity units (which may or may not include the Brown Act as a priority) are those in Alameda, Contra Costa, Fresno, Orange, Riverside, Sacramento, San Bernardino, San Diego, San Francisco and Santa Clara Counties. Still others that have no public integrity units as such but that are expressly committed to investigating Brown Act complaints are those in Amador, Marin and Ventura Counties.

§ 1-6(e): Requesting an Attorney General's Opinion

One final non-litigation approach to resolving or at least clarifying disputes or doubts about what the Brown Act requires—or does not—is to request an opinion of the California Attorney General. That office cites two case law observations indicating what authority an opinion carries. "Although an official interpretation of a statute by the Attorney General is not controlling, it is entitled to great respect." *Thorning v. Hollister School District*, 11 Cal.App.4th 1598, 1604 (1992) "Opinions of the Attorney General, while not binding, are entitled to great weight. In the absence of controlling authority, these opinions are persuasive 'since the Legislature is presumed to be cognizant of that construction of the statute.' " *Napa Valley Educators' Association. v. Napa Valley Unified School District*, 194 Cal.App.3d 243, 251(1987).

Pursuant to Government Code §12519 only certain public officials, however, are entitled to request an opinion: constitutional officers; legislators; state agencies, boards or commissions; district attorneys, city prosecutors on criminal matters (but not city attorneys who do not prosecute); county counsels and sheriffs; and appellate courts (but only through the Chief Justice or the appellate court presiding judge). But this list, advises the Attorney General, "does not authorize a designated officer to request an opinion on a question posed by someone else. A request will be declined when it is apparent that the request is made on behalf of someone not authorized by Government Code section 12519." Nonetheless, it is obvious that state legislators' requests tend to be responded to even when submitted on behalf of a local agency within their districts. For example, a request from Senator Wesley Chesbro, answered in a 2001 opinion, asked,

> May a majority of the board members of a local public agency e- mail each other to develop a collective concurrence as to action to be taken by the board without violating the Ralph M. Brown Act if the e-mails are also sent to the secretary and chairperson of the agency, the e-mails are posted on the agency's Internet website, and a printed version of each e-mail is reported at the next public meeting of the board?

(see § 1-2(d)(1)). If local agencies could not get their questions addressed to the Attorney General through their legislators, that office would have few occasions to opine on the Brown Act at all, other than in response to questions posed by county counsel on behalf of county agencies and the school districts that they advise.

When there is a genuine dispute over the meaning of the law applied to a particular situation and local body is open to having it resolved without litigation, therefore, nothing prevents a local agency from asking a legislator to request an opinion, and nothing prevents citizens interested in the issue to ask the agency to ask the legislator.

§ 1-7: Legal Remedies and Litigation Strategy

As they become more familiar with the Brown Act, people sometimes complain that it has no "teeth." Compared with open meeting laws in other states, it appears however that the Brown Act's combination of personal criminal liability for violators, declaratory and injunctive relief to prevent repeated or anticipated violations, and nullification to void action taken in certain major breaches of the law is a typical array of sanctions. But resort to court enforcement overall is in fact very rare, considering the half century of the law's existence and its applicability to quite frequent meetings of bodies governing the state's 58 counties, more than 300 cities, more than 800 school districts, and thousands of special districts. The explanation for this infrequency of legal action has something to do with the civil enforcement provisions themselves, which despite certain incentives like the award of attorney's fees to successful plaintiffs, are costly and time-consuming to pursue; with the formidable burden of proof facing prosecutors in a criminal case; and with the fact that the witnesses most consistently present to notice violations of the Act—newspaper reporters—no longer cover meetings as routinely as they once did and are typically nowhere near as familiar with the law as they might be. Cases brought by newspapers are a very small minority of the total, which is not that large in any event. Nonetheless, there are situations where the economic, political or personal stakes for some person or organization threatened or harmed by an action taken by a legislative body are substantial enough to warrant doing all that is possible to deter or reverse it, and where court action is seen as a necessary resort.

§ 1-7(a): Criminal Prosecution

The Brown Act criminalizes certain intentional misconduct by members of legislative bodies. Government Code Section 54959 states:

> Each member of a legislative body who attends a meeting of that legislative body where action is taken in violation of any provision of this chapter, and where the member intends to deprive the public of information to which the member knows or has reason to know the public is entitled under this chapter, is guilty of a misdemeanor.

Bagley-Keene Comparison
Government Code §11130.7: Each member of a state body who attends a meeting of that body in violation of any provision of this article, and where the member intends to deprive the public of information to which the member knows or has reason to know the public is entitled under this article, is guilty of a misdemeanor.

Since, in the more than 50 years of the Act's existence, only one district attorney has been known to have pursued a prosecution to a completed trial (resulting in a hung jury), there is no case law guidance as to how this provision operates. But it appears clear that in order to make a case against one or more members under this provision the burden is on the prosecutor to prove, beyond reasonable doubt, that the defendant:

- attended a "meeting" of a "legislative body" where there was "action taken" in violation of some provision of the Act;
- knew or "had reason to know" at the time that the public was entitled to information of which the violation would deprive it; and
- intended that the violation deprive the public of that information.

The first factor standing alone would implicate all members of the legislative body present when action was taken in violation of the law with the same liability, irrespective of their involvement in the Action. Adding the second factor allows a distinction to be drawn depending on awareness, but ironically might make those diligently aware of the law and what information it guarantees to the public liable for that awareness, with the ignorant members insulated, were it not for the third factor, which leaves liable only those present and aware of the law and nonetheless intending to deprive the public of public information.

Defendant's Awareness

A member of a body may know or have reason to know what information the Brown Act entitles the public to from several sources. One is simply the text of the Act itself. Government Code §54952.7 states:

> A legislative body of a local agency may require that a copy of this chapter be given to each member of the legislative body and any person elected to serve as a member of the legislative body who has not assumed the duties of office. An elected legislative body of a local agency may require that a copy of this chapter be given to each member of each legislative body all or a majority of whose members are appointed by or under the authority of the elected legislative body.

Bagley-Keene Comparison
Government Code §11121.9: Each state body shall provide a copy of this article to each member of the state body upon his or her appointment to membership or assumption of office.

Another source of awareness could be briefings by the body's legal counsel or other attorneys conducting training in the Act. Still another could be warnings issued by citizens or by the district attorney prior to the violation.

Effect of Legal Counsel's Advice

Normally reliance on the advice of legal counsel to the effect that a given practice does not violate the Brown Act would probably be protection against a criminal prosecution for being present at a meeting where that practice results in violating the law, if only because having received the reassuring advice could be cited as precluding proof that the member knew or had reason to know the contrary. On the other hand, if the district attorney had previously warned the body that the practice violated the Act (see § 1-6(d)), the fact that the body's attorney gave contradictory advice, insisting that the practice was not a violation, might not be immunizing. In *People v. Chacon,* 118 Cal.App.4th 427 (2004), the Second District Court of Appeal held, in what it deemed a case of first impression in California, that erroneous advice to a city council member by the city attorney, on which the former relied in participating in a conspiracy to change the municipal code to permit her employment as city manager, did not preclude the district attorney from prosecuting her for felony conflict of interest. Since a city attorney is not a prosecutor authorized to bring criminal actions under the Brown Act, the court reasoned, his assurances cannot bind the authorized prosecutor, the district attorney. The need for such a distinction was reinforced, the court concluded, by the political reality that a city attorney who is employed rather than elected serves at the pleasure of the council. On August 11, 2004, the California Supreme Court accepted the case (no. B164649) for review to decide whether the defense of "entrapment by estoppel" is recognized at all in California, and if so, whether it was properly rejected by the appellate court based on these facts.

§ 1-7(b): Civil Enforcement Actions by District Attorney or Others

The principal judicial enforcement mechanisms provided by the Brown Act are civil. They are designed to prevent violations that are threatened for the first time (typically using a prohibitory injunction); to obtain a judicial determination that a violation has occurred at least once (typically through a declaratory judgment); and, depending on whether that violation was an unlawful act or a failure to perform an act required by law, to prevent its repetition (typically through a prohibitory injunction or a mandamus action, respectively). A further civil action to undo an unlawfully performed action is discussed in § 1-7(g). Government Code §54960, subdivision (a) states:

> The district attorney or any interested person may commence an action by mandamus, injunction or declaratory relief for the purpose of stopping or preventing violations or threatened violations of this chapter by members of the legislative body of a local agency or to determine the applicability of this chapter to actions or threatened future action of the legislative body, or to determine whether any rule or action by the legislative body to penalize or otherwise discourage the expression of one or more of its members is valid or invalid under the laws

Bagley-Keene Comparison
Government Code §11130: (a) The Attorney General, the district attorney, or any interested person may commence an action by mandamus, injunction, or declaratory relief for the purpose of stopping or preventing violations or threatened violations of this article or to determine the applicability of this article to past actions or threatened future action by members of the state body or to determine whether any rule or action by the state body to penalize or otherwise discourage the expression of one or more of its members is valid or invalid under the laws of this state or of the United States, or to com-

pel the state body to tape record its closed sessions as hereinafter provided.

of this state or of the United States, or to compel the legislative body to tape record its closed sessions as hereinafter provided.

Standing of Non-residents

A Californian's standing as an "interested person" to bring an action against a particular local legislative body under Section 54960 does not depend on local residency, the California Court of Appeal for the Fourth District has held. More precisely, the court concluded that a resident of Los Angeles County could bring a Brown Act civil enforcement action against a school district in Orange County, since "a citizen of the State of California is an `interested person' within the meaning of sections 54960 and 54960.1 and may sue a legislative body of a local agency as provided in those sections for violations of the Brown Act." *McKee v. Orange Unified School District*, 110 Cal.App.4th 1310 (2003). By "citizen" the court may have meant resident, since the opinion notes that the Act's preamble refers to "the people of this State," and there is no discussion of United States citizenship in the opinion.

Standing of Members of the Defendant Body

In dictum, the court in *Ingram v. Flippo*, 74 Cal.App.4th 1280 (1999) observes that the plaintiff/respondent, a member of a school board,

> argues that she is a proper party to bring an action for declaratory relief under section 54960 even though she is also a member of the Board whose conduct allegedly violated the Brown Act. The statutory language providing that "any interested person" may bring such an action appears to be all-inclusive and supports appellant's position.

Id. at 1288.

But the standing of a member of a local legislative body to bring a Brown Act enforcement action against that body might be challenged as precluded by *Carsten v. Psychology Examining Committee*, 27 Cal.3d 793 (1980). In that case of first impression the California Supreme Court, by a bare 4-3 majority, held that Arlene Carsten, a member of the Psychology Examining Committee of the state Board of Medical Quality Assurance, could not sue to force the board's compliance with Business and Professions Code §2942, which set a score of 75 percent as the passing grade for the examination required to obtain state licensure as a psychologist. The board had recently decided, over *Carsten*'s dissenting vote, to adopt a standardized examination for its purposes using a national mean that effectively allowed applicants to pass with grades as low as 67.5 percent. The court concluded that Carsten had no "beneficial interest" as someone directly prejudiced, or as a citizen-taxpayer, to establish standing to seek the writ of mandate.

Carsten may however be distinguished on several grounds.

It concerns the availability of the writ of mandate generally as being confined to those with a "beneficial interest," rather than with the remedies specifically provided for violations of the Brown Act, which gives enforcement standing to the district attorney or *any* "interested person."

It defines the issue as "whether an administrative board member is, for purposes of this litigation, a mere taxpayer," and then decides to the contrary based on several factors.

• First, the court states:

> the law is clear that courts are reluctant to give advisory opinions… Since petitioner has no personal interest in the outcome of the litigation, she is in effect seeking to have the courts render an advisory opinion on the propriety of an administrative action. A judgment here would affect no person either favorably or detrimentally; it would purely and simply offer gratuitous advice to the board on how to conduct its examinations in the future as they may possibly affect some applicant other than this petitioner.

Id. at 798.

By contrast, a court's judgment or order in a Brown Act enforcement action, if successful, provides more than an "advisory opinion" or "gratuitous advice" to the body found to be in violation. It compels the body in some manner to change its conduct or even nullifies an action already taken.

• Second, the court objects,

> petitioner is in effect suing herself. She is the moving party in this litigation; the named defendant is the Psychology Examining Committee of the Board of Medical Quality Assurance, of which petitioner is part as a duly appointed member. It is unique to say the least, for one to sue herself and be both plaintiff and defendant in the same litigation. It may be said that she cannot lose the lawsuit, but we doubt that courts should encourage or permit this type of narcissistic litigation. We reach this conclusion because of the inevitable damage such lawsuits will inflict upon the administrative process.

Ibid. This observation is hard to understand, since Carsten was clearly not "suing herself" but rather, in effect, suing the committee's majority, with which she had already parted company in her dissenting vote on the regulation in question. In any case a suit to compel compliance with the Brown Act brought by a person often uniquely informed of the facts that compel him or her to resort to such litigation holds little danger of inflicting "damage" on the administrative process, but rather is calculated to keep it honest. This point is particularly clear in view of the Legislature's authorization to members of the body confidentially to blow the whistle on suspected violations to the district attorney or the grand jury, or quite publicly expressing "an opinion concerning the propriety or legality of actions taken by a legislative body of a local agency in closed session, including disclosure of the nature and extent of the illegal or potentially illegal action," all with complete immunity from liability (see § 1-5(a)(1)).

The court further takes into consideration "policy issues which militate against permitting disgruntled agency members to seek extraordinary writs from the courts."

> Unquestionably the ready availability of court litigation will be disruptive to the administrative process and antithetical to its underlying purpose of providing expeditious disposition of problems in a specialized field without recourse to the judiciary. Board members will be compelled to testify against each other, to attack members with conflicting views and justify their own positions taken in administrative hearings, and to reveal internal discussions and deliberations. Litigation -- even the threat of litigation -- is certain to affect the working relationship among board members. In addition, the defense of lawsuits brought by dissident board members -- and such suits would undoubtedly be frequent -- will severely tax the limited budgetary resources of most public agencies.
>
> From the vantage point of the judiciary such litigation has ominous aspects. It is purely and simply duplicative, a rerun of the administrative proceedings in a second, more formal forum. The dissident board member, having failed to persuade her four colleagues to her viewpoint, now has to persuade merely one judge. The number of such suits emanating from members on city, county, special district and state boards, will add significantly to court calendar congestion.

Id. at 799.

In contrast, as noted above, members of local legislatives bodies are already protected in either quietly reporting suspected violations to enforcement authorities or publicly taking issue with colleagues on the propriety of secretive practices—self-help remedies at least as potentially fraught with anti-collegial tension and disruption as filing a lawsuit. Moreover, Brown Act enforcement does not involve dragging "problems in a specialized field" of administrative law before a court, and does not, with the possible exception of a nullification action, provide a sore loser's end-run around a majority vote on a substantive policy matter—a legislative act.

As a final policy factor, the *Carsten* court states:

> While it is true that this petitioner is not only a board member but also a taxpayer, it is as a board member that she acquired her knowledge of the events upon which she bases the lawsuit. Her interest in the subject matter was piqued by service on the board, not by virtue of the neutrality of citizenship. The suit was brought in the former, not the latter capacity.
>
> The law is replete with examples of forfeiture of some rights available to others by virtue of acceptance of public service. The classic illustration is *McAuliffe v. Mayor, etc., of City of New Bedford* (1892) 155 Mass. 216 [29 N.E. 517], in which a policeman sought reinstatement to his position after discharge for exercising his right to engage in political activity. Justice Holmes, with his trenchant pen, wrote: "The petitioner may have a constitutional right to talk politics, but he has no constitutional right to be a policeman. There are few employments for hire in which the servant does not agree to suspend his constitutional rights of free speech as well as of idleness by the implied terms of his contract."

Ibid.

In the Brown Act context the apposite application of this principle is that in joining a legislative body an official foregoes several rights otherwise freely enjoyed and even constitutionally protected, including the First Amendment rights of assembly, petition, speech and association that are arguably bound up in private meetings or conversations with a majority of fellow board members. The member also takes on the duty of confidentiality with respect to lawful communications and actions in closed session, and must accept the restraint against collegial discussion of matters not on the meeting's posted agenda. But as noted above, the member is clearly not required to sacrifice his or her right publicly to dissent, on Brown Act grounds, from actions taken in closed session, or to file complaints of violations with the district attorney or grand jury. This bestowal of a protected enforcement role takes into account precisely the uncommon "knowledge of events" that a member acquires by virtue of his or her official position rather than "by virtue of the neutrality of citizenship." The conclusion of dissenting Justice Richardson with respect to the mandate issue in *Carsten* seems all the more apt with reference to a legislative body member's role in policing compliance with the Brown Act:

> The right of access to our law courts is a very important attribute of citizenship. Petitioner is a citizen and taxpayer as well as an agency board member. She, and others like her, may be particularly well informed and uniquely suited to assure that public agencies conform their procedures to statutory duty. Petitioner as an interested citizen devotes substantial amounts of time and energy toward the stated objectives of the committee. The public interest is not advanced when her willingness to serve is penalized by forfeiture of one of her important civil rights.

Id. at 807.

§ 1-7(c): Declaratory Judgment

Ripeness

The question of whether declaratory relief is available to resolve a dispute over a single alleged violation, or whether a plaintiff must await a series of incidents or a pattern of practice before seeking the relief, was resolved in the plaintiff's favor by the Fourth District Court of Appeal in *California Alliance for Utility Safety and Education (CAUSE) v. City of San Diego*, 56 Cal.App.4th 1024, 1029-31 (1997). That case involved the use of a closed session by a city council, listed on the agenda as dealing with pending litigation, to instead amend a 50-year franchise agreement, freeing the franchisee electrical utility from some of its previous obligations to place power lines underground. A consumer watchdog group sued, alleging that the city had violated the Brown Act's open meeting and agenda listing requirements by using pending litigation closed sessions for unauthorized purposes. The city demurred, contending that the action was not ripe to address potential future violations. The trial court sustained the city's demurrer without leave to amend and entered judgment in its favor. On appeal the Fourth District reversed, based on the following analysis:

> Contrary to city's argument, the ripeness doctrine does not require that to obtain declaratory relief CAUSE allege and prove a

pattern or practice of past violations. Rather, it is sufficient to allege there is a controversy over whether a past violation of law has occurred. …

Here, there can be no doubt there is a controversy between the parties over whether in reducing SDG&E's undergrounding obligation for the years 1994 through 2000, the city council met the requirements of the Brown Act and the city charter. For their part the plaintiffs believe the city council did not properly give notice of the closed session it conducted on March 28, 1995, used the closed session to discuss issues other than receiving advice from its attorneys and failed to properly give notice of the public session in which the settlement agreement with SDG&E was formally approved and failed to conduct the public hearing they believe is required by the city charter.

Notwithstanding its demurrer, for its part city does not believe any violation has occurred. City's belief as to the propriety of its action may be found not only in plaintiffs' allegation that city will engage in similar practices in the future but also in city's failure to concede that the facts alleged by plaintiffs constitute a violation of the Brown Act or the city charter. … Thus there can be no serious dispute that a controversy between the parties exists over city's past compliance with the Brown Act and the charter. On that basis alone plaintiffs are entitled to declaratory relief resolving the controversy. •••••

Not only is the controversy alleged by plaintiffs a matter of some importance, the allegations of the complaint also strongly suggest that in the absence of declaratory relief plaintiffs will have some difficulty in preventing future violations. … In this regard we note that even after the closed session had occurred and the city council had determined that it would adopt the proposed settlement, the agenda materials prepared by city failed to fully disclose the nature and scope of the settlement being considered by city. Indeed, at the time the settlement was being considered for public adoption by the council, more information about the cost of outside counsel was provided to the public than information about the settlement. The difficulty plaintiffs had in discovering the 1995 settlement suggests that in the absence of declaratory relief there is some risk that any future settlement with respect to SDG&E's undergrounding obligation will also go undetected by interested members of the public.

In sum then, the complaint alleges the existence of an actual controversy between the parties for which declaratory relief is available.

Mootness

Occasionally the conduct of a legislative body giving rise to a Brown Act violation claim—or even the body itself—may be a thing of the past by the time a court can address the matter. If so, as in other analogous circumstances, adjudicating the matter will not necessarily be foreclosed by mootness. In *Farron v. City and County of San Francisco*, 216 Cal.App.3d 1071 (1989), the court described the issue as follows:

> On February 23, 1988, following controversy over the issue of the demolition of single family houses in the City, the mayor announced the formation of the San Francisco Housing Demolition Task Force (Task Force). The purpose of the Task Force was to formulate legislation creating permanent zoning controls to replace an interim demolition moratorium that had earlier been passed by the board of supervisors. The Task Force included two members of the board of supervisors.
>
> •••••
>
> The meetings of the Task Force were closed to the public. On March 7, 1988, Ted Fang, the publisher of the San Francisco Independent, a weekly newspaper, wrote to the city attorney requesting that meetings of the Task Force be held in public because closed meetings violated the Brown Act. On March 15, 1988, the mayor responded to Fang's letter and stated that the city attorney had opined that the Brown Act was inapplicable to the Task Force because the Task Force was an informal advisory body and not a "legislative body" within the meaning of the Brown Act.
>
> Appellants contend that the trial court erred in ruling that the Action was moot. Although the Task Force completed its work prior to the trial court's hearing on appellants' motion for summary judgment, we hold that this case is not moot, because the issue of whether the Brown Act is applicable to advisory committees which include members of the board of supervisors is an issue that may recur in the future and is a question of general public interest.

Id. at 1073, 1074.

§ 1-7(d): Retaliatory Measures for Members' Speech

One remedy provided in Section 54960 is "to determine whether any rule or action by the legislative body to penalize or otherwise discourage the expression of one or more of its members is valid or invalid under the laws of this state or of the United States." This provision addresses the infrequent but unmistakable case where a board or council member is seen by the majority as unacceptably blunt, candid or revealing in his or her inquiry into agency matters or advocacy of a particular position, and where the result is either a one-time penalty of some kind or a consistent practice of prejudicial treatment. In *Degrassi v. Cook*, 29 Cal.4th 333 (2002), a case brought by a member of the city council of Glendora against the city manager, city attorney, and other council members, the plaintiff alleged that (as recited in her earlier unsuccessful federal case),

> from the time of her election . . . , the defendants . . . subjected her to a campaign of harassment and intimidation because they opposed her political views. She claims that defendants barred her from participating in Council business, prevented her from communicating with City staff, and threatened her both physically and with litigation should she disclose the wrongdoing of any City employee. Much of the conduct complained of occurred as a result of [plaintiff's] objection at a City Council meeting in 1996 to the granting of landmark status to a building in Glendora whose prior owner, she claimed, was a child molester. The owners of the building, the Andrews family, filed a [defamation] action (the Andrews action) against [plaintiff] based on her comments at the City Council meeting. [Plaintiff] claims this action, which was eventually dismissed, was filed in retaliation for her political views. [Plaintiff] sought to have the City provide her a defense against the Andrews action. On several occasions during October 1996, the City Council held closed sessions to consider [plaintiff's] demand. [Plaintiff] was excluded from these meetings. She contends this conduct was part of a continuing campaign to interfere with her First Amendment rights and to destroy her political reputation and career . . .

DeGrassi v. City of Glendora, 207 F.3d 636, 640 (2000). The California Supreme Court, in the plaintiff's second lawsuit in state court, held that even if proven, such conduct was not actionable for damages as a violation of the free speech provisions of the state constitution. But the same allegations could be the basis for a declaratory judgment action under Section 54960. Reprisals for unwelcome questioning or criticism are typically not so thoroughgoing, but may consist of a declaration of sanctions (peer disapproval), often coupled with an adoption of policy limiting opportunities for the offender to persist in the Activity felt to be insufficiently collegial, or to be imposing undue, costly or inappropriate burdens on staff or to be otherwise unbecoming of public office.

Members' Public Speech Rights

If a legislative body member is punished or more greatly burdened than colleagues for the inquiry, assertions or disclosures he or she has made in the course of official service, it is likely that any retaliatory action resulting would be hard to justify, given the First Amendment protections found in *Wood v. Georgia*, 370 U.S. 375 (1962) and of *Pickering v. Board of Education*, 391 U.S. 563 (1968) and its progeny. The former held that an elected sheriff, under investigation by a state grand jury (for suspected buying of African-American votes in rural Georgia in the 1960s), was unlawfully held in contempt of court for publicly criticizing the judges who authorized the investigation. The court observed:

> There is no evidence that the publications interfered with the performance of his duties as sheriff or with his duties, if any he had, in connection with the grand jury's investigation. We are not dealing with a situation where a sheriff refuses to issue summonses or to maintain order in the court building; nor, so far as the record shows, did the petitioner do any act which might present a substantive harm to the jury's solution of the problem placed before it. We are dealing here only with public expression.
>
> The petitioner was an elected official and had the right to enter the field of political controversy, particularly where his political life was at stake.... The role that elected officials play in our society makes it all the more imperative that they be allowed freely to express themselves on matters of current public importance.

Id. at 394.

The *Pickering* line of cases holds that even a non-elected public employee is protected from punishment by his or her employer for having spoken out publicly on a matter of public concern (as opposed to a private job grievance), so long as the speech is not fundamentally incompatible with his or her job (as it might be for a person employed to win public support for the employing agency's position on the given matter), does not otherwise preclude an effective working relationship with superiors or peers that compromises the agency's mission, and is not misrepresented as the position of the agency itself.

Members' Internal Speech Rights

Sometimes a legislative body member's speech, particularly in the form of direct communications with staff, is censured as "micromanagement"—an improper involvement in the administration of the agency that brings undue pressure on employees. The limits of this theory are illustrated in *Levy v. City of Santa Monica*, 114 Cal.App.4th 1252 (2004), which deals with a city charter provision, Section 6.10, that stated: "Except for the purpose of inquiry, the City Council and its members shall deal with the administrative service under the City Manager solely through the City Manager and neither the City Council nor any member shall give orders to any subordinates of the City Manager, either publicly or privately." A residential couple sued the city seeking, among other things, an injunction to enforce this provision in a manner that would prevent a city council member from communicating with staff about zoning enforcement matters.

The council member who had done so was responding to another constituent's complaint about a playhouse built by the plaintiffs, the complainants' next door neighbors, closer to their common property line, and higher, than the complainant felt was permitted by city regulations. The council member sent two e-mails to the city planning director. The first asked, "Could you look into this? Is this structure being built without permits? And could it be built with a permit? Please feel free to contact (the complainant) directly." The second, sent about two weeks later, asked for an update on the earlier query and said, "I just did a 'quick' review of the code. I can't say that I am necessarily accurate . . . but: Mike's letter said a 5-ft. rear setback was required. I think the code requires the same rear setback as the rear yard - - generally 15 feet (?) … I wonder if the space under the first floor should be considered a story. (I haven't found a citation to support this - yet.)" The result was a notice of violation sent to the plaintiff playhouse owners that was, once they sued, withdrawn because they had relied on earlier staff assurances that the structure was conforming. But with respect to the injunction, which the superior court was willing to grant, the Court of Appeal stated:

> Under the First Amendment, legislators are "given the widest latitude to express their views" and there are no "stricter 'free speech' standards on [them] than on the general public." (*Eller Outdoor Advertising Co. v. Board of Supervisors* (1979) 89 Cal.App.3d 76, 80.) Laws that restrict that freedom must be narrowly construed. (*Ibid.*) City officials have First Amendment protection when they respond to inquiries from the public about the city's actions on construction projects. *(Nizam-Aldine v. City of Oakland* (1996) 47 Cal.App.4th 364, 376-377.)
>
> The (plaintiffs) seek to enjoin council members from advocating their constituents' positions, applying "direct pressure" or "engaging in acts designed to influence" City administrative staff. But that is an overly broad restraint on speech which would in-

hibit constitutionally protected activity. (*Bond v. Floyd* (1966) 385 U.S. 116, 136; *Baggett v. Bullitt* (1964) 377 U.S. 360, 372; *American Civil Liberties Union of Southern California v. Board of Education*, supra, 55 Cal.2d at pp. 179-180.)

It is not easy to distinguish between inquiry and "acts" designed to influence decision. "General words create different and often particular impressions on different minds." (*Thomas v. Collins* (1945) 323 U.S. 516, 534.)

For example, in *Thomas*, a labor leader was held in contempt for violating a restraining order which prevented him from soliciting people to join a union. The Supreme Court ruled that his conviction violated the First Amendment because the trial court's order "chilled" free speech. Under the order he could discuss the attributes of the union, but was prohibited from soliciting or inviting the audience to join it. The court noted it would be difficult for the speaker to distinguish between prohibited and protected speech. He would have to anticipate how the audience might interpret his remarks. There was no guarantee that "anything he might say upon the general subject would not be understood by some as an invitation. In short, the supposedly clear-cut distinction between discussion, laudation, general advocacy, and solicitation puts the speaker . . . wholly at the mercy of the varied understanding of his hearers . . . ." (*Thomas v. Collins*, supra, 323 U.S. at p. 535.) "Such a distinction offers no security for free discussion." (*Ibid.*)

That is the case here. For some, a council member's inquiry for a constituent is advocacy simply because it calls attention to the constituent's position. To the head of a city agency, a council member's act of faxing citizen complaints about the agency might be considered an "act designed to influence" or "direct pressure." For the (plaintiffs), an inquiry is advocacy where it could change the status quo or influence the result. Under their definition, virtually all inquiries would be suspect. Council members who may make inquiries under Section 6.10 might refrain from doing so because of fear of being sued or held in contempt. For example, council members could be inhibited from calling City agencies about matters crucial to the community such as securing help for families living in substandard housing. "Free speech may not be so inhibited." (*Baggett v. Bullitt*, supra, 377 U.S. at p. 372.)

The purpose of Section 6.10 is to define the lines of authority within city government, not to prohibit protected speech. Interpreting this section to prohibit "orders" to city staff is a bright line consistent with the purpose of Section 6.10 and the First Amend-

> ment. Counsel members "are entitled to speak as they please on matters vital to them; errors in judgment . . . may be exposed, of course, but not through punishment for contempt for the expression." (*Wood v. Georgia* (1962) 370 U.S. 375, 389.) "[E]rroneous statements must be protected to give freedom of expression the breathing space it needs to survive." (Bond v. Floyd, supra, 385 U.S. at p. 136.) There are better ways to discourage improper conduct. "Under our system of government, counterargument and education are the weapons available to expose these matters, not abridgment of the rights of free speech." (*Wood*, at p. 389.)

Id. at 1261.

Conspiracy Liability for Punishing Speech

As a rare extreme, a legislative body member's speech may so provoke colleagues that they take extraordinary measures against him or her in a manner warranting a damages action. In *Awabdy v. City of Adelanto*, 368 F.3d 1062 (2004), the U.S. Court of Appeals for the Ninth Circuit held that a city councilman defeated for reelection after being charged with embezzlement can proceed with his suit to show that city officials conspired to derail him for asking questions about spending and taking other positions they found unwelcome. As described by the court in relying on Esau Awabdy's allegations:

> As a member of the Adelanto City Council, Awabdy raised questions about the expenditure of municipal funds and took positions that placed him in conflict with other officials in the San Bernardino County municipality. A conspiracy formed to use unconstitutional means to defeat him when he ran for reelection. It included Ted Hartz and Richard Althouse, also city councilmembers; Scott Burnell, a police officer; and Michael Sakamoto, the city manager (collectively "the defendants"). In addition to their political disagreements, another motive underlay the conspirators' unconstitutional scheme for bringing about Awabdy's removal from office. They made it known that they intended to "get" him because he was of "Arabic extraction."
>
> On the basis of the conspirators' false accusations that Awabdy had embezzled public funds, the San Bernardino County District Attorney's office commenced an investigation in May 1999. On October 24, 2000, just two weeks before the November election, the District Attorney charged Awabdy with embezzling public funds in violation of Cal. Penal Code § 504. Awabdy pled not guilty on October 31 and was released on his own recogni-

> zance. The election occurred a week later. Awabdy received fewer votes than any of the thirteen other candidates who were running for the three at-large seats on the Adelanto City Council. In contrast, the two other incumbents were reelected.
>
> In December 2000, Awabdy was held to answer on the embezzlement charge following a preliminary hearing. Over one year later, the state Superior Court granted a motion by a deputy District Attorney to dismiss the criminal charge against Awabdy in the interests of justice, pursuant to Cal. Penal Code § 1385. Awabdy commenced this action in May 2002.

Id. at 1065. A footnote in the court's opinion refers to a newspaper report that the charges involved some $350 in conference attendance expenses that Awabdy received reimbursement for from the conference hosts, but then turned in for reimbursement to the city as well. Awabdy sued for malicious prosecution under the federal Civil Rights Act, claiming that the defendants conspired to punish him for exercise of his free speech rights. He also sued under the Act for violation of his right to free speech and equal protection. The defendants argued that they could not be liable for malicious prosecution because it was the district attorney who used his independent discretion to go forward on the charges. The trial court granted their motion to dismiss on this and other grounds, essentially concluding that if the constitutional deprivations could not be shown as a basis for the malicious prosecution claim, they were also unavailable in a direct claim of interference under the Civil Rights Act. The Ninth Circuit disagreed, and ordered that the litigation be allowed to proceed on both causes of action. As to the second in particular, Judge Stephen Reinhardt stated for the court:

> To establish that his First Amendment rights were violated, Awabdy must prove that chilling his political speech was a substantial or motivating factor in the defendants' wrongful conduct. ... Awabdy is not merely claiming a "speculative chill due to generalized and legitimate law enforcement initiatives." ... His complaint contains specific allegations that the defendant public officials knowingly made false accusations and engaged in other wrongful, concerted conduct that resulted, as they had intended, in the institution of an unfounded criminal charge, and substantially infringed his First Amendment rights. These allegations are sufficient to state a claim under § 1983 for violation of his First Amendment rights.

Id. at 1071 (citation omitted).

§ 1-7(e): Order to Tape Closed Sessions

A remedy specific to a finding of unlawful discussion or action in closed session allows the court to order the offending body to tape record its closed sessions for a determinate period, preserving the recordings for inspection by the court should the need arise in the future. This provision acts both as a deterrent to future violations and as evidence in a future action alleging closed session abuses. Subdivision (b) of Government Code §54960 states:

(b) The court in its discretion may, upon a judgment of a violation of Section 54956.7, 54956.8, 54956.9, 54956.95, 54957, or 54957.6, order the legislative body to tape record its closed sessions and preserve the tape recordings for the period and under the terms of security and confidentiality the court deems appropriate.

(c) (1) Each recording so kept shall be immediately labeled with the date of the closed session recorded and the title of the clerk or other officer who shall be custodian of the recording.

(2) The tapes shall be subject to the following discovery procedures:

(A) In any case in which discovery or disclosure of the tape is sought by either the district attorney or the plaintiff in a civil action pursuant to Section 54959, 54960, or 54960.1 alleging that a violation of this chapter has occurred in a closed session which has been recorded pursuant to this section, the party seeking discovery or disclosure shall file a written notice of motion with the appropriate court with notice to the governmental agency which has custody and control of the tape recording. The notice shall be given pursuant to subdivision (b) of Section 1005 of the Code of Civil Procedure.

(B) The notice shall include, in addition to the items required by section 1010 of the Code of Civil Procedure, all of the following:

(i) Identification of the proceeding in which discovery or disclosure is sought, the party seeking discovery or disclosure, the date and time of the meeting recorded, and the governmental agency which has custody and control of the recording.

Bagley-Keene Comparison

Government Code Section 11130:

(b) The court in its discretion may, upon a judgment of a violation of Section 11126, order the state body to tape record its closed sessions and preserve the tape recordings for the period and under the terms of security and confidentiality the court deems appropriate.

(c) (1) Each recording so kept shall be immediately labeled with the date of the closed session recorded and the title of the clerk or other officer who shall be custodian of the recording.

(2) The tapes shall be subject to the following discovery procedures:

(A) In any case in which discovery or disclosure of the tape is sought by the Attorney General, the district attorney, or the plaintiff in a civil action pursuant to this section or Section 11130.3 alleging that a violation of this article has occurred in a closed session that has been recorded pursuant to this section, the party seeking discovery or disclosure shall file a written notice of motion with the appropriate court with notice to the governmental agency that has custody and control of the tape recording. The notice shall be given pursuant to subdivision (b) of Section 1005 of the Code of Civil Procedure.

(B) The notice shall include, in addition to the items required by Section 1010 of the Code of Civil Procedure, all of the following:

(i) Identification of the proceeding in which discovery or disclosure is sought, the party seeking discovery or disclosure, the date and time of the meeting recorded, and the governmental agency that has custody and control of the recording.

(ii) An affidavit that contains specific facts indicating that a violation of the Act occurred in the closed session.

(3) If the court, following a review of the motion, finds that there is good cause to

believe that a violation has occurred, the court may review, in camera, the recording of that portion of the closed session alleged to have violated the Act.

(4) If, following the in-camera review, the court concludes that disclosure of a portion of the recording would be likely to materially assist in the resolution of the litigation alleging violation of this article, the court shall, in its discretion, make a certified transcript of the portion of the recording a public exhibit in the proceeding.

(5) Nothing in this section shall permit discovery of communications that are protected by the attorney-client privilege.

(ii) An affidavit which contains specific facts indicating that a violation of the Act occurred in the closed session.

(3) If the court, following a review of the motion, finds that there is good cause to believe that a violation has occurred, the court may review, in camera, the recording of that portion of the closed session alleged to have violated the Act.

(4) If, following the in camera review, the court concludes that disclosure of a portion of the recording would be likely to materially assist in the resolution of the litigation alleging violation of this chapter, the court shall, in its discretion, make a certified transcript of the portion of the recording a public exhibit in the proceeding.

(5) Nothing in this section shall permit discovery of communications which are protected by the attorney-client privilege.

Triggering Closed Session Violations

The closed sessions concerning which violations may trigger the recording remedy include those involving License Applicant Appeals (see § 1-5(b)(5)), Real Property Negotiations (see § 1-5(b)(3)), Joint Powers Agency Insurance Pool Litigation (see § 1-5(b)(12)), Employee Personnel Matters (see § 1-5(b)(4)), or Employee/Union Compensation Negotiations (see § 1-5(b)(2)).

§ 1-7(f): Mandamus or Injunctive Relief

Government Code §54960 (a) prescribes mandamus or injunctive relief "for the purpose of stopping or preventing violations or threatened violations" of the Brown Act. The main difference between which approach should or can be used may often be simply whether the violation to be stopped or the threatened violation to be prevented is the omission of a mandated act or the commission of a prohibited act.

Mandamus to Compel Required Acts

The California Supreme Court observed, in *Common Cause of California v. Board of Supervisors*, 49 Cal.3d 432, 442 (1989):

> Mandamus will lie to compel a public official to perform an official act required by law. (Code Civ. Proc., § 1085.) Mandamus will not lie to control an exercise of discretion, i.e., to compel an official to exercise discretion in a particular manner. Mandamus may issue, however, to compel an official both to exercise his discretion (if he is required by law to do so) and to exercise it under a proper interpretation of the applicable law. (*Shepherd v. Supe-*

> *rior Court* (1976) 17 Cal. 3d 107, 118 ; *Anderson v. Phillips* (1975) 13 Cal. 3d 733, 737 .)

Id. at 442. Mandamus can thus be used to compel a legislative body to perform a legal duty that leaves it no discretion but that it has refused to perform, or to perform a discretionary duty correctly, in conformity with "a proper interpretation of the applicable law." Mandamus is especially appropriate where the Legislature has not provided a particular penalty or consequence for failure to perform. In the Brown Act context this compulsory function can be important where the statute requires that something be done but does not, for example, make failure to do it a basis for judicial nullification of any action taken (see § 1-7(g)). Such duties, the non-performance of which will *not* support a nullification action, include:

• adopting a set schedule of time and place for regular meetings (Government Code §54954);

• mailing copies of the "agenda packet" to those willing to pay an annual subscription price (Government Code §54954.1);

• providing copies on request of records created or received in connection with impending or future open session discussions (Government Code §54957.5);

• informing those attending a meeting that they need not sign a register or other document in order to do so (Government Code §54953.3);

• providing an opportunity for members of the public at regular meetings to address the legislative body on matters on the agenda or otherwise relevant to the agency's business (Government Code §54954.3);

• allowing non-disruptive tape recording, filming, photography or broadcasting of open meetings; preserving the agency's own tapes of its meetings for at least 30 days and providing free access to citizens who wish to listen to or view them on the agency's own equipment (Government Code §§54953.5, 54953.6);

• identifying, prior to a closed session on real property negotiations, the body's negotiators, the property parcels or addresses under negotiation, and the other party to the negotiations (Government Code §54956.8);

• informing a health care plan member of the right to have his or her complaint heard in open session (Government Code §54956.86);

• providing on request copies of records indicating the source of the "significant exposure to litigation" against the agency that justifies a closed session on pending litigation (Government Code §54956.9); and

• making public reports of action taken in closed session and releasing related records on request (Government Code §54957.1).

Injunction to Bar Prohibited Acts

Injunctive relief can be used either to prevent a threatened new violation or to stop a pattern of ongoing violations. Since the former are often either so obviously unlawful that the body can usually be persuaded to change its proposed conduct, or such an unanticipated breach that prevention is not considered, most resorts to injunctive relief are likely to focus on avoided repetition of violations already on the record. At that point the question for the court is whether proven or acknowledged violations have been such that the court will properly act to ensure they do not continue. In *Shapiro v. City Council*, 96 Cal.App.4th 904 (2002), the trial court found, in the declaratory judgment phase of a Brown Act case brought by a citizen, several violations in the council's use of closed sessions—purporting to concern real property negotiations—to discuss wide-ranging aspects of a proposed ballpark project. As described by the Court of Appeal:

> In this case, although the majority of the facts are undisputed, the trial court had to examine the minutes of the closed sessions and receive a declaration from an Assistant City Attorney in order to evaluate the City Council's continuing contention that its practices comply with the Brown Act, with respect to the amount of information required to be posted before it may hold a closed session regarding real property negotiations, and what the proper scope of discussion in such a session may be. These continuing contentions were relevant to the trial court's assessment of the need for continuing relief by injunction, to operate in the future, in order to assure the City Council's compliance with the letter and spirit of Brown Act requirements. As defined by Code of Civil Procedure section 525, an injunction is a writ or order requiring a person to refrain from a particular act. This action was brought under section 54960 by Shapiro, as an "interested person," for injunctive or declaratory relief "for the purpose of stopping or preventing violations or threatened violations of this chapter by members of the legislative body of a local agency or to determine the applicability of this chapter to actions or threatened future action of the legislative body . . .
>
> The City Council first contends that although the trial court may have been justified in issuing declaratory relief about the alleged violations of the Brown Act, injunctive relief was not proper because "relief under Section 54960 (a) must be predicated upon a finding that present violations of the Act are occurring, or that future violations of the Act are threatened," and there was no such finding here. Instead, the trial court made a finding of a past prac-

> tice, coupled with a reference to the City Council's continuing contention as to the validity of that practice, as justifying injunctive relief. The City Council further contends that since a companion section, section 54960.1, allows an agency to cure an alleged defect regarding notice of topics to be discussed at a closed session, no injunction was proper here for either of two reasons: (1) no action taken by the City Council on any topic related to the closed session has been set aside as invalid, under the cure provisions, and/or (2) because the City Council has agreed to change its practices in some respects. Accordingly, the City believes there can be no showing of any present or threatened future violations of the Act.

Id. at 912.

But, said the court, the city's very insistence of the correctness of its past practices—its refusal to acknowledge them as violation of the Brown Act—presented a clear enough prospect of repetition to justify an injunction:

> From the above discussion we may conclude that (1) our case ... involves not a one-time "offense" or alleged violation, but a legislative body's continuing contention that its practices comply with the Brown Act, with respect to the amount of information required to be posted before it may hold certain closed sessions, as well as what the proper scope of discussion in such sessions may be; and (2) so long as the allegations and proof of the legislative body's practices extend to "past actions and violations that are related to present or future ones," the Brown Act provisions are brought into play to authorize and justify injunctive relief. That is the case here, where the City Council has staked out a position that the trial court had no authority to prescribe the manner in which it should comply with the Brown Act, by posting agendas for closed sessions containing brief general descriptions of each item of business to be transacted or discussed. (§ 54954.2, subd. (a); 54954.5, subd. (b).) Also, the City Council continues to resist any judicial direction not to discuss topics in closed sessions which go beyond instructions to its negotiators regarding purchase or sale price and terms of payment of specific real property. (§ 54956.8.)

Id. at 915.

> We believe that the trial court was justified in concluding that the City Council's conduct in pursuing its contentions that it may interpret and adjust the requirements of the Brown Act as it sees fit, in dealing with a particular project, clearly demonstrates that more than past violations have occurred or will reasonably probably occur in the immediate future. We conclude the Brown Act authorizes injunctive relief that is based on, in relevant part, a showing of "*past actions and violations that are related to present or future ones,*" and there was no abuse of discretion in the trial court's grant of injunctive relief against future such actions and violations.

Id. at 917 (emphasis in the original).

§ 1-7(g): Judicial Nullification

The Brown Act permits the court to set aside, as null and void, certain actions taken in violation of certain of its central requirements. This remedy is for the plaintiff who may have no complaints about the body's general practices or concerns about future violations, but who for whatever reason wants a particular action taken by the body reversed, or at least delayed to allow time for more public attention to the decision. Government Code Section 54960.1 states:

(a) The district attorney or any interested person may commence an action by mandamus or injunction for the purpose of obtaining a judicial determination that an action taken by a legislative body of a local agency in violation of Section 54953, 54954.2, 54954.5, 54954.6, 54956, or 54956.5 is null and void under this section. Nothing in this chapter shall be construed to prevent a legislative body from curing or correcting an action challenged pursuant to this section.

(b) Prior to any action being commenced pursuant to subdivision (a), the district attorney or interested person shall make a demand of the legislative body to cure or correct the Action alleged to have been taken in violation of Section 54953, 54954.2, 54954.5, 54954.6, 54956, or 54956.5. The demand shall be in writing and clearly describe the challenged action of the legislative body and nature of the alleged violation.

(c) (1) The written demand shall be

Bagley-Keene Comparison

Government Code §11130.3: (a) Any interested person may commence an action by mandamus, injunction, or declaratory relief for the purpose of obtaining a judicial determination that an action taken by a state body in violation of Section 11123 or 11125 is null and void under this section. Any action seeking such a judicial determination shall be commenced within 90 days from the date the Action was taken.

Nothing in this section shall be construed to prevent a state body from curing or correcting an action challenged pursuant to this section.

(b) An action shall not be determined to be null and void if any of the following conditions exist:

(1) The Action taken was in connection with the sale or issuance of notes, bonds, or other evidences of indebtedness or any contract, instrument, or agreement related thereto.

(2) The Action taken gave rise to a contractual obligation upon which a party

made within 90 days from the date the Action was taken unless the Action was taken in an open session but in violation of Section 54954.2, in which case the written demand shall be made within 30 days from the date the Action was taken.

has, in good faith, detrimentally relied.

(3) The Action taken was in substantial compliance with Sections 11123 and 11125.

(4) The Action taken was in connection with the collection of any tax.

(2) Within 30 days of receipt of the demand, the legislative body shall cure or correct the challenged action and inform the demanding party in writing of its actions to cure or correct or inform the demanding party in writing of its decision not to cure or correct the challenged action.

(3) If the legislative body takes no action within the 30-day period, the inaction shall be deemed a decision not to cure or correct the challenged action, and the 15-day period to commence the Action described in subdivision (a) shall commence to run the day after the 30-day period to cure or correct expires.

(4) Within 15 days of receipt of the written notice of the legislative body's decision to cure or correct, or not to cure or correct, or within 15 days of the expiration of the 30-day period to cure or correct, whichever is earlier, the demanding party shall be required to commence the Action pursuant to subdivision (a) or thereafter be barred from commencing the Action.

(d) An action taken that is alleged to have been taken in violation of Section 54953, 54954.2, 54954.5, 54954.6, 54956, or 54956.5 shall not be determined to be null and void if any of the following conditions exist:

(1) The Action taken was in substantial compliance with Sections 54953, 54954.2, 54954.5, 54954.6, 54956, and 54956.5.

(2) The Action taken was in connection with the sale or issuance of notes, bonds, or other evidences of indebtedness or any contract, instrument, or agreement thereto.

(3) The Action taken gave rise to a contractual obligation, including a contract let by competitive bid other than compensation for services in the form of salary or fees for professional services, upon which a party has, in good faith and without notice of challenge to the validity of the Action, detrimentally relied.

(4) The Action taken was in connection with the collection of any tax.

(5) Any person, city, city and county, county, district, or any agency or subdivision of the state alleging noncompliance with subdivision (a) of Section 54954.2, Section 54956, or Section 54956.5, because of any defect, error, irregularity, or omission in the notice given pursuant to those provisions, had actual notice of the item of business at least 72 hours prior to the meeting at which the Action was taken, if the meeting was noticed pursuant to Section 54954.2, or 24 hours prior to the meeting at which the Action was taken if the meeting was noticed pursuant to Section 54956, or prior to the meeting at which the Action was taken if the meeting is held pursuant to Section 54956.5.

(e) During any action seeking a judicial determination pursuant to subdivision (a) if the court determines, pursuant to a showing by the legislative body that an action alleged to have been taken in violation of Section 54953, 54954.2, 54954.5, 54954.6, 54956, or 54956.5 has been cured or corrected by a subsequent action of the legislative body, the Action filed pursuant to subdivision (a) shall be dismissed with prejudice.

(f) The fact that a legislative body takes a subsequent action to cure or correct an action taken pursuant to this section shall not be construed or admissible as evidence of a on of this chapter.

Actions Subject to Nullification

Nullification of actions taken in violation of the Act is not available for all possible violations. This remedy is reserved for secret or surprise actions, i.e. those unlawfully taken in:

• closed sessions or entirely secret meetings, serially or otherwise (§54953 (a));
• meetings by teleconference (§54953 (b));
• open sessions at regular meetings whose agenda failed adequately to provide notice of the Action (§54954.2);
• closed sessions whose agenda listing failed adequately to provide notice of the topic pursuant to the "safe harbor" format (§54954.5);
• special meetings whose posted notice failed to include the item acted on (§54956); or
• emergency meetings whose notice failed to include the item acted on (§54956.5).

Standing to Seek Nullification Based on Notice Defects

Paragraph (5) of subdivision (d) of Section 54960.1 in effect denies standing to bring a nullification action if it is based on some defect of meeting notice and if the plaintiff had actual knowledge, throughout the required notice period, that the action in question would be taken up at the meeting. That is, if the plaintiff became aware of the fact that an item would be proposed for action at least 72 hours before a regular meeting, 24 hours before a special meeting or sometime before an emergency meeting, he or she cannot complain that the action came as an unlawful surprise justifying nullification.

Demand Letter Required

The written demand for cure or correction, and its time frame for submittal, are strict prerequisites to an action for nullification. The demand must at a minimum alert the body as to which action must be cured or corrected and why—must "clearly describe the challenged action of the legislative body and nature of the alleged violation." Although this element is not mandated, to be effective it should also specify what the body is asked to do to cure or correct the alleged violation. For example, if the alleged violation was a surprise action, taken without adequate notice on the meeting agenda, the desirable correction might be to place the matter on the agenda of the next regular meeting or, depending on the urgency of the matter and the frequency of the body's meetings, at a special meeting in the interim, to rescind the Action previously taken, and to take no further action until the public has been given full opportunity to comment. If the allegation is that the body unlawfully took action in a closed session or secret meeting, the demand might be not only to rescind the action but to release to the public all documents prepared for, used in, or resulting from that closed session, including but not limited to minutes of the discussion.

June 7, 2004

Board of Education
Bonita Unified School District
115 W. Allen Avenue
San Dimas, CA 91773

Delivery by USPS Mail, by hand & by e-mail

Subjects: **Brown Act Demand for Correction (Gov't Code § 54950 et seq.)**
Request for Copies of Public Records (Gov't Code § 6250 et seq.)

Dear Board Members,

It has been brought to my attention that the Board, at its Regular Meeting of June 2, 2004, refused to allow members of the public to directly address the Board on matters within its jurisdiction; specifically, on the topic of retirement incentives.

This refusal to allow such public comment based on the content of that speech violates Gov't Code § 54954.3, Article 1 of the California Constitution, and the First Amendment to the Constitution of the United States of America.

Even more troubling is the report that Board President Latourelle cited a Board Policy forbidding public comment on items under negotiation.

Accordingly, I seek the following:

I. Pursuant to the California Public Records Act (GC § 6250 et seq.), I request a copy of the audio tape recording of the June 2, 2004 meeting, that is prepared and retained by the District.

II. Pursuant to Government Code § 54960, I demand the Board correct its violations by publicly stating it was wrong on June 2 in denying the opportunity to address the Board to any member of the public wishing to speak on any items of business within the subject matter jurisdiction of the Board, and by reassuring the public that such a denial of rights guaranteed to the people will not occur in the future.

Without such a public assurance within the next 20 days it will be reasonably assumed that the Board will continue in the future to deny members of the public the opportunity to address the Board on some items of business within its jurisdiction at its regular meetings, as it has in the past, in violation of the requirements of the Brown Act; and such lack of timely public assurance will serve as evidence that an "actual controversy" pursuant to CCP § 1060 exists between us.

Respectfully submitted for your actions as required by law,

Richard P. McKee

Demand Letter in *McKee v. Bonita Unified School District*. See plaintiff's court papers in this successful litigation online at http://www.calaware.org.

Timelines for Submitting the Demand and Filing the Action

The periods for submitting a demand for cure or correction and dealing with the response (or non-response) to it by filing the Action operate as an effective statute of limitations. When the violation was the failure adequately to provide notice on the agenda of an action taken in open session (§54954.2), the demand must be made within 30 days of that action. In all other cases the deadline is 90 days from the time the action was taken. The California Supreme Court has held, with reference to the comparable periods in the Bagley-Keene Act, that they may not be extended to accommodate, for example, violations discovered later. *Regents of the University of California v. Superior Court (Molloy)*, 20 Cal.4th 509 (1999).

The 15-day deadline for the plaintiff to file the nullification action in superior court begins to run either 30 days after the demand for cure or correction was received by the agency, if it has made no response during that period, or, if it has responded within that period (informing the plaintiff either that a cure or correction has been made, or that none will be made), 15 days from receipt of that response.

One case shows how strictly this framework may operate. In *Boyle v. City of Redondo Beach*, 70 Cal.App.4th 1109 (1999), the plaintiff sought judicial remedies for what he believed to be violations at two city council meetings held approximately six weeks apart. Both were special meetings at which the council held closed sessions on pending litigation, an item not listed in either meeting notice. (The litigation was a federal damages suit, also captioned *Boyle v. City of Redondo Beach*, that the plaintiff had earlier brought against the city for having been ousted from a prior council meeting by the mayor.) By the time of the second meeting, the plaintiff had made a demand for correction concerning the first, and had seen it rejected. Two days after the second meeting, the plaintiff filed an action in superior court concerning the first meeting. A few days later he sent the council a demand letter concerning the second meeting, which drew no reply by the end of the city's 30 day period for response. With a Brown Act lawsuit already pending, the plaintiff could have amended his original complaint at that point to allege the violation at the second meeting. But he missed his 15-day deadline to do so by a week and a day. The court held this tardiness fatal to his second cause of action for nullification of action taken at the second meeting.

"Action Taken" Read Narrowly

The complaint in a nullification action must allege that action was taken at the meeting in question; mere discussion will not suffice. *Centinela Hospital Association v. City of Inglewood*, 225 Cal.App.3d 1586 (1990). In *Boyle*, *supra*, the court cited this ruling in finding that the first challenged meeting involved no "action taken" within the meaning of the Brown Act, since "the minutes of the May 28, 1997, meeting reflects (sic) that the City Council did no more than confer with and give direction to staff." But since Boyle's complaint sought only injunctive relief and not nullification, it is not clear why the failure to allege "action taken" should have been fatal to that cause of action.

Nullification Precluded by Corrective Action

The *Boyle* court continued:

> Second, even if the addition of the Boyle litigation item to the agenda constituted an "action taken" that violated section 54956, the City Council corrected or cured that violation. Boyle filed his demand to cure or correct the violation (§ 54960.1, subd. (b)) on June 27, 1997. The City Council minutes reflect that on July 15, 1997, the City Council rescinded all action taken at the May 28, 1997, meeting in relation to the addition of the *Boyle v. City of Redondo Beach* item after the posting of the agenda. Thus the City Council timely cured any violation within the 30-day period of section 54960.1, subdivision (c)(2).

70 Cal.App.4th 1109 at 1118. In his amended complaint, Boyle attacked

Sequence of Events in Boyle case

May 28 First alleged violation: at a special meeting, council goes into closed session to address a litigation matter not referred to in the meeting notice.

June 27 Boyle alleges notice defect at May 28 meeting in **first demand for correction.**

July 2 **City rejects** Boyle's June 27 demand for correction.

July 15 Second alleged violation: at a special meeting, council adds to the agenda a closed session item to address litigation.

July 17 **Boyle files action** alleging violation at May 28 meeting; complaint seeks injunctive relief.

July 23 Council receives **second demand for correction**, alleging violation at July 15 meeting.

Aug. 22 30-day period elapses with no council response to **second demand.**

Aug. 23 15-day period commences for Boyle to file action on **second demand**.

Sept. 8 15-day period lapses for Boyle to file action on **second demand.**

Oct. 1 **Boyle files first amended complaint re May 28 meeting**, adding allegation of violation at July 15 meeting; nullification cause of action held barred by limitations period in (c) (3).

the corrective action of July 15 as itself unlawful, having been added to the agenda only at the meeting. Had the court not concluded that Boyle's attempt to have this action nullified was time-barred, it would have had to deal with the curious question of whether an action taken to correct a previous Brown Act violation can be nullified because it was accomplished in a manner that again violated the Act.

Timing of the Corrective Action

The defendant local agency is free to secure dismissal of a nullification action at any time during its pendency by making an adequate cure or correction, as provided in subdivision (e) of Section 54960.1. The correction response is not limited in its efficacy to the 30-day period after it receives the demand. In *Bell v. Vista Unified School District*, 82 Cal.App.4th 672 (2000), the plaintiff was a high school football coach who lost that assignment after the board of education considered complaints that he had violated a key rule of the California Interscholastic Federation. Because he had not been given the required 24-hour written notice of a closed session to consider "complaints and charges" against him, the plaintiff added a Brown Act cause of action to several others in his lawsuit for reinstatement and damages, alleging action taken in violation of the employee notice requirement in Section 54957 (see § 1-5(b)(4)). With the continuity of his coaching assignment at risk, he did not give the district 30 days to respond before filling his action seeking immediate relief from the board's action. But this failure to adhere to the statutory schedule, the court concluded, was not fatal to his Brown Act claim.

> Here, it is undisputed that Bell faxed the required demand letter to VUSD's counsel on the morning of October 23, 1997, specifically identifying the section 54957 violation and requesting it be corrected. However, the lawsuit was filed that afternoon. The TRO reinstating Bell immediately as head RBV football coach pending further hearing was issued the next day. Later, after the mandamus trial, the court ruled Bell's failure to file suit after the 30-day period to respond expired neither prejudiced VUSD nor barred his mandamus action. The court noted VUSD never objected to Bell's failure to so comply until its demurrer and answer, and had more than 222 days to cure the defects of its October 16, 1997 meeting and had elected not to do so.
>
> That Bell prematurely filed his action did not prejudice VUSD. VUSD was completely aware by his statutory demand to cure the alleged Brown Act violation of its precise nature. On receiving that notice, no obstacle prevented VUSD from pursuing a

> course of correction. The premature filing of the suit and the issuance of the TRO did not restrict or diminish VUSD's option to correct the alleged violation. In fact, the statutory scheme expressly anticipates curing post filing of an action in section 54960.1, subdivision (e). VUSD simply elected not to do so.
>
> Moreover, at the TRO hearing, VUSD did not object to the jurisdiction of the court or raise this procedural deficiency. Rather, without challenging jurisdiction by a series of stipulations, VUSD agreed to leave the TRO in effect until trial. It now asserts the trial court's TRO did not clearly identify whether it rested upon some substantive or procedural due process violation or simply the alleged Brown Act violation. However, the record on appeal shows VUSD's counsel was specifically advised by the trial court the TRO and request for a preliminary injunction would become moot should VUSD hold an open meeting at which the termination of Bell as coach were confirmed. VUSD knew the trial court granted the TRO upon finding a probable violation of the Brown Act by the Board and that the ruling could be overcome by compliance with the Act. We reiterate section 54960.1, subdivision (e) anticipates potential correction following filing of the mandamus action. VUSD has neither shown the court lacked jurisdiction to intervene nor abused its discretion in issuing the TRO under the circumstances.

Id. at 685.

Actions Immune from Nullification

Subdivision (d) of Section 54960.1 bars the nullification of several kinds of action, even if they are found to have been taken in violation of the Brown Act, namely:

• an action taken in substantial compliance with the provision that is alleged to have been violated. It seems unlikely, for example, that a court would void an action taken at a special meeting on the basis of defective notice if the written notice had been posted, the members of the body notified in writing 24 hours in advance in compliance with Section 54954.6, and the eligible local media alerted in time to publish or broadcast an announcement 24 hours in advance, simply because the media notice had been conveyed orally by telephone rather than in writing as the statute specifies.

• an action taken approving a contract on which the other party to the contract, unaware of the alleged violation, has relied in good faith and, for example, spent money or engaged subcontractors as a consequence. This protection for innocent third parties does not, however, apply to the approval of an employee's salary or a fee for professional services. In any event, a copy of any demand for a cure or correction of an action approving a contract should if possible be sent to the contractor involved.

• an action taken in connection with the collection of a tax, or with the sale or issuance of notes, bonds, debt instruments or related agreements.

§ 1-7(h): Discovery

One court has held that members of a legislative body may not be compelled in discovery to disclose discussions held in closed session—even where the purpose of the litigation is to establish that the closed session unlawfully included those discussions. In *Kleitman v. Superior Court*, 74 Cal.App.4th 1231 (1999), the plaintiff, Gary Wesley, brought an action for declaratory and injunctive relief, alleging that the Mountain View City Council had held a closed session on real property negotiations that involved a proposal not alluded to on the posted agenda. That agenda listed the both the property in question and the other negotiating party as "Chamber of Commerce," and the issue under negotiation as "Lease Terms." The chamber had been leasing a building in a city park as its office, but wanted to move to another site in the park when the current lease expired. That prospect was later considered and rejected by the council in an open and public session. Wesley's case alleged as violations the failure of the agenda to highlight that the council would be considering the chamber's desire for an alternate site in the park, and the discussion of that issue in closed session without having made a previous public policy decision to amend the existing lease.

Wesley, an attorney, served each council member defendants with 16 special interrogatories, the first six of which they objected to answering. Those queries asked for the names of any and all persons in the closed session, whether terms of the existing lease had been discussed, whether the prospect of leasing another park site had been discussed, for copies of documents considered, and for a full recounting of "everything that was said" about either the existing or an alternative lease. The council members' objections stated that the requested information was protected by the official information privilege in Evidence Code §1040 and by the Brown Act itself, in that the latter authorized a confidential discussion held to give instructions to the real property negotiator (Government Code §54956.8). They added that the public interest in confidentiality outweighed the public interest in disclosure. Wesley filed a motion to compel, taking issue with these rationales and contending that the stated confidentiality either did not apply to the demanded information or had been waived by subsequent public action. The trial court's order gave Wesley most of what he had sought among the six contested interrogatories, effectively requiring council members to disclose most of their recollections of the closed session at issue.

On a writ of mandate sought by the city, the California Court of Appeal for the Sixth District concluded that while the Brown Act "does not expressly provide that the proceedings of a closed session are confidential" (this was prior to the addition of Government Code §54963; see § 1-5(a)(1)), "confidentiality may be strongly inferred from the various provisions of the Act pertaining to the recording of closed sessions." The statute permits but does not require that a minute book (or tape recording) of closed session business be kept, and provides that if kept, the minutes or recording are not subject to public disclosure, but accessible only to a court in a Brown Act enforcement suit (Government Code §54957.2). Further, the statute allows a court to order tape recording of future closed sessions as one remedy for a proven unlawful discussion or action in closed session (Government Code §54960, subd. (b)), but in that instance permits access only to a transcript of such recordings and only in a subsequent enforcement action, based on carefully prescribed standards and procedures (Government Code §54960, subd. (c) (2)).

The court observed that these two limited instances of authorized disclosure of closed session documents for *in camera* review were unmatched by any requirement that members of the body disclose their recollections, and noted that the Attorney General had taken the position that members could not make such disclosures without permission of the bodies.

> We agree with the Attorney General. Disclosure of closed session proceedings by the members of a legislative body necessarily destroys the closed session confidentiality which is inherent in the Brown Act.
>
> Further, in contrast to its provisions with respect to disclosure of minute books and tape recordings, the Brown Act makes no provision for compelled disclosure of the personal recollections of members of a legislative body regarding unrecorded closed sessions upon allegation or proof of a Brown Act violation. We conclude that it would be improper to read such a provision into the Act where none exists. The rules of statutory construction provide that " `[u]nder the guise of construction, a court should not rewrite the law, add to it what has been omitted, omit from it what has been inserted, give it an effect beyond that gathered from the plain and direct import of the terms used, or read into it an exception, qualification, or modification that will nullify a clear provision or materially affect its operation so as to make it conform to a presumed intention not expressed or otherwise apparent in the law.' " (*Frazier v. City of Richmond* (1986) 184

> Cal.App.3d 1491, 1496 (quoting 58 Cal.Jur.3d, Statutes, §86, pp. 436- 437, fns. omitted).)
>
> Had the Legislature intended that members of a legislative body be required, upon court order, to disclose their personal recollections of unrecorded closed sessions during discovery in Brown Act litigation, we are confident that such intention would have been made express in the Act.

Id. at 334.

> ...Wesley's strongest argument is that he cannot prove that the City Council members violated the Act during their unrecorded closed session of March 25, 1997, unless the council members are compelled to answer his special interrogatories. However, as we have discussed, the Act does not authorize such discovery. It does not require legislative bodies to record their closed sessions, absent court order, and provides strong protections to any minute books and tape recordings which are kept. A trial court is authorized by the Act to compel disclosure of these items only in two situations, in order to protect the confidentiality of closed sessions. Where, as here, no minute book or tape recordings are available, no disclosure of closed session proceedings can be compelled by the trial court. Therefore, respondent court abused its discretion by exceeding its legal authority when it granted Wesley's discovery motion and ordered the City Council defendants to answer special interrogatory questions about their personal recollections of unrecorded closed session proceedings.

Id. at 335.

Effect of Whistleblower Protections

Subsequent to *Kleitman* the Brown Act was amended to add Government Code §54963, which expressly makes closed session discussions confidential and authorizes various sanctions for leaks, but also immunizes members or employees present in the closed session who make

> a confidential inquiry or complaint to a district attorney or grand jury concerning a perceived violation of law, including disclosing facts to a district attorney or grand jury that are necessary to establish the illegality of an action taken by a legislative body of a local agency or the potential illegality of an action that has been the subject of deliberation at a closed session if that action were to be taken by a legislative body of a local agency.

Accordingly, while a member of a legislative body cannot under *Kleitman* be *compelled* to respond to discovery probing by disclosing recollections of closed session discussions, nothing prevents that member from voluntarily making such disclosures to a district attorney or grand jury if the member perceives them to be evidence of a Brown Act violation.

§ 1-7(i): Fee and Cost Recovery

The Brown Act gives the court discretion to order a defendant public agency to pay the court costs and attorney's fees incurred by a prevailing plaintiff in an enforcement action, and on the other hand to award the agency reciprocally if it prevails, but only on a finding that the Action was not only meritless but frivolous. Government Code §54960.5 states:

> A court may award court costs and reasonable attorney fees to the plaintiff in an action brought pursuant to Section 54960 or 54960.1 where it is found that a legislative body of the local agency has violated this chapter. The costs and fees shall be paid by the local agency and shall not become a personal liability of any public officer or employee of the local agency.
>
> A court may award court costs and reasonable attorney fees to a defendant in any action brought pursuant to Section 54960 or 54960.1 where the defendant has prevailed in a final determination of such action and the court finds that the Action was clearly frivolous and totally lacking in merit.

Bagley-Keene Comparison
Government Code §11130.5: A court may award court costs and reasonable attorney's fees to the plaintiff in an action brought pursuant to Section 11130 or 11130.3 where it is found that a state body has violated the provisions of this article. The costs and fees shall be paid by the state body and shall not become a personal liability of any public officer or employee thereof.

A court may award court costs and reasonable attorney's fees to a defendant in any action brought pursuant to Section 11130 or 11130.3 where the defendant has prevailed in a final determination of the Action and the court finds that the Action was clearly frivolous and totally lacking in merit.

Denial of Fees to Prevailing Plaintiff

While the court has discretion whether or not to award fees to the prevailing plaintiff, a court has held that denial is proper "only if the defendant shows that special circumstances exist that would make such an award unjust." *Los Angeles Times Communications v. Board of Supervisors*, 112 Cal.App.4th 1313 (2003). The newspaper had obtained a declaratory judgment finding that the board had committed three out of a claimed total of seven violations of the open meeting law. But the trial court, citing standards applied in a federal civil rights case from the Ninth Circuit, *Aho v. Clark*, 608 F.2d 365 (1979), and two successive Brown Act fee cases, *Common Cause v. Stirling*, 119 Cal.App.3d 658 (1981) (*Common Cause I*) and *Common Cause v. Stirling*, 147 Cal.App.3d 518 (1983) (*Common Cause II*), concluded that an award of fees to the Times would be unjustified because the litigation had been unnecessary, there was insufficient public injury, and the newspaper had "plenty of incentive, other than attorneys' fees, to bring this action." The

Court of Appeal disagreed, reversing the order denying fees and ordering the trial court to hold a hearing on the proper level of fees to be awarded. The events that prompted the lawsuit were, in the words of the opinion, as follows:

> In December 2001, County health care aides were backing a ballot measure to increase their pay (the health care or ballot measure). On December 18, 2001, the Board met in closed session with County Counsel Lloyd W. Pellman to discuss whether the County should sue to keep that measure off the ballot. The matter had been placed on the agenda as a closed session item under the Brown Act's exception for an agency's decision whether to initiate litigation. (§ 54956.9, subd. (c).) Because the merits of the proposed suit were unclear, Pellman floated the idea of provoking the health care aides to sue the County by refusing to submit the required ballot title and summary to the Registrar of Voters (Elec. Code, § 9105, subd. (a)), thereby keeping the measure off the ballot. Four of the five supervisors present agreed and instructed Pellman to send a letter to the ballot measure's proponents stating that Pellman would not place the measure on the ballot. Pellman changed his mind the next day - December 19 - however, and phoned three of the supervisors to let them know he had decided to comply with the law and place the measure on the ballot.
>
> The Board scheduled a closed session for January 4, 2002, under the Brown Act's exceptions for employee evaluations (§ 54957) and for conferences with legal counsel regarding exposure to litigation. (§ 54956.9, subd. (b).) In advance of that session, which was apparently prompted by concerns over Pellman's December 19 phone calls to three Board members, Supervisor Gloria Molina sent a letter to the other Board members on January 3, 2002, regarding the "violation of process that took place and [Pellman's] ability to represent our Board and our respective constituents in a fair and unbiased manner." According to Molina's letter, Pellman's phone calls to the other Board members on December 19, 2001, violated the Brown Act. Another closed session was scheduled for January 8, 2002, based on the Brown Act's employee evaluation exception. At both the January 4 and January 8 closed sessions, however, the Board also instructed its administrative officers to develop new protocols for closed sessions.
>
> Based on Molina's concerns that Pellman's December 19 phone calls violated the Brown Act, the Board adopted new closed session protocols at a public Board meeting on February 5,

> 2002. Under those new protocols, any decision to consider a matter during a closed session had to be made by the Board's chairperson, who would approve or deny the request based upon the County Counsel's advice concerning the applicability of the Brown Act. The new protocols also directed that minutes of any closed session actions be kept, but that no minutes or sound recordings be made of the closed session discussions.

Id. at 1317. The appellate court found that these circumstances undercut the trial court's conclusion that litigation had been unnecessary.

> Critical to the trial court's order was its finding that the Board remedied its Brown Act violations when Pellman shifted gears on December 19 and when the Board adopted new Brown Act protocols before appellants sued. Based on this, the trial court concluded that no repeat violations were likely and that the Action was unnecessary and conferred an insufficient public benefit to justify an award of fees. We disagree with the trial court both factually and legally.
>
> First, Pellman's change of heart the day after the Board voted to have him violate state election laws was not based on his belief that a Brown Act violation occurred on December 18. Neither was Supervisor Molina's initiation of new Brown Act procedures on January 4 and 8. Instead, as the Board's records show, it was prompted by Molina's belief that the Brown Act had been violated on December 19 when Pellman phoned three Board members to discuss his decision to comply with the election laws.
>
> Nor did the Board's later adoption of new Brown Act protocols remedy the situation. At the time suit was filed on March 29, 2002, the Board had initially adopted a new protocol which barred the taking of discussion minutes or the tape recording of closed sessions. The new protocols also left it to the Board chairperson, acting on the advice of county counsel, to decide whether a matter was properly slated for closed session under the Brown Act. However, County Counsel Pellman was then demanding the return of the documents that were accidentally disclosed to the Times while insisting that no Brown Act violations occurred. Based on this, appellants could properly conclude that their action was necessary because: (1) the Board had now made it impossible to learn what happened during a closed session by barring the taking of discussion minutes or audiotapes during closed sessions; and (2) given Pellman's insistence that no Brown Act violation occurred, along with his attempts to have the Times return the

> wayward documents and the Board's stated intention to rely on county counsel's advice when determining whether a matter could be discussed in closed session, there was a real possibility that the same violations might reoccur.
>
> Although the Board's subsequent April 2, 2002, vote permitted the taping of closed sessions and made other improvements in the Board's Brown Act procedures, that action was taken after suit was filed. On May 8, 2002, Pellman submitted to the Board a comprehensive memo on the proposed new protocols. … Even if the Board's actions after appellants sued somehow related back to the Board agenda posted the day before suit was filed, the final version of its Brown Act protocols was deficient because it still relied on Pellman's advice to determine whether the Brown Act applied. As noted, Pellman continued to maintain that no Brown Act violations occurred, sought the return of documents showing the December 18 Brown Act violation, defended this action in part on the basis that without those documents there was no proof of a violation, and tried to keep under seal the January 4 and 8 minutes which ultimately established that violations occurred on those dates. Ultimately it required a trial to disclose all the documents and determine that the Board violated the Brown Act three times.

Id. at 1330. Likewise, the appellate court found that contrary to the view of the trial court, the litigation had resulted in a significant public benefit.

> We disagree with the trial court that the net result of this litigation conferred insufficient public benefit because there was no injury apart from the three violations themselves. As discussed earlier, the litigation was necessary to uncover the January 4 and 8 violations. The trial court found those violations insignificant because they initiated an overhaul of the Board's Brown Act compliance procedures. We believe the trial court overlooked the timing and context of those two meetings, which occurred before any public disclosure of the events of December 18, 2001. Their purpose was to rectify a different perceived Brown Act violation and led to the adoption of new protocols in February that included a ban on discussion minutes or audiotapes of closed sessions. It was only after the events of December 18 became public that the Board undertook the further revisions of its Brown Act protocols. We also find the court's reasoning unpersuasive because, as discussed earlier, those changes did not address the December 18 violation and, given the Board's continued resistance to appel-

> lants' assertions, left open the possibility that the same violation could recur. Finally, we reject the notion that it was somehow proper to violate the Brown Act in order to save the Brown Act.
>
> Even though appellants lost on four of their causes of action and did not obtain injunctive or writ relief, the Brown Act expressly permits actions to "determine the applicability" of the Act. (§ 54960, subd. (a).) As a result of their petition, appellants also obtained a declaration that the Board's actions on December 18, 2001, were illegal, thus clarifying the scope of the Brown Act's initiation of litigation exception. To paraphrase the Common Cause II court, this action was brought to judicially determine the scope of that exception and, absent appellants' lawsuit, neither they nor any other person could be assured that further such Brown Act violations would not occur. ... We therefore believe that denying appellants their attorneys fees would be contrary to the legislative purpose behind section 54960.5. (*Common Cause I, supra*, 119 Cal.App.3d at p. 663 [the purpose of section 54960.5 was to "encourage private enforcement because lack of judicial interpretation hampered the Act's effectiveness . . . "

Id. at 1332. The appellate court also found, based on federal and state precedents, that "the Board's supposed good faith in defending its action" did not justify denial of the plaintiff's attorney's fees. Lastly, the court rejected the notion that the Times "had plenty of incentive, other than attorneys' fees, to bring this action" argued against an award of fees, since the fees were not needed to attract competent counsel.

> The trial court's reliance on this factor was misplaced for two reasons. First, the rule applies to plaintiffs who sue for money damages and are represented by private counsel retained under a contingent fee agreement. ... Because appellants hired private counsel on an hourly rate basis in order to obtain declaratory and other non-monetary relief, that rule is plainly inapplicable. Second, later cases have made clear that a plaintiff's ability or inability to pay private counsel are not special circumstances that would justify denying a fee award in civil rights cases. ...
>
> We think the rule is a good one and should apply to the Brown Act. Given the strong public policy behind that act and the need to spur private enforcement through an award of attorneys fees (*Common Cause I, supra*, 119 Cal.App.3d at p. 663) we see no reason to distinguish between a well-funded major metropolitan newspaper and those with fewer resources. Even the well-heeled should be encouraged to enforce the Brown Act for the

> public's benefit with full assurance that, absent special circumstances, they, too, will recover their attorneys fees.

Id. at 1334.

Fee Award Based on Market Rates

In *International Longshoremen's and Warehousemen's Union v. Los Angeles Export Terminal, Inc.*, 69 Cal.App.4th 1219 (1999) the court upheld the trial court's use of market rates for comparable attorney services, as opposed to the fee range the plaintiff actually paid its counsel, as an appropriate "touchstone" for the plaintiff's fee recovery.

> LAXT contends the $60,660 attorney fees award to ILWU is excessive. The record reflects ILWU paid its attorneys an hourly rate of $125 per hour and later, $140 per hour. However, in moving for attorney fees, ILWU requested reasonable attorney fees based on market rates, which ranged from $125 per hour to $275 per hour for the attorneys who worked on this matter. LAXT contends the trial court erred in awarding fees in excess of those actually charged by ILWU's counsel. The argument fails.
>
> In *Serrano v. Unruh* (1982) 32 Cal.3d 621, 642, which involved a claim for attorney fees under Code of Civil Procedure 1021.5, the private Attorney General statute, our Supreme Court cited with approval the view of the First Circuit, which earlier held: " `We do not think . . . that compensating a public interest organization . . . on the same basis as a private practitioner results in . . . a windfall. Indeed, we are concerned that compensation at a lesser rate would result in a windfall to the defendants.' …" *Serrano* concluded "[s]ervices compensable under section 1021.5 are computed from their reasonable market value. The trial court was entitled to use the prevailing billing rates of comparable private attorneys as the `touchstone' for determination of that value. Cost figures bore no reasonable relevance to calculation of the `touchstone' figure."
>
> The private Attorney General statute is analogous to the Brown Act's attorney fees provision in that both authorize compensation for private actions which serve to vindicate important rights affecting the public interest. (*Serrano*, supra, 32 Cal.3d at p. 632; *Common Cause*, supra, 147 Cal.App.3d at p. 524.) In *Common Cause*, a case involving attorney fees under the Brown Act, the court was guided, inter alia, by decisions involving fees under the private Attorney General theory. … Therefore, the rationale for basing an award of attorney fees on reasonable market value is

> equally applicable to section 54960.5. Accordingly, the trial court was not required to base the attorney fees award on the fees actually incurred by ILWU.

Id. at 302.

Apportionment among Multiple Causes of Action

In *Bell v. Vista Unified School District,* 82 Cal.App.4th 672 (2000), a high school athletic coach who had been relieved of his position for having violated rules of the California Interscholastic Federation sued the district on a variety of grounds, including the school board's failure to give him 24-hour written advance notice that the complaints and charges against him would be deliberated in a closed session. The trial court, in a telephonic ruling, nullified the board's decision on Brown Act grounds and ordered the district to pay the plaintiff more than $157,000 in attorney's fees and costs. The tort causes of action were settled during a subsequent trial. On appeal, the district among other things challenged the attorney fee and cost award on the basis that the court had not apportioned it among the Brown Act and other causes of action. The appellate court found this argument compelling. Under either the Brown Act or Code of Civil Procedure §1021.5, the court observed, a fee award was due only if the litigation resulted in the enforcement of an important right affecting the public interest. In ordering the trial court to recalculate the award, the appellate court concluded:

> Even if Bell conferred a significant benefit on the general public by protecting its interest in having access to VUSD meetings, reaffirming procedural due process protections, exposing serious problems at (the high school) and protecting the rights of his fellow employees, the primary focus of his litigation was personal, that is his reinstatement and quest for compensatory damages. In this context, the Brown Act violation was simply incidental to his personal and pecuniary interests in the matter. To render apportionment moot, he must establish the cost of his victory transcended his personal interests such that the necessity for pursuing the lawsuit placed a burden on him out of proportion to his individual stake in the matter. However, he was statutorily entitled to attorney fees and costs arising from the Brown Act violation under section 54960.5. He had a financial incentive in bringing the lawsuit. His litigation goal was always to obtain reinstatement and compensatory damages. He accomplished that goal by being reinstated, having the discipline rescinded and later recovering more than $125,000 in settlement. Consequently, this is not a case

> where Bell has shown his expenses in bringing the suit are disproportionate to his personal stake in the outcome of litigation, but rather one where the enforcement of the public interest is merely incidental to the obtaining of personal goals.

Id. at 691.

Allowable Costs

As to costs, the court ruled for the defendant district on the issue of which costs were allowable and how they should be apportioned.

> Finally, VUSD challenges the trial court's award of costs, asserting that approximately $4,200 of them are either explicitly or impliedly prohibited by Code of Civil Procedure section 1033.5 (i.e., photocopy, postage, telephone, facsimile and "attorney services" charges). Additionally, it challenges the costs incurred for depositions of persons unrelated to the Brown Act issue. Where a statute authorizes an award of fees and costs, but is silent as to which costs are to be awarded, Code of Civil Procedure section 1033.5 provides the courts with guidance as to those costs that may or may not be recovered in a civil action. (See *Davis v. KGO-T.V.*, Inc. (1998) 17 Cal.4th 436, 441-445; *Page v. Something Weird Video* (C.D.Cal 1996) 960 F.Supp. 1438, 1447.) Bell has not offered any reason nor can we perceive of one why that statutory guidance should not govern here under the circumstances. Accordingly, on remand, the trial court is directed to award only allowable costs after reasonable apportionment.

Ibid.

Award to Defendants Requires Written Findings

In *Boyle v. City of Redondo Beach,* 70 Cal.App.4th 1109 (1999) the court reversed a trial court order awarding the prevailing city defendants their attorneys' fees because there were no findings supporting the conclusion that the plaintiff's case was "clearly frivolous and totally lacking in merit." While the Brown Act does not expressly require written findings on the record, the court observed, these requirements are imposed as a matter of due process.

> Although it does not use the word "sanctions," the second paragraph of section 54960.5 imposes a monetary penalty as a sanction against a plaintiff who has brought an action that is not only "totally" meritless but which is also "clearly frivolous." The

> imposition of sanctions always requires procedural due process... This includes "a requirement that the person being sanctioned be told what conduct or circumstances justified the imposition of sanctions." ... Besides satisfying due process, the requirement that a court specify the circumstances justifying sanctions also enables the reviewing court to determine whether the award abused the trial court's discretion. ... "Fairness and effective appellate review require that where the court exercises its discretion to issue sanctions, it delineate the specific acts upon which the sanctions are awarded." ...
>
> For these reasons, other courts have read this requirement into statutes or rules of court which do not expressly contain it. ... Given the important public purposes underlying the Brown Act, the requirements of due process, and the need to make a record for appellate review, we conclude that pursuant to section 54960.5, a trial court must specify with particularity the basis for the awarding costs or attorney fees. The trial court must set forth the factual basis for the award either in a formal order, a minute order, or in the reporter's transcript of the hearing on the motion. ... We therefore reverse the order awarding attorney fees in favor of the City of Redondo Beach and remand for the trial court to re-enter its order with adequate justification in a manner consistent with this opinion.

Id. at 1120.

§ 1-7(j): Issues on Appeal

Mootness

In *McKee v. Orange Unified School District*, 110 Cal.App.4th 1310 (2003) the court held that the defendant's sale of the property concerning which the plaintiff had challenged its use of closed sessions did not moot the challenge. The trial court, after a hearing, had denied the plaintiff's petition on the basis that he, as a non-resident of the district, lacked standing (see § 1-7(b), *Standing of Non-residents*). The appellate court observed:

> Three months after McKee filed his notice of appeal, the board voted to sell Barham Ranch and entered into an acquisition agreement with the County. OUSD filed a motion to dismiss this appeal on the ground McKee's claims of Brown Act violations are moot because of the sale of Barham Ranch. OUSD contends any complaint about the sufficiency of agenda descriptions for discussion relating to OUSD obtaining an access easement for Barham

> Ranch over County property is moot because the sale eliminated the need for an access easement. This court ordered the motion to dismiss be considered in conjunction with the decision on appeal ... This case does not present a situation where a ruling by this court can neither have any practical impact nor provide the parties relief.
>
> McKee's motion sought, *inter alia*, an order establishing procedures for the board's meetings, geared to prevent violations of the Brown Act by, for example, requiring the board to tape-record all future closed sessions for three years, and take discussion and action only on those items of business adequately described in a regular meeting agenda or a special meeting notice. McKee's motion also sought a declaration that OUSD and the board are required to, inter alia, discuss and act only on those items of business adequately described on a regular meeting agenda or a special meeting notice.
>
> OUSD's sale of Barham Ranch does not render the above requested relief unavailable and therefore does not render this appeal moot.

Id. at 1315.

Standard of Review for Injunctions

In *Shapiro v San Diego City Council*, 96 Cal.App.4th 904 (2002), the court stated:

> The trial court's decision to grant a permanent injunction rests within its sound discretion and will not be disturbed on appeal absent a showing of a clear abuse of discretion. (*San Diego Union v. City Council* (1983) 146 Cal.App.3d 947, 952.) Such continuing relief by injunction operates in the future. (*Ibid.*) A reviewing court will exercise its independent judgment when it is required to interpret and apply a statute where the underlying facts are not in dispute. (*Ibid.*)
>
> However, to the extent the trial court had to review the evidence to resolve disputed factual issues, and draw inferences from the presented facts, an appellate court will review such factual findings under a substantial evidence standard. Our power in this regard "*begins* and *ends* with the determination as to whether there is any substantial evidence, contradicted or uncontradicted, which will support the finding of fact. [Citations.] [¶] When two or more inferences can reasonably be deduced from the facts, a reviewing court is without power to substitute its deductions for

> those of the trial court." (*Green Trees Enterprises, Inc. v. Palm Springs Alpine Estates, Inc.* (1967) 66 Cal.2d 782, 784-785.)

Id. at 912.

Nullification Not Considered for First Time on Appeal

In *County of Del Norte v. City of Crescent City*, 71 Cal.App.4th 965 (1999) the plaintiff county was challenging the validity of a policy adopted by the defendant city that it would no longer allow new utility connections outside its incorporated territory. For the first time on appeal, the county added a Brown Act theory to its attack, contending that the notice of special meeting to consider the policy's adoption was fatally inadequate and misleading and warranted nullification. The court stated:

> The County did not mention the Brown Act in any of its pleadings or papers: not in the petition/complaint, the ex parte application or the points and authorities in reply to the City's opposition. It did not seek a ruling on the purported Brown Act violation. As a general matter a party must adhere on appeal to the theory on which the matter was tried. (*Ernst v. Searle* (1933) 218 Cal. 233, 240-241; *Mattco Forge, Inc. v. Arthur Young & Co.* (1997) 52 Cal.App.4th 820, 847.) Thus we will not entertain a new theory on appeal unless it presents purely a legal question, on an uncontroverted record requiring no factual determinations. (*Mattco Forge*, supra, at p. 847.) And even then, to do so is within our discretion. (*Resolution Trust Corp. v. Winslow* (1992) 9 Cal.App.4th 1799, 1810.)
>
> We will not consider the County's Brown Act theory. First, the County has not produced evidence of any demand to cure or correct. Second, the petition/complaint was filed outside the time frame for commencing an action under Government Code section 54960.1. Third, the issue of substantial compliance requires a factual determination. In short, the County has absolutely no basis for pursuing a Brown Act argument on this appeal.

Id. at 978.

§ 1-8: Full Text of the Brown Act

The following display of all of Government Code §§54950-54963 in sequence also provides **(See)** references to sections of this chapter where each provision is discussed.

54950. In enacting this chapter, the Legislature finds and declares that the public commissions, boards and councils and the other public agencies in this State exist to aid in the conduct of the people's business. It is the intent of the law that their actions betaken openly and that their deliberations be conducted openly. The people of this State do not yield their sovereignty to the agencies which serve them. The people, in delegating authority, donor give their public servants the right to decide what is good forth people to know and what is not good for them to know. The people insist on remaining informed so that they may retain control over the instruments they have created.
(See § 1-1(c))

54950.5. This chapter shall be known as the Ralph M. Brown Act.

54951. As used in this chapter, "local agency" means a county, city, whether general law or chartered, city and county, town, school district, municipal corporation, district, political subdivision, or any board, commission or agency thereof, or other local public agency.
(See § 1-2(a))

54952. As used in this chapter, "legislative body" means: (a) The governing body of a local agency or any other local body created by state or federal statute.

(b) A commission, committee, board, or other body of a local agency, whether permanent or temporary, decision-making or advisory, created by charter, ordinance, resolution, or formal action of legislative body. However, advisory committees, composed solely of the members of the legislative body that are less than a quorum of the legislative body are not legislative bodies, except that standing committees of a legislative body, irrespective of their composition, which have a continuing subject matter jurisdiction, or a meeting schedule fixed by charter, ordinance, resolution, or formal action oaf legislative body are legislative bodies for purposes of this chapter.

(c) (1) A board, commission, committee, or other multimember body that governs a private corporation, limited liability company, or other entity that either:

(A) Is created by the elected legislative body in order to exercise authority that may lawfully be delegated by the elected governing body to a private corporation, limited liability company, or other entity.

(B) Receives funds from a local agency and the membership of whose governing body includes a member of the legislative body of the local agency appointed to that governing body as a full voting member by the legislative body of the local agency.

(2) Notwithstanding subparagraph (B) of paragraph (1), no board, commission, committee, or other multimember body that governs private corporation, limited liability company, or other entity that receives funds from a local agency and, as of February 9, 1996, has member of the legislative body of the local agency as a full voting member of the governing body of that private corporation, limited liability company, or other entity shall be relieved from the public meeting requirements of this chapter by virtue of a change in status of the full voting member to a nonvoting member.

(d) The lessee of any hospital the whole or part of which is first leased pursuant to subdivision (p) of Section 32121 of the Health and Safety Code after January 1, 1994, where the lessee exercises any material authority of a legislative body of a local agency delegated to it by that legislative body whether the lessee is organized and operated by the local agency or by a delegated authority.
(See § 1-2(b))

54952.1. Any person elected to serve as a member of a legislative body who has not yet assumed the duties of office shall conform his or her conduct to the requirements of this chapter and shall be treated for purposes of enforcement of this chapter as if he or she has already assumed office.

(See § 1-2(c))

54952.2. (a) As used in this chapter, "meeting" includes any congregation of a majority of the members of a legislative body at the same time and place to hear, discuss, or deliberate upon any item that is within the subject matter jurisdiction of the legislative body or the local agency to which it pertains.

(b) Except as authorized pursuant to Section 54953, any use of direct communication, personal intermediaries, or technological devices that is employed by a majority of the members of the legislative body to develop a collective concurrence as to action tube taken on an item by the members of the legislative body is prohibited.

(c) Nothing in this section shall impose the requirements of this chapter upon any of the following:

(1) Individual contacts or conversations between a member of legislative body and any other person.

(2) The attendance of a majority of the members of a legislative body at a conference or similar gathering open to the public that involves a discussion of issues of general interest to the public onto public agencies of the type represented by the legislative body, provided that a majority of the members do not discuss among themselves, other than as part of the scheduled program, business oaf specified nature that is within the subject matter jurisdiction of the local agency. Nothing in this paragraph is intended to allow members of the public free admission to a conference or similar gathering at which the organizers have required other participants or registrants to pay fees or charges as a condition of attendance.

(3) The attendance of a majority of the members of a legislative body at an open and publicized meeting organized to address a topic of local community concern by a person or organization other than the local agency, provided that a majority of the members do not discuss among themselves, other than as part of the scheduled program, business of a specific nature that is within the subject matter jurisdiction of the legislative body of the local agency.

(4) The attendance of a majority of the members of a legislative body at an open and noticed meeting of another body of the local agency, or at an open and noticed meeting of a legislative body of another local agency, provided that a majority of the members do not discuss among themselves, other than as part of the scheduled meeting, business of a specific nature that is within the subject matter jurisdiction of the legislative body of the local agency.

(5) The attendance of a majority of the members of a legislative body at a purely social or ceremonial occasion, provided that majority of the members do not discuss among themselves business of specific nature that is within the subject matter jurisdiction of the legislative body of the local agency.

(6) The attendance of a majority of the members of a legislative body at an open and noticed meeting of a standing committee of that body, provided that the members of the legislative body who are nonmembers of the standing committee attend only as observers.

(See § 1-2(d))

54952.6. As used in this chapter, "action taken" means a collective decision made by a majority of the members of a legislative body, collective commitment or promise by a majority of the members of legislative body to make a positive or a negative decision, or an actual vote by a majority of the members of a legislative body when sitting as a body or entity, upon a motion, proposal, resolution, order or ordinance.

(See § 1-2(e))

54952.7. A legislative body of a local agency may require that copy of this chapter be given to each member of the legislative body and any person elected to serve as a member of the legislative body who has not assumed the duties of office. An elected legislative body of a local agency may require that a copy of this chapter be given to each member of each legislative body all or a majority of whose members are appointed by or under the authority of the elected legislative body.

(See § 1-7(a))

54953. (a) All meetings of the legislative body of a local agency shall be open and public, and all persons shall be permitted to attend any meeting of the legislative body of a local agency, excepts otherwise provided in this chapter.

(See § 1-3(d))

(b) (1) Notwithstanding any other provision of law, the legislative body of a local agency may use teleconferencing for the benefit of the public and the legislative body of a local agency in connection with any meeting or proceeding authorized by law. The teleconferenced meeting or proceeding shall comply with all requirements of this chapter and all otherwise applicable provisions of law relating to a specific type of meeting or proceeding.

(2) Teleconferencing, as authorized by this section, may be used for all purposes in connection with any meeting within the subject matter jurisdiction of the legislative body. All votes taken during teleconferenced meeting shall be by roll call.

(3) If the legislative body of a local agency elects to use teleconferencing, it shall post agendas at all teleconference locations and conduct teleconference meetings in a manner that protects the statutory and constitutional rights of the parties or the public appearing before the legislative body of a local agency. Each teleconference location shall be identified in the notice and agenda of the meeting or proceeding, and each teleconference location shall be accessible to the public. During the teleconference, at least a quorum of the members of the legislative body shall participate from locations within the boundaries of the territory over which the local agency exercises jurisdiction. The agenda shall provide an opportunity for members of the public to address the legislative body directly pursuant to Section 54954.3 at each teleconference location.

(4) For the purposes of this section, "teleconference" means meeting of a legislative body, the members of which are in different locations, connected by electronic means, through either audio or video, or both. Nothing in this section shall prohibit a local agency from providing the public with additional teleconference locations.

(See § 1-3(c))

(c) No legislative body shall take action by secret ballot, whether preliminary or final.

(See § 1-3(d))

54953.1. The provisions of this chapter shall not be construed to prohibit the members of the legislative body of a local agency from giving testimony in private before a grand jury, either as individuals or as a body.

(See § 1-3(d))

54953.2. All meetings of a legislative body of a local agency that are open and public shall meet the protections and prohibitions contained in Section 202 of the Americans with Disabilities Act of 1990 (42 U.S.C. Sec. 12132), and the federal rules and regulations adopted in implementation thereof.

(See § 1-3(b))

54953.3. A member of the public shall not be required, as condition to attendance at a meeting of a legislative body of a local agency, to register his or her name, to provide other information, to complete a questionnaire, or otherwise to fulfill any condition precedent to his or her attendance. If an attendance list, register, questionnaire, or other similar document is posted at or near the entrance to the room where the meeting is to be held, or is circulated to the persons present during the meeting, it shall state clearly that the signing, registering, or completion of the document is voluntary, and that all persons may attend the meeting regardless of whether a person signs, registers, or completes the document.

(See § 1-4(b))

54953.5. (a) Any person attending an open and public meeting of legislative body of a local agency shall have the right to record the proceedings with an audio or video tape recorder or a still or motion picture camera in the absence of a reasonable finding by the legislative body of the local agency that the recording cannot continue without noise, illumination, or obstruction of view that constitutes, or would constitute, a persistent disruption of the proceedings.

(b) Any tape or film record of an open and public meeting made for whatever purpose by or at the direction of the local agency shall be subject to inspection pursuant to the California Public Records Act(Chapter 3.5 (commencing with Section 6250) of Division 7 of Title 1), but, notwithstanding Section 34090, may be erased or destroyed 30 days after the taping or recording. Any inspection of a video or tape recording shall be provided without charge on a video or tape player made available by the local agency.

(See § 1-4(d), (e))

54953.6. No legislative body of a local agency shall prohibit or otherwise restrict the broadcast of its open and public meetings in the absence of a reasonable finding that the broadcast cannot be accomplished without noise, illumination, or obstruction of view that would constitute a persistent disruption of the proceedings.

(See § 1-4(d))

54953.7. Notwithstanding any other provision of law, legislative bodies of local agencies may impose requirements upon themselves which allow greater access to their meetings than prescribed by the minimal standards set forth in this chapter. In addition thereto, unelected legislative body of a local agency may impose such requirements on those appointed legislative bodies of the local agency of which all or a majority of the members are appointed by rounder the authority of the elected legislative body.

(See §§ 1-1(d, 6-1))

54954. (a) Each legislative body of a local agency, except for advisory committees or standing committees, shall provide, by ordinance, resolution, bylaws, or by whatever other rule is required for the conduct of business by that body, the time and place for holding regular meetings. Meetings of advisory committees or standing committees, for which an agenda is posted at least 72 hours in advance of the meeting pursuant to subdivision (a) of Section 54954.2, shall be considered for purposes of this chapter as regular meetings of the legislative body.

(See § 1-3(e))

(b) Regular and special meetings of the legislative body shall beheld within the boundaries of the territory over which the local agency exercises jurisdiction, except to do any of the following:

(1) Comply with state or federal law or court order, or attend judicial or administrative proceeding to which the local agency is apart.

(2) Inspect real or personal property which cannot be conveniently brought within the boundaries of the territory over which the local agency exercises jurisdiction provided that the topic of the meetings limited to items directly related to the real or personal property.

(3) Participate in meetings or discussions of multiagency significance that are outside the boundaries of a local agency's jurisdiction. However, any meeting or discussion held pursuant to this subdivision shall take place within the jurisdiction of one of the participating local agencies and be noticed by all participating agencies as provided for in this chapter.

(4) Meet in the closest meeting facility if the local agency has no meeting facility within the boundaries of the territory over which the local agency exercises jurisdiction, or at the principal office of the local agency if that office is located outside the territory over which the agency exercises jurisdiction.

(5) Meet outside their immediate jurisdiction with elected or appointed officials of the United States or the State of California when a local meeting would be impractical, solely to discuss legislative or regulatory issue affecting the local agency and over which the federal or state officials have jurisdiction.

(6) Meet outside their immediate jurisdiction if the meeting takes place in or nearby a

facility owned by the agency, provided that the topic of the meeting is limited to items directly related to the facility.

(7) Visit the office of the local agency's legal counsel for closed session on pending litigation held pursuant to Section 54956.9, when to do so would reduce legal fees or costs.

(c) Meetings of the governing board of a school district shall beheld within the district, except under the circumstances enumerated in subdivision (b), or to do any of the following:

(1) Attend a conference on no adversarial collective bargaining techniques.

(2) Interview members of the public residing in another district with reference to the trustees' potential employment of an applicant for the position of the superintendent of the district.

(3) Interview a potential employee from another district.

(d) Meetings of a joint powers authority shall occur within the territory of at least one of its member agencies, or as provided in subdivision (b). However, a joint powers authority which has members throughout the state may meet at any facility in the state which complies with the requirements of Section 54961.

(e) If, by reason of fire, flood, earthquake, or other emergency, it shall be unsafe to meet in the place designated, the meetings shall be held for the duration of the emergency at the place designated by the presiding officer of the legislative body or his other designee in a notice to the local media that have requested notice pursuant to Section 54956, by the most rapid means of communication available at the time.

(See § 1-3(a))

54954.1. Any person may request that a copy of the agenda, or copy of all the documents constituting the agenda packet, of any meeting of a legislative body be mailed to that person. If requested, the agenda and documents in the agenda packet shall be made available in appropriate alternative formats to persons with a disability, as required by Section 202 of the Americans with Disabilities Act of 1990 (42 U.S.C. Sec. 12132), and the federal rules and regulations adopted in implementation thereof. Upon receipt of the written request, the legislative body or its designee shall cause the requested materials to be mailed at the time the agenda is posted pursuant to Section 54954.2 and 54956 or upon distribution to all, or a majority of all, of the members of legislative body, whichever occurs first. Any request for mailed copies of agendas or agenda packets shall be valid for the calendar year in which it is filed, and must be renewed following January 1 of each year. The legislative body may establish a fee for mailing the agenda or agenda packet, which fee shall not exceed the cost of providing the service. Failure of the requesting person to receive the agenda or agenda packet pursuant to this section shall not constitute grounds for invalidation of the actions of the legislative body taken at the meeting for which the agenda or agenda packet wasn't received.

(See § 1-4(a))

54954.2. (a) At least 72 hours before a regular meeting, the legislative body of the local agency, or its designee, shall post an agenda containing a brief general description of each item of business to be transacted or discussed at the meeting, including items to be discussed in closed session. A brief general description of an item generally need not exceed 20 words. The agenda shall specify the time and location of the regular meeting and shall be posted in a location that is freely accessible to members of the public. If requested, the agenda shall be made available inappropriate alternative formats to persons with a disability, as required by Section 202 of the Americans with Disabilities Act of 1990 (42 U.S.C. Sec. 12132), and the federal rules and regulations adopted in implementation thereof. The agenda shall include information regarding how, to whom, and when a request for disability-related modification or accommodation, including auxiliary aids or services may be made by a person with a disability who requires a modification or accommodation in order to participate in the public meeting. No action or discussion shall be undertaken on any item not appearing on the posted agenda, except that members of a legislative body or its staff may briefly respond to statements made or questions posed by persons exercising their public testimony rights under Section 54954.3. In addition, on their own initiative or in response to questions posed by the public, a member of a legislative body orbits staff may ask a question for clarification, make a brief announcement, or make a brief report on his or her own activities. Furthermore, a member of a legislative body, or the body itself, subject to rules or procedures of the legislative body, may provide reference to staff or other resources for factual information, request staff to report back to the body at a subsequent meeting concerning any matter, or take action to direct staff to place matter of business on a future agenda.

(b) Notwithstanding subdivision (a), the legislative body may take action on items of business not appearing on the posted agenda under any of the conditions stated below. Prior to discussing any item pursuant to this subdivision, the legislative body shall publicly identify the item.

(1) Upon a determination by a majority vote of the legislative body that an emergency situation exists, as defined in Section 54956.5.

(2) Upon a determination by a two-thirds vote of the members of the legislative body present at the meeting, or, if less than two-thirds of the members are present, a unanimous vote of those members present, that there is a need to take immediate action and that the need for action came to the attention of the local agency subsequent to the agenda being posted as specified in subdivision (a).

(3) The item was posted pursuant to subdivision (a) for a prior meeting of the legislative body occurring not more than five calendar days prior to the date action is taken on the item, and at the prior meeting the item was continued to the meeting at which action is being taken.

(See § 1-3(e))

54954.3. (a) Every agenda for regular meetings shall provide an opportunity for members of the public to directly address the legislative body on any item of interest to the public, before ordering the legislative body's consideration of the item, that is within the subject matter jurisdiction of the legislative body, provided that no action shall be taken on any item not appearing on the agenda unless the action is otherwise authorized by subdivision (b) of Section 54954.2. However, the agenda need not provide an opportunity for members of the public to address the legislative body on any item that has already been considered by a committee, composed exclusively of members of the legislative body, at a public meeting wherein all interested members of the public were afforded the opportunity to address the committee on the item, before ordering the committee's consideration of the item, unless the item has-been substantially changed since the committee heard the item, as determined by the legislative body. Every notice for a special meeting shall provide an opportunity for members of the public to directly address the legislative body concerning any item that has-been described in the notice for the meeting before or during consideration of that item.

(b) The legislative body of a local agency may adopt reasonable regulations to ensure that the intent of subdivision (a) is carried out, including, but not limited to, regulations limiting the total amount of time allocated for public testimony on particular issues and for each individual speaker.

(c) The legislative body of a local agency shall not prohibit public criticism of the policies, procedures, programs, or services of the agency, or of the acts or omissions of the legislative body. Nothing in this subdivision shall confer any privilege or protection for expression beyond that otherwise provided by law.

(See § 1-4(c))

54954.4. (a) The Legislature hereby finds and declares that Section 12 of Chapter 641 of the Statutes of 1986, authorizing reimbursement to local agencies and school districts for costs mandated by testate pursuant to that act, shall be interpreted strictly. The intent of the Legislature is to provide reimbursement for only those costs which are clearly and unequivocally incurred as the direct and necessary result of compliance with Chapter 641 of the Statutes of 1986.

(b) In this regard, the Legislature directs all state employees and officials involved in reviewing or authorizing claims for reimbursement, or otherwise participating in the reimbursement process, to rigorously review each claim and authorize only those claims, or parts thereof, which represent costs which are clearly and unequivocally incurred as the direct and necessary result of compliance with Chapter 641 of the Statutes of 1986 and for which complete documentation exists. For purposes of Section 54954.2,costs eligible for reimbursement shall only include the actual cost to post a single agenda for any one meeting.

(c) The Legislature hereby finds and declares that complete, faithful, and uninterrupted compliance with the Ralph M. Brown Act (Chapter 9 (commencing with Section 54950) of Part 1 of Division 2 of Title 5 of the Government Code) is a matter of overriding public importance. Unless specifically stated, no future Budget Act, correlated budget enactments, shall, in any manner, be interpreted to suspend, eliminate, or otherwise modify the legal obligation and duty of local agencies to fully comply with Chapter 641 of the Statutes of 1986 in a complete, faithful, and uninterrupted manner.

(See § 1-3(k))

54954.5. For purposes of describing closed session items pursuant to Section 54954.2, the agenda may describe closed sessions as provided below. No legislative body or elected official shall be in violation of Section 54954.2 or 54956 if the closed session items were described in substantial compliance with this section. Substantial compliance is satisfied by including the information provided below, irrespective of its format.

(a) With respect to a closed session held pursuant to Section 54956.7:

LICENSE/PERMIT DETERMINATION

Applicant(s): (Specify number of applicants)

(See § 1-5(b)(6))

(b) With respect to every item of business to be discussed in closed session pursuant to Section 54956.8:

CONFERENCE WITH REAL PROPERTY NEGOTIATORS

Property: (Specify street address, or if no street address, the parcel number or other unique reference, of the real property under negotiation)

Agency negotiator: (Specify names of negotiators attending the closed session) (If circumstances necessitate the absence of a specified negotiator, an agent or designee may participate in place of the absent negotiator so long as the name of the agent or designee is announced at an open session held prior to the closed session.)

Negotiating parties: (Specify name of party (not agent))

Under negotiation: (Specify whether instruction to negotiator will concern price, terms of payment, or both)

(See § 1-5(b)(3))

(c) With respect to every item of business to be discussed in closed session pursuant to Section 54956.9:

CONFERENCE WITH LEGAL COUNSEL--EXISTING LITIGATION

(Subdivision (a) of Section 54956.9)

Name of case: (Specify by reference to claimant's name, names of parties, case or claim numbers)

Or

Case name unspecified: (Specify whether disclosure would jeopardize service of process or existing settlement negotiations)

CONFERENCE WITH LEGAL COUNSEL--ANTICIPATED LITIGATION

Significant exposure to litigation pursuant to subdivision (b) of Section 54956.9: (Specify number of potential cases)

(In addition to the information noticed above, the agency may be required to provide additional information on the agenda or in an oral statement prior to the closed session pursuant to subparagraphs (B) to (E), inclusive, of paragraph (3) of subdivision (b) of Section 54956.9.)

Initiation of litigation pursuant to subdivision (c) of Section 54956.9: (Specify number of potential cases)

(See § 1-5(b)(1))

(d) With respect to every item of business to be discussed enclosed session pursuant to

Section 54956.95:
LIABILITY CLAIMS
Claimant: (Specify name unless unspecified pursuant to Section 54961)
Agency claimed against: (Specify name)
(See § 1-5(b)(12))

(e) With respect to every item of business to be discussed enclosed session pursuant to Section 54957:

THREAT TO PUBLIC SERVICES OR FACILITIES
Consultation with: (Specify name of law enforcement agency and title of officer, or name of applicable agency representative and title)
(See § 1-5(b)(5))

PUBLIC EMPLOYEE APPOINTMENT
Title: (Specify description of position to be filled)
PUBLIC EMPLOYMENT
Title: (Specify description of position to be filled)
PUBLIC EMPLOYEE PERFORMANCE EVALUATION
Title: (Specify position title of employee being reviewed)
PUBLIC EMPLOYEE DISCIPLINE/DISMISSAL/RELEASE
(No additional information is required in connection with a closed session to consider discipline, dismissal, or release of a public employee. Discipline includes potential reduction of compensation.)
(See § 1-5(b)(4))

(f) With respect to every item of business to be discussed in closed session pursuant to Section 54957.6:

CONFERENCE WITH LABOR NEGOTIATORS
Agency designated representatives: (Specify names of designated representatives attending the closed session) (If circumstances necessitate the absence of a specified designated representative, an agent or designee may participate in place of the absent representative so long as the name of the agent or designee is announced at an open session held prior to the closed session.)
Employee organization: (Specify name of organization representing employee or employees in question)
Or
Unrepresented employee: (Specify position title of unrepresented employee who is the subject of the negotiations)
(See § 1-5(b)(2))

(g) With respect to closed sessions called pursuant to Section 54957.8:

CASE REVIEW/PLANNING (No additional information is required in connection with a closed session to consider case review or planning.)
(See § 1-5(b)(13))

(h) With respect to every item of business to be discussed in closed session pursuant to Sections 1461, 32106, and 32155 of the Health and Safety Code or Sections 37606 and 37624.3 of the Government Code:

REPORT INVOLVING TRADE SECRET Discussion will concern: (Specify whether discussion will concern proposed new service, program, or facility)
Estimated date of public disclosure: (Specify month and year)
HEARINGS Subject matter: (Specify whether testimony/deliberation will concern staff privileges, report of medical audit committee, or report of quality assurance committee)
(See § 1-5(b)(14))

(i) With respect to every item of business to be discussed in closed session pursuant to Section 54956.86:

CHARGE OR COMPLAINT INVOLVING INFORMATION PROTECTED BY FEDERAL LAW (No additional information is required in connection with a closed session to discuss a charge or complaint pursuant to Section 54956.86.)
(See § 1-5(b)(18))

(j) With respect to every item of business to be discussed in closed session pursuant to Section 54956.96:

CONFERENCE INVOLVING A JOINT POWERS AGENCY (Specify by name)

Discussion will concern: (Specify closed session description used by the joint powers agency.)

Name of local agency representative on joint powers agency board: (Specify name)

(Additional information listing the names of agencies or titles of representatives attending the closed session as consultants or other representatives.)

(See § 1-5(b)(8))

(k) With respect to every item of business to be discussed in closed session pursuant to Section 54956.75:

AUDIT BY BUREAU OF STATE AUDITS

(See § 1-5(b)(7))

54954.6. (a) (1) Before adopting any new or increased general tax or any new or increased assessment, the legislative body of a local agency shall conduct at least one public meeting at which local officials shall allow public testimony regarding the proposed new or increased general tax or new or increased assessment in addition tithe noticed public hearing at which the legislative body proposes to enact or increase the general tax or assessment. For purposes of this section, the term "new or increased assessment" does not include any of the following:

(A) A fee that does not exceed the reasonable cost of providing the services, facilities, or regulatory activity for which the fee discharged.

(B) A service charge, rate, or charge, unless a special district's principal act requires the service charge, rate, or charge to conform to the requirements of this section.

(C) An ongoing annual assessment if it is imposed at the same or lower amount as any previous year.

(D) An assessment that does not exceed an assessment formula orange of assessments previously specified in the notice given to the public pursuant to subparagraph (G) of paragraph (2) of subdivision(c) and that was previously adopted by the agency or approved by the voters in the area where the assessment is imposed.

(E) Standby or immediate availability charges.

(2) The legislative body shall provide at least 45 days' public notice of the public hearing at which the legislative body proposes to enact or increase the general tax or assessment. The legislative body shall provide notice for the public meeting at the same time and in the same document as the notice for the public hearing, but the meeting shall occur prior to the hearing.

(b) (1) The joint notice of both the public meeting and the public hearing required by subdivision (a) with respect to a proposal for anew or increased general tax shall be accomplished by placing display advertisement of at least one-eighth page in a newspaper of general circulation for three weeks pursuant to Section 6063 and by first-class mailing to those interested parties who have filed written request with the local agency for mailed notice of public meetings or hearings on new or increased general taxes. The public meeting pursuant to subdivision (a) shall take place no earlier than 10 days after the first publication of the joint notice pursuant to this subdivision. The public hearing shall take place no earlier than seven days after the public meeting pursuant to this subdivision. Notwithstanding paragraph (2) of subdivision (a), the joint notice need not include notice of the public meeting after the meeting has taken place. The public hearing pursuant to subdivision(a) shall take place no earlier than 45 days after the first publication of the joint notice pursuant to this subdivision. Any written request for mailed notices shall be effective for one year from the date on which it is filed unless a renewal request is filed. Renewal requests for mailed notices shall be filed on or before April 1 of each year. The legislative body may establish reasonable annual charge for sending notices based on the estimated cost of providing the service.

(2) The notice required by paragraph (1) of this subdivision shall include, but not be limited to, the following:

(A) The amount or rate of the tax. If the tax is proposed to be increased from any previous year, the joint notice shall separately state both the existing tax rate and the proposed tax rate increase.

(B) The activity to be taxed.
(C) The estimated amount of revenue to be raised by the tax annually.
(D) The method and frequency for collecting the tax.
(E) The dates, times, and locations of the public meeting and hearing described in subdivision (a).
(F) The phone number and address of an individual, office, or organization that interested persons may contact to receive additional information about the tax.

(c) (1) The joint notice of both the public meeting and the public hearing required by subdivision (a) with respect to a proposal for anew or increased assessment on real property shall be accomplished through a mailing, postage prepaid, in the United States mail and shall be deemed given when so deposited. The public meeting pursuant to subdivision (a) shall take place no earlier than 10 days after the joint mailing pursuant to this subdivision. The public hearing shall take place no earlier than seven days after the public meeting pursuant to this subdivision. The envelope or the cover of the mailing shall include the name of the local agency and the return address of the sender. This mailed notice shall be in at least 10-point type and shall be given to all property owners proposed to be subject to the new or increased assessment by a mailing by name to those persons whose names and addresses appear on the last equalized county assessment roll or the State Board of Equalization assessment roll, as the case may be.

(2) The joint notice required by paragraph (1) of this subdivision shall include, but not be limited to, the following:
(A) The estimated amount of the assessment per parcel. If the assessment is proposed to be increased from any previous year, the joint notice shall separately state both the amount of the existing assessment and the proposed assessment increase.
(B) A general description of the purpose or improvements that the assessment will fund.
(C) The address to which property owners may mail a protest against the assessment.
(D) The phone number and address of an individual, office, or organization that interested persons may contact to receive additional information about the assessment.
(E) A statement that a majority protest will cause the assessment to be abandoned if the assessment act used to levy the assessment so provides. Notice shall also state the percentage of protests required to trigger an election, if applicable.
(F) The dates, times, and locations of the public meeting and hearing described in subdivision (a).
(G) A proposed assessment formula or range as described in subparagraph (D) of paragraph (1) of subdivision (a) if applicable and that is noticed pursuant to this section.

(3) Notwithstanding paragraph (1), in the case of an assessment that is proposed exclusively for operation and maintenance expenses imposed throughout the entire local agency, or exclusively for operation and maintenance assessments proposed to be levied on 50,000 parcels or more, notice may be provided pursuant to this subdivision or pursuant to paragraph (1) of subdivision (b) and shall include the estimated amount of the assessment of various types, amounts, rouses of property and the information required by subparagraphs (B) to (G), inclusive, of paragraph (2) of subdivision (c).

(4) Notwithstanding paragraph (1), in the case of an assessment proposed to be levied pursuant to Part 2 (commencing with Section 22500) of Division 2 of the Streets and Highways Code by a regional park district, regional park and open-space district, or regional open-space district formed pursuant to Article 3 (commencing with Section 5500) of Chapter 3 of Division 5 of, or pursuant to Division 26 (commencing with Section 35100) of, the Public Resources Code, notice may be provided pursuant to paragraph (1) of subdivision (b).

(d) The notice requirements imposed by this section shall be construed as additional to, and not to supersede, existing provisions of law, and shall be applied concurrently with the existing provisions so as to not delay or prolong the governmental decision-making process.

(e) This section shall not apply to any new or increased general tax or any new or increased assessment that requires an election of either of the following:
(1) The property owners subject to the assessment.
(2) The voters within the local agency imposing the tax or assessment.

(f) Nothing in this section shall prohibit a local agency from holding a consolidated meeting or hearing at which the legislative body discusses multiple tax or assessment proposals.

(g) The local agency may recover the reasonable costs of public meetings, public hearings, and notice required by this section from the proceeds of the tax or assessment. The costs recovered for these purposes, whether recovered pursuant to this subdivision or another provision of law, shall not exceed the reasonable costs of the public meetings, public hearings, and notice.

(h) Any new or increased assessment that is subject to the notice and hearing provisions of Article XIIIC or XIIID of the California Constitution is not subject to the notice and hearing requirements of this section.

(See § 1-3(j))

54955. The legislative body of a local agency may adjourn any regular, adjourned regular, special or adjourned special meeting to time and place specified in the order of adjournment. Less than quorum may so adjourn from time to time. If all members are absent from any regular or adjourned regular meeting the clerk or secretary of the legislative body may declare the meeting adjourned to a stated time and place and he shall cause a written notice of the adjournment to be given in the same manner as provided in Section 54956 for special meetings, unless such notice is waived as provided for special meetings. A copy of the order or notice of adjournment shall be conspicuously posted on or near the door of the place where the regular, adjourned regular, special or adjourned special meeting was held within 24 hours after the time of the adjournment. When regular or adjourned regular meeting is adjourned as provided in this section, the resulting adjourned regular meeting is a regular meeting for all purposes. When an order of adjournment of any meeting fails to state the hour at which the adjourned meeting is tube held, it shall be held at the hour specified for regular meetings by ordinance, resolution, bylaw, or other rule.

(See § 1-3(i))

54955.1. Any hearing being held, or noticed or ordered to be held, by a legislative body of a local agency at any meeting may by order or notice of continuance be continued or recombined to any subsequent meeting of the legislative body in the same manner and tithe same extent set forth in Section 54955 for the adjournment of meetings; provided, that if the hearing is continued to a time less than 24 hours after the time specified in the order or notice of hearing, a copy of the order or notice of continuance of hearing shall be posted immediately following the meeting at which the order or declaration of continuance was adopted or made.

(See § 1-3(i))

54956. A special meeting may be called at any time by the presiding officer of the legislative body of a local agency, or by a majority of the members of the legislative body, by delivering written notice to each member of the legislative body and to each local newspaper of general circulation and radio or television station requesting notice in writing. The notice shall be delivered personally or by any other means and shall be received at least 24 hours before the time of the meeting as specified in the notice. The call and notice shall specify the time and place of the special meeting and the business to be transacted or discussed. No other business shall be considered at these meetings by the legislative body. The written notice may be dispensed with as to any member who at or prior to the time the meeting convenes files with the clerk or secretary of the legislative body a written waiver of notice. The waiver may be given by telegram. The written notice may also be dispensed with as toady member who is actually present at the meeting at the time it convenes. The call and notice shall be posted at least 24 hours prior to the special meeting in a location that is freely accessible to members of the public.

(See § 1-3(f))

54956.5. (a) For purposes of this section, "emergency situation" means both of the following:

(1) An emergency, which shall be defined as a work stoppage, crippling activity, or other

activity that severely impairs public health, safety, or both, as determined by a majority of the members of the legislative body.

(2) A dire emergency, which shall be defined as a crippling disaster, mass destruction, terrorist act, or threatened terrorist activity that poses peril so immediate and significant that requiring legislative body to provide one-hour notice before holding an emergency meeting under this section may endanger the public health, safety, or both, as determined by a majority of the members of the legislative body.

(b) (1) Subject to paragraph (2), in the case of an emergency situation involving matters upon which prompt action is necessary duet the disruption or threatened disruption of public facilities, legislative body may hold an emergency meeting without complying with either the 24-hour notice requirement or the 24-hour posting requirement of Section 54956 or both of the notice and posting requirements.

(2) Each local newspaper of general circulation and radio or television station that has requested notice of special meetings pursuant to Section 54956 shall be notified by the presiding officer of the legislative body, or designee thereof, one hour prior to the emergency meeting, or, in the case of a dire emergency, at or near the time that the presiding officer or designee notifies the members of the legislative body of the emergency meeting. This notice shall be given by telephone and all telephone numbers provided in the most recent request of a newspaper or station for notification of special meetings shall be exhausted. In the event that telephone services are not functioning, the notice requirements of this section shall be deemed waived, and the legislative body, or designee of the legislative body, shall notify those newspapers, radio stations, or television stations of the fact of the holding of the emergency meeting, the purpose of the meeting, and any action taken at the meeting as soon after the meeting as possible.

(c) During a meeting held pursuant to this section, the legislative body may meet in closed session pursuant to Section 54957 if agreed to by a two-thirds vote of the members of the legislative body present, or, if less than two-thirds of the members are present, by a unanimous vote of the members present.

(d) All special meeting requirements, as prescribed in Section 54956 shall be applicable to a meeting called pursuant to this section, with the exception of the 24-hour notice requirement.

(e) The minutes of a meeting called pursuant to this section, alit of persons who the presiding officer of the legislative body, or designee of the legislative body, notified or attempted to notify, copy of the roll call vote, and any actions taken at the meeting shall be posted for a minimum of 10 days in a public place as soon after the meeting as possible.

(See § 1-3(g))

54956.6. No fees may be charged by the legislative body of a local agency for carrying out any provision of this chapter, except as specifically authorized by this chapter.

(See § 1-3(b))

54956.7. Whenever a legislative body of a local agency determines that it is necessary to discuss and determine whether an applicant for a license or license renewal, who has a criminal record, insufficiently rehabilitated to obtain the license, the legislative body may hold a closed session with the applicant and the applicant's attorney, if any, for the purpose of holding the discussion and making the determination. If the legislative body determines, as result of the closed session, that the issuance or renewal of the license should be denied, the applicant shall be offered the opportunity to withdraw the application. If the applicant withdraws the application, no record shall be kept of the discussions or decisions made at the closed session and all matters relating to the closed session shall be confidential. If the applicant does not withdraw the application, the legislative body shall take action at the public meeting during which the closed session is held or at its next public meeting denying the application for the license but all matters relating to the closed session are confidential and shall note disclosed without the consent of the applicant, except in inaction by an applicant who has been denied a license challenging the denial of the license.

(See § 1-5(b)(6))

54956.75. (a) Nothing contained in this chapter shall be construed to prevent the legislative body of a local agency that has received confidential final draft audit report from the Bureau of State Audits from holding closed sessions to discuss its response to that report.

(b) After the public release of an audit report by the Bureau of State Audits, if a legislative body of a local agency meets to discuss the audit report, it shall do so in an open session unless exempted from that requirement by some other provision of law.

(See § 1-5(b)(7))

54956.8. Notwithstanding any other provision of this chapter, legislative body of a local agency may hold a closed session with its negotiator prior to the purchase, sale, exchange, or lease of real property by or for the local agency to grant authority to its negotiator regarding the price and terms of payment for the purchase, sale, exchange, or lease. However, prior to the closed session, the legislative body of the local agency shall hold an open and public session in which it identifies its negotiators, the real property or real properties which the negotiations may concern, and the person or persons with whom its negotiators may negotiate. For purposes of this section, negotiators may be members of the legislative body of the local agency. For purposes of this section, "lease" includes renewal or renegotiation of a lease. Nothing in this section shall preclude a local agency from holding closed session for discussions regarding eminent domain proceedings pursuant to Section 54956.9.

(See § 1-5(b)(15))

54956.81. Notwithstanding any other provision of this chapter, legislative body of a local agency that invests pension funds may hold a closed session to consider the purchase or sale of particular, specific pension fund investments. All investment transaction decisions made during the closed session shall be made by rollcall vote entered into the minutes of the closed session as provided in subdivision (a) of Section 54957.2.

(See § 1-5(b)(19))

54956.86. Notwithstanding any other provision of this chapter, legislative body of a local agency which provides services pursuant to Section 14087.3 of the Welfare and Institutions Code may hold closed session to hear a charge or complaint from a member enrolled in its health plan if the member does not wish to have his or her name, medical status, or other information that is protected by federal law publicly disclosed. Prior to holding a closed session pursuant to this section, the legislative body shall inform the member, in writing, of his or her right to have the charge or complaint heard in an open session rather than a closed session.

(See § 1-5(b)(18))

54956.87. (a) Notwithstanding any other provision of this chapter, the records of a health plan that is licensed pursuant to the Knox-Keene Health Care Service Plan Act of 1975 (Chapter 2.2 (commencing with Section 1340) of Division 2 of the Health and Safety Code) and that is governed by a county board of supervisors, whether paper records, records maintained in the management information system, or records in any other form, that relate to provider rate or payment determinations, allocation or distribution methodologies for provider payments, formulas or calculations for these payments, and contract negotiations with providers of health care for alternative rates are exempt from disclosure for a period of three years after the contract is fully executed. The transmission of the records, or the information contained therein in an alternative form, to the board of supervisors shall not constitute a waiver of exemption from disclosure, and the records and information once transmitted to the board of supervisors shall be subject to this same exemption.

(b) Notwithstanding any other provision of law, the governing board of a health plan that is licensed pursuant to the Knox-Keene Health Care Service Plan Act of 1975 (Chapter 2.2 (commencing with Section 1340) of Division 2 of the Health and Safety Code) and that is governed by a county board of supervisors may order that a meeting held solely for the purpose of discussion or taking action on health plan trade secrets, as defined in subdivision (f), shall be held enclosed session. The requirements of making a public report of action taken in closed session, and the vote or abstention of every member present, may be limited to a brief general description without the information constituting the trade secret.

(c) Notwithstanding any other provision of law, the governing board of a health plan may meet in closed session to consider and take action on matters pertaining to contracts and contract negotiations by the health plan with providers of health care services concerning all matters related to rates of payment. The governing board may delete the portion or portions containing trade secrets from any documents that were finally approved in the closed session held pursuant to subdivision (b) that are provided to persons who have made the timely or standing request.

(d) Nothing in this section shall be construed as preventing the governing board from meeting in closed session as otherwise provided by law.

(e) The provisions of this section shall not prevent access to any records by the Joint Legislative Audit Committee in the exercise obits powers pursuant to Article 1 (commencing with Section 10500) of Chapter 4 of Part 2 of Division 2 of Title 2. The provisions of this section also shall not prevent access to any records by the Department of Corporations in the exercise of its powers pursuant to Article 1 (commencing with Section 1340) of Chapter 2.2 of Division 2 of the Health and Safety Code.

(f) For purposes of this section, "health plan trade secret" means trade secret, as defined in subdivision (d) of Section 3426.1 of the Civil Code, that also meets both of the following criteria:

(1) The secrecy of the information is necessary for the health plan to initiate a new service, program, marketing strategy, business plan, or technology, or to add a benefit or product.

(2) Premature disclosure of the trade secret would create substantial probability of depriving the health plan of a substantial economic benefit or opportunity.

(See § 1-5(b)(15))

54956.9. Nothing in this chapter shall be construed to prevent legislative body of a local agency, based on advice of its legal counsel, from holding a closed session to confer with, or receive advice from, its legal counsel regarding pending litigation when discussion in open session concerning those matters would prejudice the position of the local agency in the litigation. For purposes of this chapter, all expressions of the lawyer-client privilege other than those provided in this section are hereby abrogated. This section is the exclusive expression of the lawyer-client privilege for purposes of conducting closed-session meetings pursuant to this chapter. For purposes of this section, "litigation" includes any adjudicatory proceeding, including eminent domain, before a court, administrative body exercising its adjudicatory authority, hearing officer, or arbitrator. For purposes of this section, litigation shall be considered pending when any of the following circumstances exist:

(a) Litigation, to which the local agency is a party, has been initiated formally.

(b) (1) A point has been reached where, in the opinion of the legislative body of the local agency on the advice of its legal counsel, based on existing facts and circumstances, there is significant exposure to litigation against the local agency.

(2) Based on existing facts and circumstances, the legislative body of the local agency is meeting only to decide whether a closed session is authorized pursuant to paragraph (1) of this subdivision.

(3) For purposes of paragraphs (1) and (2), "existing facts and circumstances" shall consist only of one of the following:

(A) Facts and circumstances that might result in litigation against the local agency but which the local agency believes are not yet known to a potential plaintiff or plaintiffs, which facts and circumstances need not be disclosed.

(B) Facts and circumstances, including, but not limited to, an accident, disaster, incident, or transactional occurrence that might result in litigation against the agency and that are known to potential plaintiff or plaintiffs, which facts or circumstances shall be publicly stated on the agenda or announced.

(C) The receipt of a claim pursuant to the Tort Claims Act or some other written communication from a potential plaintiff threatening litigation, which claim or communication shall be available for public inspection pursuant to Section 54957.5.

(D) A statement made by a person in an open and public meeting threatening litigation on a specific matter within the responsibility of the legislative body.

(E) A statement threatening litigation made by a person outside an open and public meeting on a specific matter within the responsibility of the legislative body so long as the official or employee of the local agency receiving knowledge of the threat makes contemporaneous or other record of the statement prior to the meeting, which record shall be available for public inspection pursuant to Section 54957.5. The records so created need not identify the alleged victim of unlawful or tortuous sexual conduct or anyone making the threat on their behalf, or identify a public employee who is the alleged perpetrator of any unlawful or tortuous conduct upon which a threat of litigation is based, unless the identity of the person has been publicly disclosed.

(F) Nothing in this section shall require disclosure of written communications that are privileged and not subject to disclosure pursuant to the California Public Records Act (Chapter 3.5 (commencing with Section 6250) of Division 7 of Title 1).

(c) Based on existing facts and circumstances, the legislative body of the local agency has decided to initiate or is deciding whether to initiate litigation. Prior to holding a closed session pursuant to this section, the legislative body of the local agency shall state on the agenda or publicly announce the subdivision of this section that authorizes the closed session. If the session is closed pursuant to subdivision (a), the body shall state the title of or otherwise specifically identify the litigation to be discussed, unless the body states that to do so would jeopardize the agency's ability to effectuate service of process upon one or more unnerved parties, or that to do so would jeopardize its ability to conclude existing settlement negotiations to its advantage. A local agency shall be considered to be a "party" or to have a "significant exposure to litigation" if an officer or employee of the local agency is a party or has significant exposure to litigation concerning prior or prospective activities or alleged activities during the course and scope of that office or employment, including litigation in which it is an issue whether an activity is outside the course and scope of the office or employment.

(See § 1-5(b)(1))

54956.95. (a) Nothing in this chapter shall be construed to prevent joint powers agency formed pursuant to Article 1 (commencing with Section 6500) of Chapter 5 of Division 7 of Title 1, for purposes of insurance pooling, or a local agency member of the joint powers agency, from holding a closed session to discuss a claim for the payment of tort liability losses, public liability losses, or workers' compensation liability incurred by the joint powers agency or local agency member of the joint powers agency.

(b) Nothing in this chapter shall be construed to prevent the Local Agency Self-Insurance Authority formed pursuant to Chapter 5.5 (commencing with Section 6599.01) of Division 7 of Title 1, or local agency member of the authority, from holding a closed session to discuss a claim for the payment of tort liability losses, public liability losses, or workers' compensation liability incurred by the authority or a local agency member of the authority.
(c) Nothing in this section shall be construed to affect Section 54956.9 with respect to any other local agency.

(See § 1-5(b)(12))

54956.96. (a) Nothing in this chapter shall be construed to prevent the legislative body of a joint powers agency formed pursuant to Article 1 (commencing with Section 6500) of Chapter 5 of Division 7 of Title 1, from adopting a policy or a bylaw or including in its joint powers agreement provisions that authorize either or both of the following:

(1) All information received by the legislative body of the local agency member in a closed session related to the information presented to the joint powers agency in closed session shall be confidential. However, a member of the legislative body of a member local agency may disclose information obtained in a closed session that has direct financial or liability implications for that local agency to the following individuals:

(A) Legal counsel of that member local agency for purposes of obtaining advice on whether the matter has direct financial or liability implications for that member local agency.

(B) Other members of the legislative body of the local agency present in a closed session of that member local agency.

(2) Any designated alternate member of the legislative body of the joint powers agency who is also a member of the legislative body oaf local agency member and who is attending a properly noticed meeting of the joint powers agency in lieu of a local agency member's regularly appointed member to attend closed sessions of the joint powers agency.

(b) If the legislative body of a joint powers agency adopts policy or a bylaw or includes provisions in its joint powers agreement pursuant to subdivision (a), then the legislative body of the local agency member, upon the advice of its legal counsel, may conduct a closed session in order to receive, discuss, and take action concerning information obtained in a closed session of the joint powers agency pursuant to paragraph (1) of subdivision (a).

(See § 1-5(b)(8))

54957. (a) Nothing contained in this chapter shall be construed to prevent the legislative body of a local agency from holding closed sessions with the Attorney General, district attorney, agency counsel, sheriff, or chief of police, or their respective deputies, or a security consultant or a security operations manager, on matters posing a threat to the security of public buildings, a threat to the security of essential public services, including water, drinking water, wastewater treatment, natural gas service, and electric service, or a threat to the public's right of access to public services or public facilities.

(See § 1-5(b)(5))

(b) (1) Subject to paragraph (2), nothing contained in this chapter shall be construed to prevent the legislative body of a local agency from holding closed sessions during a regular or special meeting to consider the appointment, employment, evaluation of performance, discipline, or dismissal of a public employee or to hear complaints or charges brought against the employee by another person or employee unless the employee requests a public session.

(2) As a condition to holding a closed session on specific complaints or charges brought against an employee by another person or employee, the employee shall be given written notice of his or her right to have the complaints or charges heard in an open session rather than a closed session, which notice shall be delivered to the employee personally or by mail at least 24 hours before the time for holding the session. If notice is not given, any disciplinary or other action taken by the legislative body against the employee based on the specific complaints or charges in the closed session shall be null and void.

(3) The legislative body also may exclude from the public or closed meeting, during the examination of a witness, any or all other witnesses in the matter being investigated by the legislative body.

(4) For the purposes of this subdivision, the term "employee" shall include an officer or an independent contractor who functions as an officer or an employee but shall not include any elected official, member of a legislative body or other independent contractors. Nothing in this subdivision shall limit local officials' ability to hold closed session meetings pursuant to Sections 1461, 32106, and 32155 of the Health and Safety Code or Sections 37606 and 37624.3 of the Government Code. Closed sessions held pursuant to this subdivision shall not include discussion or action on proposed compensation except for a reduction of compensation that results from the imposition of discipline.

(See § 1-5(b)(4))

54957.1. (a) The legislative body of any local agency shall publicly report any action taken in closed session and the vote or abstention of every member present thereon, as follows:

(1) Approval of an agreement concluding real estate negotiations pursuant to Section 54956.8 shall be reported after the agreement is final, as specified below:

(A) If its own approval renders the agreement final, the body shall report that approval and the substance of the agreement in open session at the public meeting during which the closed session is held.

(B) If final approval rests with the other party to the negotiations, the local agency shall disclose the fact of that approval and the substance of the agreement upon inquiry by any person, as soon as the other party or its agent has informed the local agency of its approval.

(See § 1-5(b)(3))

(2) Approval given to its legal counsel to defend, or seek or refrain from seeking appellate review or relief, or to enter as an amicus curiae in any form of litigation as the result of consultation under Section 54956.9 shall be reported in open session at the public meeting during which the closed session is held. The report shall identify, if known, the adverse party or parties and the substance of the litigation. In the case of approval given to initiate or intervene in an action, the announcement need not identify the action, the defendants, or other particulars, but shall specify that the direction to initiate or intervene in an action has-been given and that the action, the defendants, and the other particulars shall, once formally commenced, be disclosed to any person upon inquiry, unless to do so would jeopardize the agency's ability to effectuate service of process on one or more unnerved parties, or that to do so would jeopardize its ability to conclude existing settlement negotiations to its advantage.

(See § 1-5(b)(1))

(3) Approval given to its legal counsel of a settlement of pending litigation, as defined in Section 54956.9, at any stage prior to ordering a judicial or quasi-judicial proceeding shall be reported after the settlement is final, as specified below:

(A) If the legislative body accepts a settlement offer signed byte opposing party, the body shall report its acceptance and identify the substance of the agreement in open session at the public meeting during which the closed session is held.

(B) If final approval rests with some other party to the litigation or with the court, then as soon as the settlement becomes final, and upon inquiry by any person, the local agency shall disclose the fact of that approval, and identify the substance of the agreement.

(See § 1-5(b)(1))

(4) Disposition reached as to claims discussed in closed session pursuant to Section 54956.95 shall be reported as soon as reached in manner that identifies the name of the claimant, the name of the local agency claimed against, the substance of the claim, and any monetary amount approved for payment and agreed upon by the claimant.

(See § 1-5(b)(12))

(5) Action taken to appoint, employ, dismiss, accept the resignation of, or otherwise affect the employment status of a public employee in closed session pursuant to Section 54957 shall be reported at the public meeting during which the closed session is held. Any report required by this paragraph shall identify the title of the position. The general requirement of this paragraph notwithstanding, the report of a dismissal or of the nonrenewable of unemployment contract shall be deferred until the first public meeting following the exhaustion of administrative remedies, if any.

(See § 1-5(b)(4))

(6) Approval of an agreement concluding labor negotiations with represented employees pursuant to Section 54957.6 shall be reported after the agreement is final and has been accepted or ratified by the other party. The report shall identify the item approved and the other party or parties to the negotiation.

(See § 1-5(b)(2))

(7) Pension fund investment transaction decisions made pursuant to Section 54956.81 shall be disclosed at the first open meeting of the legislative body held after the earlier of the close of the investment transaction or the transfer of pension fund assets for the investment transaction.

(See § 1-5(b)(19))

. (b) Reports that are required to be made pursuant to this section may be made orally or in writing. The legislative body shall provide to any person who has submitted a written request to the legislative body within 24 hours of the posting of the agenda, or to any person who has made a standing request for all documentation as part of request for notice of meetings pursuant to Section 54954.1 or 54956, if the requester is present at the time the closed session ends, copies of any contracts, settlement agreements, or other documents that were finally approved or adopted in the closed session. If the action taken results in one or more substantive amendments to the related documents requiring retyping, the documents need not be released until the retyping is completed during normal business hours, provided that the presiding officer of the legislative body or his or her designee orally summarizes the substance of the amendments for the benefit of the document requester or any other person present and requesting the information.

(c) The documentation referred to in paragraph (b) shall be available to any person on the next business day following the meeting in which the action referred to is taken or, in the case of substantial amendments, when any necessary retyping is complete.

(d) Nothing in this section shall be construed to require that the legislative body approve actions not otherwise subject to legislative body approval.

(e) No action for injury to a reputation, liberty, or other personal interest may be commenced by or on behalf of any employee or former employee with respect to whom a disclosure is made by legislative body in an effort to comply with this section.

(See §§ 1-5(a)(3), (4))

54957.2. (a) The legislative body of a local agency may, by ordinance or resolution, designate a clerk or other officer or employee of the local agency who shall then attend each closed session of the legislative body and keep and enter in a minute book record of topics discussed and decisions made at the meeting. The minute book made pursuant to this section is not a public record subject to inspection pursuant to the California Public Records Act (Chapter 3.5 (commencing with Section 6250) of Division 7 of Title 1), and shall be kept confidential. The minute book shall be available only to members of the legislative body or, if a violation of this chapter is alleged to have occurred at a closed session, to court of general jurisdiction wherein the local agency lies. Such minute book may, but need not, consist of a recording of the closed session.

(b) An elected legislative body of a local agency may require that each legislative body all or a majority of whose members reappointed by or under the authority of the elected legislative body keep a minute book as prescribed under subdivision (a).

(See § 1-5(a)(1))

54957.5. (a) Notwithstanding Section 6255 or any other provisions of law, agendas of public meetings and any other writings, when distributed to all, or a majority of all, of the members of legislative body of a local agency by any person in connection with matter subject to discussion or consideration at a public meeting of the body, are disc losable public records under the California Public Records Act (Chapter 3.5 (commencing with Section 6250) of Division 7 of Title 1), and shall be made available upon request without delay. However, this section shall not include any writing exempt from public disclosure under Section 6253.5, 6254, 6254.7, or 6254.22.

(b) Writings that are public records under subdivision (a) and that are distributed during a public meeting shall be made available for public inspection at the meeting if prepared by the local agency or a member of its legislative body, or after the meeting if preparedly some other person. These writings shall be made available inappropriate alternative formats upon request by a person with advisability, as required by Section 202 of the Americans with Disabilities Act of 1990 (42 U.S.C. Sec. 12132), and the federal rules and regulations adopted in implementation thereof.

(c) Nothing in this chapter shall be construed to prevent the legislative body of a local agency from charging a fee or deposit foray copy of a public record pursuant to Section 6253, except that no surcharge shall be imposed on persons with disabilities in violation of Section 202 of the Americans with Disabilities Act of 1990 (42 U.S.C. Sec. 12132), and the federal rules and regulations adopted in implementation thereof.

(d) This section shall not be construed to limit or delay the public's right to inspect or obtain a copy of any record required tube disclosed under the requirements of the California Public Records Act (Chapter 3.5 (commencing with Section 6250) of Division 7 of Title 1). Nothing in this chapter shall be construed to require legislative body of a local agency to place any paid advertisement or any other paid notice in any publication.

(See § 1-4(a))

54957.6. (a) Notwithstanding any other provision of law, legislative body of a local agency may hold closed sessions with the local agency's designated representatives regarding the salaries, salary schedules, or compensation paid in the form of fringe benefits of its represented and unrepresented employees, and, for represented employees, any other matter within the statutorily provided scope of representation. However, prior to the closed session, the legislative body of the local agency shall hold an open and public session in which it identifies its designated representatives. Closed sessions of a legislative body of a local agency, as permitted in this section, shall be for the purpose of reviewing its position and instructing the local agency's designated representatives. Closed sessions, as permitted in this section, may take place prior to and during consultations and discussions with representatives of employee organizations and unrepresented employees. Closed sessions with the local agency's designated representative regarding the salaries, salary schedules, or compensation paid in the form of fringe benefits may include discussion of an agency's available funds and funding priorities, but only insofar as these discussions relate to providing instructions to the local agency's designated representative. Closed sessions held pursuant to this section shall not include final action on the proposed compensation of one or more unrepresented employees. For the purposes enumerated in this section, a legislative body oaf local agency may also meet with a state conciliator who has intervened in the proceedings.

(b) For the purposes of this section, the term "employee" shall include an officer or an independent contractor who functions as an officer or an employee, but shall not include any elected official, member of a legislative body, or other independent contractors.

(See § 1-5(b)(2))

54957.7. (a) Prior to holding any closed session, the legislative body of the local agency shall disclose, in an open meeting, the item or items to be discussed in the closed session. The disclosure may take the form of a reference to the item or items as they are listed by number or letter on the agenda. In the closed session, the legislative body may consider only those matters covered in its statement. Nothing in this section shall require or authorize disclosure of information prohibited by state or federal law.

(b) After any closed session, the legislative body shall reconvene into open session prior to adjournment and shall make any disclosures required by Section 54957.1 of action taken in the closed session.

(c) The announcements required to be made in open session pursuant to this section may be made at the location announced in the agenda for the closed session, as long as the public is allowed to be present at that location for the purpose of hearing the announcements.

(See § 1-5(a)(2))

54957.8. Nothing contained in this chapter shall be construed to prevent the legislative body of a multijurisdictional drug law enforcement agency, or an advisory body of a multijurisdictional drug law enforcement agency, from holding closed sessions to discuss thecae records of any ongoing criminal investigation of the multijurisdictional drug law enforcement agency or of any party tithe joint powers agreement, to hear testimony from persons involved in the investigation, and to discuss courses of action in particular cases. "Multijurisdictional drug law enforcement agency," for purposes of this section, means a joint powers entity formed pursuant to Article 1 (commencing with Section 6500) of Chapter 5 of Division 7 of Title 1, which provides drug law enforcement services for the parties tithe joint powers agreement. The Legislature finds and declares that this section is within the public interest, in that its provisions are necessary to prevent the impairment of ongoing law enforcement investigations, to protect witnesses and informants, and to permit the discussion of effective courses of action in particular cases.

(See § 1-5(a)(13))

54957.9. In the event that any meeting is willfully interrupted by a group or groups of persons so as to render the orderly conduct of such meeting unfeasible and order cannot be restored by the removal of individuals who are willfully interrupting the meeting, the members of the legislative body conducting the meeting may order the meeting room cleared and continue in session. Only matters appearing on the agenda may be considered in such a session. Representatives of the press or other news media, except those participating in the disturbance, shall be allowed to attend any session held pursuant to this section. Nothing in this section shall prohibit the legislative body from establishing a procedure for readmitting an individual or individuals not responsible for willfully disturbing the orderly conduct of the meeting.

(See § 1-3(d))

54957.10. Notwithstanding any other provision of law, a legislative body of a local agency may hold closed sessions to discuss a local agency employee's application for early withdrawal of funds in deferred compensation plan when the application is based on financial hardship arising from an unforeseeable emergency due to illness, accident, casualty, or other extraordinary event, as specified in the deferred compensation plan.

(See § 1-5(b)(4))

54958. The provisions of this chapter shall apply to the legislative body of every local agency notwithstanding the conflicting provisions of any other state law.

(See § 1-1(e))

54959. Each member of a legislative body who attends a meeting of that legislative body where action is taken in violation of any provision of this chapter, and where the member intends to deprive the public of information to which the member knows or has reason to know the public is entitled under this chapter, is guilty of misdemeanor.

(See § 1-7(a))

54960. (a) The district attorney or any interested person may commence an action by mandamus, injunction or declaratory relief forth purpose of stopping or preventing violations or threatened violations of this chapter by members of the legislative body of local agency or to determine the applicability of this chapter to actions or threatened future action of the legislative body, or to determine whether any rule or action by the legislative body to penalize or otherwise discourage the expression of one or more of its members is valid or invalid under the laws of this state or of the United States, or to compel the legislative body to tape record its closed sessions as hereinafter provided.

(See § 1-7(b))

(b) The court in its discretion may, upon a judgment of violation of Section 54956.7, 54956.8, 54956.9, 54956.95, 54957, or 54957.6, order the legislative body to tape record its closed sessions and preserve the tape recordings for the period and under the terms of security and confidentiality the court deems appropriate.

(c) (1) Each recording so kept shall be immediately labeled with the date of the closed session recorded and the title of the clerk or other officer who shall be custodian of the recording.

(2) The tapes shall be subject to the following discovery procedures:

(A) In any case in which discovery or disclosure of the tape is sought by either the district attorney or the plaintiff in a civil action pursuant to Section 54959, 54960, or 54960.1 alleging that violation of this chapter has occurred in a closed session which has-been recorded pursuant to this section, the party seeking discovery or disclosure shall file a written notice of motion with the appropriate court with notice to the governmental agency which has custody and control of the tape recording. The notice shall be given pursuant to subdivision (b) of Section 1005 of the Code of Civil Procedure.

(B) The notice shall include, in addition to the items required bisection 1010 of the Code of Civil Procedure, all of the following:

(i) Identification of the proceeding in which discovery or disclosure is sought, the party seeking discovery or disclosure, the date and time of the meeting recorded, and the governmental agency which has custody and control of the recording.

(ii) An affidavit which contains specific facts indicating that violation of the act occurred in the closed session.

(3) If the court, following a review of the motion, finds that there is good cause to believe that a violation has occurred, the court may review, in camera, the recording of that portion of the closed session alleged to have violated the act.

(4) If, following the in camera review, the court concludes that disclosure of a portion of the recording would be likely to materially assist in the resolution of the litigation alleging violation of this chapter, the court shall, in its discretion, make a certified transcript of the portion of the recording a public exhibit in the proceeding.

(5) Nothing in this section shall permit discovery of communications which are protected by the attorney-client privilege.

(See § 1-7(e))

54960.1. (a) The district attorney or any interested person may commence an action by mandamus or injunction for the purpose of obtaining a judicial determination that an action taken by legislative body of a local agency in violation of Section 54953, 54954.2, 54954.5, 54954.6, 54956, or 54956.5 is null and void under this section. Nothing in this chapter shall be construed to prevent legislative body from curing or correcting an action challenged pursuant to this section.

(b) Prior to any action being commenced pursuant to subdivision(a), the district attorney or interested person shall make a demand of the legislative body to cure or correct the action alleged to have been taken in violation of Section 54953, 54954.2, 54954.5, 54954.6, 54956, or 54956.5. The demand shall be in writing and clearly describe the challenged action of the legislative body and nature of the alleged violation.

(c) (1) The written demand shall be made within 90 days from the date the action was taken unless the action was taken in an open session but in violation of Section 54954.2, in which case the written demand shall be made within 30 days from the date the action was taken.

(2) Within 30 days of receipt of the demand, the legislative body shall cure or correct the challenged action and inform the demanding party in writing of its actions to cure or correct or inform the demanding party in writing of its decision not to cure or correct the challenged action.

(3) If the legislative body takes no action within the 30-day period, the inaction shall be deemed a decision not to cure or correct the challenged action, and the 15-day period to commence the action described in subdivision (a) shall commence to run the day after the 30-day period to cure or correct expires.

(4) Within 15 days of receipt of the written notice of the legislative body's decision to cure or correct, or not to cure or correct, or within 15 days of the expiration of the 30-day period to cure or correct, whichever is earlier, the demanding party shall be required to commence the action pursuant to subdivision (a) or thereafter be barred from commencing the action.

(d) An action taken that is alleged to have been taken in violation of Section 54953, 54954.2, 54954.5, 54954.6, 54956, or 54956.5 shall not be determined to be null and void if any of the following conditions exist:

(1) The action taken was in substantial compliance with Sections 54953, 54954.2, 54954.5, 54954.6, 54956, and 54956.5.

(2) The action taken was in connection with the sale or issuance of notes, bonds, or other evidences of indebtedness or any contract, instrument, or agreement thereto.

(3) The action taken gave rise to a contractual obligation, including a contract let by competitive bid other than compensation for services in the form of salary or fees for professional services, upon which a party has, in good faith and without notice of challenge to the validity of the action, detrimentally relied.

(4) The action taken was in connection with the collection of any tax.

(5) Any person, city, city and county, county, district, or any agency or subdivision of the state alleging noncompliance with subdivision (a) of Section 54954.2, Section 54956, or Section 54956.5, because of any defect, error, irregularity, or omission in the notice given pursuant to those provisions, had actual notice of the item of business at least 72 hours prior to the meeting at which the action was taken, if the meeting was noticed pursuant to Section 54954.2, or 24 hours prior to the meeting at which the action was taken if the

meeting was noticed pursuant to Section 54956, or prior to the meeting at which the action was taken if the meeting is held pursuant to Section 54956.5.

(e) During any action seeking a judicial determination pursuant to subdivision (a) if the court determines, pursuant to a showing byte legislative body that an action alleged to have been taken in violation of Section 54953, 54954.2, 54954.5, 54954.6, 54956, or 54956.5 has been cured or corrected by a subsequent action of the legislative body, the action filed pursuant to subdivision (a) shall be dismissed with prejudice.

(f) The fact that a legislative body takes a subsequent action to cure or correct an action taken pursuant to this section shall not be construed or admissible as evidence of a violation of this chapter.

(See § 1-7(g))

54960.5. A court may award court costs and reasonable attorney fees to the plaintiff in an action brought pursuant to Section 54960 or 54960.1 where it is found that a legislative body of the local agency has violated this chapter. The costs and fees shall be paid by the local agency and shall not become a personal liability of any public officer or employee of the local agency. A court may award court costs and reasonable attorney fees to defendant in any action brought pursuant to Section 54960 or 54960.1 where the defendant has prevailed in a final determination of such action and the court finds that the action was clearly frivolous and totally lacking in merit.

(See § 1-7(1))

54961. (a) No legislative body of a local agency shall conduct any meeting in any facility that prohibits the admittance of any person, or persons, on the basis of race, religious creed, color, national origin, ancestry, or sex, or which is inaccessible to disabled persons, or where members of the public may not be present without making a payment or purchase. This section shall apply to every local agency as defined in Section 54951.

(See § 1-3(b))

(b) No notice, agenda, announcement, or report required under this chapter need identify any victim or alleged victim of tortious sexual conduct or child abuse unless the identity of the person has been publicly disclosed.

(See § 1-3(e)(1))

54962. Except as expressly authorized by this chapter, or by sections 1461, 1462, 32106, and 32155 of the Health and Safety Code or Sections 37606 and 37624.3 of the Government Code as they apply to hospitals, or by any provision of the Education Code pertaining to school districts and community college districts, no closed session may be held by any legislative body of any local agency.

(See § 1-5(b))

54963. (a) A person may not disclose confidential information that has been acquired by being present in a closed session authorized bisection 54956.7, 54956.8, 54956.86, 54956.87, 54956.9, 54957, 54957.6, 54957.8, or 54957.10 to a person not entitled to receive it, unless the legislative body authorizes disclosure of that confidential information.

(b) For purposes of this section, "confidential information" means communication made in a closed session that is specifically related to the basis for the legislative body of a local agency to meet lawfully in closed session under this chapter.

(c) Violation of this section may be addressed by the use of such remedies as are currently available by law, including, but not limited to:

(1) Injunctive relief to prevent the disclosure of confidential information prohibited by this section.

(2) Disciplinary action against an employee who has willfully disclosed confidential information in violation of this section.

(3) Referral of a member of a legislative body who has willfully disclosed confidential information in violation of this section tithe grand jury.

(d) Disciplinary action pursuant to paragraph (2) of subdivision (c) shall require that the employee in question has either received training as to the requirements of this section or otherwise has been given notice of the requirements of this section.

(See § 1-5(a)91))

(e) A local agency may not take any action authorized by subdivision (c) against a person, nor shall it be deemed a violation of this section, for doing any of the following:

(1) Making a confidential inquiry or complaint to a district attorney or grand jury concerning a perceived violation of law, including disclosing facts to a district attorney or grand jury that are necessary to establish the illegality of an action taken by legislative body of a local agency or the potential illegality of inaction that has been the subject of deliberation at a closed session if that action were to be taken by a legislative body of a local agency.

(2) Expressing an opinion concerning the propriety or legality factions taken by a legislative body of a local agency in closed session, including disclosure of the nature and extent of the illegal or potentially illegal action.

(3) Disclosing information acquired by being present in a closed session under this chapter that is not confidential information.

(f) Nothing in this section shall be construed to prohibit disclosures under the whistleblower statutes contained in Section 1102.5 of the Labor Code or Article 4.5 (commencing with Section 53296) of Chapter 2 of this code.

(See § 1-7(h))

2. Executive Branch and Related Bodies

The default law requiring open and public meetings of state bodies in the executive branch is the Bagley-Keene Open Meeting Act. But special laws or other rules govern the meetings of other state and certain education-related bodies: the University of California (U.C.) Board of Regents, auxiliary organizations in the community college and California State University (C.S.U.) systems, C.S.U. and U.C. student government bodies, and local public school site advisory committees.

§ 2-1: State Agencies Generally: The Bagley-Keene Act

The Bagley-Keene Open Meeting Act (Government Code §11120 *et seq.*) applies to the boards, commissions and like bodies in the executive branch of state government. To a great extent its provisions are similar or identical to those of the Brown Act governing local agencies, in which case they are noted for comparison in Chapter I, the Brown Act section of this guide.

§ 2-1(a): Unique Closed Session Provisions

The Bagley-Keene provisions that have *no* counterpart in the Brown Act are the following authorizations for closed sessions of particular state bodies (boldface added):

11125.8. (a) Notwithstanding Section 11131.5, in any hearing that the **State Board of Control** conducts pursuant to Section 13963.1 and that the applicant or applicant's representative does not request be open to the public, no notice, agenda, announcement, or report required under this article need identify the applicant.

(b) In any hearing that the board conducts pursuant to Section 13963.1 and that the applicant or applicant's representative does not request be open to the public, the board shall disclose that the hearing is being held pursuant to Section 13963.1. That disclosure shall be deemed to satisfy the requirements of subdivision (a) of Section 11126.3.

11126. (c) Nothing in this article shall be construed to do any of the following:

(1) Prevent state **bodies that administer the licensing of persons engaging in businesses or professions** from holding closed sessions to prepare, approve, grade, or administer examinations.

(2) Prevent **an advisory body of a state body that administers the licensing of persons engaged in businesses or professions** from conducting a closed session to discuss matters that the advisory body has found would constitute an unwarranted invasion of the privacy of an individual licensee or applicant if discussed in an open meeting, provided the advisory body does not include a quorum of the members of the state body it advises. Those matters may include review of an applicant's qualifications for licensure and an inquiry specifically related to the state body's enforcement program concerning an individual licensee or applicant where the inquiry oc-

curs prior to the filing of a civil, criminal, or administrative disciplinary action against the licensee or applicant by the state body.

(3) Prohibit a state body from holding a closed session to deliberate on a decision to be reached in a **proceeding required to be conducted pursuant to Chapter 5** (commencing with Section 11500) or similar provisions of law.

Note: The reference is to adjudicatory or trial-like hearings where the issue is whether to either grant, issue, or renew, or to revoke, suspend, condition or limit a right, authority, license or privilege. The evidentiary portion of the hearing is open as with a trial, but deliberations by the body, as with a jury, are closed.)

---

(4) Grant a **right to enter any correctional institution** or the grounds of a correctional institution where that right is not otherwise granted by law, nor shall anything in this article be construed to prevent a state body from holding a closed session when considering and acting upon the determination of a term, parole, or release of any individual or other disposition of an individual case, or if public disclosure of the subjects under discussion or consideration is expressly prohibited by statute.

*****

(6) Prevent the **Alcoholic Beverage Control Appeals Board** from holding a closed session for the purpose of holding a deliberative conference as provided in Section 11125.

*****

(8) Prevent the **California Postsecondary Education Commission** from holding closed sessions to consider matters pertaining to the appointment or termination of the Director of the California Postsecondary Education Commission.

(9) Prevent the **Council for Private Postsecondary and Vocational Education** from holding closed sessions to consider matters pertaining to the appointment or termination of the Executive Director of the Council for Private Postsecondary and Vocational Education.

(10) Prevent the **Franchise Tax Board** from holding closed sessions for the purpose of discussion of confidential tax returns or information the public disclosure of which is prohibited by law, or from considering matters pertaining to the appointment or removal of the Executive Officer of the Franchise Tax Board.

(11) Require the **Franchise Tax Board** to notice or disclose any confidential tax information considered in closed sessions, or documents executed in connection therewith, the public disclosure of which is prohibited pursuant to Article 2 (commencing with Section 19542) of Chapter 7 of Part 10.2 of the Revenue and Taxation Code.

(12) Prevent the **Board of Corrections** from holding closed sessions when considering reports of crime conditions under Section 6027 of the Penal Code.

(13) Prevent the **State Air Resources Board** from holding closed sessions when considering the proprietary specifications and performance data of manufacturers.

(14) Prevent the **State Board of Education** or the Superintendent of Public Instruction, or any committee advising the board or the superintendent, from holding closed sessions on those portions of its review of assessment instruments pursuant to Chapter 5 (commencing with Section 60600) of, or pursuant to Chapter 8 (commencing with Section 60850) of, Part 33 of the Education Code during which actual test content is reviewed and discussed. The purpose of this provision is to maintain the confidentiality of the assessments under review.

(15) Prevent the **California Integrated Waste Management Board** or its auxiliary committees from holding closed sessions for the purpose of discussing confidential tax returns, discussing trade secrets or confidential or proprietary information in its possession, or discussing other data, the public disclosure of which is prohibited by law.

(d) (1) Notwithstanding any other provision of law, any meeting of the **Public Utilities Commission** at which the rates of entities under the commission's jurisdiction are changed shall be open and public.

(2) Nothing in this article shall be construed to prevent the **Public Utilities Commission**

from holding closed sessions to deliberate on the institution of proceedings, or disciplinary actions against any person or entity under the jurisdiction of the commission.

(f) In addition to subdivisions (a), (b), and (c), nothing in this article shall be construed to do any of the following:

*****

(2) Prevent the examining committee established by the **State Board of Forestry and Fire Protection**, pursuant to Section 763 of the Public Resources Code, from conducting a closed session to consider disciplinary action against an individual professional forester prior to the filing of an accusation against the forester pursuant to Section 11503.

(3) Prevent an administrative committee established by the **California Board of Accountancy** pursuant to Section 5020 of the Business and Professions Code from conducting a closed session to consider disciplinary action against an individual accountant prior to the filing of an accusation against the accountant pursuant to Section 11503. Nothing in this article shall be construed to prevent an examining committee established by the **California Board of Accountancy** pursuant to Section 5023 of the Business and Professions Code from conducting a closed hearing to interview an individual applicant or accountant regarding the applicant's qualifications.

(4) Prevent a state body, as defined in subdivision (b) of Section 11121, from conducting a closed session to consider any matter that properly could be considered in closed session by the state body whose authority it exercises.

(5) Prevent a state body, as defined in subdivision (d) of Section 11121, from conducting a closed session to consider any matter that properly could be considered in a closed session by the body defined as a state body pursuant to subdivision (a) or (b) of Section 11121.

(6) Prevent a state body, as defined in subdivision (c) of Section 11121, from conducting a closed session to consider any matter that properly could be considered in a closed session by the state body it advises.

Note: The references in paragraphs (4), (5) and (6) are, respectively, to:

• a board, commission, committee, or similar multimember body that exercises any authority of a state body delegated to it by that state body;

• a board, commission, committee, or similar multimember body on which a member of a body that is a state body pursuant to this section serves in his or her official capacity as a representative of that state body and that is supported, in whole or in part, by funds provided by the state body, whether the multimember body is organized and operated by the state body or by a private corporation; and

• An advisory board, advisory commission, advisory committee, advisory subcommittee, or similar multimember advisory body of a state body, if created by formal action of the state body or of any member of the state body, and if the advisory body so created consists of three or more persons.

---

(7) Prevent the **State Board of Equalization** from holding closed sessions for either of the following:

(A) When considering matters pertaining to the appointment or removal of the Executive Secretary of the State Board of Equalization.

(B) For the purpose of hearing confidential taxpayer appeals or data, the public disclosure of which is prohibited by law.

(8) Require the **State Board of Equalization** to disclose any action taken in closed session or documents executed in connection with that action, the public disclosure of which is prohibited by law pursuant to Sections 15619 and 15641 of this code and Sections 833, 7056, 8255, 9255, 11655, 30455, 32455, 38705, 38706, 43651, 45982, 46751, 50159, 55381, and 60609 of the Revenue and Taxation Code.

(9) Prevent the **California Earthquake Prediction Evaluation Council**, or other body appointed to advise the Director of the Office of Emergency Services or the Governor concerning matters relating to volcanic or earthquake predictions, from holding closed ses-

sions when considering the evaluation of possible predictions.

(g) This article does not prevent either of the following:

(1) The **Teachers' Retirement Board or the Board of Administration of the Public Employees' Retirement System** from holding closed sessions when considering matters pertaining to the recruitment, appointment, employment, or removal of the chief executive officer or when considering matters pertaining to the recruitment or removal of the Chief Investment Officer of the State Teachers' Retirement System or the Public Employees' Retirement System.

(2) The **Commission on Teacher Credentialing** from holding closed sessions when considering matters relating to the recruitment, appointment, or removal of its executive director.

(h) This section shall remain in effect only until January 1, 2006, and as of that date is repealed, unless a later enacted statute, which is enacted before January 1, 2006, deletes or extends that date.

§ 2-1(b): Full Text of the Bagley-Keene Open Meeting Act

The following display of all of Government Code §§11120-11132 in sequence also provides **(See)** references to sections of the previous chapter where the Brown Act counterpart for each provision is discussed.

11120. It is the public policy of this state that public agencies exist to aid in the conduct of the people's business and the proceedings of public agencies be conducted openly so that the public may remain informed.

In enacting this article the Legislature finds and declares that it is the intent of the law that actions of state agencies be taken openly and that their deliberation be conducted openly.

The people of this state do not yield their sovereignty to the agencies which serve them. The people, in delegating authority, do not give their public servants the right to decide what is good for the people to know and what is not good for them to know. The people insist on remaining informed so that they may retain control over the instruments they have created.

This article shall be known and may be cited as the Bagley-Keene Open Meeting Act.

(See § 1-1(c))

11121. As used in this article, "state body" means each of the following:

(a) Every state board, or commission, or similar multimember body of the state that is created by statute or required by law to conduct official meetings and every commission created by executive order.

(b) A board, commission, committee, or similar multimember body that exercises any authority of a state body delegated to it by that state body.

(c) An advisory board, advisory commission, advisory committee, advisory subcommittee, or similar multimember advisory body of a state body, if created by formal action of the state body or of any member of the state body, and if the advisory body so created consists of three or more persons.

(d) A board, commission, committee, or similar multimember body on which a member of a body that is a state body pursuant to this section serves in his or her official capacity as a representative of that state body and that is supported, in whole or in part, by funds provided by the state body, whether the multimember body is organized and operated by the state body or by a private corporation.

(See § 1-2(b))

11121.1. As used in this article, "state body" does not include any of the following:

(a) State agencies provided for in Article VI of the California Constitution.

(b) Districts or other local agencies whose meetings are required to be open to the public pursuant to the Ralph M. Brown Act (Chapter 9 (commencing with Section 54950) of Part 1 of Division 2 of Title 5).

(c) State agencies provided in Article IV of the California Constitution whose meetings are required to be open to the public pursuant to the Grunsky-Burton Open Meeting Act (Article 2.2 (commencing with Section 9027) of Chapter 1.5 of Part 1 of Division 2 of Title 2).

(d) State agencies when they are conducting proceedings pursuant to Section 3596.

(e) State agencies provided for in Section 109260 of the Health and Safety Code, except as provided in Section 109390 of the Health and Safety Code.

(f) State agencies provided for in Section 11770.5 of the Insurance Code.

(g) The Credit Union Advisory Committee established pursuant to Section 14380 of the Financial Code.

(See § 1-2(b))

11121.9. Each state body shall provide a copy of this article to each member of the state body upon his or her appointment to membership or assumption of office.

(See § 1-7(a))

11121.95. Any person appointed or elected to serve as a member of a state body who has not yet assumed the duties of office shall conform his or her conduct to the requirements of this article and shall be treated for purposes of this article as if he or she has already assumed office.

(See § 1-2(c))

11122. As used in this article "action taken" means a collective decision made by the members of a state body, a collective commitment or promise by the members of the state body to make a positive or negative decision or an actual vote by the members of a state body when sitting as a body or entity upon a motion, proposal, resolution, order or similar action.

(See § 1-2(d))

11122.5. (a) As used in this article, "meeting" includes any congregation of a majority of the members of a state body at the same time and place to hear, discuss, or deliberate upon any item that is within the subject matter jurisdiction of the state body to which it pertains.

(b) Except as authorized pursuant to Section 11123, any use of direct communication, personal intermediaries, or technological devices that is employed by a majority of the members of the state body to develop a collective concurrence as to action to be taken on an item by the members of the state body is prohibited.

(c) The prohibitions of this article do not apply to any of the following:

(1) Individual contacts or conversations between a member of a state body and any other person.

(2) The attendance of a majority of the members of a state body at a conference or similar gathering open to the public that involves a discussion of issues of general interest to the public or to public agencies of the type represented by the state body, provided that a majority of the members do not discuss among themselves, other than as part of the scheduled program, business of a specified nature that is within the subject matter jurisdiction of the state body. This paragraph is not intended to allow members of the public free admission to a conference or similar gathering at which the organizers have required other participants or registrants to pay fees or charges as a condition of attendance.

(3) The attendance of a majority of the members of a state body at an open and publicized meeting organized to address a topic of state concern by a person or organization other than the state body, provided that a majority of the members do not discuss among themselves, other than as part of the scheduled program, business of a specific nature that is within the subject matter jurisdiction of the state body.

(4) The attendance of a majority of the members of a state body at an open and noticed meeting of another state body or of a legislative body of a local agency as defined by Section 54951, provided that a majority of the members do not discuss among themselves, other than as part of the scheduled meeting, business of a specific nature that is within the subject matter jurisdiction of the other state body.

(5) The attendance of a majority of the members of a state body at a purely social or ceremonial occasion, provided that a majority do not discuss among themselves business of a specific nature that is within the subject matter jurisdiction of the state body.

(6) The attendance of a majority of the members of a state body at an open and noticed meeting of a standing committee of that body, provided that the members of the state body who are not members of the standing committee attend only as observers.

(See § 1-2(d))

11123. (a) All meetings of a state body shall be open and public and all persons shall be permitted to attend any meeting of a state body except as otherwise provided in this article.

(b) (1) This article does not prohibit a state body from holding an open or closed meeting by teleconference for the benefit of the public and state body. The meeting or proceeding held by teleconference shall otherwise comply with all applicable requirements or laws relating to a specific type of meeting or proceeding, including the following:

(A) The teleconferencing meeting shall comply with all requirements of this article applicable to other meetings.

(B) The portion of the teleconferenced meeting that is required to be open to the public shall be audible to the public at the location specified in the notice of the meeting.

(C) If the state body elects to conduct a meeting or proceeding by teleconference, it shall post agendas at all teleconference locations and conduct teleconference meetings in a manner that protects the rights of any party or member of the public appearing before the state body. Each teleconference location shall be identified in the notice and agenda of the meeting or proceeding, and each teleconference location shall be accessible to the public. The agenda shall provide an opportunity for members of the public to address the state body directly pursuant to Section 11125.7 at each teleconference location.

(D) All votes taken during a teleconferenced meeting shall be by rollcall.

(E) The portion of the teleconferenced meeting that is closed to the public may not include the consideration of any agenda item being heard pursuant to Section 11125.5.

(F) At least one member of the state body shall be physically present at the location specified in the notice of the meeting.

(2) For the purposes of this subdivision, "teleconference" means a meeting of a state body, the members of which are at different locations, connected by electronic means, through either audio or both audio and video. This section does not prohibit a state body from providing members of the public with additional locations in which the public may observe or address the state body by electronic means, through either audio or both audio and video.

(See § 1-3(d))

11123.1. All meetings of a state body that are open and public shall meet the protections and prohibitions contained in Section 202 of the Americans with Disabilities Act of 1990 (42 U.S.C. Sec. 12132), and the federal rules and regulations adopted in implementation thereof.

(See § 1-3(b))

11124. No person shall be required, as a condition to attendance at a meeting of a state body, to register his or her name, to provide other information, to complete a questionnaire, or otherwise to fulfill any condition precedent to his or her attendance.

If an attendance list, register, questionnaire, or other similar document is posted at or near the entrance to the room where the meeting is to be held, or is circulated to persons present during the meeting, it shall state clearly that the signing, registering, or completion of the document is voluntary, and that all persons may attend the meeting regardless of whether a person signs, registers, or completes the document.

(See § 1-4(b))

11124.1. (a) Any person attending an open and public meeting of the state body shall have the right to record the proceedings with an audio or video tape recorder or a still or motion picture camera in the absence of a reasonable finding by the state body that the recording cannot continue without noise, illumination, or obstruction of view that constitutes, or would constitute, a persistent disruption of the proceedings.

(b) Any tape or film record of an open and public meeting made for whatever purpose by or at the direction of the state body shall be subject to inspection pursuant to the California Public Records Act (Chapter 3.5 (commencing with Section 6250) of Division 7 of Title 1), but may be erased or destroyed 30 days after the taping or recording. Any inspection of an audio or video tape recording shall be provided without charge on an audio or video tape player made available by the state body.

(c) No state body shall prohibit or otherwise restrict the broadcast of its open and public meetings in the absence of a reasonable finding that the broadcast cannot be accomplished without noise, illumination, or obstruction of view that would constitute a persistent disruption of the proceedings.

(See § 1-4(d))

11125. (a) The state body shall provide notice of its meeting to any person who requests that notice in writing. Notice shall be given and also made available on the Internet at least 10 days in advance of the meeting, and shall include the name, address, and telephone number of any person who can provide further information prior to the meeting, but need not include a list of witnesses expected to appear at the meeting. The written notice shall additionally include the address of the Internet site where notices required by this article are made available.

(b) The notice of a meeting of a body that is a state body shall include a specific agenda for the meeting, containing a brief description of the items of business to be transacted or discussed in either open or closed session. A brief general description of an item generally need not exceed 20 words. A description of an item to be transacted or discussed in closed session shall include a citation of the specific statutory authority under which a closed session is being held. No item shall be added to the agenda subsequent to the provision of this notice, unless otherwise permitted by this article.

(c) Notice of a meeting of a state body that complies with this section shall also constitute notice of a meeting of an advisory body of that state body, provided that the business to be discussed by the advisory body is covered by the notice of the meeting of the state body, provided that the specific time and place of the advisory body's meeting is announced during the open and public state body's meeting, and provided that the advisory body's meeting is conducted within a reasonable time of, and nearby, the meeting of the state body.

(d) A person may request, and shall be provided, notice pursuant to subdivision (a) for all meetings of a state body or for a specific meeting or meetings. In addition, at the state body's discretion, a person may request, and may be provided, notice of only those meetings of a state body at which a particular subject or subjects specified in the request will be discussed.

(e) A request for notice of more than one meeting of a state body shall be subject to the provisions of Section 14911.

(f) The notice shall be made available in appropriate alternative formats, as required by Section 202 of the Americans with Disabilities Act of 1990 (42 U.S.C. Sec. 12132), and the federal rules and regulations adopted in implementation thereof, upon request by any person with a disability. The notice shall include information regarding how, to whom, and by when a request for any disability-related modification or accommodation, including auxiliary aids or services may be made by a person with a disability who requires these aids or services in order to participate in the public meeting.

(See § 1-3(e))

11125.1. (a) Notwithstanding Section 6255 or any other provisions of law, agendas of public meetings and other writings, when distributed to all, or a majority of all, of the members of a state body by any person in connection with a matter subject to discussion or consideration at a public meeting of the body, are disclosable public records under the California Public Records Act (Chapter 3.5 (commencing with Section 6250) of Division 7 of

Title 1), and shall be made available upon request without delay. However, this section shall not include any writing exempt from public disclosure under Section 6253.5, 6254, or 6254.7 of this code, or Section 489.1 or 583 of the Public Utilities Code.

(b) Writings that are public records under subdivision (a) and that are distributed to members of the state body prior to or during a meeting, pertaining to any item to be considered during the meeting, shall be made available for public inspection at the meeting if prepared by the state body or a member of the state body, or after the meeting if prepared by some other person. These writings shall be made available in appropriate alternative formats, as required by Section 202 of the Americans with Disabilities Act of 1990 (42 U.S.C. Sec. 12132), and the federal rules and regulations adopted in implementation thereof, upon request by a person with a disability.

(c) In the case of the Franchise Tax Board, prior to that state body taking final action on any item, writings pertaining to that item that are public records under subdivision (a) that are distributed to members of the state body by board staff or individual members prior to or during a meeting shall be:

(1) Made available for public inspection at that meeting.

(2) Distributed to all persons who request notice in writing pursuant to subdivision (a) of Section 11125.

(3) Made available on the Internet.

(d) Prior to the State Board of Equalization taking final action on any item that does not involve a named tax or fee payer, writings pertaining to that item that are public records under subdivision (a) that are prepared and distributed by board staff or individual members to members of the state body prior to or during a meeting shall be:

(1) Made available for public inspection at that meeting.

(2) Distributed to all persons who request or have requested copies of these writings.

(3) Made available on the Internet.

(e) Nothing in this section shall be construed to prevent a state body from charging a fee or deposit for a copy of a public record pursuant to Section 6253, except that no surcharge shall be imposed on persons with disabilities in violation of Section 202 of the Americans with Disabilities Act of 1990 (42 U.S.C. Sec. 12132), and the federal rules and regulations adopted in implementation thereof. The writings described in subdivision (b) are subject to the requirements of the California Public Records Act (Chapter 3.5 (commencing with Section 6250) of Division 7 of Title 1), and shall not be construed to limit or delay the public's right to inspect any record required to be disclosed by that act, or to limit the public's right to inspect any record covered by that act. This section shall not be construed to be applicable to any writings solely because they are properly discussed in a closed session of a state body. Nothing in this article shall be construed to require a state body to place any paid advertisement or any other paid notice in any publication.

(f) "Writing" for purposes of this section means "writing" as defined under Section 6252.

(See § 1-4(a))

11125.2. Any state body shall report publicly at a subsequent public meeting any action taken, and any rollcall vote thereon, to appoint, employ, or dismiss a public employee arising out of any closed session of the state body.

(See § 1-5(b)(4))

11125.3. (a) Notwithstanding Section 11125, a state body may take action on items of business not appearing on the posted agenda under any of the conditions stated below:

(1) Upon a determination by a majority vote of the state body that an emergency situation exists, as defined in Section 11125.5.

(2) Upon a determination by a two-thirds vote of the state body, or, if less than two-thirds of the members are present, a unanimous vote of those members present, that there exists a need to take immediate action and that the need for action came to the attention of the state body subsequent to the agenda being posted as specified in Section 11125.

(b) Notice of the additional item to be considered shall be provided to each member of the state body and to all parties that have requested notice of its meetings as soon as is practicable after a determination of the need to consider the item is made, but shall be delivered

in a manner that allows it to be received by the members and by newspapers of general circulation and radio or television stations at least 48 hours before the time of the meeting specified in the notice. Notice shall be made available to newspapers of general circulation and radio or television stations by providing that notice to all national press wire services. Notice shall also be made available on the Internet as soon as is practicable after the decision to consider additional items at a meeting has been made.
(See § 1-3(e))

11125.4. (a) A special meeting may be called at any time by the presiding officer of the state body or by a majority of the members of the state body. A special meeting may only be called for one of the following purposes where compliance with the 10-day notice provisions of Section 11125 would impose a substantial hardship on the state body or where immediate action is required to protect the public interest:

(1) To consider "pending litigation" as that term is defined in subdivision (e) of Section 11126.

(2) To consider proposed legislation.

(3) To consider issuance of a legal opinion.

(4) To consider disciplinary action involving a state officer or employee.

(5) To consider the purchase, sale, exchange, or lease of real property.

(6) To consider license examinations and applications.

(7) To consider an action on a loan or grant provided pursuant to Division 31 (commencing with Section 50000) of the Health and Safety Code.

(8) To consider its response to a confidential final draft audit report as permitted by Section 11126.2.

(b) When a special meeting is called pursuant to one of the purposes specified in subdivision (a), the state body shall provide notice of the special meeting to each member of the state body and to all parties that have requested notice of its meetings as soon as is practicable after the decision to call a special meeting has been made, but shall deliver the notice in a manner that allows it to be received by the members and by newspapers of general circulation and radio or television stations at least 48 hours before the time of the special meeting specified in the notice. Notice shall be made available to newspapers of general circulation and radio or television stations by providing that notice to all national press wire services. Notice shall also be made available on the Internet within the time periods required by this section. The notice shall specify the time and place of the special meeting and the business to be transacted. The written notice shall additionally specify the address of the Internet Web site where notices required by this article are made available. No other business shall be considered at a special meeting by the state body. The written notice may be dispensed with as to any member who at or prior to the time the meeting convenes files with the clerk or secretary of the state body a written waiver of notice. The waiver may be given by telegram, facsimile transmission, or similar means. The written notice may also be dispensed with as to any member who is actually present at the meeting at the time it convenes. Notice shall be required pursuant to this section regardless of whether any action is taken at the special meeting.

(c) At the commencement of any special meeting, the state body must make a finding in open session that the delay necessitated by providing notice 10 days prior to a meeting as required by Section 11125 would cause a substantial hardship on the body or that immediate action is required to protect the public interest.

The finding shall set forth the specific facts that constitute the hardship to the body or the impending harm to the public interest. The finding shall be adopted by a two-thirds vote of the body, or, if less than two-thirds of the members are present, a unanimous vote of those members present. The finding shall be made available on the Internet. Failure to adopt the finding terminates the meeting.
(See § 1-3(f))

11125.5. (a) In the case of an emergency situation involving matters upon which prompt action is necessary due to the disruption or threatened disruption of public facilities, a state body may hold an emergency meeting without complying with the 10-day notice requirement of Section 11125 or the 48-hour notice requirement of Section 11125.4.

(b) For purposes of this section, "emergency situation" means any of the following, as determined by a majority of the members of the state body during a meeting prior to the emergency meeting, or at the beginning of the emergency meeting:

(1) Work stoppage or other activity that severely impairs public health or safety, or both.

(2) Crippling disaster that severely impairs public health or safety, or both.

(c) However, newspapers of general circulation and radio or television stations that have requested notice of meetings pursuant to Section 11125 shall be notified by the presiding officer of the state body, or a designee thereof, one hour prior to the emergency meeting by telephone. Notice shall also be made available on the Internet as soon as is practicable after the decision to call the emergency meeting has been made. If telephone services are not functioning, the notice requirements of this section shall be deemed waived, and the presiding officer of the state body, or a designee thereof, shall notify those newspapers, radio stations, or television stations of the fact of the holding of the emergency meeting, the purpose of the meeting, and any action taken at the meeting as soon after the meeting as possible.

(d) The minutes of a meeting called pursuant to this section, a list of persons who the presiding officer of the state body, or a designee thereof, notified or attempted to notify, a copy of the rollcall vote, and any action taken at the meeting shall be posted for a minimum of 10 days in a public place, and also made available on the Internet for a minimum of 10 days, as soon after the meeting as possible.

(See § 1-3(g))

11125.6. (a) An emergency meeting may be called at any time by the president of the Fish and Game Commission or by a majority of the members of the commission to consider an appeal of a closure of or restriction in a fishery adopted pursuant to Section 7710 of the Fish and Game Code. In the case of an emergency situation involving matters upon which prompt action is necessary due to the disruption or threatened disruption of an established fishery, the commission may hold an emergency meeting without complying with the 10-day notice requirement of Section 11125 or the 48-hour notice requirement of Section 11125.4 if the delay necessitated by providing the 10-day notice of a public meeting required by Section 11125 or the 48-hour notice required by Section 11125.4 would significantly adversely impact the economic benefits of a fishery to the participants in the fishery and to the people of the state or significantly adversely impact the sustainability of a fishery managed by the state.

(b) At the commencement of an emergency meeting called pursuant to this section, the commission shall make a finding in open session that the delay necessitated by providing notice 10 days prior to a meeting as required by Section 11125 or 48 hours prior to a meeting as required by Section 11125.4 would significantly adversely impact the economic benefits of a fishery to the participants in the fishery and to the people of the state or significantly adversely impact the sustainability of a fishery managed by the state. The finding shall set forth the specific facts that constitute the impact to the economic benefits of the fishery or the sustainability of the fishery. The finding shall be adopted by a vote of at least four members of the commission, or, if less than four of the members are present, a unanimous vote of those members present. Failure to adopt the finding shall terminate the meeting.

(c) Newspapers of general circulation and radio or television stations that have requested notice of meetings pursuant to Section 11125 shall be notified by the presiding officer of the commission, or a designee thereof, one hour prior to the emergency meeting by telephone.

(d) The minutes of an emergency meeting called pursuant to this section, a list of persons who the president of the commission, or a designee thereof, notified or attempted to notify, a copy of the rollcall vote, and any action taken at the meeting shall be posted for a minimum of 10 days in a public place as soon after the meeting as possible.

(See § 1-3(h))

11125.7. (a) Except as otherwise provided in this section, the state body shall provide an opportunity for members of the public to directly address the state body on each agenda item before or during the state body's discussion or consideration of the item. This section is not applicable if the agenda item has already been considered by a committee composed exclusively of members of the state body at a public meeting where interested members of the public were afforded the opportunity to address the committee on the item, before or during the committee's consideration of the item, unless the item has been substantially changed since the committee heard the item, as determined by the state body. Every notice for a special meeting at which action is proposed to be taken on an item shall provide an opportunity for members of the public to directly address the state body concerning that item prior to action on the item. In addition, the notice requirement of Section 11125 shall not preclude the acceptance of testimony at meetings, other than emergency meetings, from members of the public, provided, however, that no action is taken by the state body at the same meeting on matters brought before the body by members of the public.

(b) The state body may adopt reasonable regulations to ensure that the intent of subdivision (a) is carried out, including, but not limited to, regulations limiting the total amount of time allocated for public comment on particular issues and for each individual speaker.

(c) The state body shall not prohibit public criticism of the policies, programs, or services of the state body, or of the acts or omissions of the state body. Nothing in this subdivision shall confer any privilege or protection for expression beyond that otherwise provided by law.

(d) This section is not applicable to closed sessions held pursuant to Section 11126.

(e) This section is not applicable to decisions regarding proceedings held pursuant to Chapter 5 (commencing with Section
11500), relating to administrative adjudication, or to the conduct of those proceedings.

(f) This section is not applicable to hearings conducted by the State Board of Control pursuant to Sections 13963 and 13963.1.

(g) This section is not applicable to agenda items that involve decisions of the Public Utilities Commission regarding adjudicatory hearings held pursuant to Chapter 9 (commencing with Section 1701) of Part 1 of Division 1 of the Public Utilities Code. For all other agenda items, the commission shall provide members of the public, other than those who have already participated in the proceedings underlying the agenda item, an opportunity to directly address the commission before or during the commission's consideration of the item.

(See § 1-4(c))

11125.8. (a) Notwithstanding Section 11131.5, in any hearing that the State Board of Control conducts pursuant to Section 13963.1 and that the applicant or applicant's representative does not request be open to the public, no notice, agenda, announcement, or report required under this article need identify the applicant.

(b) In any hearing that the board conducts pursuant to Section 13963.1 and that the applicant or applicant's representative does not request be open to the public, the board shall disclose that the hearing is being held pursuant to Section 13963.1. That disclosure shall be deemed to satisfy the requirements of subdivision (a) of Section 11126.3.

(See § 2-1(a))

11125.9. Regional water quality control boards shall comply with the notification guidelines in Section 11125 and, in addition, shall do both of the following:

(a) Notify, in writing, all clerks of the city councils and county boards of supervisors within the regional board's jurisdiction of any and all board hearings at least 10 days prior to the hearing. Notification shall include an agenda for the meeting with contents as described in subdivision (b) of Section 11125 as well as the name, address, and telephone number of any person who can provide further information prior to the meeting, but need not include a list of witnesses expected to appear at the meeting. Each clerk, upon receipt of the notification of a board hearing, shall distribute the notice to all members of the respective city council or board of supervisors within the regional board's jurisdiction.

(b) Notify, in writing, all newspapers with a circulation rate of at least 10,000 within the regional board's jurisdiction of any and all board hearings, at least 10 days prior to the hearing. Notification shall include an agenda for the meeting with contents as described in

subdivision (b) of Section 11125 as well as the name, address, and telephone number of any person who can provide further information prior to the meeting, but need not include a list of witnesses expected to appear at the meeting.
(See § 1-3(e))

11126. (a) (1) Nothing in this article shall be construed to prevent a state body from holding closed sessions during a regular or special meeting to consider the appointment, employment, evaluation of performance, or dismissal of a public employee or to hear complaints or charges brought against that employee by another person or employee unless the employee requests a public hearing.

(2) As a condition to holding a closed session on the complaints or charges to consider disciplinary action or to consider dismissal, the employee shall be given written notice of his or her right to have a public hearing, rather than a closed session, and that notice shall be delivered to the employee personally or by mail at least 24 hours before the time for holding a regular or special meeting. If notice is not given, any disciplinary or other action taken against any employee at the closed session shall be null and void.

(3) The state body also may exclude from any public or closed session, during the examination of a witness, any or all other witnesses in the matter being investigated by the state body.

(4) Following the public hearing or closed session, the body may deliberate on the decision to be reached in a closed session.

(b) For the purposes of this section, "employee" does not include any person who is elected to, or appointed to a public office by, any state body. However, officers of the California State University who receive compensation for their services, other than per diem and ordinary and necessary expenses, shall, when engaged in that capacity, be considered employees. Furthermore, for purposes of this section, the term employee includes a person exempt from civil service pursuant to subdivision (e) of Section 4 of Article VII of the California Constitution.
(See § 1-5(b)(4))

(c) Nothing in this article shall be construed to do any of the following:

(1) Prevent state bodies that administer the licensing of persons engaging in businesses or professions from holding closed sessions to prepare, approve, grade, or administer examinations.

(2) Prevent an advisory body of a state body that administers the licensing of persons engaged in businesses or professions from conducting a closed session to discuss matters that the advisory body has found would constitute an unwarranted invasion of the privacy of an individual licensee or applicant if discussed in an open meeting, provided the advisory body does not include a quorum of the members of the state body it advises. Those matters may include review of an applicant's qualifications for licensure and an inquiry specifically related to the state body's enforcement program concerning an individual licensee or applicant where the inquiry occurs prior to the filing of a civil, criminal, or administrative disciplinary action against the licensee or applicant by the state body.

(3) Prohibit a state body from holding a closed session to deliberate on a decision to be reached in a proceeding required to be conducted pursuant to Chapter 5 (commencing with Section 11500) or similar provisions of law.

(4) Grant a right to enter any correctional institution or the grounds of a correctional institution where that right is not otherwise granted by law, nor shall anything in this article be construed to prevent a state body from holding a closed session when considering and acting upon the determination of a term, parole, or release of any individual or other disposition of an individual case, or if public disclosure of the subjects under discussion or consideration is expressly prohibited by statute.
(See § 2-1(a))

(5) Prevent any closed session to consider the conferring of honorary degrees, or gifts, donations, and bequests that the donor or proposed donor has requested in writing to be kept confidential.
(See § 1-5(b)(17))

(6) Prevent the Alcoholic Beverage Control Appeals Board from holding a closed session

for the purpose of holding a deliberative conference as provided in Section 11125.
(See § 2-1(a))

(7) (A) Prevent a state body from holding closed sessions with its negotiator prior to the purchase, sale, exchange, or lease of real property by or for the state body to give instructions to its negotiator regarding the price and terms of payment for the purchase, sale, exchange, or lease.

(B) However, prior to the closed session, the state body shall hold an open and public session in which it identifies the real property or real properties that the negotiations may concern and the person or persons with whom its negotiator may negotiate.

(C) For purposes of this paragraph, the negotiator may be a member of the state body.

(D) For purposes of this paragraph, "lease" includes renewal or renegotiation of a lease.

(E) Nothing in this paragraph shall preclude a state body from holding a closed session for discussions regarding eminent domain proceedings pursuant to subdivision (e).
(See § 1-5(b)(3))

(8) Prevent the California Postsecondary Education Commission from holding closed sessions to consider matters pertaining to the appointment or termination of the Director of the California Postsecondary Education Commission.

(9) Prevent the Council for Private Postsecondary and Vocational Education from holding closed sessions to consider matters pertaining to the appointment or termination of the Executive Director of the Council for Private Postsecondary and Vocational Education.

(10) Prevent the Franchise Tax Board from holding closed sessions for the purpose of discussion of confidential tax returns or information the public disclosure of which is prohibited by law, or from considering matters pertaining to the appointment or removal of the Executive Officer of the Franchise Tax Board.

(11) Require the Franchise Tax Board to notice or disclose any confidential tax information considered in closed sessions, or documents executed in connection therewith, the public disclosure of which is prohibited pursuant to Article 2 (commencing with Section 19542) of Chapter 7 of Part 10.2 of the Revenue and Taxation Code.

(12) Prevent the Board of Corrections from holding closed sessions when considering reports of crime conditions under Section 6027 of the Penal Code.

(13) Prevent the State Air Resources Board from holding closed sessions when considering the proprietary specifications and performance data of manufacturers.

(14) Prevent the State Board of Education or the Superintendent of Public Instruction, or any committee advising the board or the superintendent, from holding closed sessions on those portions of its review of assessment instruments pursuant to Chapter 5 (commencing with Section 60600) of, or pursuant to Chapter 8 (commencing with Section 60850) of, Part 33 of the Education Code during which actual test content is reviewed and discussed. The purpose of this provision is to maintain the confidentiality of the assessments under review.

(15) Prevent the California Integrated Waste Management Board or its auxiliary committees from holding closed sessions for the purpose of discussing confidential tax returns, discussing trade secrets or confidential or proprietary information in its possession, or discussing other data, the public disclosure of which is prohibited by law.
(See § 2-1(a))

(16) Prevent a state body that invests retirement, pension, or endowment funds from holding closed sessions when considering investment decisions. For purposes of consideration of shareholder voting on corporate stocks held by the state body, closed sessions for the purposes of voting may be held only with respect to election of corporate directors, election of independent auditors, and other financial issues that could have a material effect on the net income of the corporation. For the purpose of real property investment decisions that may be considered in a closed session pursuant to this paragraph, a state body shall also be exempt from the provisions of paragraph (7) relating to the identification of real properties prior to the closed session.
(See § 1-5(b)(19))

(17) Prevent a state body, or boards, commissions, administrative officers, or other representatives that may properly be designated by law or by a state body, from holding closed sessions with its representatives in discharging its responsibilities under Chapter 10 (commencing with Section 3500), Chapter 10.3 (commencing with Section 3512), Chapter 10.5

(commencing with Section 3525), or Chapter 10.7 (commencing of Section 3540) of Division 4 of Title 1 as the sessions relate to salaries, salary schedules, or compensation paid in the form of fringe benefits. For the purposes enumerated in the preceding sentence, a state body may also meet with a state conciliator who has intervened in the proceedings.

(See § 1-5(b)(2))

(18) (A) Prevent a state body from holding closed sessions to consider matters posing a threat or potential threat of criminal or terrorist activity against the personnel, property, buildings, facilities, or equipment, including electronic data, owned, leased, or controlled by the state body, where disclosure of these considerations could compromise or impede the safety or security of the personnel, property, buildings, facilities, or equipment, including electronic data, owned, leased, or controlled by the state body.

(B) Notwithstanding any other provision of law, a state body, at any regular or special meeting, may meet in a closed session pursuant to subparagraph (A) upon a two-thirds vote of the members present at the meeting.

(C) After meeting in closed session pursuant to subparagraph (A), the state body shall reconvene in open session prior to adjournment and report that a closed session was held pursuant to subparagraph (A), the general nature of the matters considered, and whether any action was taken in closed session.

(D) After meeting in closed session pursuant to subparagraph (A), the state body shall submit to the Legislative Analyst written notification stating that it held this closed session, the general reason or reasons for the closed session, the general nature of the matters considered, and whether any action was taken in closed session. The Legislative Analyst shall retain for no less than four years any written notification received from a state body pursuant to this subparagraph.

(See § 1-5(b)(5))

(d) (1) Notwithstanding any other provision of law, any meeting of the Public Utilities Commission at which the rates of entities under the commission's jurisdiction are changed shall be open and public.

(2) Nothing in this article shall be construed to prevent the Public Utilities Commission from holding closed sessions to deliberate on the institution of proceedings, or disciplinary actions against any person or entity under the jurisdiction of the commission.

(See § 2-1(a))

(e) (1) Nothing in this article shall be construed to prevent a state body, based on the advice of its legal counsel, from holding a closed session to confer with, or receive advice from, its legal counsel regarding pending litigation when discussion in open session concerning those matters would prejudice the position of the state body in the litigation.

(2) For purposes of this article, all expressions of the lawyer-client privilege other than those provided in this subdivision are hereby abrogated. This subdivision is the exclusive expression of the lawyer-client privilege for purposes of conducting closed session meetings pursuant to this article. For purposes of this subdivision, litigation shall be considered pending when any of the following circumstances exist:

(A) An adjudicatory proceeding before a court, an administrative body exercising its adjudicatory authority, a hearing officer, or an arbitrator, to which the state body is a party, has been initiated formally.

(B) (i) A point has been reached where, in the opinion of the state body on the advice of its legal counsel, based on existing facts and circumstances, there is a significant exposure to litigation against the state body.

(ii) Based on existing facts and circumstances, the state body is meeting only to decide whether a closed session is authorized pursuant to clause (i).

(C) (i) Based on existing facts and circumstances, the state body has decided to initiate or is deciding whether to initiate litigation.

(ii) The legal counsel of the state body shall prepare and submit to it a memorandum stating the specific reasons and legal authority for the closed session. If the closed session is pursuant to paragraph (1), the memorandum shall include the title of the litigation. If the closed session is pursuant to subparagraph (A) or
(B), the memorandum shall include the existing facts and circumstances on which it is based. The legal counsel shall submit the memorandum to the state body prior to the

closed session, if feasible, and in any case no later than one week after the closed session. The memorandum shall be exempt from disclosure pursuant to Section 6254.25.

(iii) For purposes of this subdivision, "litigation" includes any adjudicatory proceeding, including eminent domain, before a court, administrative body exercising its adjudicatory authority, hearing officer, or arbitrator.

(iv) Disclosure of a memorandum required under this subdivision shall not be deemed as a waiver of the lawyer-client privilege, as provided for under Article 3 (commencing with Section 950) of Chapter 4 of Division 8 of the Evidence Code.

(See § 1-5(b)(1))

(f) In addition to subdivisions (a), (b), and (c), nothing in this article shall be construed to do any of the following:

(1) Prevent a state body operating under a joint powers agreement for insurance pooling from holding a closed session to discuss a claim for the payment of tort liability or public liability losses incurred by the state body or any member agency under the joint powers agreement.

(See § 1-5(b)(12))

(2) Prevent the examining committee established by the State Board of Forestry and Fire Protection, pursuant to Section 763 of the Public Resources Code, from conducting a closed session to consider disciplinary action against an individual professional forester prior to the filing of an accusation against the forester pursuant to Section 11503.

(3) Prevent an administrative committee established by the California Board of Accountancy pursuant to Section 5020 of the Business and Professions Code from conducting a closed session to consider disciplinary action against an individual accountant prior to the filing of an accusation against the accountant pursuant to Section 11503. Nothing in this article shall be construed to prevent an examining committee established by the California Board of Accountancy pursuant to Section 5023 of the Business and Professions Code from conducting a closed hearing to interview an individual applicant or accountant regarding the applicant's qualifications.

(4) Prevent a state body, as defined in subdivision (b) of Section 11121, from conducting a closed session to consider any matter that properly could be considered in closed session by the state body whose authority it exercises.

(5) Prevent a state body, as defined in subdivision (d) of Section 11121, from conducting a closed session to consider any matter that properly could be considered in a closed session by the body defined as a state body pursuant to subdivision (a) or (b) of Section 11121.

(6) Prevent a state body, as defined in subdivision (c) of Section 11121, from conducting a closed session to consider any matter that properly could be considered in a closed session by the state body it advises.

(7) Prevent the State Board of Equalization from holding closed sessions for either of the following:

(A) When considering matters pertaining to the appointment or removal of the Executive Secretary of the State Board of Equalization.

(B) For the purpose of hearing confidential taxpayer appeals or data, the public disclosure of which is prohibited by law.

(8) Require the State Board of Equalization to disclose any action taken in closed session or documents executed in connection with that action, the public disclosure of which is prohibited by law pursuant to Sections 15619 and 15641 of this code and Sections 833, 7056, 8255, 9255, 11655, 30455, 32455, 38705, 38706, 43651, 45982, 46751, 50159, 55381, and 60609 of the Revenue and Taxation Code.

(9) Prevent the California Earthquake Prediction Evaluation Council, or other body appointed to advise the Director of the Office of Emergency Services or the Governor concerning matters relating to volcanic or earthquake predictions, from holding closed sessions when considering the evaluation of possible predictions.

(g) This article does not prevent either of the following:

(1) The Teachers' Retirement Board or the Board of Administration of the Public Employees' Retirement System from holding closed sessions when considering matters pertaining to the recruitment, appointment, employment, or removal of the chief executive officer or when considering matters pertaining to the recruitment or removal of the Chief Investment

Officer of the State Teachers' Retirement System or the Public Employees' Retirement System.

(2) The Commission on Teacher Credentialing from holding closed sessions when considering matters relating to the recruitment, appointment, or removal of its executive director.

(h) This section shall remain in effect only until January 1, 2006, and as of that date is repealed, unless a later enacted statute, which is enacted before January 1, 2006, deletes or extends that date.

(See § 2-1(a))

11126.1. The state body shall designate a clerk or other officer or employee of the state body, who shall then attend each closed session of the state body and keep and enter in a minute book a record of topics discussed and decisions made at the meeting. The minute book made pursuant to this section is not a public record subject to inspection pursuant to the California Public Records Act (Chapter 3.5 (commencing with Section 6250) of Division 7 of Title 1), and shall be kept confidential. The minute book shall be available to members of the state body or, if a violation of this chapter is alleged to have occurred at a closed session, to a court of general jurisdiction. Such minute book may, but need not, consist of a recording of the closed session.

(See § 1-5(a)(1))

11126.2. (a) Nothing in this article shall be construed to prohibit a state body that has received a confidential final draft audit report from the Bureau of State Audits from holding closed sessions to discuss its response to that report.

(b) After the public release of an audit report by the Bureau of State Audits, if a state body meets to discuss the audit report, it shall do so in an open session unless exempted from that requirement by some other provision of law.

(See § 1-5(b)(7))

11126.3. (a) Prior to holding any closed session, the state body shall disclose, in an open meeting, the general nature of the item or items to be discussed in the closed session. The disclosure may take the form of a reference to the item or items as they are listed by number or letter on the agenda. If the session is closed pursuant to paragraph (2) of subdivision (d) of Section 11126, the state body shall state the title of, or otherwise specifically identify, the proceeding or disciplinary action contemplated. However, should the body determine that to do so would jeopardize the body's ability to effectuate service of process upon one or more unserved parties if the proceeding or disciplinary action is commenced or that to do so would fail to protect the private economic and business reputation of the person or entity if the proceeding or disciplinary action is not commenced, then the state body shall notice that there will be a closed session and describe in general terms the purpose of that session. If the session is closed pursuant to subparagraph (A) of paragraph (2) of subdivision (e) of Section 11126, the state body shall state the title of, or otherwise specifically identify, the litigation to be discussed unless the body states that to do so would jeopardize the body's ability to effectuate service of process upon one or more unserved parties, or that to do so would jeopardize its ability to conclude existing settlement negotiations to its advantage.

(b) In the closed session, the state body may consider only those matters covered in its disclosure.

(c) The disclosure shall be made as part of the notice provided for the meeting pursuant to Section 11125 or pursuant to subdivision
(a) of Section 92032 of the Education Code and of any order or notice required by Section 11129.

(d) If, after the agenda has been published in compliance with this article, any pending litigation (under subdivision (e) of Section 11126) matters arise, the postponement of which will prevent the state body from complying with any statutory, court-ordered, or other legally imposed deadline, the state body may proceed to discuss those matters in closed session and shall publicly announce in the meeting the title of, or otherwise specifically identify, the litigation to be discussed, unless the body states that to do so would jeopardize the body's ability to effectuate service of process upon one or more unserved parties, or that to do so would jeopardize its ability to conclude existing settlement negotiations to its advantage. Such an announcement shall be deemed to comply fully with the requirements of this section.

(e) Nothing in this section shall require or authorize a disclosure of names or other information that would constitute an invasion of privacy or otherwise unnecessarily divulge the particular facts concerning the closed session or the disclosure of which is prohibited by state or federal law.

(f) After any closed session, the state body shall reconvene into open session prior to adjournment and shall make any reports, provide any documentation, and make any other disclosures required by Section 11125.2 of action taken in the closed session.

(g) The announcements required to be made in open session pursuant to this section may be made at the location announced in the agenda for the closed session, as long as the public is allowed to be present at that location for the purpose of hearing the announcement.

(See § 1-5(a)(2))

11126.5. In the event that any meeting is willfully interrupted by a group or groups of persons so as to render the orderly conduct of such meeting unfeasible and order cannot be restored by the removal of individuals who are willfully interrupting the meeting the state body conducting the meeting may order the meeting room cleared and continue in session. Nothing in this section shall prohibit the state body from establishing a procedure for readmitting an individual or individuals not responsible for willfully disturbing the orderly conduct of the meeting. Notwithstanding any other provision of law, only matters appearing on the agenda may be considered in such a session.

Representatives of the press or other news media, except those participating in the disturbance, shall be allowed to attend any session held pursuant to this section.

(See § 1-3(d))

11126.7. No fees may be charged by a state body for providing a notice required by Section 11125 or for carrying out any provision of this article, except as specifically authorized pursuant to this article.

(See § 1-4(b))

11127. Each provision of this article shall apply to every state body unless the body is specifically excepted from that provision by law or is covered by any other conflicting provision of law.

(See § 1-1(e))

11128. Each closed session of a state body shall be held only during a regular or special meeting of the body.

(See § 1-3(i))

11128.5. The state body may adjourn any regular, adjourned regular, special, or adjourned special meeting to a time and place specified in the order of adjournment. Less than a quorum may so adjourn from time to time. If all members are absent from any regular or adjourned regular meeting, the clerk or secretary of the state body may declare the meeting adjourned to a stated time and place and he or she shall cause a written notice of the adjournment to be given in the same manner as provided in Section 11125.4 for special meetings, unless that notice is waived as provided for special meetings. A copy of the order or notice of adjournment shall be conspicuously posted on or near the door of the place where the regular, adjourned regular, special, or adjourned special meeting was held within 24 hours after the time of the adjournment. When a regular or adjourned regular meeting is adjourned as provided in this section, the resulting adjourned regular meeting is a regular meeting for all purposes. When an order of adjournment of any meeting fails to state the hour at which the adjourned meeting is to be held, it shall be held at the hour

specified for regular meetings by law or regulation.
(See § 1-3(i))

11129. Any hearing being held, or noticed or ordered to be held by a state body at any meeting may by order or notice of continuance be continued or recontinued to any subsequent meeting of the state body in the same manner and to the same extent set forth in Section 11128.5 for the adjournment of meetings. A copy of the order or notice of continuance shall be conspicuously posted on or near the door of the place where the hearing was held within 24 hours after the time of the continuance; provided, that if the hearing is continued to a time less than 24 hours after the time specified in the order or notice of hearing, a copy of the order or notice of continuance of hearing shall be posted immediately following the meeting at which the order or declaration of continuance was adopted or made.
(See § 1-3(1)

11130. (a) The Attorney General, the district attorney, or any interested person may commence an action by mandamus, injunction, or declaratory relief for the purpose of stopping or preventing violations or threatened violations of this article or to determine the applicability of this article to past actions or threatened future action by members of the state body or to determine whether any rule or action by the state body to penalize or otherwise discourage the expression of one or more of its members is valid or invalid under the laws of this state or of the United States, or to compel the state body to tape record its closed sessions as hereinafter provided.

(b) The court in its discretion may, upon a judgment of a violation of Section 11126, order the state body to tape record its closed sessions and preserve the tape recordings for the period and under the terms of security and confidentiality the court deems appropriate.

(c) (1) Each recording so kept shall be immediately labeled with the date of the closed session recorded and the title of the clerk or other officer who shall be custodian of the recording.

(2) The tapes shall be subject to the following discovery procedures:

(A) In any case in which discovery or disclosure of the tape is sought by the Attorney General, the district attorney, or the plaintiff in a civil action pursuant to this section or Section 11130.3 alleging that a violation of this article has occurred in a closed session that has been recorded pursuant to this section, the party seeking discovery or disclosure shall file a written notice of motion with the appropriate court with notice to the governmental agency that has custody and control of the tape recording. The notice shall be given pursuant to subdivision (b) of Section 1005 of the Code of Civil Procedure.

(B) The notice shall include, in addition to the items required by Section 1010 of the Code of Civil Procedure, all of the following:

(i) Identification of the proceeding in which discovery or disclosure is sought, the party seeking discovery or disclosure, the date and time of the meeting recorded, and the governmental agency that has custody and control of the recording.

(ii) An affidavit that contains specific facts indicating that a violation of the act occurred in the closed session.

(3) If the court, following a review of the motion, finds that there is good cause to believe that a violation has occurred, the court may review, in camera, the recording of that portion of the closed session alleged to have violated the act.

(4) If, following the in-camera review, the court concludes that disclosure of a portion of the recording would be likely to materially assist in the resolution of the litigation alleging violation of this article, the court shall, in its discretion, make a certified transcript of the portion of the recording a public exhibit in the proceeding.

(5) Nothing in this section shall permit discovery of communications that are protected by the attorney-client privilege.
(See § 1-7(b))

11130.3. (a) Any interested person may commence an action by mandamus, injunction, or declaratory relief for the purpose of obtaining a judicial determination that an action taken by a state body in violation of Section 11123 or 11125 is null and void under this section.

Any action seeking such a judicial determination shall be commenced within 90 days from the date the action was taken. Nothing in this section shall be construed to prevent a state body from curing or correcting an action challenged pursuant to this section.

(b) An action shall not be determined to be null and void if any of the following conditions exist:

(1) The action taken was in connection with the sale or issuance of notes, bonds, or other evidences of indebtedness or any contract, instrument, or agreement related thereto.

(2) The action taken gave rise to a contractual obligation upon which a party has, in good faith, detrimentally relied.

(3) The action taken was in substantial compliance with Sections 11123 and 11125.

(4) The action taken was in connection with the collection of any tax.

(See § 1-7(g))

11130.5. A court may award court costs and reasonable attorney's fees to the plaintiff in an action brought pursuant to Section 11130 or 11130.3 where it is found that a state body has violated the provisions of this article. The costs and fees shall be paid by the state body and shall not become a personal liability of any public officer or employee thereof.

A court may award court costs and reasonable attorney's fees to a defendant in any action brought pursuant to Section 11130 or 11130.3 where the defendant has prevailed in a final determination of the action and the court finds that the action was clearly frivolous and totally lacking in merit.

(See § 1-7(i))

11130.7. Each member of a state body who attends a meeting of that body in violation of any provision of this article, and where the member intends to deprive the public of information to which the member knows or has reason to know the public is entitled under this article, is guilty of a misdemeanor.

(See § 1-7(a))

11131. No state agency shall conduct any meeting, conference, or other function in any facility that prohibits the admittance of any person, or persons, on the basis of race, religious creed, color, national origin, ancestry, or sex, or that is inaccessible to disabled persons, or where members of the public may not be present without making a payment or purchase. As used in this section, "state agency" means and includes every state body, office, officer, department, division, bureau, board, council, commission, or other state agency.

(See § 1-3(b))

11131.5. No notice, agenda, announcement, or report required under this article need identify any victim or alleged victim of crime, tortious sexual conduct, or child abuse unless the identity of the person has been publicly disclosed.

(See § 1-5(b)(1))

11132. Except as expressly authorized by this article, no closed session may be held by any state body.

(See § 1-5(b))

§ 2-2: The U.C. Board of Regents

The University of California is governed by a Board of Regents, which under Article IX, Section 9 of the California Constitution has "full powers of organization and governance" subject only to very specific areas of legislative control. The article states that "the university shall be entirely independent of all political and sectarian influence and kept free therefrom in the appointment of its Regents and in the administration of its affairs." The board consists of 26 members:

- 18 Regents are appointed by the Governor for 12-year terms;
- one is a student appointed by the Regents to a one-year term;
- seven are ex officio members -- the Governor, Lieutenant Governor, Speaker of the Assembly, Superintendent of Public Instruction, president and vice president of the Alumni Associations of UC and the UC president. In addition, two faculty members—the chair and vice chair of the Academic Council—sit on the board as non-voting members.

The Regents operate through seven standing committees: Audit, Educational Policy, Finance, Grounds and Buildings, Health Services, Investments and Oversight of the Department of Energy Laboratories. The Regents meet six times a year, every other month, in two-day meetings. Meeting dates, sites and agendas for the Board of Regents and its committees are posted on the Internet at http://www.universityofcalifornia.edu/regents/meetings.html

Public access to these meetings is governed by Education Code §§92020-92033, which subject the Regents and their committees to the Bagley-Keene Open Meeting Act, with some exceptions. None of these provisions has been interpreted by a court, but action by the Regents was the subject of a case concerning remedies under the Bagley-Keene Act in *Regents of University of California v. Superior Court (Molloy)*, 20 Cal.4th 509 (1999).

92020. As used in this article, "Regents of the University of California" means the Board of Regents of the University of California and its standing and special committees or subcommittees, other than groups of not more than three regents appointed to advise and assist the university administration in contract negotiations.

92030. All meetings of the Regents of the University of California shall, except as otherwise provided in this article, be subject to Article 9 (commencing with Section 11120) of Chapter 1 of Part 1 of Division 3 of Title 2 of the Government Code.
(Editor's note: The reference is to the Bagley-Keene Open Meeting Act.)

92032. Notwithstanding any provision of Article 9 (commencing with Section 11120) of Chapter 1 of Part 1 of Division 3 of Title 2 of the Government Code:

(a) The Regents of the University of California may, as occasioned by necessity, hold special meetings. The regents shall give public notice for these meetings. This notice shall be given by means of a notice hand delivered or mailed to each newspaper of general circulation and television or radio station that has requested notice in writing, so that the notice may be published or broadcast at least 72 hours before the time of the meeting. The notice shall specify the time, place, and agenda of the special meeting. The regents shall not consider any business not included in the agenda portion of the notice. Failure to satisfy the provisions of this subdivision shall not be excused by the fact that no action was taken at the special meeting.

(b) The Regents of the University of California may conduct closed sessions when they meet to consider or discuss:

(1) Matters affecting the national security.
(2) The conferring of honorary degrees or other honors or commemorations.
(3) Matters involving gifts, devises, and bequests.
(4) Matters involving the purchase or sale of investments for endowment and pension

funds.

(5) Matters involving litigation, when discussion in open session concerning those matters would adversely affect, or be detrimental to, the public interest.

(6) The acquisition or disposition of property, if discussion of these matters in open session could adversely affect the regents' ability to acquire or dispose of the property on the terms and conditions they deem to be in the best public interest.

(7) Matters concerning the appointment, employment, performance, compensation, or dismissal of university officers or employees, excluding individual regents other than the president of the university. Consideration of compensation for the principal officers of the regents and the officers of the university, as listed in Figure 9 on page F-37 of the Analysis of the 1993-94 Budget Bill by the Legislative Analyst's office, shall not include action by the regents on compensation proposals. Action by the regents on those proposals shall be only in open session. Compensation for the principal officers of the regents and the officers of the university shall include salary, benefits, perquisites, severance payments (except those made in connection with a dismissal or a litigation settlement), retirement benefits, or any other form of compensation.

(8) Matters relating to complaints or charges brought against university officers or employees, excluding individual regents other than the president of the university, unless the officer or employee requests a public hearing.

(c) While a witness is being examined during any open or closed session, any or all other witnesses in the investigation may be excluded from the proceedings by the regents.

(d) Committees of the regents may conduct closed sessions on Medi-Cal contract negotiations.

(e) The nominating committee of the regents may conduct closed sessions held for the purpose of proposing officers of the board and members of the board's various committees.

(f) Committees of the regents may conduct closed sessions held for the purpose of proposing a student regent.

(g) The regents shall not be required to give public notice of meetings of special search or selection committees held for the purpose of conducting interviews for university officer positions.

92032.5. (a) It is the intent of the Legislature that no proposal relating to the salary, benefits, perquisites, severance payments (except those made in connection with a dismissal or a litigation settlement), or retirement benefits, or any other form of compensation paid to an officer of the University of California shall become effective unless both of the following occur:

(1) (A) Notice of the meeting at which the proposal is to be considered has been given to each regent.

(B) Information and materials regarding the proposal, including a full disclosure of the fiscal impact, have been made available to each regent in advance of the meeting at which the proposal is to be considered.

(C) The fact that the board of regents intends to vote on a proposal concerning the compensation of an officer has been displayed in the meeting notice made available to the public in accordance with the requirements of Article 9 (commencing with Section 11120) of Chapter 1 of Part 1 of Division 1 of the Government Code or, in the case of a special meeting, in accordance with subdivision (a) of Section 92032.

(D) The specific proposal has been made available, prior to the commencement of the open session of the regents at which adoption of the proposal is to be considered, to members of the public present at the open session. The proposal shall be acted upon by the regents as the final open session item for action.

(2) The proposal has been approved by the making of a motion and its adoption by a majority vote of the regents present at an open session. Nothing in this section shall preclude in open session the full discussion of the contents of the motion or the reasons why it should or should not be adopted.

(b) As used in this section, "officer" means each principal officer of the Regents of the University of California and the officers of the university, as listed in Figure 9 on page F-37 of the Analysis of the 1993-94 Budget Bill by the Legislative Analyst's office.

92033. The Regents of the University of California shall provide a copy of this article and Article 9 (commencing with Section 11120) of Chapter 1 of Part 1 of Division 3 of Title 2 of the Government Code, to each regent upon his or her appointment to the board or assumption of the office of regent.

§ 2-3: Higher Education Auxiliary Organizations

Individual community colleges, the statewide community college system as a whole, and campuses of the California State University have supporting entities called auxiliary organizations. Typically organized as nonprofit corporations, auxiliary organizations may operate campus bookstores or administer student association or organization activities; alumni activities; gifts, bequests, devises, endowments and trusts; or public relations programs. The Education Code specifies several organizational and financial requirements for these entities, including open meeting mandate. The community college auxiliary organizations are declared subject to the Brown Act, while those at CSU campuses have special rules governing their meetings. Meeting dates, sites and agendas for a community college district's auxiliary organizations would ordinarily be posted at the same place used for agendas of the college district board. Meeting dates, sites and agendas for a C.S.U. campus's auxiliary organizations are not required to be posted on the Internet, and may require some inquiry to locate.

§ 2-3(a) : Community College Auxiliary Organizations

72670. The governing board of a community college district may establish auxiliary organizations for the purpose of providing supportive services and specialized programs for the general benefit of its college or colleges. As used in this article, "auxiliary organization" may include, but is not limited to, the following entities:

(a) Any entity in which any official of a community college district participates as a director as part of his or her official position.

(b) Any entity formed or operating pursuant to Article 4 (commencing with Section 76060) of Chapter 1 of Part 47.

(c) Any entity which operates a commercial service for the benefit of a community college or district on a campus or other property of the district.

(d) Any entity whose governing instrument provides in substance both of the following:

(1) Its purpose is to promote or assist a community college or district, or to receive gifts, property and funds to be used for the benefit of the community college or district or any person or organization having an official relationship therewith.

(2) Any of its directors, governors, or trustees are either appointed or nominated by, or subject to, the approval of the governing board of the district, an official of the district, or selected, ex officio, from the membership of the student body or the faculty or the governing board or the administrative staff of the district.

(e) Any entity which is designated as an auxiliary organization by the district governing board.

72670.5. (a) The Board of Governors of the California Community Colleges may establish auxiliary organizations for the purpose of providing supportive services and specialized programs for the general benefit of the mission of the California Community Colleges.

(b) As used in this article:

(1) "Auxiliary organization" may include, but is not limited to, the following entities:

(A) Any entity whose governing instrument provides in substance both of the following:

(i) That its purpose is to promote or assist the Board of Governors of the California Community Colleges, or to receive gifts, property, and funds to be used for the benefit of the Board of Governors of the California Community Colleges or any person or organization having an official relationship therewith.

(ii) That any of its directors, governors, or trustees are either appointed or nominated by, or subject to, the approval of the Board of Governors of the California Community Colleges or an official of the California Community Colleges, or selected, ex officio, from the membership of the Board of Governors or the administrative staff of the California Community Colleges.

(B) Any entity which, exclusive of the foregoing subdivisions of this section, is designated as an auxiliary organization by the Board of Governors of the California Community Colleges.

72674. Each auxiliary organization formed pursuant to this article, shall have a board of directors composed, both as to size and categories of membership, in accordance with regulations established by the district governing board.

Each board of directors shall, during each fiscal year, hold at least one business meeting each quarter. The board of directors shall have the benefit of the advice and counsel of at least one attorney admitted to practice law in this state and at least one licensed certified public accountant. Neither the attorney at law nor the certified public accountant need be members of the board of directors.

No auxiliary organization shall accept any grant, contract, bequest, trust, or gift, unless it is so conditioned that it may be used only for purposes consistent with policies of the district governing board.

Each board of directors of an auxiliary organization shall conduct its business in public meetings in accordance with the provisions of Chapter 9 (commencing with Section 54950) of Part 1 of the Government Code.

§ 2-3(b) : California State University Auxiliary Organizations

89901. As used in this article, the term "auxiliary organization" includes the following entities:

(a) Any entity in which any official of the California State University participates as a director as part of his or her official position.

(b) Any entity formed or operating pursuant to Article 1 (commencing with Section 89300) of Chapter 3.

(c) Any entity which operates a commercial service for the benefit of a campus of the California State University on a campus or other property of the California State University.

(d) Any entity whose governing instrument provides in substance both of the following:

(1) That its purpose is to promote or assist any campus of the California State University, or to receive gifts, property, and funds to be used for the benefit of such campus or any person or organization having an official relationship therewith.

(2) That any of its directors, governors, or trustees are either appointed or nominated by, or subject to, the approval of an official of any campus of the California State University, or selected, ex officio, from the membership of the student body or the faculty or the administrative staff of campus.

(e) Any entity whose governing instrument provides in substance both of the following:

(1) That its purpose is to promote or assist the trustees of the California State University, or to receive gifts, property, and funds to be used for the benefit of the trustees of the California State University or any person or organization having an official relationship therewith.

(2) That any of its directors, governors, or trustees are either appointed or nominated by, or subject to, the approval of the trustees or an official of the California State University, or selected, ex officio, from the membership of the trustees or the administrative staff of the California State University.

(f) Any entity which, exclusive of the foregoing subdivisions of this section, is designated as an auxiliary organization by the trustees.

89902. This article shall not apply to any student body organization not formed or operating pursuant to Article 1 (commencing with Section 89300) of Chapter 3 nor to any student or faculty society, social club, fraternity, or sorority, nor to any alumni association, whether officially recognized as a campus organization or not, unless it is described in Section 89901.

This section shall not be construed to alter or limit the powers of the trustees to establish rules and regulations governing organizations which maintain an official relationship with any campus of the California State University or which use the name or facilities of the campus.

89920. Each governing board, or any subboard of the governing board, of an auxiliary organization shall conduct its business in public meetings. All governing board and subboard meetings shall be open and public, and all persons shall be permitted to attend any meeting of the governing board or subboard of an auxiliary organization, except as otherwise provided in this article.

89921. Each governing board and subboard shall annually establish, by resolution, bylaws, or whatever other rule is required for the conduct of business by that body, the time and locations for holding regular meetings. Each governing board and subboard shall, at least one week prior to the date set for the meeting, give written notice of every regular meeting, and any special meeting which is called, at least one week prior to the date set for the meeting, to any individual or medium that has filed a written request for notice. Any request for notice filed pursuant to this section shall be valid for one year from the date on which it is filed unless a renewal request is filed.

89922. A special meeting may be called at any time by the presiding officer of a governing board or subboard, or by a majority of the members of the governing board or subboard, by delivering personally or by mail written notice to each member of the board or subboard, and to any medium or other party to be directly affected by a meeting, or any other person who has requested notice in writing. The call and notice of a special meeting shall be delivered at least 24 hours prior to any meeting and shall specify the time and place of the special meeting and the business to be transacted. No other business shall be considered at these meetings by the governing board or subboard. Written notice may be dispensed with as to any member who, at or prior to the time the meeting convenes, files with the clerk or the secretary of the governing board or subboard a written waiver of notice. The waiver may be given by telegram. Written notice may also be dispensed with as to any member who is actually present at the meeting at the time it convenes.

89923. Any governing board or subboard may hold closed sessions to consider matters relating to litigation, collective bargaining, or the appointment, employment, evaluation of performance, or dismissal of an employee, or to hear complaints or charges brought against an employee by another person or employee, unless the employee requests a public hearing. For the purposes of this section, "employee" does not include any person elected or appointed to an office. A board or subboard, upon a favorable majority vote of its members, may also hold a closed session to discuss investments where a public discussion could have a negative impact on the auxiliary organization's financial situation. In this case, a final decision shall only be made during public sessions.

89924. No governing board or subboard shall take action on any issue until that issue has been publicly posted for at least one week.

89925. Each auxiliary organization shall establish, by constitution, statute, bylaws, or resolution, provisions for elections of officers and board members. These provisions shall be designed to allow all those eligible to vote complete access to all information on issues and candidates. These provisions shall include, but not be limited to, provisions for sample ballots, numbers of days and hours for voting, polling locations, and notice of elections.

89926. Where the constitution or articles of incorporation of an associated students auxiliary organization provides for a judiciary or judicial council with powers separate from the governing board of the auxiliary organization, decisions rendered by the judiciary or judicial council shall be final.

89927. Each member of a governing board pursuant to this article who attends a meeting of the governing board where action is taken in violation of any provision of this article, with knowledge of the fact that the meeting is in violation of this article, is guilty of a misdemeanor.

89928. This article is not applicable to either of the following:
(a) Any entity formed or operating pursuant to Section 89300.
(b) The governing board of any statewide student organization that represents the students of the California State University.

§ 2-4: California State University Student Government Bodies

Unlike those at community colleges or the University of California, student government bodies at C.S.U. campuses have their own open meeting statute, the Gloria Romero Open Meetings Act (Education Code §89305 *et seq.*) The Romero Act is closely modeled on the Brown Act, with mostly identical provisions. Meeting dates, sites and agendas are not required to be posted on the Internet, but may be. For example, the Associated Students, Inc. of California State University, Sacramento, posts its meeting agendas on its calendar of events at http://www.asi.csus.edu.

89305. This article shall be known, and may be cited, as the Gloria Romero Open Meetings Act of 2000.

89305.1. (a) A legislative body of a student body organization shall conduct its business in public meetings. All meetings of the legislative body shall be open and public, and all persons shall be permitted to attend any meeting of the legislative body, except as otherwise provided in this article.
(b)(1) As used in this article:
(A) "Legislative body" means any or all of the following:
(i) The governing body of any entity formed or operating pursuant to Section 89300.
(ii) The governing body of any statewide student organization that represents either the students of the California State University or the governing bodies of the student body organizations of the campuses of the California State University, or both.
(iii) A commission, committee, board, subboard, or other body, whether permanent or temporary, created by charter, resolution, or formal action of a legislative body described in clause (i) or (ii). However, an advisory committee is not a legislative body, except that a standing committee of a legislative body, irrespective of its composition, that has a continuing subject matter jurisdiction, or a meeting schedule established by charter, resolution, or formal action of a legislative body is a legislative body for purposes of this article.
(B) "Meeting" includes any congregation of a majority of the membership of a legislative body at the same time and place to hear, discuss, or deliberate upon any item that is within the subject matter jurisdiction of the legislative body to which it pertains. "Meeting" does not include, and nothing in this section imposes the requirements of this article upon, any of the following:
(i) Individual contacts or conversations between a member of a legislative body and any other person.

(ii) The attendance of a majority of the members of a legislative body at a conference or similar gathering open to the public that involves a discussion of issues of general interest to the public or to higher education of the type represented by the legislative body, provided that a majority of the members do not discuss among themselves, other than as a part of the scheduled program, business of a specified nature that is within the subject matter jurisdiction of the legislative body. Nothing in this clause is intended to allow members of the public free admission to a conference or similar gathering at which the organizers have required other participants or registrants to pay fees or charges as a condition of attendance.

(iii) The attendance of a majority of the members of a legislative body at an open and noticed meeting of another body or entity created or formed by the legislative body, provided that a majority of the members do not discuss among themselves, other than as a part of the scheduled meeting, business of a specific nature that is within the subject matter jurisdiction of the legislative body.

(iv) The attendance of a majority of the members of a legislative body at a purely social or ceremonial occasion, provided that a majority of the members do not discuss among themselves business of a specific nature that is within the subject matter jurisdiction of the legislative body.

(2) For the purposes of this section, "teleconference" means a meeting of a legislative body, the members of which are in different locations, connected by electronic means, through either audio or video, or both.

(c)(1) Notwithstanding any other provision of law, the legislative body may use teleconferencing for the benefit of the public and the legislative body in connection with any meeting or proceeding authorized by law. The teleconferenced meeting or proceeding shall comply with all requirements of this chapter and all otherwise applicable provisions of law.

(2) Teleconferencing, as authorized by this section, may be used for all purposes in connection with any meeting within the subject matter jurisdiction of the legislative body. All votes taken during a teleconferenced meeting shall be by rollcall.

(3) If the legislative body elects to use teleconferencing, it shall post agendas at all teleconference locations and conduct teleconference meetings in a manner that protects the statutory and constitutional rights of the parties or the public appearing before the legislative body. Each teleconference location shall be identified in the notice and agenda of the meeting or proceeding, and each teleconference location shall be accessible to the public. The agenda shall provide an opportunity for members of the public to address the legislative body directly pursuant to Section 89306 at each teleconference location.

(d) Nothing in this section shall prohibit a student body organization from providing the public with additional teleconference locations.

(e) No legislative body shall take action by secret ballot, whether preliminary or final.

89305.4. As used in this article, "action taken" means a collective decision made by a majority of the members of a legislative body, a collective commitment or promise by a majority of the members of a legislative body to make a positive or a negative decision, or an actual vote by a majority of the members of a legislative body when sitting as a body or entity, upon a motion, proposal, report, resolution, order, or recommendation.

89305.5. (a) Each legislative body shall annually establish, by resolution, bylaws, or whatever other rule is required for the conduct of business by that body, the time and locations for holding regular meetings.

(b)(1) At least 72 hours before a regular meeting, the legislative body, or its designee, shall post an agenda containing a brief general description of each item of business to be transacted or discussed at the meeting, including items to be discussed in closed session. A brief general description of an item generally need not exceed 20 words. The agenda shall specify the time and location of the regular meeting and shall be posted in a location that is freely accessible to members of the public.

(2) No action or discussion shall be undertaken on any item not appearing on the posted agenda, except that a member of a legislative body, or a member of his or her staff, may briefly respond to statements made or questions posed by a person exercising his or her public testimony rights under Section 89306. In addition, on his or her own initiative or in

response to questions posed by the public, a member of a legislative body, or a member of his or her staff, may ask a question for clarification, make a brief announcement, or make a brief report on his or her own activities. Furthermore, a member of a legislative body, or the body itself, subject to the rules or procedures of the legislative body, may provide a reference to staff or other resources for factual information, request staff to report back to the body at a subsequent meeting concerning any matter, or take action to direct staff to place a matter of business on a future agenda.

(c) Notwithstanding subdivision (b), the legislative body may take action on items of business that do not appear on the posted agenda, but are publicly identified under any of the following conditions:

(1) Upon a determination, pursuant to Section 89306.5, by the membership of the legislative body that an emergency situation exists.

(2) Upon a determination by a two-thirds vote of the members of the legislative body present at the meeting, or, if less than two-thirds of the members are present, a unanimous vote of those members present, that there is a need to take immediate action and that the need for action came to the attention of the legislative body subsequent to the agenda being posted as specified in subdivision (b).

(3) The item was posted pursuant to subdivision (b) for a prior meeting of the legislative body occurring not more than five calendar days prior to the present meeting.

89305.7. Any person may request that a copy of the agenda, or a copy of all the documents that constitute the agenda packet, of any meeting of a legislative body be mailed to that person. Upon receipt of the written request, the legislative body or its designee shall cause the requested materials to be mailed at the time the agenda is posted pursuant to Section 89305.5 or upon distribution to all, or a majority of all, of the members of a legislative body, whichever occurs first. Any request for mailed copies of agendas or agenda packets shall be valid for the calendar year in which it is filed, and shall be renewed following January 1 of each year. The legislative body may establish a fee for mailing the agenda or agenda packet, and that fee shall not exceed the cost of providing the service. Failure of the requesting person to receive the agenda or agenda packet pursuant to this section shall not constitute grounds for invalidation of the Actions of the legislative body taken at the meeting for which the agenda or agenda packet was not received.

89306. (a)(1) Every agenda for regular meetings shall provide an opportunity for members of the public to directly address the legislative body on any item affecting higher education at the campus or statewide level, provided that no action shall be taken on any item not appearing on the agenda unless the Action is otherwise authorized by subdivision (c) of Section 89305.5.

(2) Notwithstanding paragraph (1), the agenda need not provide an opportunity for members of the public to address the legislative body on any item that has already been considered by a committee, composed exclusively of members of the respective legislative body at a public meeting wherein all interested members of the public were afforded the opportunity to address the committee on the item, before or during the committee's consideration of the item, unless the item has been substantially changed, as determined by the legislative body, since the committee heard the item.

(3) Every notice for a special meeting shall provide an opportunity for members of the public to directly address the legislative body concerning any item that has been described in the notice for the meeting before or during consideration of that item.

(b) A legislative body may adopt reasonable regulations to ensure that the intent of subdivision (a) is carried out, including, but not necessarily limited to, regulations limiting the amount of time allocated for public testimony on a particular issue and for each individual speaker.

(c) A legislative body shall not prohibit public criticism of anything related to the student body organization, the legislative body, or both. Nothing in this subdivision shall confer any privilege or protection for expression beyond that otherwise provided by law.

89306.5. (a) A special meeting may be called at any time by the presiding officer of a legislative body, or by a majority of the membership of the legislative body, by providing written notice to each member of the legislative body, and to each local newspaper of general circulation and radio or television station that has requested notice of special meetings at least 24 hours prior to the meeting. The written notice shall specify the time and place of the meeting and the business to be transacted or discussed. No other business shall be considered at these meetings by the legislative body. Written notice may be dispensed with as to any member who, at or prior to the time the meeting convenes, provides the clerk or the secretary of the legislative body with a waiver of written notice. Written notice may also be dispensed with as to any member who is actually present at the meeting at the time it convenes.

(b) The call and notice shall be posted at least 24 hours prior to the special meeting in a location that is freely accessible to members of the public.

(c) In the case of an emergency situation involving matters upon which prompt action is necessary due to the disruption or threatened disruption of public facilities, a legislative body may hold an emergency meeting without complying with either the 24-hour notice requirement or the 24-hour posting requirement of subdivision (b), or both.

(d)(1) For purposes of this section, "emergency situation" means either of the following:

(A) Work stoppage or other activity that severely impairs public health, safety, or both, as determined by a majority of the membership of the legislative body.

(B) Crippling disaster that severely impairs public health, safety, or both, as determined by a majority of the membership of the legislative body.

(2) Each local newspaper of general circulation and radio or television station that has requested notice of special meetings pursuant to subdivision (a) shall be notified by the presiding officer of the legislative body, or his or her designee, one hour prior to the emergency meeting by telephone. If necessary, the presiding officer or designee shall use all of the telephone numbers provided in the most recent request of that newspaper or station for notification of special meetings to notify the newspaper or radio of the special meeting.

(3) If telephone services are not functioning, the notice requirements of this section shall be deemed waived, and the legislative body, or designee, shall notify those newspapers, radio stations, or television stations of the fact of the holding of the emergency meeting, the purpose of the meeting, and any action taken at the meeting as soon after the meeting as possible.

(e) Notwithstanding subdivision (c) of Section 89307, the legislative body shall not meet in closed session during a meeting called pursuant to this section.

(f) All special meeting requirements prescribed in subdivision (a) shall be applicable to a meeting called pursuant to subdivision (c), with the exception of the 24-hour notice requirement.

(g) The legislative body shall post in a public place, as soon after the meeting as possible and for a minimum of 10 days, the minutes of a meeting called pursuant to subdivision (c), a list of persons who the presiding officer of the legislative body, or designee, notified or attempted to notify, a copy of the rollcall vote, and any actions taken at the meeting.

89307. (a) Any legislative body may hold a closed session under any of the following circumstances:

(1) A closed session with its negotiator prior to the purchase, sale, exchange, or lease of real property by or for the student body organization to grant authority to its negotiator regarding the price and terms of payment for the purchase, sale, exchange, or lease. Prior to the closed session, the legislative body shall hold an open and public session in which it identifies its negotiators, the real property or real properties that the negotiations may concern, and the person or persons with whom its negotiators may negotiate.

(2) For purposes of this subdivision:

(A) A negotiator may be a member of the legislative body.

(B) "Lease" includes renewal or renegotiation of a lease.

(b)(1) Based on advice of its legal counsel, holding a closed session to confer with, or receive advice from, its legal counsel regarding a liability claim or pending litigation when discussion in open session concerning the matter would prejudice the position of the student body organization in the litigation.

(2) For purposes of this subdivision, all applications of the lawyer-client privilege other than those provided in this section are hereby abrogated. This section is the exclusive

expression of the lawyer-client privilege for purposes of conducting closed-session meetings pursuant to this article.

(3) For purposes of this subdivision, "litigation" means any adjudicatory proceeding, including, but not limited to, eminent domain, court proceeding, or a proceeding of an administrative body exercising its adjudicatory authority, hearing officer, or arbitrator.

(4) For purposes of this subdivision, litigation shall be considered pending when any of the following circumstances exist:

(A) Litigation, to which the student body organization is a party, has been initiated formally.

(B) A point has been reached where, in the opinion of the legislative body on the advice of its legal counsel, based on existing facts and circumstances, there is a significant exposure to litigation against the student body organization.

(C) Based on existing facts and circumstances, the legislative body is meeting only to decide whether a closed session is authorized pursuant to subparagraph (B).

(D) Based on existing facts and circumstances, the legislative body has decided to initiate, or is deciding whether to initiate, litigation.

(5) For purposes of subparagraphs (B), (C), and (D) of paragraph (4), "existing facts and circumstances" shall consist only of one of the following:

(A) Facts and circumstances that might result in litigation against the student body organization, but which the organization believes are not yet known to a potential plaintiff or plaintiffs, which facts and circumstances need not be disclosed.

(B) Facts and circumstances, including, but not necessarily limited to, an accident, disaster, incident, or transactional occurrence, that might result in litigation against the student body organization and that are known to a potential plaintiff or plaintiffs, which facts or circumstances shall be publicly stated on the agenda or announced.

(C) The receipt of a claim pursuant to the Tort Claims Act (Division 3.6 (commencing with Section 810) of Title 1 of the Government Code) or some other written communication from a potential plaintiff threatening litigation.

(D) A statement made by a person in an open and public meeting threatening litigation on a specific matter within the responsibility of the legislative body.

(E) A statement threatening litigation made by a person outside an open and public meeting on a specific matter within the responsibility of the legislative body, so long as the official or employee of the student body organization receiving knowledge of the threat makes a contemporaneous or other record of the statement prior to the meeting. The records so created need not identify the alleged victim of unlawful or tortious sexual conduct or anyone making the threat on their behalf, or identify a public employee who is the alleged perpetrator of any unlawful or tortious conduct upon which a threat of litigation is based, unless the identity of the person has been publicly disclosed.

(6) Nothing in this section shall require disclosure of written communications that are privileged and not subject to disclosure pursuant to the California Public Records Act (Chapter 3.5 (commencing with Section 6250) of Division 7 of Title 1 of the Government Code).

(7) Prior to holding a closed session pursuant to this section, the legislative body shall state on the agenda or publicly announce and identify the provision of this section that authorizes the closed session. If the session is closed pursuant to paragraph (1), the legislative body shall state the title of or otherwise specifically identify the litigation to be discussed, unless the legislative body states that to do so would jeopardize the ability of the student body organization to effectuate service of process upon one or more unserved parties, or that to do so would jeopardize its ability to conclude existing settlement negotiations to its advantage.

(8) For purposes of this subdivision, a student body organization shall be considered to be a "party" or to have a "significant exposure to litigation" if an officer or employee of the student body organization is a party or has significant exposure to litigation concerning prior or prospective activities or alleged activities during the course and scope of that office or employment, including litigation in which it is an issue whether an activity is outside the course and scope of the office or employment.

(c)(1) Nothing contained in this section shall be construed to prevent a legislative body from holding closed sessions with the Attorney General, district attorney, sheriff, or chief of police, or their respective deputies, on matters posing a threat to the security of public buildings or a threat to the public's right of access to public services or public facilities, or from holding closed sessions during a regular or special meeting to consider the appointment, employment, evaluation of performance, discipline, or dismissal of an employee of the student body organization or to hear complaints or charges brought against the employee by another person or employee unless the employee requests a public session.

(2) As a condition to holding a closed session on specific complaints or charges brought against an employee by another person or employee, the employee shall be given written notice of his or her right to have the complaints or charges heard in an open session rather than a closed session, which notice shall be delivered to the employee personally or by mail at least 24 hours before the time for holding the session. If notice is not given, any disciplinary or other action taken by the legislative body against the employee based on the specific complaints or charges in the closed session shall be null and void.

(3) A legislative body also may exclude from the public or closed meeting, during the examination of a witness, any or all other witnesses in the matter being investigated by the legislative body.

(4) For the purposes of this subdivision, the term "employee" shall include an officer or an independent contractor who functions as an officer or an employee of the student body organization, but shall not include any elected official, member of a legislative body, or other independent contractor. Closed sessions held pursuant to this section shall not include discussion or action on proposed compensation except for a reduction of compensation that results from the imposition of discipline.

(d)(1) A legislative body shall publicly report any action taken in closed session and the vote or abstention of every member present thereon, as follows:

(A) Approval of an agreement concluding real property negotiations pursuant to subdivision (a) shall be reported after the agreement is final, as follows:

(i) If its own approval renders the agreement final, the legislative body board or subboard shall report that approval and the substance of the agreement in open session at the public meeting during which the closed session is held.

(ii) If final approval rests with the other party to the negotiations, the legislative body shall disclose the fact of that approval and the substance of the agreement upon inquiry by any person, as soon as the other party or its agent has informed the legislative body of its approval.

(B) Approval given to its legal counsel to defend, or seek or refrain from seeking appellate review or relief, or to enter as an amicus curiae in any form of litigation, as the result of a consultation under subdivision (b) shall be reported in open session at the public meeting during which the closed session is held. The report shall identify, if known, the adverse party or parties and the substance of the litigation. In the case of approval given to initiate or intervene in an action, the announcement need not identify the Action, the defendants, or other particulars, but shall specify that the direction to initiate or intervene in an action has been given and that the Action, the defendants, and the other particulars shall, once formally commenced, be disclosed to any person upon inquiry, unless to do so would jeopardize the ability of the student body organization to effectuate service of process on one or more unserved parties, or that to do so would jeopardize its ability to conclude existing settlement negotiations to its advantage.

(C) Approval given to its legal counsel of a settlement of pending litigation, as defined in subdivision (b), at any stage prior to or during a judicial or quasi-judicial proceeding shall be reported after the settlement is final, as follows:

(i) If a legislative body accepts a settlement offer signed by the opposing party, the legislative body shall report its acceptance and identify the substance of the agreement in open session at the public meeting during which the closed session is held.

(ii) If final approval rests with some other party to the litigation or with the court, then, as soon as the settlement becomes final, and upon inquiry by any person, the legislative body shall disclose the fact of that approval and identify the substance of the agreement.

(D) Action taken to appoint, employ, dismiss, accept the resignation of, or otherwise affect the employment status of an employee of the employee organization in closed session pursuant to subdivision (c) shall be reported at the public meeting during which the closed session is held. Any report required by this subparagraph shall identify the title of the employee's position. Notwithstanding the general requirement of this subparagraph, the report of a dismissal or of the nonrenewal of an employment contract shall be deferred until the first public meeting following the exhaustion of administrative remedies, if any.

(E) Approval of an agreement concluding labor negotiations with represented employees pursuant to subdivision (e) shall be reported after the agreement is final and has been accepted or ratified by the other party. The report shall identify the item approved and the other party or parties to the negotiation.

(2) Reports that are required to be made pursuant to this subdivision may be made orally or in writing. A legislative body shall provide to any person who has submitted a written request to the legislative body within 24 hours of the posting of the agenda, or to any person who has made a standing request for all documentation as part of a request for notice of meetings pursuant to Section 89306.5, if the requester is present at the time the closed session ends, copies of any contracts, settlement agreements, or other documents that were finally approved or adopted in the closed session. If the Action taken results in one or more substantive amendments to the related documents requiring retyping, the documents need not be released until the retyping is completed during normal business hours, provided that the presiding officer of the legislative body, or his or her designee, orally summarizes the substance of the amendments for the benefit of the document requester or any other person present and requesting the information.

(3) The documentation referred to in paragraph (2) shall be available to any person on the next business day following the meeting in which the Action referred to is taken or, in the case of substantial amendments, when any necessary retyping is complete.

(4) Nothing in this subdivision shall be construed to require that a legislative body approve actions not otherwise subject to the approval of that legislative body.

(5) No action for injury to a reputational, liberty, or other personal interest may be commenced by or on behalf of any employee or former employee with respect to whom a disclosure is made by a legislative body in an effort to comply with this subdivision.

(e)(1) Notwithstanding any other provision of law, a legislative body may hold closed sessions with the designated representative of the student body organization regarding the salaries, salary schedules, or compensation paid in the form of fringe benefits of its represented and unrepresented employees, and, for represented employees, any other matter within the statutorily provided scope of representation. However, prior to the closed session, the legislative body shall hold an open and public session in which it identifies its designated representatives.

(2)(A) Closed sessions of a legislative body, as permitted in this subdivision, shall be for the purpose of reviewing its position and instructing the designated representative of the student body organization.

(B) Closed sessions, as permitted in this subdivision, may take place prior to and during consultations and discussions with representatives of employee organizations and unrepresented employees.

(C) Closed sessions with the designated representative of the student body organization regarding the salaries, salary schedules, or compensation paid in the form of fringe benefits may include discussion of the available funds and funding priorities of the student body organization, but only insofar as these discussions relate to providing instructions to the designated representative of the student body organization.

(D) Closed sessions held pursuant to this subdivision shall not include final action on the proposed compensation of one or more unrepresented employees.

(E) For the purposes enumerated in this subdivision, a legislative body may also meet with a state conciliator who has intervened in the proceedings.

(3) For the purposes of this subdivision, the term "employee" includes an officer or an independent contractor who functions as an officer or an employee of the student body organization, but shall not include any elected official, member of a legislative body, or other independent contractors.

(f)(1) Prior to holding any closed session, the legislative body shall disclose, in an open meeting, the item or items to be discussed in the closed session. The disclosure may take the form of a reference to the item or items as they are listed by number or letter on the agenda. In the closed session, the legislative body may consider only those matters covered in its statement. Nothing in this subdivision shall require or authorize a disclosure of information prohibited by state or federal law.

(2) After any closed session, the legislative body shall reconvene into open session prior to adjournment, and shall make any disclosures required by subdivision (d) of action taken in the closed session.

(3) The disclosure required to be made in open session pursuant to this subdivision may be made at the location announced in the agenda for the closed session, as long as the public is allowed to be present at that location for the purpose of hearing the announcements.

89307.1. In the event that any meeting is willfully interrupted by a group or groups of persons so as to render the orderly conduct of that meeting unfeasible, and order cannot be restored by the removal of individuals who are willfully interrupting the meeting, the members of the legislative body conducting the meeting may order the meeting room cleared and continue in session. Only matters appearing on the agenda may be considered in that session. Representatives of the press or other news media, except those participating in the disturbance, shall be allowed to attend any session held pursuant to this section. Nothing in this section shall prohibit the legislative body from establishing a procedure for readmitting an individual or individuals not responsible for willfully disturbing the orderly conduct of the meeting.

89307.2. (a) No legislative body of a local agency shall conduct any meeting in any facility that prohibits the admittance of any person, or persons, on the basis of race, religious creed, color, national origin, ancestry, or sex, or which is inaccessible to disabled persons, or where members of the public may not be present without making a payment or purchase. This section shall apply to every legislative body as defined in Section 89305.1.

(b) No notice, agenda, announcement, or report required under this article need identify any victim or alleged victim of tortious sexual conduct or child abuse unless the identity of the person has been publicly disclosed.

89307.4. Each member of a legislative body who attends a meeting of that legislative body where an action is taken in violation of any provision of this article, with knowledge that the meeting is in violation of this article, is guilty of a misdemeanor.

§ 2-5: University of California Student Government

No statutes govern meetings of the Associated Students organizations at campuses of the University of California. Instead, access to these meetings is governed by the organizations' own constitutions or similar charter provisions. For example, the A.S.U.C. Constitution at U.C. Berkeley states:

ARTICLE VIII – MEETINGS
SECTION 1: CLOSED SESSION

A. All meetings of ASUC boards, councils, committees, and other organizations shall be open and public, except as provided in this article.

B. The ASUC Senate, the Judicial Council, the Graduate Assembly, and subordinate units of these bodies may hold closed sessions only if two-thirds (2/3) of their entire membership approve. Such closed sessions may be held only for the discussion or consideration of the following:

1. Matters involving litigation, when discussing in open session concerning those matters would adversely affect the interests of the ASUC.

2. The acquisition or disposition of property, if discussion of these matters in open session could adversely affect the ability of the ASUC to acquire or dispose of the property on the terms and conditions it deems to be in the best interest of the Association.

3. Matters concerning the appointment, employment, performance, compensation, or

dismissal of ASUC employees, excluding elected and appointed officers.

4. Deliberation on a case in order to arrive at a judgment, for the ASUC Judicial Council only.

5. Matters relating to labor-related negotiations between the Association and the University.

6. Matters involving investments, when discussion in open session could have a negative impact on the Association's financial situation.

C. The agenda for closed sessions shall be approved in open session and no further items shall be considered in closed session. No items shall be voted on during a closed session.

SECTION 2: PUBLIC NOTICE

A. The ASUC Senate, the Judicial Council, and the Graduate Assembly shall not take action on any main motion unless and until that motion has been publicly posted for at least one week.

B. Notice of the agenda for each regular meeting must be given to all ASUC Executive Officers and all members of the respective body and any individual or medium that has filed a request for it at least one week prior to the meeting.

C. The call and notice of a special meeting shall be posted and given at least 48 hours in advance and shall specify the business to be transacted. No other business shall be considered at these meetings.

D. The requirements of this article may be waived by two-thirds vote of the entire membership of a body mentioned in Section A in the case of the following emergency situations involving matters upon which prompt action is necessary.

1. Work stoppage.
2. Crippling disaster.
3. Pending litigation.

The presiding officer of the bodies mentioned in Section A shall provide notice and public posting of such situations and actions as soon as practicable.

SECTION 3: VOTING BY PROXY

Members of the ASUC Senate or any board, council, or other organization of the Association may not vote by proxy in any ASUC matter.

§ 2-6: Local Public School Site Advisory Committees

As the result of certain specialized public education programs, citizens with no powers other than to advise public institutions sometimes occupy seats on permanent multimember bodies that the legislature wishes to exempt from the full complexities of the Brown Act. Education Code Section 35147 exempts "schoolsite advisory committees" from the Brown Act, which would otherwise govern them since they are multimember bodies created by a school board. The section instead provides a few open meeting rules whose only enforcement sanction is the prospect of having to redo an action if it has violated these basic requirements. The bodies governed by this section are subject to very elementary requirements, with no sanctions for violations, only a possible exposure to revisiting a matter dealt with in conflict with the rules. Education Code Section 35147 states:

(a) Except as specified in this section, any meeting of the councils or committees specified in subdivision (b) is exempt from the provisions of this article, the Bagley-Keene Open Meeting Act (Article 9 (commencing with Section 11120) of Chapter 1 of Division 3 of Title 2 of the Government Code), and the Ralph M. Brown Act (Chapter 9 (commencing with Section 54950) of Division 2 of Title 5 of the Government Code).

(b) The councils and schoolsite advisory committees established pursuant to Sections 52012 (school improvement programs), 52065 (repealed), 52176 (bilingual-bicultural education), and 52852 (school-based program coordination), subdivision (b) of Section 54425 (compensatory education), Sections 54444.2 (migrant education), 54724 (dropout recovery), and 62002.5, and committees formed pursuant to Section 11503 or Section 2604 of Title 25 of the United States Code, are subject to this section.

(c) Any meeting held by a council or committee specified in subdivision (b) shall be open to the public and any member of the public shall be able to address the council or committee during the meeting on any item within the subject matter jurisdiction of the council or committee. Notice of the meeting shall be posted at the schoolsite, or other appropriate place accessible to the public, at least 72 hours before the time set for the meeting. The notice shall specify the date, time, and location of the meeting and contain an agenda describing each item of business to be discussed or acted upon. The council or committee may not take any action on any item of business unless that item appeared on the posted agenda or unless the council or committee members present, by unanimous vote, find that there is a need to take immediate action and that the need for action came to the attention of the council or committee subsequent to the posting of the agenda. Questions or brief statements made at a meeting by members of the council, committee, or public that do not have a significant effect on pupils or employees in the school or school district or that can be resolved solely by the provision of information need not be described on an agenda as items of business. If a council or committee violates the procedural meeting requirements of this section and upon demand of any person, the council or committee shall reconsider the item at its next meeting, after allowing for public input on the item.

(d) Any materials provided to a schoolsite council shall be made available to any member of the public who requests the materials pursuant to the California Public Records Act (Chapter 3.5 (commencing with Section 6250) of Division 7 of Title 1).

3. The Legislature

The laws governing open meetings of the California Legislature are found in the Constitution, the Government Code and the Joint Rules of the Senate and Assembly. To date, there are no reported cases or other public authorities interpreting these laws. Compared with the Brown Act and the Bagley-Keene Act they are relatively compact, distinguished mainly by the authorization for closed party caucuses at the house or even committee level. Committee hearing dates for a bill can be found as part of the status report on its web page, which can be found by entering the bill number at either
http://www.assembly.ca.gov/acs/acsframeset2text.htm
or
http://info.sen.ca.gov/cgi-bin/pagequery?type=sen_bilinfo&site=sen&title=Bill+Information
A list of all the bills to be considered at a particular committee hearing, plus the time and location of the hearing, can be found in the daily file of the Assembly, at
http://www.assembly.ca.gov/acs/defaulttext.asp
or of the Senate, at
http://www.senate.ca.gov/~newsen/schedules/schedules.htp

§ 3-1: The Constitutional Provisions

Article IV, Section 7, subdivision (c) of the California Constitution states:

(c) (1) The proceedings of each house and the committees thereof shall be open and public. However, closed sessions may be held solely for any of the following purposes:

(A) To consider the appointment, employment, evaluation of performance, or dismissal of a public officer or employee, to consider or hear complaints or charges brought against a Member of the Legislature or other public officer or employee, or to establish the classification or compensation of an employee of the Legislature.

(B) To consider matters affecting the safety and security of Members of the Legislature or its employees or the safety and security of any buildings and grounds used by the Legislature.

(C) To confer with, or receive advice from, its legal counsel regarding pending or reasonably anticipated, or whether to initiate, litigation when discussion in open session would not protect the interests of the house or committee regarding the litigation.

(2) A caucus of the Members of the Senate, the Members of the Assembly, or the Members of both houses, which is composed of the members of the same political party, may meet in closed session.

(3) The Legislature shall implement this subdivision by concurrent resolution adopted by rollcall vote entered in the journal, two-thirds of the membership of each house concurring, or by statute, and shall prescribe that, when a closed session is held pursuant to paragraph (1), reasonable notice of the closed session and the purpose of the closed session shall be provided to the public. If there is a conflict between a concurrent resolution and statute, the last adopted or enacted shall prevail.

§ 3-2: The Statutory Provisions

The implementing statute comprises the following Government Code sections:

9027. Except as otherwise provided in this article, all meetings of a house of the Legislature or a committee thereof shall be open and public, and all persons shall be permitted to attend the meetings. As used in this article, "meeting" means a gathering of a quorum of the members of a house or committee in one place for the purpose of discussing legislative or other official matters within the jurisdiction of the house or committee. As used in this article, "committee" includes a standing committee, joint committee, conference committee, subcommittee, select committee, special committee, research committee, or any similar body.

9028. Any meeting that is required to be open and public pursuant to this article, including any closed session held pursuant to subdivision (a) of Section 9029, shall be held only after full and timely notice to the public as provided by the Joint Rules of the Assembly and Senate.

9029. (a) A house of the Legislature or a committee thereof may hold a closed session solely for any of the following purposes:

(1) To consider the appointment, employment, evaluation of performance, or dismissal of a public officer or employee, to consider or hear complaints or charges brought against a Member of the Legislature or other public officer or employee, or to establish the classification or compensation of an employee of the Legislature.

(2) To consider matters affecting the safety and security of Members of the Legislature or its employees or the safety and security of any buildings and grounds used by the Legislature.

(3) To confer with, or receive advice from, its legal counsel regarding pending or reasonably anticipated, or whether to initiate, litigation when discussion in open session would not protect the interests of the house or committee regarding the litigation.

(b) A caucus of the Members of the Senate, the Members of the Assembly, or the Members of both houses, which is composed of members of the same political party, may meet in closed session.

9029.5. (a) A closed session may be held pursuant to paragraph (3) of subdivision (a) of Section 9029 under any of the following circumstances:

(1) An adjudicatory proceeding before a court, administrative body exercising its adjudicatory authority, hearing officer, or arbitrator, to which a house of the Legislature or a committee,
Member, or employee thereof is a party, has been initiated formally.

(2) Based on existing facts and circumstances, a point has been reached where, in the opinion of a house of the Legislature or a committee thereof, on the advice of its legal counsel, litigation against the house or a committee, Member, or employee thereof is reasonably anticipated.

(3) Based on existing facts and circumstances, a house of the Legislature or a committee thereof has decided to initiate or is deciding whether to initiate litigation.

(4) To confer with, or receive advice from, its legal counsel and negotiator prior to the purchase, sale, exchange, or lease of real property by or for the house or committee regarding the price and terms of payment for the purchase, sale, exchange, or lease.

(b) Prior to holding a closed session pursuant to paragraph (3) of subdivision (a) Section 9029 and this section, the presiding officer of the house or the chair of the committee shall state publicly which paragraph of subdivision (a) is applicable. If the closed session is held pursuant to paragraph (1) of subdivision (a), the presiding officer or chair shall state the title of or otherwise specifically identify the litigation to be discussed, unless the presiding officer or chair states that to do so would jeopardize the ability to effectuate service of process upon one or more unserved parties, or that to do so would jeopardize the ability of the house or the committee to conclude existing settlement negotiations to its advantage. If the closed session is held pursuant to paragraph (4) of subdivision (a), the notice of the closed session shall identify the real property which the negotiations may concern and the person with whom the negotiations may take place.

(c) The legal counsel of the house or the committee shall prepare and submit to the house or the committee a memorandum stating the specific reasons and legal authority for the closed session. If the closed session is held pursuant to paragraph (1) of subdivision (a), the memorandum shall include the title of or other identification of the litigation. If the closed session is held pursuant to paragraph (2) or (3) of subdivision (a), the memorandum shall set forth the existing facts and circumstances on which the closed session is based. The legal counsel shall submit the memorandum to the house or the committee prior to the closed session, if feasible, or, in any case, not later than one week after the closed session. The memorandum shall be exempt from disclosure under the Legislative Open Records Act (Article 3.5 (commencing with Section 9070) of Chapter 1.5 of Part 1 of Division 2 of Title 2).

(d) For purposes of paragraph (3) of subdivision (a) of Section 9029 and this section, "litigation" includes any adjudicatory proceeding, including eminent domain, before a court, administrative body exercising its adjudicatory authority, hearing officer, or arbitrator.

(e) For purposes of this article, all expressions of the lawyer-client privilege other than those provided in this section are hereby abrogated. This section is the exclusive expression of the lawyer-client privilege for the purposes of conducting closed-session meetings pursuant to this article.

(f) Disclosure of a memorandum required under this section shall not be deemed a waiver of the lawyer-client privilege provided for under Article 3 (commencing with Section 950) of Chapter 4 of Division 8 of the Evidence Code.

9030. Each Member of the Legislature who attends a meeting of the Assembly, the Senate, or any committee or subcommittee thereof, where action is taken in violation of Section 9027, with knowledge of the fact that the meeting is in violation thereof, is guilty of a misdemeanor.

9031. Any interested person may commence an action by mandamus, injunction, or declaratory relief for the purpose of stopping or preventing violations or threatened violations of this article by Members of the Legislature or to determine the applicability of this article to actions or threatened future action of a house of the Legislature or a committee thereof.

§ 3-3: The Joint Rule on Conference Committees

The statutory provisions have been supplemented by one of the Joint Rules of the Senate and the Assembly, which states:

29.5. (a) All meetings of any conference committee on the Budget Bill shall be open and readily accessible to the public.

A conference committee on any bill may not meet, consider, or act on the subject matter of the bill except in a meeting that is open and readily accessible to the public, unless the Action is on a report determined by the Legislative Counsel to be nonsubstantive. The Legislative Counsel shall examine each proposed report and shall note upon the face of the report that the amendments proposed are "substantive" or "nonsubstantive" as the case may be.

The chairman or chairwoman of the conference committee of each house shall give notice to the File Clerk of their respective houses of the time and place of the meeting. Notice of each public meeting shall be published in the Daily File of each house one calendar day prior to the meeting, except that the notice is not required for a meeting of a conference committee on the Budget Bill. When this subdivision is waived with respect to a meeting of any public conference committee, or when there is a meeting of a conference committee on the Budget Bill, every effort shall be made to inform the public that a meeting has been called. When this subdivision has been waived with respect to the meeting of any public conference committee, the chairman or chairwoman of the conference committee of each house shall immediately notify the chairman or chairwoman of the policy committee of their respective houses that considered the bill in question of the waiver, and of the time and place of the meeting.

4. Judicial Branch Bodies

The bodies governing or administering various aspects of the judicial branch include the California Judicial Council, the Commission on Judicial Appointments, the Commission on Judicial Performance, the Board of Governors of the State Bar, the State Bar Court, and the board of the Habeas Corpus Resource Center. With the exception of the last, these bodies' meetings or proceedings are required to be open to some extent by a rule of court, a constitutional provision or a statute. To date, only the constitutional provision governing proceedings of the Commission on Judicial Performance has been interpreted by a court.

§ 4-1 California Judicial Council

The Judicial Council is the state body established by the California Constitution to set the priorities, rules and standards for management of the statewide court system, the largest in the nation. The Council comprises 27 members: the Chief Justice, who serves as its chair; 14 judges appointed by the Chief Justice (one associate justice of the Supreme Court, three justice of the Courts of Appeal, and 10 trial court judges); four attorney members appointed by the State Bar Board of Governors; and one member from each house of the Legislature. Six advisory members include representatives of the California Judges Association and state court administrative agencies. The Council is aided by five standing committees and more than 20 advisory committees and task forces. It meets six to eight times a year and is supported by its staff agency, the Administrative Office of the Courts. Meetings of the Council are governed by the provision of the California Rules of Court below. Meeting dates, sites and agendas for the Judicial Council are posted on the Internet at http://www.courtinfo.ca.gov/courtadmin/jc.

Rule 6.6. Judicial Council meetings

(a) [Open meeting policy] Business meetings are open to the public unless they are closed under subdivision (b) of this rule. Other meetings, such as orientation, planning, and educational meetings, may be made open to the public at the discretion of the Chief Justice. The Chief Justice may seek a recommendation from the Executive and Planning Committee on whether all or part of any meeting should be open or closed. Any discussion or decision of the full council at a business meeting regarding a trial court budget allocation must take place in an open meeting of the council, except for an executive session as provided in subdivision (b).

(b) [Closed sessions] The Chief Justice may close all or part of a business meeting because of the nature of the meeting or of matters to be discussed. The following matters will ordinarily be discussed in closed session:

(1) A personnel matter or a discussion of the character, competence, or physical or mental

health of an individual;

(2) Claims or litigation in which the Judicial Council has an interest;

(3) Contract, labor, or legislative negotiations;

(4) The purchase, sale, or lease of real property;

(5) Security plans or procedures;

(6) Allegations of criminal or professional misconduct; and

(7) Discussions protected by the attorney-client privilege.

(c) [Conduct at meeting] Members of the public who attend open meetings must remain orderly. The Chief Justice may order the removal of any disorderly persons.

(d) [Requests to speak-general] The Executive and Planning Committee, in its discretion, may allow a member of the public to speak at a business meeting. Unless the Chief Justice waives this requirement, any member of the public who wishes to speak at a business meeting must submit a request of no more than two pages to the chair of the Executive and Planning Committee by delivering it to the Administrative Office of the Courts at least four business days before the meeting.

(1) *(Contents of the request)* The request must include the following:

(A) A description of the agenda item to be addressed;

(B) A specific recitation of the proposed statement with an explanation of its relevance to the agenda item and the reasons it would be of benefit to the council in its deliberations;

(C) The name, residence, and occupation of the person asking to speak and, if applicable, the name, address, and purpose of the agency or organization that the speaker represents;

(D) If available, telephone and fax numbers and e-mail address of the person asking to speak and, if applicable and available, telephone and fax numbers of the agency or organization that the speaker represents;

(E) The words "Request to Speak at Judicial Council Meeting" displayed prominently in letters at least one-quarter-inch high on the envelope containing the request; and

(F) A copy of any written materials the speaker proposes to distribute at the meeting.

(2) (*Notice of decision*) The Executive and Planning Committee must respond to the request at least two business days before the meeting. The committee may grant the request in part or whole, request additional information, circulate any written materials, or take other action it deems appropriate.

(e) [Presentation of information on trial court budget matters]

(1) *(Presentation of written information)* Any designated employee representative has a right to provide written information on trial court budget allocations to the council.

(2) *(Oral presentation)* Any designated employee representative who wishes to make an oral presentation to the Judicial Council must make a written request to the Administrative Office of the Courts (attention Secretariat Office) no later than 24 hours before the meeting unless the issue has arisen within the last five business days before the meeting, in which case the written request may be made on the day of the meeting.

(3) *(Limit on number and time)* The Chief Justice or his or her designee may limit the number and time of speakers in order to avoid cumulative discussion.

(f) [Video recording, photographing, and broadcasting at meeting] The Chief Justice may permit video recording, photographing, or broadcasting of a meeting. Any such video recording, photographing, or broadcasting is subject to regulations that ensure the meeting's security and dignity. A request to record, photograph, or broadcast a council meeting must be received by the Chief Justice at least two business days before the meeting.

(g) [Minutes as official records] The Secretary of the Judicial Council must prepare written minutes of each council meeting for approval at the next council meeting. When approved by the council, the minutes constitute the official record of the meeting.

§ 4-2: Commission on Judicial Appointments

When the Governor appoints candidates to the Supreme Court or the Courts of Appeal, the appointees must be confirmed by the Commission on Judicial Appointments, a body established by the California Constitution. The commission has three members: the Chief Justice, the Attorney General, and the senior presiding justice of the Court of Appeal of the affected appellate district. When a Supreme Court appointee is being considered, the third member of the commission is the state's senior presiding justice of the Courts of Appeal. The commission holds one or more public hearings to review the appointee's qualifications and may confirm or veto the appointment. Hearing dates, sites and agendas for the Commission are not required to be posted on the Internet, but are issued by press release. Guidelines governing these hearings, adopted by the Commission in 1999, are as follows.

Guideline 4. Pre-hearing procedures (a) [Scheduling, notice, and location of public hearing] The chairperson shall schedule the confirmation hearing within a reasonable time after the nomination and shall issue a press release announcing the time, place, and subject of the hearing.

(b) [Commission on Judicial Nominees Evaluation (Gov. Code § 12011.5)] The chairperson shall request the Commission on Judicial Nominees Evaluation of the State Bar (JNE) to:

(1) Submit to the commission as soon as practicable, but in no event later than the time specified in paragraph (d) of this guideline, its written recommendations to the commission concerning the nominee, and the reasons therefor, and, if specifically requested, all prior JNE recommendations, including the date of evaluation and the court for which the nominee was evaluated; and

(2) Designate a representative to testify at the hearing as to the JNE evaluation of the nominee.

(c) [Communications with the commission] All communications regarding a nominee must be made in writing to the commission and/or by testimony at the hearing. Communications regarding a nomination or nominee should be made to the commission as a whole rather than to any commission member individually, and shall be distributed promptly to the members of the commission. Communications may be sent to the commission by United States Mail, overnight delivery, messenger service, or fax, to arrive within the time specified in these guidelines. The commission generally will not formally acknowledge receipt of written presentations concerning a nominee's qualifications.

(d) [Written presentations and requests to testify; time for submission]

(1) Individuals, including the nominee, who submit a written presentation to or request to testify before the commission must identify themselves by name, residence, and occupation, and, if applicable, shall identify the name, address, and purpose of any agency or organization for which they are acting in a representative capacity. Telephone numbers and any fax numbers of these individuals and organizations must be included.

(2) All requests to testify before the commission, other than those under paragraph (g), must be in writing and must specifically describe the proposed testimony, its relevance to the nominee's qualifications, and the facts upon which the testimony and opinion will be based. All written presentations or requests to testify must be received by the commission no later than 5:00 p.m. on the fifth court day before the hearing. (For example, if a hearing is to be held on a Monday, the fifth court day before the hearing would be the preceding Monday, unless a judicial holiday falls in between. Each intervening judicial holiday requires an additional court day's notice.)

(e) [Permissible testimony] The commission shall review requests to testify and shall permit testimony that is relevant to the nominee's qualifications. Testimony relating to the judicial system generally or the overall nomination or confirmation process will not be received. Testimony that is unduly cumulative to or repetitive of other testimony may be excluded. A person whose request to testify is denied shall be so informed by the commission as soon as possible before the hearing, by telephone or fax.

(f) [Notice to nominee] The commission promptly shall provide the nominee with a copy of all the written presentations or requests to testify it receives and shall afford the nominee an opportunity to refute, clarify, or comment, either at the hearing or before the hearing in writing, or both. Similarly, if the commission receives any record, public or private, or any other communication relating to the nominee's qualifications, it promptly shall provide the nominee with a copy thereof, and afford the nominee an opportunity to refute, clarify, or comment on that record or communication (consistent with the provisions of Cal. Const. art. VI, § 18.5). All written responses by the nominee must be received by the commission no later than 5:00 p.m. on the third court day before the hearing.

(g) [Nominee's witness list] The nominee shall present the commission with a list of any witnesses he or she wishes to testify at the hearing. This list must include the information required by paragraph (d)(i) and shall be received by the commission no later than 5:00 p.m. on the third court day before the hearing.

(h) [Release of lists of speakers and communications] No later than 2:00 p.m. on the second court day before the scheduled hearing, the commission shall release to the public the following:

(1) The names of witnesses who will testify at the hearing;

(2) The names of any individuals or organizations that have submitted written communications to the commission;

(3) Correspondence and public reports received by the commission concerning the nominee's qualifications, including any reports submitted by JNE pursuant to paragraph (b), and the nominee's Personal Data Questionnaire submitted by the Governor to the commission. The commission, however, may delete any confidential personal information such as an individual's residential address, or social security or driver's license number. The written material released shall be made available for copying at the requesting party's expense.

Guideline 5. Hearing procedures (a) [Conference] The commission members may confer before the confirmation hearing to consider procedural issues.

(b) [Absence of commission member] Concurrence of at least two commission members present at the hearing is necessary to confirm a nominee. If the Chief Justice is recused or unavailable, the Acting Chief Justice shall serve as the Chairperson. If the presiding justice described in Guideline 2 is recused or unavailable, the presiding justice of the affected district who has presided next longest, or, in districts with a single presiding justice, the Acting presiding justice, or for a nomination to the Supreme Court, the presiding justice who has presided next longest on any Court of Appeal, shall serve. (See Cal. Const, art. VI, §§ 2, 3, and 7.) A request that a commission member not participate in proceedings of the commission shall be decided by that member alone. The hearing may proceed if two members of the commission are present.

(c) [Witnesses] Witnesses shall be heard in the following order:

(1) Witnesses in support of the nominee;

(2) Witnesses in opposition to the nominee;

(3) The JNE representative;

(4) The nominee.

(d) [Exhibits and demonstrative evidence] Witnesses must testify orally and have no right to present exhibits or demonstrative evidence at the hearing.

(e) [Record of hearing] The hearing proceedings shall be recorded by audio or video recorder, court reporter, or any other means appropriate for preserving the testimony. A nominee who wishes to make his or her own arrangements to record the hearing by video recorder or other means shall notify the commission in writing. This notice must be received by the commission no later than 5:00 p.m. on the second court day before the hearing.

(f) [Public attendance and broadcasting] The hearing shall be open to the public and to the media. Any request to broadcast, photograph, or record the hearing requires the approval of the chairperson, upon written application received no later than 5:00 p.m. on the second court day before the hearing.

(g) [Announcement of decision] The commission may deliberate privately, but shall announce its decision publicly at the hearing, as well as by subsequent news release. If necessary, the hearing may be continued to a future date for further proceedings.

(h) [Official record] The commission's minutes shall be the official record of the hearing.

Guideline 6. Staff to the commission The chairperson of the commission may designate a person to act as secretary to the commission and one or more persons to act as assistant secretaries. The secretary shall maintain custody of the commission's files. The Administrative Office of the Courts, at the chairperson's direction, shall provide additional staff and financial support as necessary to enable the commission to perform its duties.

Guideline 7. Access to the commission's files; post-hearing procedures After the conclusion of any nomination proceedings of the commission subject to these guidelines, a person, agency, or organization, upon written request to the commission's secretary, may obtain access to the public portions of the commission's files, as defined in guideline 4(h), and the record of the testimony as defined in guideline 5(e), for inspection and copying at the requesting party's expense pursuant to internal guidelines established by the commission.

§ 4-3: Commission on Judicial Performance

This Commission, established in the California Constitution to deal with charges of serious misconduct or disability among judges, is also constitutionally required to provide access to its proceedings and records. The 11-member body consists of one judge of a Court of Appeal and two superior court judges, each appointed by the Supreme Court; two members of the State Bar who have practiced law in here for 10 years, each appointed by the Governor; and six citizens who are not judges, retired judges, or members of the State Bar, two of whom are appointed by the Governor, two by the Senate Committee on Rules, and two by the Speaker of the Assembly. The anti-secrecy provisions were added by the voters' approval of Proposition 190 of 1994. The Commission's authority and the public access provisions are found in the following subdivisions of Article VI, Section 18.

(a) A judge is disqualified from acting as a judge, without loss of salary, while there is pending (1) an indictment or an information charging the judge in the United States with a crime punishable as a felony under California or federal law, or (2) a petition to the Supreme Court to review a determination by the Commission on Judicial Performance to remove or retire a judge.

(b) The Commission on Judicial Performance may disqualify a judge from acting as a judge, without loss of salary, upon notice of formal proceedings by the commission charging the judge with judicial misconduct or disability.

(c) The Commission on Judicial Performance shall suspend a judge from office without salary when in the United States the judge pleads guilty or no contest or is found guilty of a crime punishable as a felon under California or federal law or of any other crime that involves moral turpitude under that law. If the conviction is reversed, suspension terminates, and the judge shall be paid the salary for the judicial office held by the judge for the period of suspension. If the judge is suspended and the conviction becomes final, the Commission on Judicial Performance shall remove the judge from office.

(d) Except as provided in subdivision (f), the Commission on Judicial Performance may (1) retire a judge for disability that seriously interferes with the performance of the judge's duties and is or is likely to become permanent, or (2) censure a judge or former judge or remove a judge for action occurring not more than 6 years prior to the commencement of the judge's current term or of the former judge's last term that constitutes willful misconduct in office, persistent failure or inability to perform the judge's duties, habitual intemperance in the use of intoxicants or drugs, or conduct prejudicial to the administration of justice that brings the judicial office into disrepute, or (3) publicly or privately admonish a judge or former judge found to have engaged in an improper action or dereliction of duty. The commission may also bar a former judge who has been censured from receiving an assignment, appointment, or reference of work from any California state court. Upon petition by the judge or former judge, the Supreme Court may, in its discretion, grant review of a determination by the commission to retire, remove, censure, admonish, or disqualify pursuant to subdivision (b) a judge or former judge. When the Supreme Court reviews a determination of the commission, it may make an independent review of the record. If the Supreme Court has not acted within 120 days after granting the petition, the decision of the commission shall be final.

*****

(f) A determination by the Commission on Judicial Performance to admonish or censure a judge or former judge of the Supreme Court or remove or retire a judge of the Supreme Court shall be reviewed by a tribunal of 7 Court of Appeal judges selected by lot.

*****

(i) The Commission on Judicial Performance shall make rules implementing this section, including, but not limited to, the following:

(1) The commission shall make rules for the investigation of judges. The commission may provide for the confidentiality of complaints to and investigations by the commission.

(2) The commission shall make rules for formal proceedings against judges when there is cause to believe there is a disability or wrongdoing within the meaning of subdivision (d).

(j) When the commission institutes formal proceedings, the notice of charges, the answer, and all subsequent papers and proceedings shall be open to the public for all formal proceedings instituted after February 28, 1995.

Disclosure of Members' Votes

In *The Recorder v. Commission on Judicial Performance*, 72 Cal.App.4th 258 (1999), the California Court of Appeal for the First District rejected the Commission's contention that it need not disclose the individual votes of commissioners to the public. The court stated:

> We conclude the vote of the members on whether or not to impose judicial discipline is such an essential and integral part of the formal proceedings of the commission—perhaps the single most important act a member takes in his or her capacity as such—that it would be plainly unreasonable to accept the commission's interpretation of its authority under section 18(i) and 18(j). That is, when California voters overwhelmingly approved a requirement that all "proceedings" subsequent to the filing of formal disciplinary charges "shall be open to the public" (§ 18(j)), they must have intended the commission to vote in public or at least to disclose the full results of its vote, including how each commission member voted.

Id. at 263. But, the court decided, public disclosure did not demand that the commissioners conduct their deliberations openly.

> We further conclude, however, that—like an intermediate appellate court, or an administrative agency acting in an adjudicative capacity—the commission is not required to conduct its "delibera-

> tions" in public. Section 18(j) was clearly not intended as an "open meeting" law but, rather, as a provision relating to adjudicatory proceedings, as to which it is well settled and universally recognized that the judicial "thought process" need not be publicly revealed. (Ibid.)
> *****
> … the point is that when the commission acts in an adjudicatory capacity—as it does when it conducts "formal proceedings" for judicial discipline—the proponents of Proposition 190 intended the commission to conduct its formal "proceedings" as a court does in a criminal case and as the State Bar Court does in attorney discipline cases. It was and is widely understood that internal "deliberations" of American and California courts are, and always have been, conducted in secrecy and that the "judicial thought process" need not be disclosed to the public. Likewise, the *deliberations* of the judges of the State Bar Court are excluded from the provision requiring all State Bar Court proceedings to be public.

Id. at 281 (emphasis in the original).

§ 4-4: Board of Governors of the State Bar

The State Bar is governed by a 23-member Board of Governors. Fifteen are lawyers elected by members of the State Bar. A 16th lawyer is elected by the California Young Lawyers Association (CYLA) Board of Directors. Since 1977, the State Bar has operated with increased involvement by the public. Beginning that year, six "public" or nonlawyer members were appointed to the Board of Governors – four by California's governor, one by the state Senate Committee on Rules and one by the Speaker of the Assembly. The Board meets approximately eight times a year to debate organizational, policy and professional issues. Each meeting includes a public and a confidential session. Meeting dates and locations, and a person to contact for agenda information, are found at http://www.calbar.ca.gov/state/calbar/calbar_extend.jsp?cid=10117&id=1030&filter=BOG . The open meeting requirement is in Business and Professions Code § 6026.5.

Every meeting of the board shall be open to the public except those meetings, or portions thereof, relating to:

(a) Consultation with counsel concerning pending or prospective litigation.

(b) Involuntary enrollment of active members as inactive members due to mental infirmity or illness or addiction to intoxicants or drugs.

(c) The qualifications of judicial appointees, nominees, or candidates.

(d) The appointment, employment or dismissal of an employee, consultant, or officer of the State Bar or to hear complaints or charges brought against such employee, consultant, or officer unless such person requests a public hearing.

(e) Disciplinary investigations and proceedings, including resignations with disciplinary investigations or proceedings pending, and reinstatement proceedings.

(f) Appeals to the board from decisions of the Board of Legal Specialization refusing to certify or recertify an applicant or suspending or revoking a specialist's certificate.

(g) Appointments to or removals from committees, boards, or other entities.

(h) Joint meetings with agencies provided in Article VI of the California Constitution.

§ 4-5: State Bar Court

The attorney disciplinary process in California consists of a series of investigations by the State Bar. If not resolved, the case is forwarded to the State Bar Court. Created in 1988, the State Bar Court is an arm of the California Supreme Court. It decides all attorney discipline cases in California, subject to discretionary (non-mandatory) review by the Supreme Court. Business and Professions Codes Section 6086.1 states:

(a) (1) Subject to subdivision (b), and except as otherwise provided by law, hearings and records of original disciplinary proceedings in the State Bar Court shall be public, following a notice to show cause.

(2) Subject to subdivision (b), and except as otherwise provided by law, hearings and records of the following matters shall be public:

(A) Filings for involuntary inactive enrollment or restriction under subdivision (a), (c), (d), or (e) of Section 6007.

(B) Petitions for reinstatement under Section 6078.

(C) Proceedings for suspension or disbarment under Section 6101 or 6102.

(D) Payment information from the Client Security Fund pursuant to Section 6140.5.

(E) Actions to cease a law practice or assume a law practice under Section 6180 or 6190.

(b) All disciplinary investigations are confidential until the time that formal charges are filed and all investigations of matters identified in paragraph (2) of subdivision (a) are confidential until the formal proceeding identified in paragraph (2) of subdivision (a) is instituted. This confidentiality requirement may be waived under any of the following exceptions:

(1) The member whose conduct is being investigated may waive confidentiality.

(2) The Chief Trial Counsel or President of the State Bar may waive confidentiality, but only when warranted for protection of the public. Under those circumstances, after private notice to the member, the Chief Trial Counsel or President of the State Bar may issue, if appropriate, one or more public announcements or make information public confirming the fact of an investigation or proceeding, clarifying the procedural aspects and current status, and defending the right of the member to a fair hearing. If the Chief Trial Counsel or President of the State Bar for any reason declines to exercise the authority provided by this paragraph, or disqualifies himself or herself from acting under this paragraph, he or she shall designate someone to act in his or her behalf. Conduct of a member that is being inquired into by the State Bar but that is not the subject of a formal investigation shall not be disclosed to the public.

(3) The Chief Trial Counsel or his or her designee may waive confidentiality pursuant to Section 6044.5. (c) Notwithstanding the confidentiality of investigations, the State Bar shall disclose to any member of the public so inquiring, any information reasonably available to it pursuant to subdivision(o) of Section 6068, and to Sections 6086.7, 6086.8, and 6101, concerning a member of the State Bar which is otherwise a matter of public record, including civil or criminal filings and dispositions.

5. Boards of Planned Community Associations

Certain associations of homeowners—"common interest development associations"—governing gated communities, condominium developments and the like, while not public agencies, must provide residents with access to the meetings of their boards of directors.

§ 5-1: Planned Community Governance

As stated by the court in *Damon v. Ocean Hills Journalism Club*, 85 Cal.App.4th 468, 475 (2000),

In exchange for the benefits of common ownership, the residents elect a legislative/executive board and delegate powers to this board. This delegation concerns not only activities conducted in the common areas, but also extends to life within "the confines of the home itself." … A homeowners association board is in effect "a quasi-government entity paralleling in almost every case the powers, duties, and responsibilities of a municipal government." …

> Because of a homeowners association board's broad powers and the number of individuals potentially affected by a board's actions, the Legislature has mandated that boards hold open meetings and allow the members to speak publicly at the meetings. … These provisions parallel California's open meeting laws regulating government officials, agencies and boards. (Ralph M. Brown Act, Gov. Code, § 54950 et seq.) Both statutory schemes mandate open governance meetings, with notice, agenda and minutes requirements, and strictly limit closed executive sessions.

The court refers to associations governed by the Davis-Stirling Act, which among other things defines the entities subject to the Common Interest Development Open Meeting Act.

§ 5-2: Davis-Stirling Act (Civil Code §1351 et seq.)

1351. As used in this title, the following terms have the following meanings:

(a) "Association" means a nonprofit corporation or unincorporated association created for the purpose of managing a common interest development.

•••••

(c) "Common interest development" means any of the following:

(1) A community apartment project.

(2) A condominium project.

(3) A planned development.
(4) A stock cooperative.
(d) "Community apartment project" means a development in which an undivided interest in land is coupled with the right of exclusive occupancy of any apartment located thereon.
•••••
(f) A "condominium project" means a development consisting of condominiums. A condominium consists of an undivided interest in common in a portion of real property coupled with a separate interest in space called a unit, the boundaries of which are described on a recorded final map, parcel map, or condominium plan in sufficient detail to locate all boundaries thereof. ... The portion or portions of the real property held in undivided interest may be all of the real property, except for the separate interests, or may include a particular three-dimensional portion thereof, the boundaries of which are described on a recorded final map, parcel map, or condominium plan...
•••••
(k) "Planned development" means a development (other than a community apartment project, a condominium project, or a stock cooperative) having either or both of the following features:
(1) The common area is owned either by an association or in common by the owners of the separate interests who possess appurtenant rights to the beneficial use and enjoyment of the common area.
(2) A power exists in the association to enforce an obligation of an owner of a separate interest with respect to the beneficial use and enjoyment of the common area by means of an assessment which may become a lien upon the separate interests...
•••••
(m) "Stock cooperative" means a development in which a corporation is formed or availed of, primarily for the purpose of holding title to...improved real property, and all or substantially all of the shareholders of the corporation receive a right of exclusive occupancy in a portion of the real property, title to which is held by the corporation. ... A "stock cooperative" includes a limited equity housing cooperative which is a stock cooperative that meets the criteria of Section 33007.5 of the Health and Safety Code.

§ 5-2: Common Interest Development Open Meeting Act

1363.05. (a) This section shall be known and may be cited as the Common Interest Development Open Meeting Act.
(b) Any member of the association may attend meetings of the board of directors of the association, except when the board adjourns to executive session to consider litigation, matters relating to the formation of contracts with third parties, member discipline, personnel matters, or to meet with a member, upon the member's request, regarding the member's payment of assessments, as specified in Section 1367 or 1367.1. The board of directors of the association shall meet in executive session, if requested by a member who may be subject to a fine, penalty, or other form of discipline, and the member shall be entitled to attend the executive session.
(c) Any matter discussed in executive session shall be generally noted in the minutes of the immediately following meeting that is open to the entire membership.
(d) The minutes, minutes proposed for adoption that are marked to indicate draft status, or a summary of the minutes, of any meeting of the board of directors of an association, other than an executive session, shall be available to members within 30 days of the meeting.
The minutes, proposed minutes, or summary minutes shall be distributed to any member of the association upon request and upon reimbursement of the association's costs for making that distribution.
(e) Members of the association shall be notified in writing at the time that the pro forma budget required in Section 1365 is distributed, or at the time of any general mailing to the entire membership of the association, of their right to have copies of the minutes of meetings of the board of directors, and how and where those minutes may be obtained.

(f) As used in this section, "meeting" includes any congregation of a majority of the members of the board at the same time and place to hear, discuss, or deliberate upon any item of business scheduled to be heard by the board, except those matters that may be discussed in executive session.

(g) Unless the time and place of meeting is fixed by the bylaws, or unless the bylaws provide for a longer period of notice, members shall be given notice of the time and place of a meeting as defined in subdivision (f), except for an emergency meeting, at least four days prior to the meeting. Notice shall be given by posting the notice in a prominent place or places within the common area and by mail to any owner who had requested notification of board meetings by mail, at the address requested by the owner. Notice may also be given, by mail or delivery of the notice to each unit in the development or by newsletter or similar means of communication.

(h) An emergency meeting of the board may be called by the president of the association, or by any two members of the governing body other than the president, if there are circumstances that could not have been reasonably foreseen which require immediate attention and possible action by the board, and which of necessity make it impracticable to provide notice as required by this section.

(i) The board of directors of the association shall permit any member of the association to speak at any meeting of the association or the board of directors, except for meetings of the board held in executive session. A reasonable time limit for all members of the association to speak to the board of directors or before a meeting of the association shall be established by the board of directors.

6. Sunshine Ordinances

The best way to ensure the most satisfactory open government policy for a given local agency is by persuading it to adopt its own "sunshine ordinance"—a commitment to make extra efforts to do public business in the open.

§ 6-1: Why a Local Ordinance Is Possible and Desirable

Anyone with experience observing local government leadership in action knows that the laws supporting access to public meetings often don't completely accommodate the needs of citizens attempting to be informed participants in their community's policy-making. The Brown Act simply doesn't always guarantee the quality, ease or completeness of informed participation that citizens might desire. And changing these state laws can be a daunting and even frustrating task. Do citizens have to wait for state law to change in order to get better access policy from their city councils, county supervisors, school boards and special district directors? Fortunately, the answer is no. A little-noticed fact about the Brown Act is that it does not pre-empt or discourage local agencies from adopting their own more accommodating rules. On the contrary, it expressly authorizes them to do so. The Brown Act provides, in Government Code Section 54953.7: "Notwithstanding any other provision of law, legislative bodies of local agencies may impose requirements upon themselves which allow *greater access to their meetings* than prescribed by the minimum standards set forth in this chapter... " (emphasis added). Thus the Brown Act, by its own terms, is not a *ceiling* on the access rights that citizens may expect, but instead a *floor* below which their rights may not descend: "minimum standards" for public participation and information. Accordingly, several local jurisdictions in the state adopted their own improved access rules. The City and County of San Francisco adopted its Sunshine Ordinance in the summer of 1993, and shortly thereafter the City of Richmond adopted a version applying to records only. In early 1995 the Contra Costa County Board of Supervisors enacted an even farther-reaching law than San Francisco's—Better Government Ordinance. The City of Oakland followed suit not long thereafter. At this writing the City of Benicia had adopted its version after more than a year of study.

What's the Effect of a Local Sunshine Law?

The beauty of this approach is its flexibility. The rules proposed to one's local body can be the ones most responsive to the recurrent procedural and policy problems encountered in dealing with the body. Some agencies (school and other special districts) do not adopt "ordinances", but nothing precludes them from adopting open government bylaws or other policies they will commit to abide by. Some typical goals for local ordinances:

- Extend open meeting requirements to more situations
- Require clearer, more meaningful agendas
- Require earlier or better access to agenda-related documents
- Reduce the frequency of closed sessions
- Require more disclosure about closed sessions, before and after
- Create a permanent oversight commission of citizens to assure that the sunshine law works

What Does It Take to Get a Sunshine Law Passed?

The indispensable elements so far have usually been:

• A Body Open to Change -- No matter how hard one tries, it will be impossible to pass a sunshine ordinance through a council or board that has a majority leery of or hostile to greater and more informed public participation. In such circumstances the cause isn't lost forever, but will have to wait for one or more new elected members with the will to take it seriously.

• An Effective Author -- That is, an elected public official on the local body who will lead the effort to get his or her peers to adopt the measure. This torchbearer must be politically adept with the combination of intelligence, insight and credibility needed to secure support for what some might otherwise view as threatening.

• Adequate Media Backing -- It's not essential that a newspaper be the leading proponent of the measure, but it helps greatly if least one influential newspaper lets the agency in question know that it considers the measure very important, and underscores that point by having its top executives— the editor and publisher—on the scene now and then to boost the process along.

• A Knowledgeable Attorney Guide -- Ending up with rules that actually improve on existing state law requires the extended attention and advice of a lawyer who knows what those requirements are and what specific language will or won't make a difference in the final product. While the body's own attorney may be knowledgeable, it's vital to for the proponents to have a counselor of their own to be active in the negotiation and review process. Californians Aware can suggest an effective

Getting Started:
Contact Californians Aware

If you'd like your county, city or other local agency to adopt a Sunshine policy, you can start brainstorming by using the ideas here, and if you have questions by calling Californians Aware General Counsel Terry Francke at (916) 487-7000, or sending him e-mail at terry@calaware.org.

attorney for this role.

• A Corps of Committed Citizen Participants -- Both independent civic activists and organizational representatives from groups like the League of Women Voters, the Parent-Teachers Association, a business or taxpayer group, or a homeowners or senior citizens association are important to help build support for and contribute ideas to sunshine law efforts. These people should help advise and lobby for the proposal from the outset.

• Months of Patient Negotiation -- It takes time to negotiate fair terms for a local sunshine ordinance. Numerous meetings need to be held between supporters and agency staff and attorneys. These negotiations are required to fine-tune whatever proposals the process starts with into something that resolves the host of reservations, alarms and objections that predictably will be expressed by those whose work routines or responsibilities will be affected by the new rules.

§ 6-2: Some Issues and Solutions in Existing Ordinances

The full text of the lengthy San Francisco Sunshine Ordinance, which will be referred to repeatedly below is found at http://www.sfgov.org/site/sunshine_index.asp?id=4673plus But note:

• The San Francisco ordinance began its development at a time before the Brown Act was revised effective in 1994, so many if not most of the open meeting rules are now in the Brown Act, and to that extent would not need to be duplicated in a new ordinance. Compare the ordinance with the current text of the Brown Act, in other words, to determine how much of the former has been duplicated by the latter and is already in effect statewide.

• Before lifting language wholesale, be aware of how the nomenclature you use may need to vary depending on whether you are dealing with a city, a school board or some other local agency, the titles of bodies, officials and department heads, etc.

The following are some issues for consideration that are addressed in the San Francisco Sunshine Ordinance (SFSO) and the San Diego Right to Know Ordinance (San Diego Municipal Code Chapter 2: Government; Rule 30.3 Noticing and Conduct of Closed Sessions).

What constitutes a "meeting" governed by the ordinance?

> See especially SFSO 67.3 (b) (2) and (3)

SEC. 67.3. Definitions.

Whenever in this Article the following words or phrases are used, they shall have the following meanings:

(a) "City" shall mean the City and County of San Francisco.

(b) "Meeting" shall mean any of the following:

(1) A congregation of a majority of the members of a policy body at the same time and place;

(2) A series of gatherings, each of which involves less than a majority of a policy body, to hear, discuss or deliberate upon any item that is within the subject matter jurisdiction of the City, if the cumulative result is that a majority of members has become involved in such gatherings; or

(3) Any other use of personal intermediaries or communications media that could permit a majority of the members of a policy body to become aware of an item of business and of the views or positions of other members with respect thereto, and to negotiate consensus thereupon.

What meetings other than those governed by the Brown Act should be included, at least for passive (observational only) attendance by the public?

> See SFSO 67.3 (c), 67.4.

SEC. 67.3. Definitions.

Whenever in this Article the following words or phrases are used, they shall have the following meanings:

(c) "Passive meeting body" shall mean:

(1) Advisory committees created by the initiative of a member of a policy body, the Mayor, or a department head;

(2) Any group that meets to discuss with or advise the Mayor or any Department Head on fiscal, economic, or policy issues;

(3) Social, recreational or ceremonial occasions sponsored or organized by or for a policy body to which a majority of the body has been invited.

(4) "Passive meeting body" shall not include a committee that consists solely of employees of the City and County of San Francisco created by the initiative of a member of a policy body, the Mayor, or a department head;

(5) Notwithstanding the provisions of paragraph (4) above, "Passive meeting body" shall include a committee that consists solely of employees of the City and County of San Francisco when such committee is reviewing, developing, modifying, or creating city policies or procedures relating to the public health, safety, or welfare or relating to services for the homeless;

SEC. 67.4. Passive Meetings.

(a) All gatherings of passive meeting bodies shall be accessible to individuals upon inquiry and to the extent possible consistent with the facilities in which they occur.

(1) Such gatherings need not be formally noticed, except on the City's website whenever possible, although the time, place and nature of the gathering shall be disclosed upon inquiry by a member of the public, and any agenda actually prepared for the gathering shall be accessible to such inquirers as a public record.

(2) Such gatherings need not be conducted in any particular space for the accommodation of members of the public, although members of the public shall be permitted to observe on a space available basis consistent with legal and practical restrictions on occupancy.

(3) Such gatherings of a business nature need not provide opportunities for comment by members of the public, although the person presiding may, in his or her discretion, entertain such questions or comments from spectators as may be relevant to the business of the gathering.

(4) Such gatherings of a social or ceremonial nature need not provide refreshments to spectators.

(5) Gatherings subject to this subsection include the following: advisory committees or other multimember bodies created in writing or by the initiative of, or otherwise primarily formed or existing to serve as a non-governmental advisor to, a member of a policy body, the Mayor, the City Administrator, a department head, or any elective officer, and social, recreational or ceremonial occasions sponsored or organized by or for a policy body to which a majority of the body has been invited. This subsection shall not apply to a committee which consists solely of employees of the City and County of San Francisco.

(6) Gatherings defined in subdivision (5) may hold closed sessions under circumstances allowed by this Article.

(b) To the extent not inconsistent with state or federal law, a policy body shall include in any contract with an entity that owns, operates or manages any property in which the City has or will have an ownership interest, including a mortgage, and on which the entity performs a government function related to the furtherance of health, safety or welfare, a requirement that any meeting of the governing board of the entity to address any matter relating to the property or its government related activities on the property, or performance under the contract or grant, be conducted as provided in subdivision (a) of this section. Records made available to the governing board relating to such matters shall be likewise available to the public, at a cost not to exceed the actual cost up to 10 cents per page, or at a higher actual cost as demonstrated in writing to such governing board.

Should the press at least have longer lead time for notice of special meetings? Should the lead time be even longer if the body is meeting at some unusual place?

> See SFSO 67.6 (f).

SEC. 67.6. Conduct of Business: Time and Place for Meetings.

(f) Special meetings of any policy body, including advisory bodies that choose to establish regular meeting times, may be called at any time by the presiding officer thereof or by a majority of the members thereof, by delivering personally or by mail written notice to each member of such policy body and the local media who have requested written notice of special meetings in writing. Such notice of a special meeting shall be delivered as described in (e) at least 72 hours before the time of such meeting as specified in the notice. The notice shall specify the time and place of the special meeting and the business to be transacted. No other business shall be considered at such meetings. Such written notice may be dispensed with as to any member who at or prior to the time the meeting convenes files with the presiding officer or secretary of the body or commission a written waiver of notice. Such waiver may be given by telegram. Such written notice may also be dispensed with as to any member who is actually present at the meeting at the time it convenes. Each special meeting shall be held at the regular meeting place of the policy body except that the policy body may designate an alternate meeting place provided that such alternate location is specified in the notice of the special meeting; further provided that the notice of the special meeting shall be given at least 15 days prior to said special meeting being held at an alternate location. This provision shall not apply where the alternative meeting location is located within the same building as the regular meeting place.

How understandable should meeting agendas be? What about Internet posting as a backup? How should related reports and other documents be made available? Should the standards allowing action on "surprise" (off-agenda) items be tightened? What agenda format accommodations for the disabled? How about a standard agenda advisory about learning more from or submitting complaints/concerns to the oversight commission, in San Francisco called the "task force?"

> See SFSO 67.7. On agenda intelligibility, see also San Diego Ordinance, Rule 30.3 (a) (2)

SEC. 67.7. Agenda Requirements: Regular Meetings.

(a) At least 72 hours before a regular meeting, a policy body shall post an agenda containing a meaningful description of each item of business to be transacted or discussed at the meeting. Agendas shall specify for each item of business the proposed action or a statement the item is for discussion only. In addition, a policy body shall post a current agenda on its Internet site at least 72 hours before a regular meeting.

(b) A description is meaningful if it is sufficiently clear and specific to alert a person of average intelligence and education whose interests are affected by the item that he or she may have reason to attend the meeting or seek more information on the item. The description should be brief, concise and written in plain, easily understood English. It shall refer to any explanatory documents that have been provided to the policy body in connection with an agenda item, such as correspondence or reports, and such documents shall be posted adjacent to the agenda or, if such documents are of more than one page in length, made available for public inspection and copying at a location indicated on the agenda during normal office hours.

(c) The agenda shall specify the time and location of the regular meeting and shall be posted in a location that is freely accessible to members of the public.

(d) No action or discussion shall be undertaken on any item not appearing on the posted agenda, except that members of a policy body may respond to statements made or questions posed by persons exercising their public testimony rights, to the extent of asking a question for clarification, providing a reference to staff or other resources for factual information, or requesting staff to report back to the body at a subsequent meeting concerning the matter raised by such testimony.

(e) Notwithstanding subdivision (d), the policy body may take action on items of business not appearing on the posted agenda under any of the following conditions:

(1) Upon a determination by a majority vote of the body that an accident, natural disaster or work force disruption poses a threat to public health and safety.

(2) Upon a good faith, reasonable determination by a two-thirds vote of the body, or, if less than two-thirds of the members are present, a unanimous vote of those members present, that (A) the need to take immediate action on the item is so imperative as to threaten serious injury to the public interest if action were deferred to a subsequent special or regular meeting, or relates to a purely commendatory action, and (B) that the need for such action came to the attention of the body subsequent to the agenda being posted as specified in subdivision (a).

(3) The item was on an agenda posted pursuant to subdivision (a) for a prior meeting of the body occurring not more than five calendar days prior to the date action is taken on the item, and at the prior meeting the item was continued to the meeting at which action is being taken.

(f) Each board and commission enumerated in the charter shall ensure that agendas for regular and special meetings are made available to speech and hearing impaired persons through telecommunications devices for the deaf, telecommunications relay services or equivalent systems, and, upon request, to sight impaired persons through Braille or enlarged type.

(g) Each policy body shall ensure that notices and agendas for regular and special meetings shall include the following notice:

> KNOW YOUR RIGHTS UNDER THE SUNSHINE ORDINANCE
>
> (Chapter 67 of the San Francisco Administrative Code)
>
> Government's duty is to serve the public, reaching its decisions in full view of the public.
>
> Commissions, boards, councils and other agencies of the City and County exist to conduct the people's business. This ordinance assures that deliberations are conducted before the people and that City operations are open to the people's review.
>
> FOR MORE INFORMATION ON YOUR RIGHTS UNDER THE SUNSHINE ORDINANCE OR TO REPORT A VIOLATION OF THE ORDINANCE, CONTACT THE SUNSHINE ORDINANCE TASK FORCE.

(h) Each agenda of a policy body covered by this Sunshine Ordinance shall include the address, area code and phone number, fax number, e-mail address, and a contact person's name for the Sunshine Ordinance Task Force. Information on how to obtain a free copy of the Sunshine Ordinance shall be included on each agenda.

What about personalized notices to residents of neighborhoods that are especially affected by a certain proposal?

> See SFSO 67.7-1.

SEC. 67.7-1. Public Notice Requirements

(a) Any public notice that is mailed, posted or published by a City department, board, agency or commission to residents residing within a specific area to inform those residents of a matter that may impact their property or that neighborhood area, shall be brief, concise and written in plain, easily understood English.

(b) The notice should inform the residents of the proposal or planned activity, the length of time planned for the activity, the effect of the proposal or activity, and a telephone contact for residents who have questions.

(c) If the notice informs the public of a public meeting or hearing, then the notice shall state that persons who are unable to attend the public meeting or hearing may submit to the City, by the time the proceeding begins, written comments regarding the subject of the meeting or hearing, that these comments will be made a part of the official public record, and that the comments will be brought to the attention of the person or persons conducting the public meeting or hearing. The notice should also state the name and address of the person or persons to whom those written comments should be submitted.

Should closed sessions be tape recorded to either deter or document violations? Should the tapes ever become public? Should the agency's attorney tell a requester when and if an "anticipated" case is actually filed?

> See SFSO 67.8-1.

SEC. 67.8-1. Additional Requirements for Closed Sessions

(a) All closed sessions of any policy body covered by this Ordinance shall be either audio recorded or audio and video recorded in their entirety and all such recordings shall be retained for at least ten years, or permanently where technologically and economically feasible. Closed session recordings shall be made available whenever all rationales for closing the session are no longer applicable. Recordings of closed sessions of a policy body covered by this Ordinance, wherein the justification for the closed session is due to "anticipated litigation" shall be released to the public in accordance with any of the following provisions: two years after the meeting if no litigation is filed; upon expiration of the statute of limitations for the anticipated litigation if no litigation is filed; as soon as the controversy leading to anticipated litigation is settled or concluded.

Should closed sessions be transcribed by a court reporter instead of being taped?

> See San Diego Ordinance, Rule 30.3 (d)

Rule 30.3 Noticing and Conduct of Closed Sessions

(d) Transcription of Closed Sessions: All closed sessions shall be transcribed by a court certified reporter. All transcripts shall be retained.

Agenda backup material: Internet posting? Public access even before distribution to the body? A per-page fee cap?

> See SFSO 67.9.

SEC. 67.9. Agendas and Related Materials: Public Records

(a) Agendas of meetings and any other documents on file with the clerk of the policy body, when intended for distribution to all, or a majority of all, of the members of a policy body in connection with a matter anticipated for discussion or consideration at a public meeting shall be made available to the public. To the extent possible, such documents shall also be made available through the policy body's Internet site. However, this disclosure need not include any material exempt from public disclosure under this ordinance.

(b) Records which are subject to disclosure under subdivision (a) and which are intended for distribution to a policy body prior to commencement of a public meeting shall be made available for public inspection and copying upon request prior to commencement of such meeting, whether or not actually distributed to or received by the body at the time of the request.

(c) Records which are subject to disclosure under subdivision (a) and which are distributed during a public meeting but prior to commencement of their discussion shall be made available for public inspection prior to commencement of, and during, their discussion.

(d) Records which are subject to disclosure under subdivision (a) and which are distributed during their discussion at a public meeting shall be made available for public inspection immediately or as soon thereafter as is practicable.

(e) A policy body may charge a duplication fee of one cent per page for a copy of a public record prepared for consideration at a public meeting, unless a special fee has been established pursuant to the procedure set forth in Section 67.28(d). Neither this section nor the California Public Records Act (Government Code sections 6250 et seq.) shall be construed to limit or delay the public's right to inspect any record required to be disclosed by that act, whether or not distributed to a policy body.

Permitted closed sessions: To consider hiring outside lawyers?

> See SFSO 67.10.

SEC. 67.10. Closed Sessions: Permitted Topics.

A policy body may, but is not required to, hold closed sessions:

*****

(d) Based on advice of its legal counsel, and on a motion and vote in open session to assert the attorney-client privilege, to confer with, or receive advice from, its legal counsel regarding pending litigation when discussion in open session concerning those matters would likely and unavoidably prejudice the position of the City in that litigation. ...

*****

(3) A closed session may not be held under this section to consider the qualifications or engagement of an independent contract attorney or law firm, for litigation services or otherwise.

Litigation Log: How should the body's attorney keep members and the public updated on the number and status of court cases the agency is involved in?

> See San Diego Ordinance, Rule 30.3 (f).

Rule 30.3 Noticing and Conduct of Closed Sessions

The City Council may impose upon itself requirements which allow greater access to its meetings than prescribed by the minimum legal standards set forth in the California Open Meeting Law, commonly known as the Brown Act.

•••••

(f) Litigation Log: The City Attorney, in coordination with the City Clerk, shall provide to the Mayor and City Council a weekly listing of all litigation filed against or by the City of San Diego, its officers or employees, any City boards, redevelopment agencies, and commissions (collectively "the City") that has been served upon the City. The list shall include the court in which the case was filed, the name of the litigants, the date filed, and the Court case number. A copy of the list shall be kept on file in the Office of the City Clerk and available for members of the public. The list shall be provided every week, and shall report on cases served the immediate preceding week.

Pre-closed session disclosures: Should the staff or attorney publicly brief the body on what's known to both sides about the progress of negotiations or litigation before retiring to closed session to discuss strategy? Should members of the body or of the public be allowed to make statements or ask questions at that point?

> See San Diego Ordinance, Rule 30.3 (a) (4), (b), (c).

Rule 30.3 Noticing and Conduct of Closed Sessions

The City Council may impose upon itself requirements which allow greater access to its meetings than prescribed by the minimum legal standards set forth in the California Open Meeting Law, commonly known as the Brown Act.

(a)

*****

(4) In open session, before public comment or City Council discussion of any closed session item, the City Attorney or appropriate staff shall provide an oral update or progress report on matters under litigation, real property negotiations or employee unit bargaining.

•••••

(b) Public Participation

The public shall have the opportunity to directly address the City Council on any closed session item on the agenda, prior to City Council questions and discussion on the item and after the oral report by the City Attorney or appropriate staff.

(c) Council questions and discussion in Open Session: At the regular or special meeting of the City Council, the Mayor and Councilmembers shall have the opportunity to discuss the basis for convening into closed session, ask questions, and respond to questions from the public.

(d) Transcription of Closed Sessions: All closed sessions shall be transcribed by a court certified reporter. All transcripts shall be retained.

Post-closed session disclosures: What, if anything, can be revealed, and should the body be required to vote up or down on sharing certain information after every closed session? Should proposed litigation settlements, especially those involving more than just smaller sums of money, be sunshined to the public before final approval? What specifics should be announced about personnel actions -- positive or otherwise? What about those separation agreements used to buy an employee's resignation with no fuss? Should this information be posted, as well as announced?

> See SFSO 67.12.

SEC. 67.12. Disclosure of Closed Session Discussions and Actions

(a) After every closed session, a policy body may in its discretion and in the public interest, disclose to the public any portion of its discussion that is not confidential under federal or state law, the Charter, or non-waivable privilege. The body shall, by motion and vote in open session, elect either to disclose no information or to disclose the information that a majority deems to be in the public interest. The disclosure shall be made through the presiding officer of the body or such other person, present in the closed session, whom he or she designates to convey the information.

(b) A policy body shall publicly report any action taken in closed session and the vote or abstention of every member present thereon, as follows:

*****

(3) Settlement: A policy body shall neither solicit nor agree to any term in a settlement which would preclude the release of the text of the settlement itself and any related docu-

mentation communicated to or received from the adverse party or parties. Any written settlement agreement and any documents attached to or referenced in the settlement agreement shall be made publicly available at least 10 calendar days before the meeting of the policy body at which the settlement is to be approved to the extent that the settlement would commit the City or a department thereof to adopting, modifying, or discontinuing an existing policy, practice or program or otherwise acting other than to pay an amount of money less than $50,000. The agenda for any meeting in which a settlement subject to this section is discussed shall identify the names of the parties, the case number, the court, and the material terms of the settlement. Where the disclosure of documents in a litigation matter that has been settled could be detrimental to the city's interest in pending litigation arising from the same facts or incident and involving a party not a party to or otherwise aware of the settlement, the documents required to be disclosed by subdivision (b) of this section need not be disclosed until the other case is settled or otherwise finally concluded.

(4) Employee Actions: Action taken to appoint, employ, dismiss, transfer or accept the resignation of a public employee in closed session pursuant to Government Code Section 54957 shall be reported immediately in a manner that names the employee, the action taken and position affected and, in the case of dismissal for a violation of law or of the policy of the City, the reason for dismissal. "Dismissal" within the meaning of this ordinance includes any termination of employment at the will of the employer rather than of the employee, however characterized. The proposed terms of any separation agreement shall be immediately disclosed as soon as presented to the body, and its final terms shall be immediately disclosed upon approval by the body.

(5) Collective Bargaining: Any collectively bargained agreement shall be made publicly available at least 15 calendar days before the meeting of the policy body to which the agreement is to be reported.

(c) Reports required to be made immediately may be made orally or in writing, but shall be supported by copies of any contracts, settlement agreements, or other documents related to the transaction that were finally approved or adopted in the closed session and that embody the information required to be disclosed immediately shall be provided to any person who has made a written request regarding that item following the posting of the agenda, or who has made a standing request for all such documentation as part of a request for notice of meetings pursuant to Government Code Sections 54954.1 or 54956.

(d) A written summary of the information required to be immediately reported pursuant to this section, or documents embodying that information, shall be posted by the close of business on the next business day following the meeting, in the place where the meeting agendas of the body are posted.

Attendance barriers: What happens if the crowd overflows the meeting room? Accommodations for deaf or others disabled?

> See SFSO 67.13.

SEC. 67.13. Barriers to Attendance Prohibited.

(a) No policy body shall conduct any meeting, conference or other function in any facility that excludes persons on the basis of actual or presumed class identity or characteristics, or which is inaccessible to persons with physical disabilities, or where members of the public may not be present without making a payment or purchase. Whenever the Board of Supervisors, a board or commission enumerated in the charter, or any committee thereof anticipates that the number of persons attending the meeting will exceed the legal capacity of the meeting room, any public address system used to amplify sound in the meeting room shall be extended by supplementary speakers to permit the overflow audience to listen to the proceedings in an adjacent room or passageway, unless such supplementary speakers would disrupt the operation of a City office.

Tapes of the meeting made by the agency: Should all covered meetings be at least audiotaped? Should the tapes be preserved longer than the Brown Act's 30 days?

> See SFSO 67.14.

SEC. 67.14. Tape Recording, Filming and Still Photography.

*****

(b) Each board and commission enumerated in the charter shall audio record each regular and special meeting. Each such audio recording, and any audio or video recording of a meeting of any other policy body made at the direction of the policy body shall be a public record subject to inspection pursuant to the California Public Records Act (Government Code Section 6250 et seq.), and shall not be erased or destroyed. Inspection of any such recording shall be provided without charge on an appropriate play back device made available by the City.

Addressing the body: Should the presiding officer announce up front which if any agenda items have been reshuffled in order or continued to a later meeting?

> See SFSO 67.15.

SEC. 67.15 Public Testimony.

*****

(e) To facilitate public input, any agenda changes or continuances shall be announced by the presiding officer of a policy body at the beginning of a meeting, or as soon thereafter as the change or continuance becomes known to such presiding officer.

Meeting minutes: What content should be required? How much inclusion of citizens' comments to the body? How soon should the draft minutes be ready for public access?

> See SFSO 67.16.

SEC. 67.16. Minutes.

The clerk or secretary of each board and commission enumerated in the charter shall record the minutes for each regular and special meeting of the board or commission. The minutes shall state the time the meeting was called to order, the names of the members attending the meeting, the roll call vote on each matter considered at the meeting, the time the board or commission began and ended any closed session, the names of the members and the names, and titles where applicable, of any other persons attending any closed session, a list of those members of the public who spoke on each matter if the speakers identified themselves, whether such speakers supported or opposed the matter, a brief summary of each person's statement during the public comment period for each agenda item, and the time the meeting was adjourned. Any person speaking during a public comment period may supply a brief written summary of their comments which shall, if no more than 150 words, be included in the minutes.

The draft minutes of each meeting shall be available for inspection and copying upon request no later than ten working days after the meeting. The officially adopted minutes shall be available for inspection and copying upon request no later than ten working days after the meeting at which the minutes are adopted. Upon request, minutes required to be produced by this section shall be made available in Braille or increased type size.

§ 6-3: Some Other Issues That Could Be Covered

The following are *not* addressed in either the San Francisco or San Diego ordinances, but do relate to issues that arise from time to time, and could be candidates for consideration, if they address problems or controversies noticeable in the agency's practices.

Use of the Internet and e-mail to maximum sunshine advantage. In addition to posting meeting agendas and materials on the agency site (see a good example for small agencies at http://www.riverbank.org/council/agendas.html and for large agencies at http://bos.co.la.ca.us/Categories/Agenda/AgendaHome.asp), consider creating a listserv that sends an e-mail alert link to the currently posted agenda to anyone who signs up for it.

Clear rules on how e-mail can and can't be used for communications to and among members of legislative bodies. See the Attorney General's opinion on the subject at http://www.cfac.org/AGOpinions/AG_Op_-_E-mail.html.

No closed personnel sessions relating to the chief executive officer. This is the single most influential and consequential individual in the government agency, and how he/she is hired, evaluated, etc. is essential not only to understanding how the big problems of the agency are dealt with, but to holding accountable the elected officials in performing their single most significant function. The CEO is the lens on the whole operation, and one the public has a right and a need to look through. Those who are not ready for this scrutiny can serve elsewhere or, to put it more positively, those who are ready for the scrutiny are the kind of people one would want to provide leadership and execute local public policy.

Sunshining of all proposed closed session actions that lock in policy commitments (not just the payment of money), to allow time for informed public comment. Not just settlements, but collective bargaining and real property agreements as well. No more secretly bargained deals done behind the community's back and then announced afterward as a *fait accompli*.

Allowance of citizens to place agency-relevant matters on a future (one or two meetings hence) agenda, at least with concurrence of two out of five members. Education Code Section 35145.5 provides for something like this (no concurrence required) with respect to school boards (see . This doesn't require that the body say or do anything in particular about the issue, but it does remove the Brown Act barrier—"We can't talk about it because it's not on the agenda."

No removal or arrest of a citizen speaker unless both his or her allegedly disruptive activity and the removal have been videotaped, to be kept as evidence. This would apply to those addressing the body during a period designated for public comment, not to a person rising spontaneously in interruption from the audience.

No routine one-on-one serial briefings of a majority of the body by the CEO or other key staff on coming agenda issues --- or anything else. This practice, probably more widespread than most people realize, may not constitute a prohibited serial meeting if it is not used to allow the members of the body to deliberate or exchange views through the staff as an intermediary. But it has three other glaring problems that warrant its discontinuance. It wastes time, putting the staff through three to five times as many repeated presentations as a one-time briefing at the body's open meeting would be. It risks manipulation, allowing staff to tailor its remarks differently depending on the member's known preferences, prejudices, priorities or perspectives. The result: three to five compartmentalized decision-makers, each with a unique understanding of a proposal, and unaware of what was asked by or said to the others. Finally, the public is cheated of hearing the members ask their questions and get the answers, and thus cannot intelligently do the principal thing that the Brown Act supposedly enables them to do—hold the members accountable for their actions or omissions. Private briefings may not involve secret member-to-member deliberation. But in eliminating true deliberation altogether, they have much the same effect, if not a worse one.

7. The Constitutional Open Government Right

Proposition 59 was approved by voters in the November 2004 election by an overwhelming 83.4 percent margin, adding to the California Constitution a fundamental right to open government. It swept all 58 counties, ranging in voter approval between 76 and 88 percent. It adds a new subdivision (b) to Section 3 of Article I, and affects the enactment and interpretation of laws governing the meetings of government bodies and the records of public agencies and officials.

§ 7-1: Introduction

Proposition 59 is about public scrutiny of governmental conduct. Paragraph (1) of subdivision (b) of Section 3 of Article I states: "The people have the right of access to information concerning the conduct of the people's business, and, therefore, the meetings of public bodies and the writings of public officials and agencies shall be open to public scrutiny."

Proposition 59 is not simply another law. As a provision added to the Declaration of Rights in the California Constitution, it has the same fundamental gravity as the rights of privacy, speech, assembly or petition, for example. It is a law to which less fundamental laws such as acts of the Legislature, and to which actions of government generally, must conform. Practices running contrary to Prop 59 are not simply to be avoided. They are unconstitutional, meaning that actions and decisions made possible by such practices may be directly attacked as invalid.

§ 7-2: Other Rights and Laws Left in Place

Privacy

Proposition 59 does not affect how privacy rights are to be interpreted. Paragraph (3) of subdivision (b) of Section 3 of Article I states:

> Nothing in this subdivision supersedes or modifies the right of privacy guaranteed by Section 1 or affects the construction of any statute, court rule, or other authority to the extent that protects that right to privacy, including any statutory procedures governing discovery or disclosure of information concerning the official performance or professional qualifications of a peace officer.

Other Constitutional Rights

Proposition 59 does not affect how other basic rights are to be interpreted. Paragraph (4) of subdivision (b) of Section 3 of Article I states:

> Nothing in this subdivision supersedes or modifies any provision of this Con-

stitution, including the guarantees that a person may not be deprived of life, liberty, or property without due process of law, or denied equal protection of the laws, as provided in Section 7.

Exemptions from Access Laws

Prop 59 leaves in place the laws stating what is public and not public. Paragraph (5) of subdivision (b) of Section 3 of Article I states:

> This subdivision does not repeal or nullify, expressly or by implication, any constitutional or statutory exception to the right of access to public records or meetings of public bodies that is in effect on the effective date of this subdivision, including, but not limited to, any statute protecting the confidentiality of law enforcement and prosecution records.

§ 7-3: How Access Laws Are to Be Interpreted

Proposition 59 affects how most statutes and other rules are to be interpreted. Those not dealing with personal privacy, while not "repealed or nullified," may be "modified" in effect depending on how their broadly or narrowly their terms are construed by the courts. Paragraph (2) of subdivision (b) of Section 3 of Article I states: "A statute, court rule, or other authority, including those in effect on the effective date of this subdivision, shall be broadly construed if it furthers the people's right of access, and narrowly construed if it limits the right of access." When, in other words, there is room in what a statute says or does not say for doubt as to the required scope of disclosure vis-à-vis the permitted scope of non-disclosure, the doubt must be resolved in favor of disclosure. For example, where the Brown Act permits but does not require a closed session for certain discussions, the practice of treating that rule as a license for routine, invariable secrecy rather than an allowance for discretionary confidentiality to avoid certain harm may be subject to attack.

Equally, a practice of stretching the use of closed sessions or other confidentiality to cover all related information just because it is somehow related may be likewise vulnerable. For example, if an exception to the Brown Act's rule of access has a clearly defined purpose such as keeping a litigation or bargaining adversary uninformed as to the facts known to a public agency or its position on a given issue, that purpose is not served by keeping the public ignorant of what the adversary already knows, or of information it has itself provided to the agency. Interpreting limits to the right of access narrowly means using discretionary confidentiality judiciously, to protect what must be protected and avoid what needs to be avoided, to the extent necessary—but no more than that.

§ 7-4: How New Limits on Access Are to be Justified

Proposition 59 affects how new limitations on access are to be justified. Paragraph (2) of subdivision (b) of Section 3 of Article I states:

> A statute, court rule, or other authority adopted after the effective date of this subdivision that limits the right of access shall be adopted with findings demonstrating the interest protected by the limitation and the need for protecting that interest.

This requirement applies not only to the Legislature, Judicial Council and state regulatory agencies but to any level of government creating a policy or procedure that limits access to meetings of government bodies, or to records of government officials or agencies. The phrase "findings demonstrating" probably refers to factual determinations, not simply expressions of opinion or preference. What *is* the public interest to be protected? Why is the proposed access limitation (as opposed to others) the *necessary* one? What experience *demonstrates* these conclusions?

§ 7-5: The Limited Exemption for the Legislature

Proposition 59 exempts the Legislature from its own terms, but not from public scrutiny otherwise. The Legislature is already bound by another provision of the Constitution, namely Article 4, Section 7, which states:

> (c) (1) The proceedings of each house and the committees thereof shall be open and public. However, closed sessions may be held solely for any of the following purposes:
>
> (A) To consider the appointment, employment, evaluation of performance, or dismissal of a public officer or employee, to consider or hear complaints or charges brought against a Member of the Legislature or other public officer or employee, or to establish the classification or compensation of an employee of the Legislature.
>
> (B) To consider matters affecting the safety and security of Members of the Legislature or its employees or the safety and security of any buildings and grounds used by the Legislature.
>
> (C) To confer with, or receive advice from, its legal counsel regarding pending or reasonably anticipated, or whether to initiate, litigation when discussion in open session would not protect the interests of the house or committee regarding the litigation.
>
> (2) A caucus of the Members of the Senate, the Members of the Assembly, or the Members of both houses, which is composed of the members of the same political party, may meet in closed session.
>
> (3) The Legislature shall implement this subdivision by concurrent resolution adopted by rollcall vote entered in the journal, two-thirds of the membership of each house concurring, or by statute, and shall prescribe that, when a closed session is held pursuant to paragraph (1), reasonable notice of the closed session and the purpose of the closed session shall be provided to the public. If there is a conflict between a concurrent resolution and statute, the last adopted or enacted shall prevail.

Documents of the Legislature are presumed to be public under the Legislative Open Records Act (Government Code Section 9070), which has far fewer exemptions than the California Public Records Act. There are no reported cases brought under either the constitutional or the statutory access laws.

§ 7-6: Application to the Judicial Branch

Proposition 59 applies to the administrative meetings and records of judicial branch agencies—if it did not, there would have been no purpose in its several references to "court rules" as separate and distinct from statutes. It does not apply to court proceedings and records in civil or criminal cases, but access to them is already presumed under the First Amendment, state statutes and common law. It does apply, however, to meetings of the California Judicial Council, and probably to local superior court administrative bodies—executive committees of judges, for example—as well.

§ 7-7: The Effect on Public Agencies' Policies and Practices

Proposition 59 will be interpreted officially only gradually in court decisions over the next generation. But meanwhile it will probably expose perceived excessive secrecy in local and state government to somewhat readier and more frequent challenge. Some agencies and officials will anticipate Proposition 59's thrust and adapt their practices accordingly. Others will wait to be forced to change their ways, if change is required. But since 83.4 percent of voters lent their assent to the change, it is likely that most Californians will begin to judge the officials and agencies they encounter with a higher, if not altogether defined, expectation of openness from now on.

TABLE OF AUTHORITIES

Cases

Statutes

CALIFORNIA LAW

Constitution

Government Code

Bagley-Keene Open Meeting Act

Attorney General's Opinions

INDEX LETTERS

Publications

Agenda Posting

TOPICAL INDEX

A

B

D

E

F-G

H-I-J-L

M-N-O

P

Q-R

S-W